THE OLDWAYS TABLE

THE
Oldways
Table

ESSAYS & RECIPES
FROM THE CULINARY
THINK TANK

K. DUN GIFFORD & SARA BAER-SINNOTT

with contributions from around the food world

TEN SPEED PRESS
Berkeley | Toronto

Ten Speed Press
PO Box 7123
Berkeley, California 94707
www.tenspeed.com

Distributed in Australia by Simon & Schuster Australia, in
Canada by Ten Speed Press Canada, in New Zealand by South-
ern Publishers Group, in South Africa by Real Books, and in the
United Kingdom and Europe by Publishers Group UK.

Design by Nancy Austin
Composition by Katy Brown and Chloe Rawlins

Library of Congress Cataloging-in-Publication Data
Gifford, K. Dun.
 The Oldways table : essays and recipes from the culinary think
tank / K. Dun Gifford and Sara Baer-Sinnott ; with contribu-
tions from around the food world.
    p. cm.
 Includes index.
 ISBN-13: 978-1-58008-490-1
 ISBN-10: 1-58008-490-7

 1. Nutrition. 2. Food. 3. Cookery. 4. Oldways Preservation &
Exchange Trust. I. Baer-Sinnott, Sara. II. Oldways Preservation
& Exchange Trust. III. Title.
 TX357.G48 2007
 641.3—dc22
                           2006025176

First printing, 2007
Printed in Canada

1 2 3 4 5 6 7 8 9 10 — 11 10 09 08 07

CONTENTS

PREFACE

K. DUN GIFFORD

From its first stirrings in my imagination, in the late 1980s, I saw Old-ways as an agent of change, as a new organization that would challenge the corporate world's assumptions about the future of our food—about growing, processing, preparing, eating, drinking, and enjoying it. It was clear to me that our food chain was awry, skewed by industrial farming, intense processing, technical advances, and television advertising.

I was dead certain that the "old ways" were sounder than the "new ways" for just about everything to do with our food, and I was determined to challenge these discouraging trends with positive advocacy about the healthful pleasures of real food.

These discouraging new ways were all about "techno foods," with only bare genuflection to real foods. Techno foods were steadily washing away the wonderful, warm, and glorious traditions of the old ways of food. Evidence was steadily accumulating, too, that radical departures from the traditional food and eating patterns were seeding a grim harvest of killer chronic diseases (cancer, heart disease, and diabetes). Finally, studies were beginning to appear in medical and health journals that linked the growing accessibility of techno foods with an upturn in worldwide weight gain.

The old ways, on the other hand, were the patterns of millions of years eating and living that formed our genes, those microscopic marvels that control everything about our bodies. Genes change only slowly, and I was sure that the cascade of new "wonder chemicals" in our ever more industrial food system were lodging in our bodies faster than our genes could adjust, which helped to account for the escalating rates of diet-related diseases.

Equally grim was the decline in food literacy, as fewer and fewer people grew their food, cooked their food, ate seasonally, understood nutrition basics, were healthy, or avoided silly fad diets.

Our dietary professionals were stuck in the past; the words and graphics of their advice and messages to consumers were virtually unchanged from the 1950s, when television was black and white and a big screen was ten inches on the diagonal. No one in the late 1980s, when every living room in America had a big-screen color TV, paid much attention to 1950s-era messages about diet and nutrition.

Compounding the problem, great mountains of packages of frozen meals and microwavable snack-packs were replacing fresh groceries in family kitchens, and the vast cooking knowledge we once had as a human race was slipping into the history books. Now, our children are taught only perfunctorily about their food, meaning that as adults they are less likely to know the countless pleasures of the kitchen and of the table.

Just think for a minute about the traditional Thanksgiving dinner, the one meal we still seem to celebrate with actual cooking and with family members (or friends) helping out in the kitchen. Try to imagine the Thanksgiving dinners of tomorrow; they'll arrive "with all the trimmings," precooked in a microwavable freezer pack. No muss, no fuss, no pots to clean, and no crowd hanging around in the kitchen fussing with the gravy and all of Thanksgiving's other wonderful traditional goodies.

These perceptions were not really rocket science in the late 1980s, and they are not rocket science today, either, since agricultural and health experts continue to warn regularly and darkly about the implications of a factory-based food system. It's just that not many people were listening in the 1980s, and the challenge I chose for Oldways was to make the old ways hip, cool, and groovy—to make people listen.

I wanted Oldways to be a different kind of "healthy eating" advocacy organization—to be sure, a critic of outrageous techno foods and chemically intensive agriculture—but much more, I wanted Oldways to focus on wise solutions and positive approaches. The government, private organizations, physicians, and dietitians were everywhere urging people to "eat a balanced diet and exercise regularly," but very few Americans paid any attention. Cynical fad diet books seemed everywhere, hawked on late-night television and making their promoters rich, but not doing much good; Americans were growing fatter and getting lazier. This is the disconnect I focused on.

I was certain that the nutrition science needed some tweaking and updating, but was in the right ballpark. But I knew the messaging used to promote it was terrible. "People do not eat nutrients, they eat food," the sociologist Margaret Mead said famously in 1944, but that key lesson was lost in the mists of history. A U.S. Senate panel led by George McGovern had brutally challenged the federal government's ineffective nutrition programs in 1977 and had forced important changes. So for me, at the end of the 1980s, some combination of Mead and McGovern—an emphasis on food and the techniques of politics—seemed as strong a combination as bacon and eggs, pretzels and beer, or oatmeal and brown sugar.

THE OLD WAYS OF FOOD

I love most things about the old ways of food—seeds, planting, farms, growing, harvesting, picking wild berries and grapes, fishing, hunting, cooking, preserving, eating, drinking, wine tastings, cheese samplings, oysters and clams on the half shell, all kinds of restaurants, cookouts on the beach or in the backyard, BBQs, Fenway franks, Thanksgiving turkey, Fourth of July salmon, grilled fresh foie gras, and much more, too.

I am fascinated by the contradictions of wildly ranging food preferences. Hamburgers are a delight for most of us, but anathema to vegetarians and animal rights advocates. Flinty or sweet, fresh icy oysters are joy to some, but gross to others. Organic is a firm principle for a growing number of consumers, but ignored by the great majority. The list of religious dietary rules about pork is dizzying, but a comforting tradition to many. Calf's testicles and sheep's eyeballs are delicacies for cowboys and shepherds, but horrific for most of us. In effect, the only safe generalization about food preferences may be that we choose the things we like, and avoid the ones we don't.

The great majority of what we eat and drink is, to a small or large degree, processed, and there is nothing intrinsically wrong with processed food. After all, we process most of what we eat. We boil grains and potatoes for soups. We scramble or boil or fry eggs because we don't like them raw, and we roast raw meat and raw fish for the same reason. We boil strawberries to make jam and boil rolled oats to make oatmeal. We salt pork and freeze green peas. We fry bacon and pancakes. We ferment hops to make beer, and ferment grapes to make wine. We pasteurize milk so it does not go sour, ferment it to make cheese, and freeze it to make ice cream. We make trail mix in ways not very different from the way Roman and Greek and Saracen and Arab warriors did thousands of years ago as they marched and fought their way back and forth across thousands of Mediterranean miles.

So, for eons we have busily processed raw foods to make them edible and palatable. We chop and slice, marinate and salt, boil and steam, fry and bake, toast and roast, ferment and acidify.

To transform our raw and fresh foods, we process them. The fact of the matter is that we eat only minor amounts of unprocessed foods—apples and bananas, walnuts and pecans, oysters and clams, celery and carrot sticks, and other things like that.

But what is it, then, that makes today's techno foods different from yesterday's processed or transformed foods? Basically, it's just about everything. For example, yesterday's fresh foods were rarely cosmetically perfect. They often were wrinkled, misshapen, and not of uniform size. Why? Because unlike today's factory farm fruits and vegetables, they had not been bred for uniformity of size and shape and color in order to pack better on shipping boxes, to resist bruising during mechanical harvesting and ripening with externally applied ethylene gas, and to rack better in geometrical stacks in supermarkets.

Old ways foods were picked ripe when they reached full flavor, and, if not eaten fresh, were "put up" (preserved) in mason jars, made into jellies and jams and preserves (berries, tomatoes, fruits, and melons), pickled (cucumbers and onions), or dried (beans and corn). They tasted better, not as flat as today's techno foods do.

Most of the food we eat today is processed and packaged, and in some sense, almost pre-eaten. It's "meals ready-to-eat," or MREs, which is actually the name of the "open and eat" foods served to the armed forces. It is the direction that meals in schools, hospitals, and prisons are taking. It's the "heat and serve," or "open and eat" crowding supermarket shelves. It's the take-out and drive-through. By some estimates, this accounts for two-thirds of the meals that Americans eat.

Without a determined effort to educate families—parents and children—about all of what we stand to lose in a techno-food future, we'll keep on going down the slippery slope to factory food and artificial flavors and tastes, and starve ourselves of the micronutrients we need.

Fifteen years later, and after growing Oldways into an effective and respected international influence, I realized that a book about Oldways, and the "old ways," would spread our messages to a wider audience. We would write this book to capture the fun, excitement, and pleasures of food and wines; to explain what was at stake if we passively accepted a techno-food future; and to map out simple steps to stem the erosion of the old ways in our everyday food system.

Sara Baer-Sinnott, my partner at Oldways for most of these Oldways years, enthusiastically agreed with this idea of an Oldways book, and so we began to write. A key element is contributions we have gathered from many friends of Oldways, who are themselves leading authorities on the pleasures of the table and the importance of the old ways.

OLDWAYS, FROM THE BEGINNING

The idea for Oldways came to me in Qufu, the birthplace of Confucius, during a 1987 visit to China. We'd had a three-hour traditional banquet in the replica of the Confucius family home, during which an astonishing parade of thirty-six dazzling dishes and drinks expressed the Confucian ideal of harmony among earth, body, and spirit. Luckily, each dish was only the size of a half-dollar, and each drink (some alcoholic, some not) was only a thimbleful, so the entire feast wasn't much more than thirty-six tastes.

During the banquet, Nina Simonds, the China food expert I'd asked to put this trip together, and Dr. Wan You Kui, a noted Confucian scholar, explained how each of these surprising spoonfuls—some spicy and some mild, some smooth and some crunchy, all of them wondrous—played its own harmonic role "in the whole, which is beyond words."

I woke up the next morning surprised to see that the banquet had painted in my mind's eye a clear image of what would become Oldways—a new nonprofit advocacy organization to research and promote a harmony of traditional food patterns, sustainable agriculture,

and healthy eating and drinking. It would combine "the best of the old ways" with "the best of the new ways," and stand in strong contrast to "techno foods" that, oxymoronically, remain "fresh" for months on grocery store and kitchen shelves.

In 1987 China was still shuddering from the Cultural Revolution, and in Shanghai and Chengdu, we'd listened as survivors of the Cultural Revolution haltingly told us about the thousands of chefs (among many other thousands of its educated population) who were dispatched for "reeducation" to far-distant collective farms from which many never returned. The Revolution's Red Guards had shuttered culinary schools during this grim convulsion, and hauled entire libraries of books and scrolls detailing China's vast and glorious culinary history into the streets and burned them in bonfires. The survivors' vivid and compelling stories struck me hard— from childhood I had a passion for books, and in college I had fallen in love with illuminated manuscripts in Harvard's rare book collections. This destruction of China's culinary treasures appalled me.

But in some ineffable way, the harmonies of our Confucian banquet were ying for the destruction's yang—they marked the power of food traditions to survive even the worst kinds of police-state brutalities. Food memories are among our most indelible, whether they're the intense smells of foods cooking, the evocative tastes of familiar favorites, the warmth of a memorable family meal, or a romantic candlelight dinner. Some rituals are so associated with food—marriage, religion, birth, and death are among them—that they seem fixed in our genes, and not easily erased.

The images in that Qufu morning after the banquet knotted together many of my life's threads, and I returned to Boston determined to develop a new organization to promote the values (if not the literal specifics) of the "foodways of the old ways." Oldways would, like Janus, look back and forward simultaneously for a harmonious balance among good nutrition, pleasurable traditional foods, and respect for the earth, all to help modern humans live healthier and happier lives.

Later in 1987, in the autumn, my close friend Nancy Harmon Jenkins helped me organize an extensive culinary trip to northern Italy, which turned out to be a well-matched bookend to the China trip in the spring. Nancy writes prodigiously and beautifully about food, and she had just finished a long stint as a *New York Times* food writer. She is as fluent in Italian as Nina Simonds is in Chinese, essential ingredients since I spoke neither.

We organized this Italian trip as a kind of triangle, beginning in the top left-hand side of Italy's boot, the Piedmont region; then heading northeast across its top to the border with Austria and what was then Yugoslavia; and then finally turning southwest to finish in Tuscany.

The others in our merry band were themselves highly accomplished food authorities: Marian Morash, then chef of the Straight Wharf Restaurant on Nantucket; Thekla Sanford, who grew up in a Milwaukee brewing family and was the co-owner with her winemaker husband, Richard, of the prize-winning Sanford Winery in Santa Barbara; and Sheryl Julian, a food writer for the *Boston Globe* and a cookbook author with an impeccable instinct for recipe authenticity.

After two and a half weeks, we reached Nancy's farmhouse in the mountains of eastern Tuscany, outside Cortona, where we cooked birds and beef and vegetables and woodsy porcini mushrooms over oak embers in her great stone fireplace with her farm's fresh olive oil and Sicilian sea salt and drank dark, powerful Tuscan country wines. We agreed we had eaten like the Medicis and loved every traditional mouthful.

This Italian culinary adventure was an exhilarating immersion into a second of the world's great traditional "oldways" cultures, where the sensory elements of the foods and wines are inseparable from a joyous way of living. It was a seductive Italian sensuality balanced against intense Chinese complexity in Qufu, and strong validation of my image and purposes for Oldways.

So, when I got back to Boston from this extraordinary Italian pilgrimage, I called my lawyer and we set the paperwork in motion to establish Oldways as a non-profit educational organization. Appropriately, Nancy Jenkins and Nina Simonds joined me as the first members of its Board of Directors.

LIFE LESSONS

I am extraordinarily lucky; I grew up and have lived my life immersed in good food and wine, political activism, environmental campaigns, strong traditions, and nutrition awareness. The lessons of this life are central both to Oldways and to *The Oldways Table*.

My mother was raised in a Rhode Island family that cared very much about its food, and she brought forward to her own children the steady determination that every day we eat oatmeal, fresh vegetables, whole-wheat bread, chicken, and fruit and drink three glasses of milk. Although this did make her something of a retrograde, my mom wore a coat of many colors—we were the first family in our neighborhood to have a pressure cooker and a Waring blender, so she was certainly no Luddite.

My father grew up on a farm in Kentucky and brought this experience with him to his marriage, career, and child-rearing in Providence. He was deeply into foraging in the wholesale food markets of Providence, which were vibrant in part because of the city's large Italian immigrant population. He regularly brought home for us crates of beautiful food—meat, lobsters, strawberries, mangoes, avocados, peas, parsnips, and some things we didn't like very much, like rutabagas (but believe me, we ate them). He was also a wine collector and built a notable cellar. His bon vivant approach was much more about enjoying wine than it was about labels, although he took care to have a decent inventory of spectacular wines, too.

During part of World War II we lived on a navy base, and I remember hoarding food rationing stamps, saving bacon fat for "the war effort," and eating poor cuts of meat so "our fighting men would have the best cuts." When Dad was sent to the Pacific, I was sent to live with his father, who had a large Victory Garden at his place outside New York City. Granpadad and I went out to his garden each morning at sunup to harvest the day's vegetables, and also so he could shoot at the never-ending waves of hungry rabbits who pillaged his garden. He taught me to skin a rabbit when I was six, and when I had learned to do a skinning to his satisfaction, he stopped calling me "Boy" and began calling me "Little Man." I understood why.

As we grew up in the late 1940s and early 1950s, after Dad was back from the war, he taught me and my two brothers and my sister to catch small harbor fish like scup and tautog and large ocean fish like bluefish and striped bass, and to clean and fillet them. We dug quahogs and soft-shelled clams, caught blue crabs and Nantucket bay scallops, and we learned how to open them for the kitchen, and cook them, too.

We were manic berry pickers and jam and jelly makers. On perfect summer afternoons we went off to the moors and woodlands to pick blueberries and blackberries and beach plums, returning home to make intense, deep-dish pies and all kinds of lush jams and jellies.

I remain passionate about all this and share the berry passion with my equally passionate children, grandchildren, and my sister, and naturally she and I spar about whose jams and jellies are superior. I share the fishing passion with my friend Russ. He'll call to say, "Hey, the blues are running, wanna throw some [fishing] plugs?" Or, "tide's dead low at eight, wanna dig some 'hogs' [quahogs]?"

But the real point is that the intense berrying and fishing experiences of my childhood are very much part of my life today, fifty years later. I can vouch for the pleasure and power of food memories, and their pleasures. They are part of the backbone of Oldways' emphasis on traditional foods.

I am also drawn to gardening, and during the spells in my life when I had time for it, my gardens were lush with vegetables and fruits. Like all gardeners, I fought with torturing bastards like horned tomato caterpillars, swore at the damn deer who just flew over my tall fences as if they were escapees from Santa. But my chil-dren and I grew corn eight feet tall; so many tomatoes we threw overripe ones at each other; and so much sorrel we sold it to my brother's restaurant.

My wife, Pebble, taught herself to be a very good cook, and the meals she cooks consistently draw praise. This may well be her way of putting behind her memories of fresh bright green peas turning inexorably into mushy gray ones.

My own four children are now good at fishing and harvesting shellfish, too, and they know how to clean and cook their catch. They like to garden and pitch in to help with my gardens without being asked. It looks as if my grandchildren are well on their way to developing these skills; they love to fish off the docks, and to plant seeds in small pots and then set them out in the garden.

Cooking has fascinated me for as long as I can remember—something miraculous happens when smelly googly fish become delicious; gooey eggs change into luscious scrambled eggs; hard beach plums become silky, sweet jelly; scary-looking quahogs settle into comforting chowders; and leftover vegetables and meats are transformed into a warming stew. It's sort of e pluribus unum: right before your eyes, a bunch of individuals are transformed into a unity.

I bless the gods of parents, jobs, friends, farms, foods, and flavors for these experiences, because they are the sensory and pleasure nerves of the Oldways idea.

The lesson I took away from my time in Washington was well said by Margaret Mead: "Never doubt that a small group of thoughtful committed citizens can change the world: indeed, it's the only thing that ever has."

MAKING A DIFFERENCE

During summer break at law school in 1964 I worked as a legislative officer for Senator Claiborne Pell of Rhode Island, researching, writing, and—the high point—sitting with him on the Senate floor as his researcher while he argued, and won approval, for his legislation establishing the Sea Grant program.

I returned to Washington after graduating from law school to work in the then-new Department of Housing and Urban Development, as a member of the group developing the White House proposals for the "urban crisis" of the mid-1960s. It was intense and difficult work, but it was electrifying to see actual words and phrases that I had written down on my yellow legal pad appear in presidential proposals and speeches.

A year later, in early 1967, I went back to Capitol Hill to work as legislative assistant to Senator Ted Kennedy. The next year his brother Senator Robert Kennedy ran for president, and I was a national campaign coordinator during his short campaign. I helped to subdue his assassin, rode in the ambulance with the mortally wounded senator and his wife and sister Jean to the hospital, and grieved mightily with millions of others over the murder of this courageous and charismatic man. I continued to work for Ted Kennedy until 1970, when I returned with my wife and three young sons to Cambridge.

These Washington experiences absolutely persuaded me that an individual can make a big difference if he or she chooses to do so, and this belief is also a motivating force for Oldways. This is an obvious truth in personal matters—we can get fat or remain thin, get married or stay single, and do volunteer work or avoid it. But not very many people decide they want to make changes on a large scale, such as by running for president or governor or mayor, or for Congress or a state or local legislature. The lesson I took away from my time in Washington was well said by Margaret Mead: "Never doubt that a small group of thoughtful committed citizens can change the world: indeed, it's the only thing that ever has."

CHARLES RITZ AND TRADITIONS

In the 1970s I worked for the astute founder of a large real estate firm who, among other things, owned the Ritz-Carlton Hotel in Boston. Through him, I grew friendly with Charles Ritz, owner of the Ritz Hotel in Paris. Like me, Charles was an avid fisherman, and over the years we talked fishing for days and days. More important, he lectured me endlessly about the values of tradition in food and its preparations, insistent that this was a key ingredient of the Ritz's success.

He took me repeatedly to a room in the Ritz lined with impeccably bound volumes of old Ritz menus and recipes that his father, Cesar Ritz, had collected. He opened one book after another, reminiscing about meals, foods, delights, pleasures. We also returned again and again to the Ritz's astounding wine cellars, not so much to drink (though we tasted), but for him to instruct me about how the Boston Ritz must build and maintain a similar cellar.

The last time I visited with him he was too ill to fish, and when we said goodbye, he gave me a clutch of his beautiful French split-bamboo rods. It is my talisman for remembering what he taught me about the power of traditions.

EARTH DAY

The 1970s woke me to "the environment," at least in its organizational sense. Like most thinking people who fish, search for wild foods, and garden, I was a conservationist, a great fan of Rachel Carson, and ripe to become an environmentalist. I was a member of the Senate staff group that helped Senator Gaylord Nelson flesh out the details for the first Earth Day in 1970. I advised Senator Kennedy when he developed legislation to extend the Cape Cod National Seashore to parts of the offshore islands on Martha's Vineyard and Nantucket. With other committed individuals I organized and was president of a very aggressive land conservation group, which is now twenty-five years old. I wrote articles for legal journals about land conservation techniques. And for many years I kept bees, watching my hives gradually diminish in strength as the increasing spread of flower-garden pesticides ate into my bees' vitality, finally killing them all off.

JULIA AND FRIENDS

In the 1980s I was deeply into the restaurant business, and during these years my food, wine, and cookery educators were formidable.

Chief among them was Julia Child, a friend for two decades. We both had knee replacements, for example, and visited each other in the hospital. Another time, when she was immobilized at home from a back operation, I picked up a double order of her favorite hot french fries from her favorite fast food joint (shh: it was McDonald's) and rushed with them to her house, stirred the cocktail-hour, on-the-rocks gin martinis all set up on a big tray she'd laid out in her pantry, and carried all of it up to her bedroom. We ate the french fries and drank the martinis (two for each), and caught up on "the news."

She joined my family for Thanksgiving dinner (my children were terrified about whether she'd like our favorite gravy, and she did) and for regular dinners and dinner parties, and we went out together to restaurant dinners with friends. She loved to talk politics, and we had a wonderful time talking about what was happening in the White House. We agreed on just about everything except the nutrition police (even though she ate the kind of nutritionally balanced meals most nutritionists dream that everyone would eat).

We lunched in her kitchen from time to time, too, where she almost always made an omelet while toasting bread in the oven broiler, tossed a green salad with vinaigrette, and set out a fruit and cheese plate, while I poured two glasses of very cold white wine. This was classic Julia: a few bites of a simple but elegant lunch, a bite of business, a bite of gossip, a bite of politics. It was a regular routine for her, a way of keeping up with her

friends when her knees went south, and it was not easy for her to get out. Her ease in the kitchen was, of course, astounding, but one thing always puzzled me: she never once missed getting the toast just right, and she never used a timer.

Julia had a strong influence on me—not only about recipes and cooking techniques, but about food, its culture, finding excellence in simplicity, and enjoying mealtimes as a celebration of life.

Julia introduced me to Robert Mondavi, with whom I have also been friends for two decades. If there is a more gentlemanly individual who has had such spectacular success in the cutthroat wine business on his own, I have not met him. His understanding—like Julia's—of the power of "excellence" was profoundly analogous to the similar understandings of most very successful politicians. In those years Mondavi's mission was popularizing the strong scientific support for links between wine and good health, and his passion amplified my formative ideas about the relationships between food and health.

Russell Morash and Marian Morash are very talented, classy people. Russ has a forty-year string of successful public television shows: he was the producer/director of Julia Child's first twenty-five years of cooking shows, the longtime producer/director of *The Victory Garden*, and the developer and producer/director of *The New Yankee Workshop* and *This Old House*. Marian was Julia's assistant and executive chef in the early years, was the founding chef of the superb Straight Wharf Restaurant in Nantucket (owned by one of my brothers and his former wife), is the author of two longtime best-selling cookbooks, and was the television chef of *The Victory Garden*. Russ and Marian and I have caught, picked, bought, cooked, and eaten all manner of food together over the years. We have also eaten a vast number of meals together in great, good, and some not-so-good restaurants together here and overseas, learning about good wines, the tastes of extra virgin olive oil, and lush ripe avocados. These two wonderful people are another of my life's blessings.

I cooked wild ducks and drank wonderful wines and

sat in saunas with Benjamin Thompson, the late genius architect who brought us Faneuil Hall Marketplace (and other vibrant marketplaces in New York and Baltimore) and who was obsessed with connecting people with their food through the mediums of architecture and design. Ben and I and his wife, Jane, were partners in Harvard Square's Harvest Restaurant, which Ben had started, and which was an incubator for a dozen well-known chefs. Many of these chefs have subsequently won top awards for excellence in their own restaurants, and they remain friends and colleagues who have helped to shape Oldways. They are part of the reason Oldways organized the Chefs Collaborative in 1993 as a group of like-minded food professionals who were willing to use their knowledge and reputations to promote sustainable farming (see page 54).

CHANGING CONVENTIONAL WISDOM

Nancy Jenkins and I have learned much about all of this together. She concedes no ground to me about "absolute knowledge" of food and wine, and I ask for none, because she is generous with her knowledge, and for many years and in many ways has been a "seeing eye" for me. I have been one for her, too. She was a key sister-in-arms during the incubation of Oldways, and she has remained a trusted resource and counselor ever since.

Greg Drescher was also with us in the early development of Oldways, and his formidable networking was a big help in the early voyages on the stormy seas of gastronomy and nutrition.

Fausto Luchetti, impresario of the International Olive Oil Council in Madrid for nearly two decades, encouraged us enthusiastically in our consolidation of the scattered nutrition science evidence for the healthfulness of the Mediterranean diet. Fausto didn't stop with nutrition; he and his wife, Mar, also encouraged and taught us about wonderful Mediterranean ingredients in home and restaurant cooking through the enjoyment of many meals in of Italy, Spain, and the rest of the Mediterranean.

There are many other wonderful people who helped me stitch threads into the Oldways tapestry over the years, and many of them have also graciously and generously contributed recipes, descriptions, explanations, and ideas for this book. These threads include the "healthy food" threads from my early years, the "one man can make a difference" threads from my political years, the culinary traditions threads from my Ritz years, the emotional power and pleasure of beautifully cooked meals threads of my "foodie" years, the sustainability thread from my environmental activities, and the nutrition science thread from my Oldways advocacy years.

Despite these many threads of the Oldways tapestry, we try hard to keep our focus on our simple triangle: nutrition, tradition, and sustainability, with healthy people eating delicious, healthy, and wonderful meals in its center. The Oldways idea is that "wise eaters" keep this simple image in their minds when they buy and eat their food and drink, and that because they do, they increase the odds that they will have long and healthy lives and be happier along its pathways.

It is clear that Oldways broke important new ground in the last decade in changing the conventional wisdom about what constitutes a "good, healthy diet." With *The Oldways Table*, I am sure that Oldways will break even more new ground, persuading people that they can eat well and wisely, with pleasure.

My partner in carrying this Oldways message forward for the last fourteen years has been Sara Baer-Sinnott, who is a great communicator and manager of people. I think about what Oldways should do, she thinks about how we can do it, and then together we do it, enlisting our staff, friends, associates, and supporters along the way. She understood immediately that because the Oldways idea was a direct challenge to the nutrition establishment, to the fast-food/junk-food/techno-food merchants, and to big agriculture, life at Oldways would be no picnic in the park on a fine summer day. Fortunately, she welcomed that challenge, and it is rewarding to have Sara at my side.

INTRODUCTION

K. DUN GIFFORD AND SARA BAER-SINNOTT

The food and drink we put into our bodies every day truly matters—for the bodily and mental health of each one of us, for the children we bear and raise, and for the very viability of the planet that sustains us. We need our planet to continue supplying us our food and drink, and so we must not poison and deplete it in ways that dampen its abilities to grow our food and provide our water.

There are some simple truths, some lasting principles, and some common-sense guidelines about food and drink. Principal among them are the human senses of sight, smell, and taste. At an elemental, hardwired biological level, these senses send our conscious minds warnings about foods to avoid (rotten or poisonous) and acceptance about foods to consume (sweet or familiar).

Another principle is that eating and drinking are times when we share our lives with others; there is something very intimate about eating, chewing, drinking, and swallowing in the close company of friends, co-workers, family, colleagues, or even enemies. We actually don't think much about these connections between dining and intimacy because we take them for granted.

But we break bread (religions), we cut cakes (weddings), we raise a glass (closing deals), we spray champagne (victories), we mount banquets (awards, diplomatic events), we mark holidays (Christmas, Hanukkah, Kwanza, Ramadan), we have men's business lunches and ladies' nights out, and on and on. Eating and drinking together are truly a kind of societal glue.

We have often wondered if it were possible to compute the number of ways that people have made palatable dishes and drinks, always concluding that it's incalculable because the number is certainly as high as the number of stars in the sky. But that's not an impediment to thinking clearly about people with consuming passions who have written so wonderfully about dishes and drinks.

Julia Child, one of these people, was agitated toward the end of her life about what she called "the nutrition police." As joyously candid as ever in one of her last books, she wrote at the conclusion of its introduction, "Because of media hype and woefully inadequate information, too many people nowadays are deathly afraid

Our agenda is to uncover what elements of the old ways of food and drink are of value and healthy in our contemporary society, and to enable individuals and families to incorporate them conveniently into life in the twenty-first century.

of their food." Julia's feelings about this were intense; this was but a relatively mild rebuke. Her solution? "The pleasures of the table—that lovely old-fashioned phrase—depict food as an art form, as a delightful part of civilized life. In spite of food fads, fitness programs, and health concerns, we must never lose sight of a beautifully conceived meal."

About a hundred years earlier (1896) Fannie Farmer published *The Boston Cooking-School Cook Book,* which in later editions morphed into *The Fannie Farmer Cookbook,* of which about fifteen editions have since been published. We are sure she and Julia would have liked each other; here are Fannie's opening words in the 1896 edition: "Every meal should be a small celebration. If you acknowledge so joyous a fact of life, the pride you take in your efforts in the kitchen won't be confined to company occasions."

The felicitous writer Marian Cunningham wrote the revised thirteenth edition of *The Fannie Farmer Cookbook* in 1990, and opened her preface this way: "Today, more than ever, I sense a hankering for home cooking, for a personal connection to our food, despite all the statistics that no one is cooking at home any more." She explains: "Part of that yearning is an unconscious loss of the family center. Food is more than fodder. It is an act of giving and receiving because the experience at the table is a communal sharing."

WHAT IS OLDWAYS?

Oldways, the organization, takes the basic idea that a sensible update of the literal old ways is easily incorporated into today's harried lifestyles—and puts it into practice.

This has not always been easy, however, because few among us want to return to root cellars or give up our microwaves and refrigerators. We certainly don't, either, so turning back the clock is not on the agenda of Oldways.

Our agenda is to uncover what elements of the old ways of food and drink are of value and healthy in our contemporary society, and to enable individuals and families to incorporate them conveniently into life in the twenty-first century.

Here are some specific things that Oldways does.

We encourage professionals in the nutrition sciences to understand that people do not eat nutrition, but eat food that they have shopped for, cooked, or bought at a take-out or restaurant. We encourage journalists to treat single nutrition studies as but one piece in a very large and complicated mosaic, and not as a "magic bullet" answer. We encourage physicians to learn the rudiments of nutrition to help their patients recover more rapidly, because the only nutrition education that most medical students receive is the nutrition of tube feeding for comatose or stomach-disabled patients. And we encourage consumers to think about the essential concept of balance as they make their food choices—balance among food groups, and a balance of calories taken in and calories burned off.

We challenge fad diets for being, well, fads. They come and they go, promoted heavily by individuals selling books, pills, diet products, "easy weight loss," cancer protection, and, basically, snake oil. We keep an ever-growing list of fad diets, and collect magazine covers heralding them and subsequently announcing their demise. It's startling to see how new diet fads are promoted—low-fat rises high into the magazine cover sky, and then falls to the earth a few years later as low-carb becomes the next diet-fad cover story. We also keep the stories from the business pages reporting on the bankruptcies and business failures of these former high-flyers.

The ups and downs are bookends of the failed hopes of millions of gullible people hoping for a quick fix. Eating soundly is a long-term proposition, like managing relationships: it requires willpower and steadfast nurturing.

In the same way, we encourage consumers to understand that eating a lot of one food (or, heaven forbid, a lot of one supplement) is unwise; our bodies thrive on variety. We encourage people in the communica-tions business to ignore promoters touting quack remedies for losing weight, adding muscle, or living longer. And we encourage people to continually seek out the joys and pleasures of foods they like, well prepared and eaten (and drunk, too) with pleasure, in the company of family and friends.

THE NEW OLDWAYS APPROACH TO FOOD

Once the concept of what became Oldways had jelled, it needed a name that fit its unconventional nature. Dun did not want a weird word (like Exxon is weird for gasoline and Song is weird for an airline), so he kept returning to that portmanteau word—Oldways—that suggested what our new organization was all about. With that decision, he established its specific goals, and set out to get the Oldways message into the public consciousness. The message was about the lost values of traditional food systems—growing, preparing, and eating—and the agricultural systems that produced the food.

We had determined that the healthiest eating pattern most familiar to Americans is the Mediterranean. Because even the best products are "more sold than bought," and since we did not have the funding to undertake an advertising campaign, we opted for a series of public seminar-type events as the most cost-effective course of introducing Oldways to the opinion leaders in food, wine, nutrition, and environmentalism.

We organized this series of coming-out parties for Oldways in 1991:

In March, in Miami and Palm Beach, we celebrated the first stirrings of an olive oil consciousness with four days of seminars, tastings, and Mediterranean-inspired meals.

In May, in New York City, we challenged top-flight chefs and food writers in two day-long colloquiums, one of them focused on issues in contemporary food writing and journalism, and the other on the future of American cooking in the United States, as waves of immigrants were rapidly transforming us into a global village.

In September, in Los Angeles, we organized a three-day international conference called "Cultural Models for Healthy Eating: From Asia to the Mediterranean." It challenged a cross section of top leaders in gastronomy to consider the impact that "global cuisine" (then all the rage in culinary circles) would have on the traditional foods, drinks, and foodways of the world's rainbow of cultures.

In October, in Greece, we organized a five-day international symposium called "The Food and Wines of Greece," and held it at a splendid seaside resort hotel in Porto Carras in Thessaloníki. This was a large gathering, and it focused on what was happening to traditional Mediterranean cuisine under the spread of the dreaded and increasingly ubiquitous "international cuisine" of the tourist industry. It was at once a celebration of the great Mediterranean traditions, and a warning that these traditions were eroding in the face of standardized formula cuisine that dumbed down the glorious traditional tastes and flavors. We spent a lot of time with hands-on cooking and eating and put our toes in the water about the then-quaint idea of sustainable agriculture.

We invited a winner's circle of experts in many food and wine disciplines to these symposiums, ranging from chefs to journalists and writers, broadcasters, farmers, winemakers, nutrition scientists, historians, and government officials. By the end of the year the number of people who'd attended our events was about one thousand.

All of these conferences aggressively challenged the inevitability of a monolithic industrial food and drink future, and we asked everyone to think how to reverse what appeared to be an irreversible, slippery downhill slope.

In Los Angeles Dun had put it this way at the opening of the conference:

"In many respects the world finds itself at a fork in the culinary road. If we rush headlong down the techno-food route, then manufactured, highly processed, and engineered foods are our future, and the rich garden of the world's culinary traditions will die.

"But if, instead, we accelerate our efforts to preserve and understand these culinary traditions, and incorporate the best of them into today's dietary practices, then we will meet twin goals.

"First, food growing and production will reflect much higher attention to sustainable agriculture practices—an environmental imperative.

"Second, the full and exciting tastes of the foods of other cultures will encourage major changes in dietary patterns—a public health imperative."

This thread ran through all four of these conferences in 1991 that launched Oldways, and it conveyed the rationale for setting up Oldways in the first place: that the old ways were still alive, and even if they were endangered, their values were worth fighting to preserve and propagate. It was thrilling that the serious people who joined us at these meetings caught the Oldways fever, and from that year we have never looked back.

It gradually became clear that journalists and consumers wanted specifics about the Mediterranean diet that Oldways was putting forward as the healthy alternative to the increasingly unhealthy U.S. eating patterns. So the question we sought to answer was, "What is the best way to convey nutrition information to consumers so they understand it and can readily incorporate it into their everyday and time-pressured lives?"

A DIETARY GUIDE FOR THE PEOPLE

If one thing was clear, it was that the conventional approaches to healthy eating advice for consumers were falling on deaf ears. Rates of diet-related chronic diseases were steadily rising, despite the fact the best possible scientific evidence underlaid programs trying to steer consumers toward healthy eating and lifestyles. We struggled to decipher the reasons for this disconnect, and gradually began to understand what was wrong. It was all to do with language.

Dietary guides were written in the language of nutrition-speak—eat more fruits and vegetables, avoid saturated fat, have three servings of grains a day, limit meat to seven ounces a day, and so on. But consumers speak about what they are going to eat in words of specific foods and in the cultures of food. "How about some Chinese take-out tonight?" "Want to go to that little French bistro place and have a romantic dinner?" "I feel like some pasta and red wine, how about we go to over Mario's after the movie?"

This is the familiar language of food. It's specific about details, usually focuses on a "main dish," and is decidedly practical. It is not about servings, serving sizes, or food groups. Because it is how consumers communicate about food, we must figure out ways to communicate our own eating guides in the lingua franca of people-speak.

It turns out to be a stubborn problem. No one was quite sure how to convey dietary guidelines for healthy eating and drinking to consumers effectively.

After decades of experimenting with food guides shaped like plates, graphs, wheels, ladders, rainbows, and others, a sort of international consensus has emerged that a pyramid or triangle shape is an "optimal" way to picture clearly and simply the healthy eating patterns that nutrition scientists believe promote lifelong good health. This is because pyramids are hierarchical, with a wide base that suggests greater quantity or frequency, but narrowing as they rise to suggest reduced quantities or frequency.

In 1992 the U.S. government released a new food guide pyramid to explain its diet guidelines, which were much criticized for kneeling to the meat and dairy lobbies. But this pyramid quickly became a well-recognized icon, printed in untold numbers of magazines and posted in schools, hospitals, and cafeterias everywhere.

Toward the end of 1992, we were closely watching how this food guide pyramid was received by consumers, because we were preparing to present our "Traditional Healthy Mediterranean Diet" to a large high-

So the question we sought to answer was, "What is the best way to convey nutrition information to consumers so they understand it and can readily incorporate it into their everyday and time-pressured lives?"

level international scientific and culinary conference in early January. Over the course of a year a committee of U.S. and European scientists, coordinated by Oldways with the Harvard School of Public Health and the World Health Organization, had written a precise and quite lengthy nutrition science text that carefully described the evidence and the specific elements of the healthy Mediterranean eating patterns. The text was drafted and redrafted during many months of faxes in 1992, resulting in a final version in the late fall. During a planning meeting shortly before the conference, Dun suddenly thought—*no consumer will ever read this! No consumer media will reproduce it! We've got to have a simple-to-understand graphic!* He was certain our wonderful text would have little consumer impact without some way to convey it simply.

So, we adopted the government's pyramid shape, and made it our own—the "Traditional Healthy Mediterranean Diet Pyramid," which was accompanied by the explanatory scientific text (see page 8). It depicted the makeup of the traditional Mediterranean diet, low in red meat and moderately high in olive oil. It also had a bottle and glass of red wine along one side, and a man and woman jogging on its other side. This was the first diet pyramid to picture an alcoholic beverage (because it was a traditional meal accompaniment) and to picture the close association of exercise with a healthy lifestyle. The one regret we have is that we could not persuade our scientific colleagues to include coffee and tea, despite their prevalence in the Mediterranean diet and their being a source of calories.

When we released our new pyramid at the conference, it touched off what the *Washington Post* called "Mediterranean Madness" in the headline of its story about how Mediterranean foods and dishes were sweeping into stores, restaurants, food pages, cookbooks, and home kitchens. And many newspapers and magazines had nice stories about the Traditional Healthy Mediterranean Diet and that olive oil was a healthy fat—and included a graphic of the Mediterranean diet pyramid!

With this success, Oldways rapidly became known as a resource for information about how to eat healthy foods that actually tasted good without having to count servings and portions. Also, we continued an extensive program of familiarization trips to the Mediterranean for journalists, chefs, retailers, and various others in the food business.

On the basis of this success, during the following three years we developed an Asian diet pyramid (see page 8), a Latin American diet pyramid (see page 11), and a Vegetarian diet pyramid (see page 12) as food guides for three other classic cuisines, which were popular with two important ethnic groups in the United States and the growing number of vegetarians.

These four Oldways pyramids quickly reached deeply into the culture of food choices and nutrition guidance; they were reprinted in hundreds of nutrition texts, healthy eating books and manuals, magazines, and newspapers.

We think that there are three principal reasons for the rapid and continuing successes of these pyramids.

First, these pyramids challenged the conventional wisdom that all fats are bad fats. We and our scientific advisors argued that type of fat was more important than amount of fat in eating patterns consistent with overall healthy guidelines. We also argued that the promotion of low-fat diets by the government and private groups

was sure to spawn an entire new family of low-fat and no-fat "fake" foods that would increase levels of obesity.

We were strongly attacked for this position by the nutrition establishment in 1993, but seven years later the official U.S. dietary guidelines adopted our position that a moderate amount of healthy fat was the correct course. By this time it had escaped only those in denial that the surge in sales of low-fat and no-fat foods coincided with the steep rise in rates of obesity. To make low-fat, no-fat foods palatable, manufacturers had to pack them with salt and sugar because they had low levels of fats (or none at all), people did not "feel full" and so ate more and more of them, ending up with more calories than with moderate-fat foods.

Second, these Oldways pyramids drove home the then-radical but now-accepted principle that in the dietary guides business, one size does not fit all, just as in the clothing or automobile business. The United States is increasingly polyglot; Americans come in all sizes and shapes, some older, some younger, some taller and some shorter, some men and some women, some children and some seniors, some Anglo and some Asian or Hispanic or Black. All these Americans seek out foods from many cultures—burritos, pita, rice paper roll-ups, pizzas, stir-fries, jerk chicken, and more.

A dietary guide written as if America was white and middle-class was doomed to fail with the two-thirds of Americans who were neither white nor middle class,

Oldways rapidly became known as a resource for information about how to eat healthy foods that actually tasted good without having to count servings and portions.

and it did. The 1992 U.S. Food Guide Pyramid is such a pyramid; it has failed to stem the plague of obesity.

The U.S. government's website, MyPyramid.com, introduced in April 2005 is a tremendous improvement over its previous versions. For the first time it incorporates exercise and recognizes that one size does not fit all, with a mirror site in Spanish. It is Internet based and can be individualized for each user. We don't know how successful it will be, but Americans are not ignoring it. In the first few days after its release, over 42 million Americans clicked onto the Pyramid's website. It has great potential. People do care about what they eat and drink.

TRADITIONAL HEALTHY DIET PYRAMIDS

Oldways is probably best known for its four Traditional Healthy Diet pyramids—Mediterranean, Asian, Latin American, and Vegetarian. They are the result of years of work figuring out ways to reach consumers with information that helps to change unhealthy eating habits.

They are the response to this question: What is the clearest way to picture for consumers the nutrition pattern that represents what scientists believe is the healthiest way to eat and drink?

The solution is not simple, because the science is very complex, steadily evolving, and complicated by attention-grabbing fad diets that come in and go out as regularly as the tides.

It is made even more complex because we consumers are quite different from one another. We have different tastes, preferences, shapes, metabolism, and ages. We grew up in different cultures, economic circumstances, climates, and religions. Some of us live in cities and some in the country, some in the plains and some on the coasts.

Moreover, consumers do not shop for carbohydrates or proteins, order dietary pattern take-out, browse menus for calories, or cook food guides at home. They eat food and drink drinks. As a result, it is a truism that fashioning persuasive dietary recommendations and eating guides is a daunting task.

Eating well must be cast not as work, but as companionable, nurturing, pleasant, and fun. This is why Oldways set out to evaluate the traditional diets of the world's diverse cultures. All of today's world is a melting pot, and diversity of racial and cultural backgrounds is a manifest feature of cities everywhere. To reach peoples of differing backgrounds with effective dietary guidance messages, it is essential to speak to them in a vernacular that they understand. After all, are any of us uncertain about whether we are tasting a plate of Chinese or Italian or Mexican food?

Not all food pyramids need look like the great Egyptian pyramids; they can accommodate to cultural sensitivities. China, for example, uses a pagoda shape, and the Oldways Latin American pyramid is a series of small pyramids within the main pyramid, respecting Mayan, Aztec, and Inca heritage.

All these different pyramids convey clear messages of proportionality and food groups to eat "more of," or "less of."

Pyramid Patterns

Humans are astonishingly adept at recognizing patterns. Young children in an instant can pick out a parent's face from among hundreds of others, and parents their child's.

Adults can recognize a familiar face in a large crowd, at a distance or up close, and do so even after twenty years of separation and even with the effects of twenty years of aging.

Even the most powerful computers cannot do this—it is a human quality developed over millions of years of evolution.

Pyramid-shaped food guides show a pattern of frequencies and proportions that, if followed, promote good health. And they are flexible enough to accommodate regular exercise, drinks, and other key elements of a healthy lifestyle.

It's the pyramid pattern that conveys these messages, and it is powerfully recognizable.

Daily Beverage
Recommendations:
6 Glasses of Water

MEAT — Monthly

SWEETS
EGGS — Weekly
POULTRY
FISH

Wine in
moderation

CHEESE & YOGURT

OLIVE OIL

FRUITS | BEANS, LEGUMES & NUTS | VEGETABLES — Daily

BREAD, PASTA, RICE, COUSCOUS, POLENTA,
OTHER WHOLE GRAINS & POTATOES

Daily Physical Activity

In 1947, when the first beginning steps were unknowingly taken by a small group of scientists asking residents of Crete a very large number of questions, there was no such thing as the Mediterranean diet. There was only the history of the eating patterns of the people who for 40 centuries had populated the shores of the Mediterranean.

These peoples ate close to the land and, some of them, close to the sea as well. The rhythms of their growing and harvesting and fishing refracted the rhythms of the seasons. They ate simply during their six-day workweek, usually with their immediate families. On the seventh day they feasted, usually in the festive company of extended families, neighbors, and, during religious celebrations, often with entire villages. They lived an old ways lifestyle.

In 1947 a group of scientists began the task of planning for the reconstruction of war-devastated Crete, "to see if the level of living in Crete could be raised." These scientists did what good scientists always do—they gathered masses of raw data, they sifted it, and then applied their intelligence and training to ordering it. And these were the best scientists, led by Leland Allbaugh and others drawn both from the staffs of the Rockefeller Foundation and from the highest level of Greek universities and public agencies. Their meticulous data and detailed records of Crete, published in 1953, are as evocative of the daily lives of the islanders of Crete as are the paintings of the Brueghels.

A major surprise in the public health conclusions of the Rockefeller study, which was organized by Dr. W. A. McIntosh, had to do with chronic diseases—the postwar residents of Crete were healthier than their postwar American peers (even without cod liver oil, steak, and orange juice!). This startling result piqued the interest of small groups of nutrition experts, and out of their insights (especially those of Ancel Keys) was eventually born the Mediterranean diet.

What then, is this Mediterranean diet?

It's pasta and couscous, olives and olive oil, octopus and dorade, lamb and ham, grains and greens, eggplants and onions, lemons and figs, cheese and yogurt, wine and ouzo. It's the food of the Mediterranean regions of Greece, Italy, Spain, Turkey, Morocco, Tunisia, and France—glorious food, distinguished by bold flavors and simplicity of preparation.

But it's not a "diet" in the common English language usage of the word—a prescribed menu plan designed to control weight or remediate disease. The Mediterranean "diet" we are talking about is a way of eating, drinking, and living. Perhaps the words "pattern" or "rhythm" or "style" are better describers than "way." In many Mediterranean languages there is a single word for this phrase, but unhappily it translates into English as "alimentation," a singularly unattractive word and not at all suited to describe the vibrant cuisines of the Mediterranean.

Ancel Keys himself wrestled with this linguistics dilemma for many years. He and his wife, Margaret, published a pioneering book in 1975 and called it *How to Eat Well and Stay Well the Mediterranean Way*. Their title anticipated the popularity of "Mediterranean," but it rejected "alimentation" and did not adopt "diet." "Way" did not catch on, however, and gradually the "Mediterranean diet" came to be the lingua franca for the healthy, traditional foods, wines, and eating patterns of Mediterranean peoples at mid-century.

Has this remarkable conjunction of scientific knowledge and culinary heritage that we call the Mediterranean diet had any influence or lasting impact on our everyday lives? Though this question is difficult to measure, one indicator is the influence that the work of Allbaugh, Keys, and their associates had upon the U.S. Dietary Guidelines, which are arguably the most influential of all the dietary guidance documents published anywhere in the world.

The prestige of the Rockefeller Foundation gave credibility to its startling conclusions about the healthfulness of Crete residents. The reputation and astounding magnetic energy of Ancel Keys brought individuals of enormous influence into the ambit of his Seven Countries Studies. Paul Dudley White (President Eisenhower's White House physician) wrote the foreword to Keys's 1957 book while in Heraklion

with Keys. Jean Mayer (chairman of president Nixon's White House Conference on Nutrition and a nutrition professor at Harvard before becoming president of Tufts University) wrote the foreword to Keys's 1975 book. Keys died at the age of one hundred in 2004, but a number of his colleagues in the original Seven Countries Studies remain active even today.

Each passing week, nutrition and clinical scientists uncover additional reasons to explain why Mediterranean populations who eat in healthy traditional Mediterranean diet patterns live longer and are healthier in their senior years than people who eat the "American" or "Western" diet. Some of these reasons are discovered at the metabolic level. Some are discoveries that the Mediterranean diet has impacts in other medical areas than chronic disease—gastroenterology, or old age, or women's health issues, for example.

In fact, by the time of the tenth anniversary conference of the Mediterranean diet pyramid in 2003, the scientific literature had begun to describe the Mediterranean eating pattern as "the gold standard." How far we had come!

The most effective way to preserve and promote the Traditional Healthy Mediterranean Diet is to honor its science and celebrate its culinary pleasures—to paraphrase Jean Mayer, to make the virtue of hewing to the best in science and medicine a profound and attractive pleasure at the table. We must continue to advance the scientific understanding of the mechanisms that define the traditional healthy Mediterranean eating patterns, and educate people everywhere about the ease and the pleasures of cooking in Mediterranean ways.

> The most effective way to preserve and promote the healthy traditional Mediterranean diet is to honor its science and celebrate its culinary pleasures—to paraphrase Jean Mayer, to make the virtue of hewing to the best in science and medicine a profound and attractive pleasure at the table.

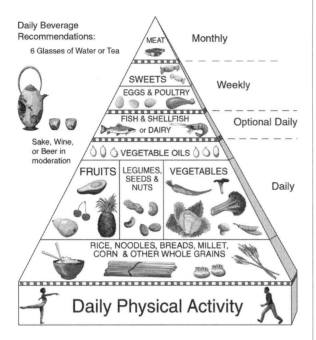

Daily Beverage
Recommendations:
6 Glasses of Water or Tea

MEAT — Monthly

SWEETS — Weekly
EGGS & POULTRY

FISH & SHELLFISH
or DAIRY — Optional Daily

Sake, Wine,
or Beer in
moderation

VEGETABLE OILS

FRUITS — LEGUMES, SEEDS & NUTS — VEGETABLES — Daily

RICE, NOODLES, BREADS, MILLET,
CORN & OTHER WHOLE GRAINS

Daily Physical Activity

The foods of Asia are exciting, aromatic, mysterious, captivating. Why is this so?

Because over many centuries, the Asian peoples designed their meals this way, making them a riotous collection of foods, spices, and traditions. The dishes gradually became as much a part of the culture and traditions of Asians as did pagodas and mysticism.

Even on a quick examination we discover the eight flavors that Chinese cooks must balance; the five flavors blended in Thai cooking; the deft use of aromatics in Indian cooking; the balance of cooked, uncooked, and barely cooked foods in Japanese cuisine; the nuoc mam fish sauce in Vietnam; and stunning adaptations of these in Hong Kong.

And at Asian tables we smell, taste, and savor crispy-skinned Peking duck; exquisitely seasoned shrimp, fish, and shellfish in Hong Kong; the gorgeous sushi and sashimi of Kyoto and Tokyo; parades of trolleys filled with dim sum; soothing, aromatic sobu noodles steeping in a broth of lemongrass with a kick of spicy pepper; symbolic and extravagant "food as art" in formal Chinese banquets; a magnificent Indonesian rijst-

tafel; steaming Mongolia hotpots; the dizzying variety of flavors and shapes of bread from the wheat-growing regions of India's north; delicate pad thai noodles; rices—steamed, curried, fried, boiled; and Vietnamese spring rolls, with fresh vegetables, shrimp, chicken, and cilantro wrapped in crisp rice paper.

Generations of Asians and visitors to Asia have marveled at its foods and dishes. Nutrition science is only now discovering the reasons why these delicious, variegated, and traditional cuisines are healthier than "modern" food.

Like the traditional Mediterranean diet, the traditional Asian diet is built upon a base of healthy grain (rice), buttressed by leafy green vegetables and soybeans, small amounts of fish and meat (pork and chicken), bounteous spices and herbs—all tied together with healthy soy and peanut oils.

> Generations of Asians and visitors to Asia have marveled at its foods and dishes. Nutrition science is only now discovering the reasons why these delicious, variegated, and traditional cuisines are healthier than "modern" food.

LATIN AMERICAN DIET PYRAMID

Daily Beverage
Recommendations:
6 Glasses of Water

MEAT,
SWEETS
& EGGS

WEEKLY

PLANT OILS

Alcohol in
moderation

FISH
& SHELLFISH

DAIRY

POULTRY

DAILY

WHOLE GRAINS, TUBERS,
PASTA, BEANS & NUTS

AT EVERY
MEAL

FRUITS

VEGETABLES

Daily Physical Activity

The Healthy Traditional Latin American Food Guide Pyramid is derived from the very best and most up-to-date nutrition science. It speaks in the familiar vernacular of the foods of Latino ethnic groups and describes the foods and their diverse individual cultures.

The Latin American diet pyramid incorporates the foods, the culinary traditions, the practicalities of food availability, and the sustainability of diets ranging throughout the vastness of Latin America. It reflects the ethnic backgrounds, genetic makeup, and the economic, educational and social status of the more than half a billion people in Latin America—just about twice as many people as live in the United States. It reflects agricultural harvests from the northwestern corner of Mexico to Tierra del Fuego—a distance of 7,000 miles, or twice the distance from Boston to San Diego. And it reflects the acculturation of waves of migration and spasms of conquests.

It also reflects the experience of the border region, where interplay between the cultures of the southern half of the American continents and those of the northern half is a daily fact of life.

The foods of the Latin American diet pyramid are not strange; they are potatoes, beans, tomatoes, chiles, corn, avocados, tortillas, and chocolate. There are a hundred varieties of potatoes readily available in Latin American markets; corn kernels as big as table grapes are common in parts of the Andes mountains; and pasta in soups is eaten nearly as often as tortillas. In addition, the people of Latin America drink alcohol in amounts not far different from other of the world's populations.

Chris Schlesinger and John Willoughby have written about the "unconscious healthfulness" of many ethnic cuisines around the world, which "were created not specifically to be healthful, but to be as tasty as possible using available ingredients—largely grain, legumes, vegetables and spices."

"The resulting dishes turn out to be good for you," they conclude. This innate healthfulness is a hallmark of the Traditional Healthy Latin American Diet pyramid, and if it is widely popularized, it can help to encourage and enable people to eat in healthy patterns—healthy for our bodies, and healthy for our earth.

Chris Schlesinger and John Willoughby have written about the "unconscious healthfulness" of many ethnic cuisines around the world, which "were created not specifically to be healthful, but to be as tasty as possible using available ingredients—largely grain, legumes, vegetables and spices."

The development of this Vegetarian diet pyramid followed a different pattern than did the development of the Mediterranean, Latin American, and Asian pyramids. The three geographically determined pyramids drew upon analyses of populations and eating patterns with many culturally homogenous characteristics. For example, the dominant grain of the Mediterranean diet is wheat; in Latin America it is corn; and in Asia, rice. Since grains are the foundation of all healthy population-wide eating patterns, this "grain determinant" is a principal identifier of the region's dietary patterns and foodways.

But this is not so with vegetarian eating patterns, since there are vegetarians in the Mediterranean, Latin America, Asia, the United States, and elsewhere. Consequently, the analysis underlying the Vegetarian diet pyramid rests upon the epidemiology of groups of vegetarians in all parts of the world.

Data from vegetarians show that they enjoy the lowest recorded rates of chronic diseases and the highest adult life expectancy, and the healthfulness of this pattern is corroborated by epidemiological and experimental nutrition. In a time when overweight and obesity have reached epidemic proportions in the United States, this way of eating offers a powerful route for intervention and behavior modification—since, as a group, vegetarians are leaner than nonvegetarians.

Here, as described by the Oldways conference scientists and depicted in the Vegetarian diet pyramid are the characteristics of the Traditional Healthy Vegetarian Diet.

1. Multiple daily servings of foods from these groups: fruits and vegetables, whole grains.

2. Daily servings from nuts and seeds, plant oils, egg whites, soy milks and dairy.

3. Occasional or small-quantity servings of eggs and sweets.

4. Attention to consuming a variety of foods from all seven of these groups.

5. Daily consumption of enough water throughout the day to assure good health.

6. Regular physical activity at a level that promotes healthy weight, fitness, and well-being.

7. Reliance upon whole foods and minimally processed foods in preference to highly processed foods.

8. Moderate regular intake of alcoholic beverages such as wine, beer, or spirits (optional).

9. Daily consumption of unrefined plant oils.

10. Dietary supplements as necessary, based upon factors such as age, sex, and lifestyle, with special attention to those avoiding dairy and/or eggs (vitamins D and B_{12}).

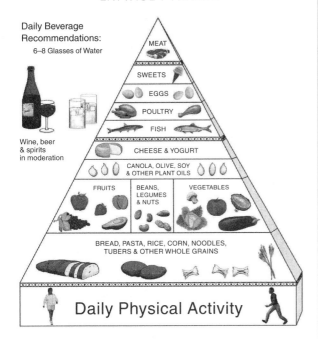

EATWISE PYRAMID

Daily Beverage
Recommendations:
6–8 Glasses of Water

MEAT

SWEETS

EGGS

POULTRY

FISH

CHEESE & YOGURT

CANOLA, OLIVE, SOY
& OTHER PLANT OILS

FRUITS

BEANS,
LEGUMES
& NUTS

VEGETABLES

BREAD, PASTA, RICE, CORN, NOODLES,
TUBERS & OTHER WHOLE GRAINS

Wine, beer
& spirits
in moderation

Daily Physical Activity

At the end of the 1990s, the Mediterranean diet eating pattern began to be recognized as a model for international population-wide dietary guidance. During our 2001 International Conference on Traditional Eating Patterns in Beijing, this concept was much discussed among the international attendees, in the context that the pattern of types of foods was the key and not the literal Mediterranean foods themselves.

Over the next two years, articles in leading scientific and medical journals adopted this approach referring to the "Med-type dietary pattern" as the gold standard, which could be adapted to the foods of individual cultures throughout the world. As a result, this Mediterranean eating pattern has gradually become the measuring stick against which other eating patterns are judged.

The reasons are not complicated. The Mediterranean diet has a healthful balance among the essential nutrients—fats, carbohydrates, and proteins. The fats are balanced in healthful ways among saturated and unsaturated (both polyunsaturated and monounsaturated); the carbohydrates are a healthful balance between simple and complex carbohydrates; and the proteins are

a healthful mix of animal, fish, and plant. The alcohol of Mediterranean peoples is wine, almost always drunk with meals, the most sensible way to drink.

We realized that not everyone could, or would, eat the classic Mediterranean diet, and would not work in the fields and walk every day through the village or city squares, meeting and greeting. In advancing the concept of the "Med-type diet," we encourage substitution of local foods. We used examples such as dried beans for Italian fava beans, or spinach instead of broccoli rabe, or rice noodles in place of wheat pasta.

To represent this global gold standard Med-style diet we introduced the fifth and final Oldways pyramid, the EatWise pyramid. It is a kind of stew: the gold standard eating pattern in a pyramid shape, picturing the foods of many different cultures. It is the gold standard, multicultural food guide pyramid.

Some Nomenclature

There is little doubt about the gulf that separates "nutrition" and "food."

Nutrition speaks of proteins, carbohydrates, fats, glycemic index, hydration, and hundreds and hundreds of other scientific words and concepts. Food speaks of cheeseburgers, oatmeal, Caesar salad, ice cream, pita pockets, burritos, stir-fries, pasta, baguettes, crisp apples, juicy plums, and thousands more. The real question is whether these twain shall ever meet.

The Oldways approach is to acknowledge the twain and not try to force them to merge. We have five food pyramids—Mediterranean, Asian, Latin American, Vegetarian, and Eatwise—that present the healthy eating nutrition patterns of these cultures, but do so using pictures of foods actually eaten by their peoples.

In *The Oldways Table*, we have pulled the many threads of our Oldways tapestry together, and we hope that it stirs larger challenges to the spread of techno foods. The patterns of the old ways of food, drink, and agriculture are sounder for the health of each one of us.

"All over the world, most of us make our daily bread from grain."

—K. DUN GIFFORD

"The Whole Grains Council aims to educate consumers about whole grains, and I hope that with more attention and awareness, the consumption of whole grains will increase."

—MIKE ORLANDO

GRAINS

Grains are bound so tightly to us—and we to them—that we characterize entire cultures by the major grains the people eat.

Chinese are "rice people," for example, while South and Central Americans are "corn people." North Americans and Mediterraneans are "wheat people," North Europeans are "oats and rye people," and Africans are "millet and sorghum people."

Galaxies of Grains— Grain and Culture
K. DUN GIFFORD

As with most things about what we humans eat and drink, however, it's not quite that simple. India, the second most populated country in the world, is divided among wheat, barley, and rice people. Chinese and Indians use sorghum flour to make breads; the Chinese make strong alcoholic beverages from sorghum and Indians make beer. Americans eat oatmeal made by rolling oats and drink beer made from fermenting barley. South and Central Americans eat pasta from wheat and drink chicha beer from corn. Each of the world's cultures seems to have its own preferences, and grains truly are the staff that supports life as we know it. All over the world most of us make our daily bread from grain, and we make a lot of our booze (mostly beer and spirits) from it, too.

Which grain grows where has a lot to do with climate. Rice grows where it pours rain, wheat and corn where it rains middling amounts, and sorghum and millet where it doesn't rain much at all. Everyone, everywhere, complains about the weather, but rice farmers pray for sun, wheat farmers pray for a balance of sun and rain, and sorghum farmers pray for rain.

FLATBREADS AROUND THE WORLD

A human universal version of grains is flatbread, which tracks back to the times before pots, pans, stoves, and ovens, when our ancestors made do with rock, water, and fire. They picked grains and ground them between rocks, mixed this rough flour up with water (sometimes adding fresh milk) to make dough, then spread this dough to cook over hot rocks heated by their cooking fires.

Flatbreads are good travelers. Pita breads from the Middle East are familiar in Western countries and so are rice papers; they make pockets and roll-ups for many varieties of quick foods. The French make crepes, Americans make pancakes (and bread slices), Brits make tea muffins, Indians make chapatis, Italians make pizza, Mexicans make tortillas, Norwegians make lefse, Russians make blinis—the list of culturally distinct flatbreads is dizzyingly long.

There are thousands of other versions of flatbreads, but one thing they all have in common is that they are grain-based delivery vehicles. They deliver other great foods—all sorts of vegetables, meats, cheeses, and more. But you do not need to stretch your mind very far to think of fruit pies as flatbreads, too—they're basically fruit between sheets of pastry. And people everywhere put fruits on bread—as jams, jellies, tarts, fruit spreads, and inside bread as fillings.

Another key reason for the endurance of flatbreads on the human menu is that they usually taste pretty good, and of all the foods readily available, they are both inexpensive and easily transportable. Think of the Roman legions marching from Rome to London, or the pilgrims trekking to Jerusalem—bread was their staff of life.

NOODLES AROUND THE WORLD

In addition to making flatbreads from their iconic grain, people all over the world also turn grains into culturally distinct slippery foods. The obvious examples are rice noodles and buckwheat noodles (soba) in Asia, and durum wheat pasta and couscous in the Mediterranean. Everyone puts grains into soups and stews, including rice, barley, wheat, corn, sorghum, and millet and all their cousins. All these grains are slippery foods; humans do not have the large molars and jaw muscles to chew uncooked grains. As is the case with flatbreads, these slippery grain foods provide a base for adding protein foods, fats, and other vegetables, generating untold legions of great pasta, soup, and stew dishes.

Pasta, like flatbreads, is a terrific delivery vehicle for delicious foods from other food groups—tomato sauces are the quick-to-mind example, but meat sauces, clam sauces, cheeses, and olive oil are everyday pasta partners. When the Atkins craze threatened to take over America's sanity in 2003 and 2004, Oldways organized a scientific conference on the healthy pasta meal (see page 25) to reintroduce a pasta dish as a healthy and delicious, almost-perfect meal.

Pasta has also long been a staple in the soups and stews of Northern Europe, Russia, China, Latin America, Africa, and the Caribbean. It is a staple base of meals in cultures spread out along the shoreline of the Mediterranean; couscous, for example, is just round-shaped pasta. Joining pasta in these soups and stews are vegetables, red and white meats, fish and shellfish, herbs and spices, cheese, olive oil, butter, salt and pepper, and (sometimes) whatever else seems to be hanging around the pantry or refrigerator.

Moving to Asia, stir-fries have pasta's aura of ubiquitousness—and since stir-fries are served over rice, it has always seemed to me that pasta and stir-fries are fraternal twins. Rice and pasta dishes both deliver vegetables and meat and a lot of other partners with their grain base.

Let's not overlook chicken noodle soup, the elemental comfort cure-all food of countless cultures as diverse as Middle American farm families and kosher Jewish families.

THE BREAD OF LIFE

Then there's bread itself. It is indispensable for religious ceremonies and sustaining pilgrims, for breakfast and coffee breaks, for filling lunch boxes and picnic baskets, for stuffing turkeys and feeding pigeons, for carrying cheeseburgers and Frenching toast, and for countless Asian, Latin, African, and Mediterranean equivalents.

It is often written that the aromas of baking breads, pies, pastries, pizza, and tortillas speak to tribal memories common to all humans, much as roasting meat does. Is this evidence that being masters of fire is what separates us from our cousins, the chimpanzees?

Grains in Human Evolution

JEFF DAHLBERG, PhD

Oldways has brought focus to grains as the base food of human eating, and grains form the base of all the Oldways pyramids (Mediterranean, Asian, Latin, Vegetarian, and EatWise). But we didn't start talking about why grains are healthy until we began our PAX (phytonutrients and antioxidants) Initiative in the spring of 2001. At this project's first conference, we met two gentlemen from Lubbock, Texas, who represented the National Sorghum Producers. We didn't know then much about sorghum, but we soon did—about how healthy, useful, and tasty sorghum can be. We found their research director, a world-traveling agronomist named Jeff Dahlberg, to be a plain-talking Texan with a vast knowledge of plants and agriculture. So when the time came to explain the ABCs of grains for this book, we looked no further than the gentleman from Lubbock.

For most of the two million plus years we have inhabited the earth, humans were hunter-gatherers. Roughly 99.995 percent of our time on earth has been spent hunting and gathering our basic food needs. In fact, several researchers have concluded that one could adequately gather enough food from wild stands of grasses to provide sufficient supplies of grains to supplement other foods in a diverse diet.

Something happened about ten thousand years ago that helped set our paths on the road to agriculture. Agriculture is a dynamic, changing (human), evolutionary (plants and animals) system, which continues developing an interactive relationship between the humans and their environment. From this relationship, products are produced.

Roughly ten million people occupied the earth ten thousand years ago, and there have been several debates as to what changed these people from hunter-gatherers to agriculturalists. Was it population pressure? Change in the climate? Cultural changes? We discovered it? Gods or goddesses handed it down to us? No matter what happened, we did something to change how we dealt with plants and animals. In the simplest sense, we "domesticated" plants and animals. To domesticate means to bring into the household. The first act of domestication was to select plants that did not shatter their seeds and therefore these plants became dependent upon humans for their survival and dispersal.

This had consequences for us, also. We began to settle into cities and towns. Language, art, culture, and education became more developed. In many ways, we became domesticated. Paleoethnobotanist Dr. Jack Harlan best summed up the impact domestication of plants and animals had upon us: "Man has become so utterly dependent on the plants that he grows that, in a sense, the plants have 'domesticated' him."

Today, there are many types of grass seeds used by humans in food preparations; however, six cereals dominate our agriculture heritage. These six cereals are wheat, rice, maize, barley, sorghum, and millet.

Wheat clearly dominates as the most important cereal crop worldwide in terms of the amount of hectares that are planted; however, with improved plant breeding, rice actually produces more than wheat on a per hectare basis. Clearly, there are other cereal crops that play important roles in agricultural systems throughout the world. Teff, grown almost exclusively in Ethiopia, is a major cereal crop that is an integral part of the Ethiopian agricultural landscape. Fonio is another important cereal that is grown in the semi-arid regions of West Africa and is still a major staple of many people's diets. With this in mind, here's a brief summary about some of the most important cereal crops that make up our diet, along with some others unfamiliar to most of us.

WHEAT

The origins of cultivated wheat are extremely complex. The Fertile Crescent is thought to be the most likely site of the origin of wheat, and it is believed that around eight thousand years ago an event led to the creation of wild emmer wheat, which is the ancestor to most of the wheat cultivated today. Wheat was probably first introduced into the Americas by the Spanish, and English colonists most likely brought it to the United States. These early introductions did not grow well, and the Mennonites are one of the few groups that had much early success with wheat. Immigrants from Russia brought "Turkey" wheat to the United States in 1870, and this was well adapted to hot, dry climates.

We use several types of wheat for various food products today. Hard red winter wheat is grown primarily in Nebraska, Kansas, Oklahoma, and the Texas panhandle. Wheat flour is used primarily for bread making and it seems to thrive in areas where cold, freezing winters and poor moisture conditions are common. Soft red winter wheat is grown throughout the United States and is typically found in more humid areas of the country (central Texas, around the Great Lakes, and east toward the Atlantic). This flour is used to produce cookies, cakes, snack foods, crackers, and other pastries. Hard red spring wheat, used primarily in breads, is grown in the northern plains. Two other types of wheat

"Today, a great many types of grass seeds (also known as cereal grains, and just plain grains) are used by humans in food preparations; however, six cereals dominate our agriculture heritage. These six cereals are wheat, rice, maize, barley, sorghum, and millet."

—JEFF DAHLBERG, PhD

are grown in the United States—durum and white wheat. Durum wheat, the hardest of the other wheats, with high levels of protein, is used in the production of pastas. White wheat, similar to soft red winter wheat, is used for bakery products.

RICE

There are over 120,000 varieties of rice around the world. *Oryza sativa,* the rice most familiar to the world, was probably domesticated in China and/or Southeast Asia. *Oryza glaberrima,* called African rice, was domesticated in Africa. Debate surrounds the date of domestication; however, it can be argued that the domestication of rice was probably one of the most important agricultural developments ever to take place, since rice has fed more people for a longer period of time than any other crop. The earliest evidence for domesticated rice was found in remains dating to 4000 B.C. in Thailand.

Rice is highly adaptable and can be grown in diverse environments. It is grown on both irrigated uplands and rain-fed, flood-prone lowlands. More than three-quarters of all rice harvested is grown on irrigated lands. Many of the world's poorest people depend upon rice grown in upland areas and on rain-fed lowlands. A paddy is a field that is flooded, and this paddy rice is also known as rough rice, still containing the hull. Brown rice is simply rice that has had its hull removed. We most often see white rice in the markets; this is brown rice that has had its bran removed and the grain polished. Many products are made from rice—rice noodles, rice flour, rice cakes—but most Americans consume rice simply boiled in water for 20 minutes.

MAIZE

Native American folklore tells of a beautiful woman giving corn to a lonely man, and that when he sees silk on the cornstalks he is reminded of that beautiful woman and no longer feels alone. Maize, or corn as it is more commonly referred to in the United States, is believed to have been domesticated in the Tehuacan Valley of Mexico. Corncobs as old as 5,600 years have been unearthed in archaeological sites in New Mexico. Corn played an extremely important role in the daily lives of many Native Americans. It was extensively grown in ancient America and was first brought to Europe soon after its discovery in Cuba by Christopher Columbus's men in 1492.

There are currently several types of corn, and they are typically classified as dent, flint, popcorn, sweet, waxy, and pod corn. Much of this classification is based on end uses.

Corn is one of the most highly researched crops in the world and is planted in some of the best agricultural land in the world. The world record for corn yield is over twenty thousand pounds per acre. It typically requires good levels of moisture and does not tolerate drought stress very well. It has a wide range of uses, and it is estimated that of the ten thousand food items available in a typical grocery store, twenty-five hundred of those items contain corn or a corn by-product.

BARLEY

There is good evidence to suggest that about ten thousand years ago, in the Fertile Crescent, barley was first domesticated. It has been argued that this might be the first domesticated cereal. The grain was probably ground to make porridge or flatbreads; however, moist barley was quite susceptible to fermentation. Egyptians and Greeks talk about fermented beverages, breads, and porridges made from barley. Christopher Columbus probably introduced barley to North America.

Barley is one of the most highly adaptable cereals and can be grown from sub-Arctic to sub-tropical climates. Because it grows well in cool, dry conditions, it is found mostly in the northern plain states and the Pacific Northwest. Over 6.6 billion gallons of malted beverages are produced in the United States, and malted barley is used in beer, liquor, and malted milk and as flavoring in other products.

SORGHUM

The center of origin for sorghum was in Ethiopia in East Africa. The oldest recorded find of sorghum (eight thousand years old) was in southern Egypt. Nomadic tribes and traders traversing the numerous caravan routes throughout Africa exposed the wild ancestors of sorghum to variable climates and geography and through this exposure, five major races of sorghum evolved. Each race is distinctive in its environmental adaptation.

In Africa and Asia, sorghum is used for various food products, including flatbreads, porridges, and couscous. It can be malted and made into traditional or lager beer and other malted products. Its stems and stalks are used as animal feed, and the stalks are utilized as building material. Sorghum was first described in the United States by Benjamin Franklin, who introduced the country to broomcorn, which is actually a type of sorghum. Sorghum is extremely drought tolerant, and it is grown primarily in areas in the United States that are prone to prolonged drought and heat stress. In the United States, most sorghum is either used in livestock feeding or is exported. People on the East Coast may recognize it as sorghum syrup or molasses, while others in the United States are using it as a gluten-free flour. One of the fastest-growing uses of sorghum is in ethanol production.

PEARL MILLET

Pearl millet is considered one of the "lost crops of Africa" because most people outside of Africa and India have never heard of it. Pearl millet is the sixth most important cereal crop worldwide and was most likely domesticated four thousand years ago in what is now the heart of the Sahara Desert. Approximately ten thousand years ago, the Sahara Desert was considered a vast, lush savanna where wild cereals were abundant. As the climate changed and the Sahara began to dry up, several important cereal crops were domesticated and moved throughout the continent of Africa. Pearl millet is a staple crop in some of the harshest climates in the world and is grown on hot, dry, sandy soils. In the United States it is considered primarily an animal feed and fodder; but in Africa and India, it is a versatile foodstuff. Compared to other cereals, it is relatively nutritious and is used mainly as whole, cracked, or ground flour or as a ricelike product.

TEFF

Because of an interest in foods from international destinations, teff has begun to show up in the United States and Europe. Ethiopian restaurants in major cities have introduced teff to those people outside of Ethiopia, where it is a major cereal crop. Teff is so popular in Ethiopia that its production exceeds that of most other cereals, and in parts of the country, it provides about two-thirds of the protein in a typical diet. Most teff is made into a flat, spongy, and slightly sour bread called injera, which looks similar to a crepe or bubbly pancake the size of a serving platter. It is torn and used to scoop up spicy stews and food dishes. Though it is only grown in Ethiopia, it has potential in other countries, since it grows well under difficult growing conditions. Because of the small size of its grains, it is eaten in the whole-grain form and consequently has better food value than some of the other cereal grains that are typically refined.

FONIO

Fonio is thought to be the oldest African cereal grain and, for thousands of years, has been cultivated in dry savannas in West Africa. Despite its ancient heritage, little is known of this crop outside of West Africa, and this is in part due to some misunderstanding by outsiders. Europeans called this crop "hungry rice," and it was thought to be a crop only harvested when native people were starving and hungry.

QUINOA

Quinoa has been cultivated for more than five thousand years in the Andean highlands, and the Incas considered it the "mother grain." Technically, quinoa is considered a pseudocereal and is adapted to cold, dry climates. It is handled like rice in its seed processing. The Incas recognized its nutritional importance early on and mixed it with corn to create a balanced meal. It has an almost perfect amino acid composition and is high in calcium, phosphorus, and iron and low in sodium. The seeds are covered with a resinlike substance called saponin, which must be removed before eating. The crop is extremely salt-tolerant and will grow from three to six feet in height. It is typically prepared whole, similar to rice, or made into flour for breads and biscuits.

THE INFLUENCE OF GRAINS ON HISTORY

Clearly, domestication of cereals had a tremendous influence upon our history, and today we consume a wide variety of plants in our daily search for food. We continue to learn about new or "lost" crops that broaden our culinary dictionary. As the world becomes smaller and we learn more about the important role of different plants in different cultures, we will benefit from the rich knowledge and history of our ancestors and the role plants played in their development.

Breakfasts of Champions

SARA BAER-SINNOTT

We often wonder: Do top nutritionists really "walk the walk," or do they just "talk the talk?" In other words, do leading nutrition scientists eat for breakfast what they tell us is good for us to eat for breakfast? We think you'll be fascinated to learn that whole-grain cereal makes the breakfast menu of all the nutrition leaders we surveyed!

FROM PENNY KRIS-ETHERTON, PhD, PENNSYLVANIA STATE UNIVERSITY

To answer your question about my very favorite breakfast: I have come to love McCann's oatmeal doctored up in many different ways. It is steel-cut oatmeal from Ireland. It comes in a can and is available in State College, Pennsylvania, so I presume you can find it all over the country. I always serve it mixed with applesauce and with fruit, nuts, and whipped yogurt on top. Here are some versions you might consider:

- Oatmeal (with berry-flavored applesauce) and berries (fresh or dried blueberries are great, too), toasted almonds, and whipped vanilla yogurt

- Oatmeal with unflavored, unsweetened applesauce and dates, pecans, and whipped peach yogurt

- Oatmeal with unflavored, unsweetened applesauce on top, with bananas, toasted coconut, flavored walnuts, and whipped vanilla yogurt

- Oatmeal with peach applesauce and canned peaches, whipped peach yogurt, and walnuts

If you don't use whipped yogurt, any yogurt will do. And, you can come up with all sorts of neat and interesting variations.

Along with the oatmeal, freshly squeezed orange juice and latte makes any of these breakfasts taste great!

FROM JENNIE BRAND-MILLER, PhD, UNIVERSITY OF SYDNEY

This morning I had muesli mixed half and half with raw oats and a whole mango. (It's mango season here and we buy them by the box. I'll be yellow soon!) I find raw oats keep me going from 7 A.M. to 1 P.M. without any thought of hunger. Breakfast is usually a breakfast cereal of some sort, but I make sure they are low GI ones (see page 26 for information on GI, or glycemic index) and that I eat them with a low-fat milk. Sometimes I'll put a sliced banana and a drizzle of one of Australia's pure floral honeys on top. We tested these recently and showed they had remarkably low glycemic index values. On a nice, slow weekend, I'll cook up some poached eggs on a muffin with extra lean bacon and grilled tomato with basil sprinkled on top.

FROM WALTER WILLETT, MD, DrPH, HARVARD SCHOOL OF PUBLIC HEALTH

For breakfast, I usually have a packet of Kashi or a mix of oats, brown rice, wheat, and other grains. I add two tablespoons of flaxseed for omega-3 fatty acids and cook for forty-five minutes. It cooks while I'm out running. (The cereal can also be cooked the night before.) Then I add dried fruit or fresh fruit and a few nuts, and sometimes a little bit of milk. I also have orange juice diluted with carbonated water.

FROM JOHN FOREYT, PhD, BAYLOR COLLEGE OF MEDICINE

Before I leave for the office I always have oatmeal with skim milk and a glass of orange juice; when I get to the office, I have one cup of black coffee.

Whole Grains: A Special Case

K. DUN GIFFORD

All grains are created whole, but by the time they have traveled from field to table, it is extremely unlikely they have remained whole—the vast proportion have been refined into fine white enriched flour.

Down through the millions of years of human evolution, our forebears ate only whole, intact grains; they were not able to "refine" and "highly process" their grains. But as archaeologists regularly report from their excavations, ancient peoples did grind them; museum dioramas teach us that the men went out hunting for meat and fish, while the women and children picked wild grains and then, using stones, ground them. Stone-ground grains were all that they knew.

In relatively recent times—say, the last few hundred years—we learned how to "mill" grain by stripping away its bran (outer shell and source of fiber) and its germ (embryo and source of key nutrients and unsaturated fatty acids), and then processing what remains (its endosperm, which is starch) into very fine flour. We learned how to refine it further by bleaching, and to fortify it by adding back vitamins and minerals that were removed during milling, processing, and refining, and even adding some that were never in them to begin with.

From the perspective of nutrition and health, this continuum has two important consequences, both of which bear on overweight and obesity. The first is the rate of digestion and nutrient absorption, and the second is the laying down of body fat.

DIGESTION AND ABSORPTION

Let's stop and take a look at how our stomachs and intestines attack and break down whole grains on the one hand, and refined white flour, on the other.

When whole grains are delivered, stomachs and intestines must work hard to break through the bran's protective layer and move it along; to unpack the nutrients and disassemble the pesky fats and nutrients in the germ; and then to get to work on the endosperm, which they confront as a lump and not as small particles. All this work takes some time, and it stretches out significantly the length of time it takes to turn them into sugars.

There are two key points here: the digestion time differentials between refined flours and whole grains (it takes longer to digest whole grains); and what's in whole grains that's not in white flour (bran and germ, among others). This "absorption time factor" is a very important connection between eating and drinking, and obesity and overweight.

LAYING DOWN BODY FAT

Starch is transformed mostly into glucose, a sugar. Glucose is an essential building block delivered by the digestive system to the rest of the body. It is the fuel that powers cells, which in turn power muscles (heart, lung, eye, stomach, leg, and so on). Glucose is essential for life.

Bodies are very efficient in handling glucose; it is rapidly absorbed into the bloodstream and quickly carried to the nooks and crannies of brains and the tips of fingers and toes. As an indication of just how quickly, an average adult has about twelve pints of blood, and since his/her heart pumps about ten pints of blood per minute, the heart handles nearly all of a body's blood in just over a minute.

So far, so good—unless there is too much refined flour in the stomach. When there is, then too much glucose can be churned out too rapidly, and then too much glucose is absorbed, and then there is a flood of glucose in the bloodstream. When it senses a glucose flood, the body tries to restore balance by producing an immediate corresponding flood of insulin, because insulin lowers the levels of glucose in the blood.

If the glucose flood is strong, as it would be after eating, say, a large white flour bagel, then, in its anxiety, the body can overreact and produce too much insulin, which lowers the blood glucose levels too far, which then sends alarm signals to the brain to get more glucose, which then revs up the body's appetite urge, and the body sends out hunger signals. Then the body wants to eat more food, which means more calories, more weight gain, and more body fat.

If, however, this bagel had been whole grain, there would be no glucose flood, but instead a gradual flow of glucose, which would not raise any hunger alarms.

Refined white flour can contribute to overeating because of the "yo-yo effect" of a glucose rush/insulin response, followed by a glucose need/appetite signal, resulting in the normal instinct to respond to this signal by eating and drinking.

National dietary guides and recommendations, a phenomenon of the last hundred years, recognize grains as the "base" of a healthy eating pattern and recommend multiple servings of grains every day. There are both evolutionary as well as nutrition science reasons for this. For survival, bodies need fats, proteins, carbohydrates, and water. For millions of years of evolution, protohumans and then humans got all the nutrients they needed from the natural whole foods they ate and what they drank. They did not have and did not need supplements, fortification, and additives.

Whole grains stored for the winter months supplied proteins, carbohydrates, and some fats; during the rest of the year, vegetables, fruits, nuts, legumes, fish, and game joined grains to supply the necessities for life.

In a phrase, "we ignore whole grains at our peril."

The Next Part of the Story: Oldways and the Whole Grains Council

CYNTHIA HARRIMAN

Oldways has long encouraged whole grains as part of the gold standard Mediterranean diet. For more than a decade most of our conferences—whatever the city or theme—included sessions on the health benefits of whole grains. Our conference chefs created delicious dishes featuring whole grains from their entire range—amaranth and bulgur to sorghum and wheat berries.

Along the way we made friends with dozens of people who farmed, milled, and baked whole grains; with the scientists and health professionals who studied them; and with chefs who experimented with new ways to cook and serve whole grains. All of these friends urged us to create an ongoing, focused effort to promote whole grains.

So it was that the idea for the Whole Grains Council was born at the Oldways Whole Grains Summit in

April of 2002. After a year of informally brainstorming goals and purposes, the group held its initial meeting in July of 2003, and the council soon had its first nine industry members. A dozen scientists and a handful of culinary experts signed on as well to ensure that the council received the best advice on health, grain science, and cooking issues.

The group had lofty goals, all centered on the need to remove consumer barriers to enjoying more whole grains—to make whole grains a mainstream product. We learned that consumers—and many manufacturers—do not understand what a whole grain is, so the council crafted a consumer-friendly definition of whole grain. We realized that shoppers have trouble identifying whole-grain products on grocery shelves, and we developed the eye-catching black and gold "Whole Grain" stamp for whole-grain foods. We discovered that manufacturers were eager to understand the market for whole grains and some of the technological issues in switching to whole grains, and we convened a major industry conference to educate companies. We found that the media needed a reliable source for whole-grain facts and recipes, and we filled the information void.

By January of 2006, the Whole Grains Council had grown to more than one hundred members, with more joining every week. The country's leading grain manufacturers joined the effort, alongside small artisan companies, all committed to producing more whole-grain

Definition of Whole Grains

Whole grains or foods made from them contain all the essential parts and naturally occurring nutrients of the entire grain seed. If the grain has been processed (e.g., cracked, crushed, rolled, extruded, lightly pearled, and/or cooked), the food product should deliver approximately the same rich balance of nutrients that are found in the original grain seed.

Examples of generally accepted whole-grain foods and flours are amaranth, barley (lightly pearled), brown and colored rice, buckwheat, bulgur, corn and whole cornmeal, emmer, farro, grano (lightly pearled wheat), Kamut grain, millet, oatmeal and whole oats, popcorn, quinoa, sorghum, spelt, triticale, whole rye, whole or cracked wheat, wheat berries, and wild rice.

This definition has been approved and endorsed by the Whole Grains Council, May 2004.

WHOLE GRAIN STAMP

The 2005 Dietary Guidelines for Americans call on everyone to eat at least three servings of whole grains daily. However, many consumers are unsure about what is a whole-grain product and what isn't. In 2005, Oldways and its Whole Grains Council unveiled the "Whole Grain" stamp, a graphic that identifies foods containing a half serving or a full serving of whole grains per labeled serving. In 2006, the stamps appeared on more than eight hundred products, including breads, cereals, crackers, soups, cookies, and granola bars.

BASIC STAMP

A half serving of whole grains

At least 8g whole grain per labeled serving

100% STAMP

A full serving of whole grains

At least 16g whole grain per labeled serving *and* no refined grain

products and closing the whole grains gap. The "Whole Grain" stamp began to appear on products in supermarkets across the land, and consumers who saw the stamp on the *Today Show* and on *Oprah* started using the stamp to guide their purchases of more whole-grain products.

As the Whole Grains Council moves forward, we are working with schools, restaurants, and convenience stores to add more whole grains to the many meals that consumers eat outside the home. We want people everywhere to discover the delicious nutty taste and long-lasting energy that come with eating "Whole Grains at Every Meal"—the council's simple but compelling slogan.

A Bird's-Eye View of Milling— Transforming Edible Seeds into Flour

ROBERT SERRANO

To unravel the mystery about how grains go from the ground to a box, we asked one of the most respected grain millers around–Robert Serrano from (of course) Grain Millers.

Milling" means "grinding," as when windmills or watermills ground farmers' corn and wheat kernels into flour. Technical milling today is the factory process of grinding clean, whole grain and other edible seeds, cereals, legumes, and pulses into flour.

At the end of World War II, wheat processors began to refine whole wheat by removing, in whole or in part, the most nutritious portions of the wheat kernel, the bran layers, during the milling. This produced "refined" white flour to satisfy the market demand for "cosmetically" appealing white bread. Variability in degree and extent of refinement, together with bleaching agents, produced nonuniform white bread and wide nutrient variability. In response, the Food and Drug Adminis-

tration identified a public health need to standardize wheat flour (and ultimately bread) by creating standards of identity for both bread and flour. This FDA action established controlled enrichment and standardized bleaching standards for refined flour. It recognized the need for color uniformity and for the replacement of valuable nutrients (such as vitamins and minerals) lost during the refinement process.

While mill and equipment design differ according to the type of edible seed to be converted into flour, the principles of wheat flour milling are, with very few exceptions, interchangeable. Seeds are cleaned, tempered or conditioned with water and/or steam, ground into flour, and refined. Tempering or conditioning is used to "mellow" the seed's components and help the grinding. Grinding is done on the whole seed. The materials used in the construction of the milling equipment are basically a function of efficiency, product purity, quality, and capital investment.

It's a far cry from the days of milling with stones (hence the term *stone-ground flour*), but the goal is the same—the creation of flours.

Pasta Fights Back! The Special Case of the Pasta Meal

K. DUN GIFFORD AND SARA BAER-SINNOTT

As the Atkins diet and other low-carb diet crazes swept the United States (and other parts of the world) in the early 2000s, we were mindful that the low-fat and no-fat fad diets of the 1990s coincided with a steep increase in rates of obesity. We worried that the "doctrine of unintended health consequences" could crop up from the low-carb craze, too. We were sure that consumers would forget that calories—not carbs or fat—add pounds and inches to their waistlines.

As this low-carb craze heated up, dieters were urged in vast media coverage to avoid all white foods—bread, pasta, and rice included. We concluded this was bad science, bad public policy, and a prescription for increased obesity. Consumers were whipsawed and confused. What was it to be: Low carb? No carb?

The anti-carbohydrate fad (the Atkins diet and its cousins) was launched in July 2002 when the *New York Times* put a luscious color photo of a juicy steak smothered in butter on the cover of its *Sunday Times* magazine. Inside was an article promoting the virtues of a low-carb, Atkins-type diet and criticizing scientists who warned about the health dangers of too much saturated fat. The Atkins frenzy burst on the scene almost immediately.

This Atkins craze was, of course, not the first fad diet. In the lands of plenty in this twenty-first century, consumers try to lose weight by following any diet that promises quick results. Like the Atkins diet, most of these diets fail in the long run.

The media's focus is generally on the present, with the goal of selling today's newspaper, this week's magazines, and keeping their advertisers happy—with the added pressure of always giving the readers "something new."

This was the atmosphere that nourished the Atkins frenzy.

To throw water on this unhealthy frenzy, Oldways organized a scientific and media conference in Rome in January 2004, called "The Healthy Pasta Meal," to examine the evidence. Based on numerous detailed presentations by leading experts from many countries, the scientific committee drew up a "Scientific Consensus Statement," and presented it to the media and the public.

This consensus statement detailed the nutritional evidence for considering that carbohydrates are at the heart of healthy diets and lifestyles. It also presented the details of the scientific reasons that pasta meals are an excellent example of the nutrient profile at the heart of a healthy balanced meal and lifestyle.

Why a pasta meal? Pasta is rarely (if ever!) eaten solo; its regular partners on the plate include olive oil and cheese, fish and meat, and vegetables and nuts. The combined impact of these ingredients results in dramatically slower rates of aborption, digestion, and insulin impact. This effect helps to account for the gold standard status of the traditional Mediterranean diet.

The Scientific Consensus Statement about the healthfulness of the pasta meal wasn't the only result of the conference. Called "Pasta Fights Back" by the press, the conference generated hundreds of news and feature articles about the healthfulness and delicious pleasures of the pasta meal. It was a huge relief to us and to pasta lovers around the world when our work and that of others helped prove that Dr. Atkins and other low-carb faddists were proved to be just a flash in the pan.

Glycemic Index: A Brief Explanation

The glycemic index (or GI) ranks carbohydrate foods according to how rapidly they are converted into the blood sugar glucose, which is the fuel for a human body's trillions of cells.

Foods with a low GI, like whole grains, apples, and pasta meals, are absorbed gradually, avoiding a spike in blood sugar. On the other hand, foods with a high glycemic index, like french fries and doughnuts, are absorbed rapidly and may cause a rush in blood sugar, straining the body's sugar-management abilities.

Traditional foods have a lower GI, while highly processed foods generally have a higher GI.

In its education programs, Oldways promotes an emphasis on traditional foods, and cautions about highly processed foods. With attention to this kind of balance, and avoidance of overdoing it, there is room in a healthy eating pattern for all kinds of foods and drinks, including traditional and highly processed.

The glycemic index, and its partner glycemic load (a ranking system for carbohydrate content in servings of food), will be much in the news in the next few years, and understanding what lessons they have for helping to avoid diabetes and other blood sugar disorders is a key public and personal health issue.

Corn Is as High as an Elephant's Eye

K. DUN GIFFORD

The corn is as high as an elephant's eye, and it looks like it's climbing right up to the sky," sang Curly joyously in the wonderful 1940s Broadway musical *Oklahoma*, as he expressed his contentment with his life on the farm (and to attract Laurey, of course). In the 1940s and 1950s Americans had still-vivid memories of the Dust Bowl and the Great Depression of the 1930s and grim years of grinding poverty, desperate food shortages, soup kitchens, factory closings, and mortgage foreclosures on homes and farms.

And so the bountiful harvests of our farm heartland were a rebirth for the people of the United States and became a strong metaphor for the nation's strength and power. We are so good at farming that in the decades since, we have produced enough farmland bounty to export millions and millions of tons of farm products, most of them grain. It's no accident that "Oh beautiful, for spacious skies, for amber waves of grain" is an evocative phrase in one of our national songs.

Corn does not grow in amber waves, of course, but it grows in vast abundance of tall green rows in America's midsection, the rich earth giving not only food for us and our animals (furred and feathered alike), but also sugars that sweeten our foods and starches for making plastics and hundreds of other goods.

And we eat it in many ways—we have popcorn, corn muffins, corn pone, johnnycakes, corn bread, corn dogs, cornflakes, canned corn, grits, and—best of all for many of us—fresh-picked corn on the cob.

We were not first with corn. The honor of domesticating corn goes to the early Aztecs and Incas, from whom it spread north to the Native Americans and to Europe when Christopher Columbus returned to Spain with it.

Latin Americans still eat their corn today in tortillas, soups, stews, and tamales. Italians in the lush farmlands of their north took quickly to corn, and polenta is now one of Italy's national and even gourmet dishes.

In my family, the fresh-corn-on-the-cob ritual is firmly established among members of three generations now alive. On summer mornings we go to a farm or farmstand and pick out the best-looking ears from that dawn's harvest and keep them in a cool place back at home until we strip the husks and silk just before sliding them into the kettle of boiling, roiling water.

We all like boiling best, though we have other ways and recipes for cooking fresh corn. But when all is done, with corn, simple is always better! Butter, salt, and pepper: that's it. Bite into the hot and juicy sweet kernels, and then chew up and down the ear's neat rows (unless, of course, you're one of those odd-ball round-and-round eaters). How sweet it is!

Tortillas

ZARELA MARTINEZ

Zarela Martinez is one of the pioneering chefs who introduced true and traditional Mexican foods to American tables. No matter whether it's through Zarela (her restaurant in midtown Manhattan), through her three highly accessible cookbooks, or through the vibrant personality that brightens her television program, Zarela has revolutionized what Americans know about authentic Mexican cuisine.

Daily bread is a window on the soul. At least that's true of Mexican tortillas. They were the people's bread centuries before they received a Spanish name meaning "little round cakes." Like French loaves, Arabic pita, or Indian chapatis, they have powerful symbolic meaning for the entire culture.

Tortillas basically consist of alkali-treated corn kernels (*nixtamal*) ground to make a dough (*masa*), patted into small rounds, and baked on a griddle (*comal*).

Everything that goes into them is an emblem of tradition dating back to pre-Hispanic times: the majestic corn plant, the stone metate over which generations of women knelt to grind the treated kernels, the skilled actions of forming the round and sliding it onto the *comal,* and flipping it with a quick pressure of the hand to make it puff slightly. Tortillas are "slow cooking" at its most archetypal—that is, the actual cooking takes only seconds, but the soaking and patient, laborious grinding traditionally occupied hours of every day.

The genius of pre-Hispanic cooks played hundreds of regional and other variations on this simple food—using different kinds of corn, separating out the delicate starch, working other ingredients into the dough, molding all kinds of shapes, pleating the surface, coating the tortillas with flavorful sauces, rolling or forming them around fillings. Every crumb of leftover tortilla went into still other dishes.

In a few remote regions you may still find women soaking their own corn, grinding masa on a metate, and expertly patting out the dough between their palms or on a bare knee. But the tortilla hasn't exactly stood still over the centuries. The first big change was the introduction of wheat by the Spanish. This created the flour tortillas that people in northern wheat-growing states love the way other Mexicans love corn tortillas. Another novelty was European cooking fats, such as lard, for working into flour dough or for frying. Soon cooks learned to combine corn masa with wheat flour for special tortilla variations, such as gorditas, which puff up into delicious balloons when fried.

For about a century, machines have been superseding the daily labor of preparing tortilla dough. First came small commercial mills to grind the masa, sparing housewives hours bent over the metate. Handle-operated presses replaced manual patting-out almost everywhere. Meanwhile, manufacturers devised instantized "flour" mixes from dried corn masa—Maseca, Quaker Masa Harina, and others. Many companies started making preformed packaged tortillas, both wheat-flour and corn.

Today tortillas of true non-instantized masa are virtually extinct in the United States and only sometimes to be found in Mexico. Corn tortillas made from dried mixes are now the norm. Even in my own restaurant, we are no longer able to make tortillas from real masa.

It's a sad loss. In the state of Oaxaca there's a movement to bring back artisanal masa, and I'd rejoice if it could spread to this country. Meanwhile, we all make do—and I have to say that in some tortilla variations traditionally made with a combination of masa and some flavorful starch like mashed beans or plantains, the absence of fresh masa doesn't matter as much. See page 38 for one of my favorites.

Rice around the World

K. DUN GIFFORD

Quick! What do you think of when you hear the word *rice*? Sushi? Rice and beans? Boiled rice with turkey and gravy? Chicken and rice soup? Rice pilaf? Risotto? A photograph of rice paddies? Throwing it at a wedding?

If you are an agricultural economist, you might be wondering how this year's production will rank against last year's. Will rice still be the world's largest food crop?

If you are a demographer, you might be wondering how long it will be that more people eat rice than any other of the world's great grains (wheat and corn).

If you are an Asian, you probably remember a favorite dish your mother or your grandmother made for you, which you dream about but have never been quite able to reproduce.

If you are me, you think of the chicken and rice soup my mother always made for us when we were sick in bed with a cold, sometimes with shredded chicken, sometimes not. And how I like rice and green peas together, with olive oil and French sea salt. I have clear recall of eating meals that treated rice as a centerpiece, and not as a side dish.

One such meal was in Istanbul, with our friend Engin Akin, a richly cultured woman whose family and husband's family have deep roots in Turkey's dense food history (see page 30). One evening I went with them to their friend Cigdem Simar's magnificent home over the Bosporus for a long dinner. All of it was sensational, but best of all for me was the rice course.

The server carried to the table a large silver platter, easily three feet in diameter, on which was a perfect mound covered with a steaming white cloth. Slightly bowing, he presented it to the host, while another server lifted the cloth to reveal the rice, from which billows of steam swirled upward. Wonderful aromas quickly spread across the table, with the strong scent of good rice and some sort of very slight floral perfume.

"Oh," Engin said when I asked her what it was. "Every house has its own personal way of making rice, like their own signature. Usually it's the husband's, but that's changing now. I think this is her family's; it's seasoned with flowers that grow near their vacation home in the south, near Bodrum."

I had Dutch friends when we lived in Washington in the 1970s, and every once in awhile they would lay on an authentic rijsttafel, which is a meal of hybrid dishes that evolved out of the more-than-one-hundred-year Dutch occupation of Indonesia. I loved these rijsttafels; they were more a seated buffet than a meal—an eating event, really—because the procession of small dishes that flavored the rices seemed as long as the Macy's Thanksgiving Day parade.

The big mistake at a rijsttafel is not to understand this, because then you don't know to hold back in the beginning and so are just too stuffed halfway through to enjoy the wonders that just keep on parading out of the kitchen.

The foundation of it all is rice; Indonesians are proud of their native rices, and once you've had good rice—good traditional strains, minimally processed, cooked just to perfection (boiled or steamed, it seemed not to make a difference) so it was not sticky, and served steaming hot—you crave more of it and are constantly on the lookout for it.

The Moroccans, too, celebrate rice in their high-style cooking. My first exposure to it came also in Washington, during elegant dinners at the Moroccan Embassy—candlelit salons, guests sitting on gorgeous carpets on the floor around large embossed hassocks for tables, a succession of great trays of food set down in the center, eating with our fingers, and plenty of notable Moroccan wines.

Years later, during an Oldways symposium in Morocco, we were treated to a luncheon feast by Morocco's leading agricultural businessman, who threw a memorable lunch in his country "house" for all two hundred of us. It followed the embassy dinner pattern, right down to the hassocks, parades of waiters with vast platters of food, but including a first for me. For the main course, each of the waiters in the parade carried an entire leg of roasted baby lamb on an oval tray—not a haunch, but the entire leg (*mechoui*). It was spectacular.

Later we visited the Royal Cooking School and learned that the graduates were posted to Moroccan embassies around the world for a minimum six-year stage. As a result, these embassies could serve authentic Moroccan specialties, and the traditions of Moroccan cuisine would be carried on when these graduates returned to live and work in Morocco after completing their embassy *stages*. Learning this closed the loop for me about the extraordinary attention to tradition in the meals of the Moroccan Embassy in Washington.

People who think about food know (in imagination if not in fact) of the great richness of rice-based cooking in the rice cultures of Asia, and are probably familiar with other traditional national rice dishes that can rise to great gastronomic heights—the spicy paellas of Spain, creamy risottos of Italy, the fillings of dolmas in Greece and Turkey, and the rice and beans of the Caribbean and Latin America.

Rice: An Essential Ingredient of Turkish Cuisine

ENGIN AKIN

We met Engin Akin in Istanbul when we were organizing our 1993 International Symposium on Turkish Foods and Wines. Since then she's become a newspaper columnist, radio show host, cookbook author, and a much-in-demand speaker on Turkish food. 🖂

Turkish cuisine is a friendly cuisine with its ingredients common to most people and other cuisines. Dishes made with tomatoes, olive oil, butter, pepper, garlic, vegetables like eggplant, legumes, and grains used throughout the Mediterranean basin appear on everyday tables all around Turkey. These ingredients are either cooked with meat or made into soups; almost all vegetables may be simmered in olive oil. Always using fresh and seasonal ingredients, Turkish cuisine is probably one of the healthiest.

Yogurt, another symbolic health food, is one of the oldest ingredients of our cuisine. It can be made into a drink or a sauce, or served as an accompaniment, but surely it is a favorite since childhood.

Turkish cuisine has long been a fusion cuisine in the sense that many ingredients from all over the world have been integrated into our gastronomy long before fusion became known to the world. Rice is one ingredient that has been carried to Anatolia all the way from our first homeland. Rice appears snugly in dolma or within the warmth of a chicken soup, or as an incredibly tasty duet with sugar and spices, such as saffron and mastic in numerous desserts. Our love of rice is, however, crowned by the flaky rice *pilav* that appears nearly every day on family tables and always on festive tables.

As rice comes in many disguises, so does the unleavened bread of the nomadic Turkish tribes. Countless pastries, savory and sweet, including böreks, the flaky baklava, and others with more erotic names—like woman's navel or lip of the beloved—are all made from yufka, the see-through muslin-thin sheet of pastry made with a rolling pin. The wonderfully aromatic butter the pastries are dressed with only makes sure that they will be an everlasting taste memory. Our love of dough and bread has led to numerous kinds of bread, *pide* (pita) being one of the tastiest and most famous.

Turkish cuisine can best be summarized as being innovative and sophisticated with an expertise that has been achieved by our respect for food and taste everywhere; be it a small village or the Imperial Ottoman Palace, where sultans dined on jewel-bedecked cushions.

"National dietary guides and recommendations, a phenomenon of the last hundred years, reflect this. The first national dietary guideline was American, in 1916, and now virtually all developed nations have them. Guidelines recognize grains as the "base" of a healthy eating pattern and recommend multiple servings of grains every day."

—K. DUN GIFFORD

Back to the Future: In-School Cooking Classes

SARA BAER-SINNOTT

Oldways is passionate that a healthy future depends on teaching children about good, healthy, clean, and fresh food from farms based on these principles: (1) what we eat can keep us healthy or make us sick; (2) when we support our local farm families, we are acting to sustain our environment instead of plundering it, and we are helping to keep our farm communities alive instead of abandoning them; and (3) the farms, food, and cooking of any society are just as much markers of its culture as are its music, dance, literature, religion, and geopolitics. This human food legacy needs to be treasured equally for the societal values that it represents.

To help fulfill the obligation we share to teach our children about food, cooking, culture and history, nutrition, and the environment, we worked with a group of chefs in 1998 to develop an in-school cooking program for children. This "High Five!" program is a step toward safeguarding the health of our children and the health of our earth.

High Five! is an eight-part lesson plan designed to teach children about the foods children eat in other countries. Each class includes an introduction to the history and culture of different countries, some special ingredients, and cooking techniques that make the food distinctive.

The lessons are tailored for children aged eight through twelve in elementary school, but they can easily be adapted to the interests and skill levels of children of any age, from kindergarten to high school, and even for senior citizens in assisted living centers, HMO classes, or to any group interested in learning about healthy eating. The lesson plans are professionally designed so that chefs, teachers, parents, grandparents, and other food people will be comfortable teaching them, and they have easily followed step-by-step guides for preparing and teaching.

We wanted this program to be a hands-on program—one where kids and teachers in school could actually cook in the classroom. Since ovens are not typically found in classrooms, we decided that cooking in a skillet, using a hot plate, was our only alternative.

Each lesson is based on a different flatbread, because of the importance of bread (and particularly flatbreads made of different grains) in all cultures around the globe. Flatbread is the unifying element that ties the eight lessons together, and each lesson includes a recipe for the foods traditionally prepared and eaten with it.

Flatbreads are perfect for the program. First, they can easily be prepared in a skillet; second, they provide a wonderful structure to the lessons (every culture has a fantastic flatbread that helps to define the cuisine); and third, the ingredients that are eaten with flatbreads usually complement the breads, together making a complete meal (fats, proteins, carbohydrates).

Naomi Duguid and Jeffrey Alford, award-winning cookbook authors, agreed to help us with the program, and they graciously allowed us to adapt their recipes for flatbreads for the program. We also worked closely with Rick and Deann Bayless of Frontera Grill and Topolobampo restaurants in Chicago, to develop this program (in its first release) for chefs to teach kids in classrooms. The program started in October 1998 with President Gerald Ford teaching the first lesson at the Gerald Ford Elementary School in Palm Springs, California, and continues today, from coast to coast.

Every time I teach (and I've taught High Five! for six years), the school halls are filled with the smells of freshly cooked bread, olive oil, or lemon or even garlic! Teachers and other students come out of other classrooms, wondering what's going on, and why their classrooms don't have these same wonderful smells.

Best of all are the reactions of the students. My all-time favorite response was the second grader who said, as we were rolling filling up in the rice papers during the Vietnam lesson, "I didn't know Vietnam had a war."

VIETNAMESE RICE PAPER ROLL-UPS

NAOMI DUGUID AND JEFFREY ALFORD

This dish is so simple, so delicious, and so healthy that the fifth-grade teacher who allowed us to "test" High Five! in her classroom added it to her weight loss program. 🍲

MAKES ENOUGH FOR A CLASS OF 20 TO 25, OR A MEAL FOR 6 TO 8 PEOPLE

- 1 (8-ounce) package thin dried rice noodles (rice sticks)
- 1 cup mung bean sprouts
- 20 to 25 dried rice papers (banh uot)
- 1 large head Boston, bibb, or tender leaf lettuce
- 1/2 cup firmly packed fresh cilantro leaves, chopped
- 1/2 cup firmly packed fresh mint leaves, chopped
- 1/2 cup firmly packed fresh basil leaves, chopped
- 1/2 small fresh pineapple, peeled and diced (optional)
- 2 large tomatoes, diced

Prepare the rice noodles following the instructions on the package. Blanch the bean sprouts. Moisten the dried rice papers one by one by plunging them in warm water. Lay a lettuce leaf flat. Place a moistened rice wrapper on the lettuce leaf. Top with a little cilantro, mint, basil, pineapple, tomato, rice noodles, and bean sprouts. Fold in the sides and roll up. Serve immediately.

Note: It is much easier to keep the rice paper on the outside with the lettuce and filling inside. You may want to do it this way.

ORECCHIETTE CON CIME DI RAPE

NANCY HARMON JENKINS

Cime di rape are the greens sold in American produce markets as broccoli di rape or broccoli rabe. This magnificent vegetable is both delicious, with a better bite that is extraordinarily pleasing, and nutritious, with all the remarkable properties of the cabbage family—loaded with antioxidants and other healthy things. If you are unable to find broccoli rabe, you may substitute ordinary broccoli, but the dish will lack the complex flavors that come from the combination of bitter broccoli rabe, sweet garlic, oil, salty anchovies, and pungent chile peppers. 🍲

SERVES 4

- 1/2 cup extra virgin olive oil
- 2 cloves garlic, sliced
- 6 anchovy fillets, boned and coarsely chopped
- 1 small dried hot red chile pepper, coarsely chopped, or 1/2 teaspoon crushed red pepper flakes
- 1 pound (2 bunches) broccoli rabe
- 1 pound orecchiette
- Sea salt and freshly ground black pepper

Pour the oil into a saucepan over medium heat and add the garlic slices. When they begin to soften and turn color (don't let them brown), add the anchovies. Cook over medium heat, crushing the anchovy fillets into the oil with the back of a fork to make a coarse paste. When all the anchovy fillets are mashed into the oil, add the hot pepper. Stir to mix well and set aside in a warm place until you are ready to use it.

Clean the broccoli rabe, discarding any yellow, old, or tough outer leaves and the thick stems. Coarsely chop the leaves and thinner stems, leaving the little flower clusters intact.

Bring a large pot of lightly salted water to a rolling boil, drop in the broccoli rabe pieces and pasta, and boil, uncovered, for about 15 minutes, or until the pasta is al dente. Drain in a colander, transfer to a heated bowl, and toss with the anchovy-garlic sauce. Or, if the pan in which the sauce cooked is large enough, turn the drained broccoli rabe and pasta into the sauce and cook briefly, just long enough to impregnate the pasta with the flavors of the sauce. Taste and add salt if necessary (the anchovies may give it sufficient salt) and a lot of black pepper. Serve immediately.

ORZO WITH FETA, OLIVES, TOMATOES, AND DILL

SUSAN KRON

This great summer dish is really a nonrecipe, since all of the ingredients are added according to taste and sight. In other words, when it looks like a nice, balanced combination of all of the ingredients and it tastes great, it's ready! Serve this with a good peasant bread, a side salad of mesclun greens in vinaigrette, and wine, and you've got a perfect summer lunch. ❧

SERVES 4

> 8 ounces orzo
> Extra virgin olive oil, to lightly coat the orzo
> 1 pint cherry or grape tomatoes, halved
> Sliced Kalamata olives
> Feta cheese
> Fresh dill, minced
> Sea salt and freshly ground black pepper

Bring a large pot of lightly salted water to a rolling boil. Add the orzo and cook until al dente. Drain quickly in a colander in the sink and immediately cool by letting water flow over it. Set aside until completely cool and drained. Transfer to a large mixing bowl.

Add olive oil to coat but not drench the pasta. Add tomatoes, olives, and feta to taste. Add chopped dill and salt and pepper to taste. Mix well. Serve immediately.

PASTA RINGS WITH CAULIFLOWER AND BREAD CRUMBS

JULIA DELLA CROCE

You can use water in place of the small quantity of vegetable broth, and still wind up with plenty of flavor in the finished dish. ❧

SERVES 3 TO 4

> 1 medium head cauliflower, trimmed and cut into florets
> 1½ tablespoons coarse sea salt
> 6 tablespoons extra virgin olive oil
> 2 large cloves garlic, minced
> 1 medium onion, minced
> 1 cup vegetable broth
> 8 ounces pasta rings (anelli)
> ¼ cup fresh bread crumbs
> 2 tablespoons chopped fresh flat-leaf parsley
> Sea salt and freshly ground black pepper

Bring 5 quarts water to a rapid boil. Add the cauliflower and the 1½ tablespoons salt. Boil until tender, 7 minutes. Use a slotted spoon to retrieve the cauliflower; cut into dice and set aside. Reserve the water.

In a large skillet over medium-high heat, warm 4 tablespoons of the olive oil. Add the garlic and onion and sauté until softened, 4 minutes. Stir in the cauliflower and broth. Continue to sauté, stirring constantly until the cauliflower is lightly colored, about 5 minutes.

Cook the pasta rings in the cauliflower water until they are al dente. Drain and add them to the skillet with the cauliflower.

In a small skillet, heat the remaining 2 tablespoons olive oil and add the crumbs. Stir constantly until the crumbs are golden and add the parsley. Sprinkle the crumbs and parsley over the pasta and add salt and pepper to taste. Serve immediately.

SPAGHETTI ZUCCHINI CARBONARA

RENZO AND MARGHERITA RIZZO

This recipe, from Renzo Rizzo, R&D chief of Barilla Pasta Meals, is rooted in the gastronomy of Puglia, the family cuisine of Renzo's wife. She inherited the region's taste for simple recipes, using a lot of fresh local vegetables and insisting on high-quality ingredients and clean and recognizable flavors. This recipe is the Rizzo family's Pugliese interpretation of the original pasta carbonara from Rome. Instead of the bacon of the traditional recipe they actually like to use an Italian lean smoked ham, a specialty from the Alps called "Speck" (see page 188). Or use a lean smoked raw ham, or prosciutto di Parma. As with the traditional cuisine from Puglia, vegetables appear in most of the family's recipes, and their trick is to prepare them in ways that appeal to young children. Like all Italian children, Renzo's children love pasta (they don't even call it a meal if pasta is not there!). What better way to make vegetables appealing than mixing them with pasta?

This pasta meal is excellent as a main dish; it provides a good balance of healthy proteins, carbs, vegetables, and oil (yes, also a bit of butter, but not too much!)—all in one delicious dish. We hope you'll enjoy it. 🍽

SERVES 4

> 2 cloves garlic
> 3 tablespoons high-quality extra virgin olive oil
> 2 medium zucchini (approximately 1 pound), thinly sliced and quartered, if desired
> 1 large egg

> 2 tablespoons freshly grated Parmigiano-Reggiano
> 2 tablespoons milk, plus more as needed
> 1/4 pound prosciutto di Parma (or Speck or ham)
> 1 teaspoon butter
> 8 ounces spaghetti

In a large skillet, simmer the garlic in the olive oil (keep the garlic whole, don't slice it—the taste is going to be lighter). When the garlic begins to turn golden, add the zucchini. Cover the skillet and let it simmer until the zucchini is soft but still retaining some crispiness and shape. The time depends on the size of the zucchini and the slices you made, so you'll have to watch it.

While the zucchini cooks, mix the egg in a small bowl with the Parmigiano and milk until it is well blended (more so than you would do for scrambled eggs).

Next, prepare a crispy prosciutto. Melt the butter in a large skillet over medium heat, add the prosciutto, and cook, turning for about 5 minutes, until crisp. Bring 6 cups of salted water to a boil in a large pot. Add the spaghetti and cook until al dente (cook 1 to 2 minutes less than what the package recommends). Drain and return to the pan in which it cooked.

At this point, pour the egg mixture on the pasta in its pan (but not on the heat), and stir till the egg starts to set (the pasta and egg must remain moist). Pour the pasta and egg mixture into the skillet with the zucchini. Add the crispy prosciutto on top and mix lightly so that the ingredients blend and pasta absorbs some of the accompaniments and becomes tastier. If need be, add a drop of milk to make the sauce more fluid. Serve quite hot.

Note: If you have leftovers, you can make a pasta frittata. Scramble 2 large eggs with 2 tablespoons freshly grated Parmigiano-Reggiano and 2 tablespoons milk. Add the leftover pasta. Heat 2 tablespoons extra virgin olive oil in a large skillet over medium heat, pour in the pasta mixture, and cook until the egg is firm and the liquid is absorbed.

BARBARA LYNCH'S BRIOCHE PIZZAS WITH PROSCIUTTO AND FIGS

BARBARA LYNCH

This pizza recipe is an interpretation of a New World pizza. Barbara Lynch first started making pizzas in 1992 at Todd English's original Figs Restaurant in Charlestown (in those days there was just one Olive's and only one Figs). She moved on to owning her own award-winning Boston restaurants (No. 9 Park and B&G Oyster) and winning her own Beard Award. We think she makes one of the best pizzas in Boston, and we're sure you'll agree with us.

This is an hors d'oeuvre that borrows from the French and the Italians--pizza, but with a crust made from brioche. The topping could be anything that adds a hint of salt, though Barbara thinks the combination of the prosciutto and fig is pretty good. Note that the dough needs to chill overnight, and that you should form it while it is cold—otherwise it's too sticky. You can also make it ahead and freeze it—just thaw overnight in the refrigerator before proceeding with the rolling and topping. 🖾

MAKES 12 HORS D'OEUVRES

BRIOCHE

1/3 cup warm water or milk

1/4 ounce (1 packet) active dry yeast

5 large eggs

3 1/2 cups all-purpose flour, plus up to 3 tablespoons more as needed

1/3 cup sugar

1 teaspoon sea salt

6 ounces unsalted butter, softened

TOPPING

12 paper-thin slices prosciutto di Parma

12 fresh figs (black or green) sliced in half lengthwise

2 tablespoons extra virgin olive oil

Sea salt and freshly ground black pepper

Pour the warm milk into a bowl and sprinkle the yeast over. Let stand for 10 minutes. Add 1 of the eggs and 1 cup of the flour and mix thoroughly until well combined. Sprinkle a second cup of the flour over the top of the dough (do not mix in) and let the mixture rest for 30 to 40 minutes.

After this "sponge" has rested, transfer it to the bowl of an electric mixer fitted with a dough hook attachment. Add the sugar, salt, remaining 4 eggs, and 1 cup of the remaining flour. Mix for 1 minute at medium speed, then add the final 1/2 cup flour, and beat continuously on medium speed for 15 minutes. If after 15 minutes the dough is not cohesive, add additional flour up to 3 tablespoons. With the mixer running, add the butter in small pieces. Continue beating until the dough comes together, about 5 minutes more. The dough will be soft and sticky. Transfer the dough to an oiled bowl, cover, and let rise until doubled, about 1 hour.

After the dough has risen, deflate it by gently pressing down on it, then cover tightly with plastic, and refrigerate overnight.

The following day, preheat the oven to 375°F. Divide the dough into 12 pieces (each piece should be roughly 1 ounce) and, on a floured surface, flatten the dough balls into small rounds and prick all over with the tines of a fork. Transfer the rounds to a baking sheet and top each round with a slice of prosciutto and a fig, cut side down. Drizzle with olive oil and sprinkle with salt and pepper.

Bake in the oven until the dough is lightly browned, about 10 minutes. Serve immediately.

PANZEROTTI SPERANZA

ROSSELLA SPERANZA

We first ate panzerotti at the birthday party of our friend Rossella Speranza at her home in Santo Spirito, just outside of Bari, in the heel of Italy's boot. We'd met Rossella when we organized a symposium in Puglia in 1999 and she represented Bari's Chamber of Commerce. Later on, she became the face and voice of Oldways Italia. Since then we've enjoyed panzerotti in a few restaurants in the United States, but although delicious, they've never matched the ones we had in Italy. We begged Rossella to share her mother's recipe. If you love pizza and love fresh mozzarella, you must try Panzerotti Speranza.

By dividing the dough into two sections you can cook half and freeze the remaining dough to use at a later time for more panzerotti, or even a pizza!

MAKES 24 PANZEROTTI

DOUGH

> 1/4 ounce (1 packet) active dry yeast
> 1 1/2 cups warm water
> 4 1/2 cups unbleached white flour
> 1 teaspoon sea salt
> 1 tablespoon high-quality extra virgin olive oil, plus more for frying (of a lower price)

STUFFING

> 2 pounds peeled tomatoes, fresh or canned
> 4 fresh mozzarella balls
> 1/2 cup Parmigiano-Reggiano cheese, freshly grated
> Sea salt

To make the dough, mix the yeast with water in a large bowl. Add the flour, salt, and olive oil, gradually, mixing as you go. Mix and knead into a ball and transfer to an oiled bowl. Cover and let it rise for 1 to 1 1/2 hours, until doubled.

After the dough has doubled, punch down and divide the dough into four parts, to have a manageable amount of dough to work with. Roll out one piece of the dough on a floured surface until the dough is approximately 1/4 inch thick. Cut the dough into 12 by 12-inch squares. Repeat with the remaining dough to make a total of 24 squares.

To make the stuffing, chop the tomatoes and mozzarella into small pieces about the size of silver dollars. Mix together the tomatoes, mozzarella, Parmigiano, and salt in a colander, squeezing both the tomatoes and mozzarella to drain away excess liquid.

Place 1 tablespoon of the mixture on each square of dough, and seal the pouch carefully.

In a deep saucepan filled with 4 or 5 inches of oil, deep-fry the panzerotti pouches, 1 or 2 at a time, for 1 to 2 minutes, until the dough turns a light brown. Lift out of the oil, and place on brown paper bags or paper towels to drain. Serve immediately.

BAGUETTE

SARA BAER-SINNOTT

While this may never rival the splendid baguettes of Poilâne in Paris, the pleasures of making the dough, watching it rise, shaping it, smelling the wonderful aroma of baking bread, and then finally eating it hot from the oven, are almost as good as being in Paris.

MAKES 4 BAGUETTES

> 2 1/2 cups lukewarm water, plus more for glaze
> 1/4 ounce (1 packet) active dry yeast
> 2 tablespoons sugar
> 1 tablespoon sea salt

5 cups unbleached white flour, or 3 cups unbleached white flour and 2 cups whole-wheat
  flour, plus more as needed
2 tablespoons extra virgin olive oil or canola oil
1 large egg white

Combine the water, yeast, sugar, and salt in a large mixing bowl. Slowly add the flour, mixing as you go, until
the dough is stiff. Put the dough on a wooden board,
lightly dusted with flour. Knead the dough for approximately 10 minutes, until it is a shiny ball. Add extra
flour, if needed. Coat the sides of the mixing bowl with
the oil. Place the dough into the bowl, cover with a wet
cloth, and let the dough rise until it has doubled in size,
1 to 1½ hours.

Punch the dough down and knead again briefly. Here,
it is up to you: If you want the bread to be less coarse,
you can let the bread rise until doubled in size again, 1
to 1½ hours. If not, divide the dough into four equal
parts. Shape each of the four parts into a long baguette
shape—either by rolling like a jelly roll or rolling
between your hands.

Preheat the oven to 450°F. Grease a baking sheet or 4
baguette pans. Slash the top of each loaf with a knife—
about 4 or 5 short diagonal slashes about ¼ inch deep
all the way down the loaf. Beat the egg white with an
equal amount of water, and brush the top of each loaf
with the mixture, to make the loaf crusty.

Bake for 15 minutes; turn the temperature down to
350°F and continue baking for 30 minutes. Cool before
serving.

CRETE'S CRACKED WHEAT BREAD

NARSAI DAVID

*Narsai David made this spectacular wheat bread as
part of the Crete Experiment during the 1997 Oldways symposium on the Island of Crete. "Magical
Narsai" disappeared into the storerooms of the large
restaurant kitchen used for the afternoon and reap-
peared wearing a baker's hat and smiling like the
Cheshire cat. He found mixing bowls, mixed grains
and water and salt, and kneaded away happily. He
presented the wonderful bread to us, saying, "This is
bread my grandmother knew."*

MAKES 2 LOAVES

2 cups warm water
2 cups unbleached all-purpose flour
4 cups bread flour
1 cup whole-wheat flour
¾ cup trahana (soured cracked wheat, available
  at Greek markets; coarse cracked wheat or
  bulgur may be substituted)
3 tablespoons grape syrup or honey
¼ ounce (1 packet) active dry yeast
2 teaspoons sea salt
3 tablespoons extra virgin olive oil
2 tablespoons sesame seeds

Combine all water, flours, trahana, grape syrup, yeast,
salt, and oil in a large mixing bowl and stir well to create
a dough. The dough will appear soft at first. But, as the
cracked wheat starts to absorb moisture, it will firm up
into a proper dough.

Knead the dough by hand or machine. If by hand, turn
it out onto a floured board and work it until it is smooth
and elastic, approximately 10 minutes. If using a dough
hook on an electric mixer, knead the dough at a slow
speed for 8 to 10 minutes.

Cover the bowl with a kitchen towel and set it in a warm, draft-free place to rise until the dough has just about doubled in bulk, 60 to 75 minutes. (A perfect place in cool weather is a gas oven with the slight heat given off by the pilot light; an electric oven, turned on low for only 2 minutes, then turned off, but with the oven light left on, works equally well.)

When the dough has doubled, turn it onto a floured board, punch it down, and divide it into two loaves. Form round loaves, taking time to round them up evenly until there are no wrinkles on top of the loaves. Moisten the top of the loaves with a wet towel or a sprayer and sprinkle with sesame seeds.

Place the loaves on a sheet pan dusted with flour or cornmeal. Cover the loaves with a towel on the counter and let them rise until almost doubled, about 1 hour.

With a razor blade, cut four deep gashes to form a very large square on the surface of each loaf. Cover again with the towel, and let them rise another 10 to 15 minutes.

While the loaves are rising, preheat the oven to 400°F with the rack positioned so that the bread will bake in the middle of the oven. If using a baking tile, it should be heating in the oven at the same time.

Place the loaves in the oven and spray them well with a fine mist of water. Repeat the misting two more times at 10-minute intervals. Bake for about 45 minutes, until a nice firm crust has formed. Test for doneness by rapping the bottom with your knuckle. The loaf should be firm and make a hollow sound. Cool on a wire rack.

CORN MASA-GREEN PLANTAIN TORTILLAS (*TORTILLAS DE MASA Y PLÁTANO VERDE*)

ZARELA MARTINEZ

Plain corn tortillas were the Mexican staff of life when the Spanish arrived, and still are. But in Veracruz there are also some fascinating hybrid tortillas born of marriages between pre-Columbian and post-conquest elements. This example extends and enriches the original corn masa with the starchy plantains that came to the whole Caribbean region during the slave era. You can use them as you would any fresh corn tortilla, but Zarela finds that they tend to stick to the griddle more in baking—no problem if you grease the griddle a little more often and more generously than usual. Her first introduction to these delicious tortillas came from the anthropologist-cook Raquel Torres.

MAKES ABOUT 15 (5- TO 6-INCH) TORTILLAS

> 1 small or ½ large green plantain
> 1 pound masa, fresh, or reconstituted by mixing 2 cups masa harina with about 1⅛ cups water
> 1 teaspoon sea salt
> 2 to 3 tablespoons unbleached all-purpose flour (optional)
> 2 to 3 tablespoons vegetable oil, or as needed, for oiling the griddle

Peel the plantain. Using the medium-fine side of a box grater, grate it into a large mixing bowl. Add the masa and salt and work with your hands to combine thoroughly. It should form a somewhat stiff but pliable dough but not too pasty to handle. If it is difficult to work with, add a little flour (about 1 tablespoon at a time) and knead in thoroughly until the consistency is smoother.

Shape the mixture into about 15 golfball-sized balls. Press them out into 5- to 6-inch rounds about $^1/_{16}$ inch thick. Griddle-bake as for regular tortillas. Serve hot.

SUMMER CORN

NORMA BAER

This is a fun and colorful alternative to the great American summer tradition, corn on the-cob that Sara's mother served when Sara was young.

SERVES 6 TO 8

6 tablespoons extra virgin olive oil or butter

3 cups uncooked corn kernels

$^1/_4$ cup chopped red bell peppers

$^1/_4$ cup chopped green bell peppers

$^1/_4$ cup chopped onions or shallots

2 large tomatoes, peeled, seeded, and chopped

1 tablespoon chopped fresh basil

$^1/_2$ teaspoon sea salt

$^1/_2$ teaspoon freshly ground black pepper

Pinch of sugar

In a large skillet over medium heat, heat the olive oil. Add the corn kernels, chopped red and green peppers, and onion and sauté for 5 minutes, making sure that the corn does not stick. Stir in the tomatoes, basil, salt, pepper, and sugar. Cover and cook, stirring once or twice, for 10 minutes. Serve hot.

WILD RICE AND LENTIL SALAD

ELLEN ECKER OGDEN

This main-dish salad combines flavors and textures that can easily be adapted depending on the season. While this recipe calls for arugula and vine-ripened tomatoes, which are at their peak in the summer, it is equally delicious in the fall or winter substituting kale and pine nuts. The key is the rice and lentil foundation, which gives it substance and absorbs the dressing to keep the whole dish moist and savory. Excellent for a picnic or potluck, it is ideally made early in the day and left to marinate until lunch or dinner.

SERVES 6 TO 8

1 cup vegetable or chicken stock

1 cup brown rice or wild rice blend

1 cup dry French green lentils

$^1/_2$ cup extra virgin olive oil

$^1/_4$ cup freshly squeezed lemon juice

$^1/_4$ cup red wine vinegar

2 garlic cloves, minced and mashed

6 scallions, coarsely chopped

2 cups halved cherry tomatoes or diced regular tomatoes

2 cups coarsely chopped fresh arugula

1 cup crumbled goat or sheep feta cheese

Combine 1 cup water and the stock in a saucepan over high heat and bring to a boil. Add the rice, cover, and simmer over medium heat until all the liquid has been absorbed, about 30 minutes.

Meanwhile, place lentils in a saucepan over medium heat and cover with $1^1/_2$ cups water. Simmer until just tender, about 15 minutes. Drain and let cool. In a large salad bowl, combine the cooked rice and lentils.

Prepare a vinaigrette by whisking together the olive oil, lemon juice, vinegar, and garlic in a small bowl. Pour the dressing over the lentils and rice. Add the chopped scallions and cherry tomatoes. Place in the refrigerator and chill for at least 2 hours. Just before serving, add the chopped arugula and crumbled feta cheese.

PAELLA

ANNE BANVILLE

Anne Banville travels the world for the USA Rice Federation to find interesting ways to teach consumers how to cook and enjoy rice. This classic Spanish dish from Valencia is delicious and healthy; it makes a complete meal on one plate and is a great illustration of the versatility of rice.

SERVES 6

- I clove garlic, minced
- I tablespoon extra virgin olive oil
- $^1/_2$ pound hot or sweet Italian sausage links
- $^1/_2$ pound boneless, skinless chicken breast, cut into I-inch pieces
- I cup rice of your choosing
- I cup chopped onion
- I$^1/_2$ cups chicken broth
- I (8-ounce) can stewed tomatoes, with juice, chopped
- $^1/_2$ teaspoon sweet paprika
- $^1/_8$ to $^1/_4$ teaspoon ground red pepper
- $^1/_8$ teaspoon ground saffron
- $^1/_2$ pound medium shrimp, peeled and deveined
- $^1/_2$ cup red bell pepper strips
- $^1/_2$ cup green bell pepper strips
- $^1/_2$ cup frozen green peas

Heat the garlic and oil in a large skillet or paellero (special paella pan) over medium-high heat. Remove the sausage meat from its casings. Add the chicken and sausage to the oil and stir until browned, about 10 min-

utes. Spoon off all but 1 tablespoon drippings from the skillet. Add the rice and onion. Cook, stirring, until the onion is transparent and rice is lightly browned, about 5 minutes. Add the broth, tomatoes and their juice, paprika, red pepper, and saffron. Bring to a boil; reduce heat, cover, and simmer for 10 minutes. Add the shrimp, red and green pepper strips, and peas. Cover and simmer for 10 minutes, or until rice is tender and liquid is absorbed. Serve immediately.

OLEANA TURKISH TOMATO RICE WITH FARMER CHRIS'S BEEFSTEAK TOMATOES

ANA SORTUN

This recipe sealed the match of award-winning chef Ana Sortun and her farmer-husband Chris Kurth when he went looking for a chef who wanted really perfect tomatoes, and she was looking for a farmer who grew really perfect tomatoes. This dish is simple to make and just right for a robust side dish for a crowd.

SERVES 6 TO 8

- 4 cups medium-grain rice, such as a paella rice
- 2 tablespoons butter
- I tablespoon extra virgin olive oil
- I small white onion, finely minced
- 6 beefsteak tomatoes
- Water
- Sea salt and freshly ground black pepper

Cover the rice in lukewarm water and soak for 1 hour.

Gently melt the butter over medium-low heat with the oil in a heavy saucepan with lid. Don't brown or boil the butter. Add the onions and sweat over low heat for 5 to 8 minutes, until translucent.

Cut the tomatoes in half vertically and grate on the large-holed end of a hand grater until all you have left is the skin in your hand. Place tomatoes in a glass measure and add enough water to make them equal to 8 cups of liquid. Season the liquid with salt and pepper, and add the rice.

Add the liquid and rice to the onions in the heavy saucepan. Cover and cook over low heat for 15 to 20 minutes, until all liquid is completely gone and rice is tender. Take the cover off of the saucepan. *Do not stir.* Cover the pot with a clean towel and let stand for another 5 minutes. The trick to this rice is getting a little bit of a crust on top.

PERUVIAN QUINOA AND ORANGE SALAD

ELISABETH LUARD

This simple salad from Elisabeth Luard, author of a book on Latin American cooking, can be served as an accompaniment in which the nutty sweetness of the quinoa is balanced by the acidity of the citrus.

Serve with thick slices of corn bread or thick tortillas made with the snowy white corn of the Andes—hot from the griddle. ▨

SERVES 4 TO 6

    I pound quinoa
    Water
    I chayote or a small cucumber, diced
    6 scallions, white and tender green parts,
        chopped
    Small handful chopped flat-leaf parsley
    Small handful chopped mint
    I to 2 oranges, segments divided and zest finely
        grated
    2 green or red jalapeño chiles, seeded and
        chopped
    6 tablespoons extra virgin olive oil

    2 tablespoons freshly squeezed lemon or Seville
        orange juice
    Sea salt

Rinse the quinoa under cold running water until the water runs clear.

In a large pan, cover the grains with double its own volume of water. Bring to a boil, then lower the heat to a simmer with the lid on loosely. Cook for about 20 minutes or so, until the grains are translucent and the water has all been absorbed.

Combine the warm quinoa with the chayote, scallions, parsley, mint, oranges and orange zest, jalapeños, olive oil, lemon juice, and salt to taste. Taste and add whatever's needed—maybe a little more salt or an extra squeeze of lemon. Serve warm or cold.

"Quinoa has been cultivated for more than five thousand years in the Andean highlands, and the Incas considered it the 'mother grain.'"

—JEFF DAHLBERG, PhD

HIGHLAND OATCAKES

ELISABETH LUARD

*Oats are the traditional grain of the Scottish High-
lands, eaten as porridge for breakfast (and at any
other meal) and stored in the form of oatcakes, which
will keep almost indefinitely buried in the oatmeal
chest. Traditionally they're baked on a heavy iron
plate, known as a girdle on the west coast and as
a griddle elsewhere in Scotland, and then dried on
a rack in front of a peat fire. Fine-ground oatmeal
makes a smooth, crisp oatcake to eat for breakfast
with butter and marmalade (Elisabeth's Edinburgh-
born grandmother never let her have both). A proportion of coarse-ground oatmeal, as here, gives
a crunchy texture suitable for eating with fresh
cream cheese. Make sure you have ground oatmeal—
porridge-oats won't do. Butter or oil can replace the
traditional dripping or lard. Elisabeth suggests that
the oatcakes are a perfect accompaniment to her
One-Pot Hebrides Stew (see page 166).*

MAKES 24 OATCAKES

- 16 ounces oatmeal
- 1/2 teaspoon sea salt
- 2 to 3 tablespoons melted bacon drippings, lard,
  butter, or canola oil
- About 1 cup boiling water

Preheat the oven to 300°F.

Using a rolling pin, grind half of the oatmeal until
coarsely ground, then grind the remaining half of the
oatmeal until finely ground. Toss the two oatmeals in
a bowl together with the salt. Mash in the bacon drippings and boiling water to make a firm dough. Pat it out
between 2 sheets of plastic wrap and roll it until it is 1
inch thick. Use a whisky tumbler or water glass to cut it
into rounds. Work the trimmings into a ball, roll it out,

and cut out as many as you can. Transfer the rounds to
a baking sheet.

Bake for 30 to 40 minutes, until the oatcakes are dry—
don't let them brown. Transfer to a wire rack. They'll
become crisp as they cool. Store in an airtight tin. If
they soften, warm them up again in a low oven.

MILO SALAD WITH OREGANO,
FETA CHEESE, AND CUCUMBERS

JESSE COOL

*Sometimes sorghum is called milo, and sometimes
milo is called sorghum. Whatever you call it, Jesse's
milo salad is a fresh, clean, and delicious dish. The
National Sorghum Producers (www.sorghumgrow
ers.com) can put you in touch with a source for sorghum (milo).*

SERVES 12

- 9 cups water
- 3 cups milo
- 3/4 cup chopped fresh oregano
- 6 scallions, white and tender green parts,
  chopped
- 3/4 cup extra virgin olive oil
- 9 tablespoons freshly squeezed lemon juice
- 3 tablespoons grated lemon zest
- 3 cups chopped English cucumbers
- 1 cup toasted pine nuts
- 3 cups crumbled feta cheese
- 1/2 teaspoon ground red pepper
- 1 tablespoon sea salt

Bring the water to a boil in a large saucepan and add the
milo. Simmer the milo, uncovered, for 30 to 40 minutes, or until all the water is absorbed and the milo is
the consistency of cooked rice. Cool the milo to room
temperature, fluffing with a fork occasionally.

In a medium bowl, combine the oregano, the scallions, olive oil, lemon juice, lemon zest, cucumbers, pine nuts, feta cheese, red pepper, and salt.

Add the cooked milo. Adjust the salt and red pepper.

BULGUR PILAF WITH TOASTED NOODLES

PAULA WOLFERT

Remember that bulgur easily overcooks and turns mushy if too much liquid is used. Don't soak it; cook in about 1¾ cups hot meat or chicken broth for every 1 cup of large grains.

SERVES 4

- 4 tablespoons butter
- ½ cup broken spaghetti or vermicelli (3- or 4-inch pieces)
- 1 teaspoon sea salt
- 1 cup coarse-grain bulgur
- 1½ cups chicken or meat broth, boiling
- ½ teaspoon freshly ground black pepper

Melt 3 tablespoons of the butter in a medium saucepan over medium heat. Add the spaghetti or vermicelli and fry, stirring often, for about 5 minutes, until golden brown. Add the salt and the bulgur, stirring. Pour in broth and allow the mixture to boil for about 3 minutes. Cover, reduce the heat, and cook at a simmer for 10 more minutes, or until all the liquid has been absorbed.

Place a kitchen towel or double layer of paper towels on the grains, replace the cover, remove from the heat, and let stand 10 to 15 minutes before serving.

Heat the remaining 1 tablespoon butter; add the pepper and let sizzle. Pour over the bulgur and serve.

LENTIL SOUP WITH GRANO

MIKE ORLANDO

Grano (Italian for "grain") is polished durum wheat, which has a nutty flavor. Mike Orlando is the chairman of Sunnyland Mills, a seller of whole grains. His father, Carl, is 100 percent Sicilian and is very much into food. He took one of Mike's recipes and added his own flair and Italian style to create a soup "like my mother used to make." It harkens back to the simplicity and wholesomeness of the old days in the Sicilian countryside where Mike's grandparents grew up. Va bene!

SERVES 4

- 2 tablespoons extra virgin olive oil, plus more to drizzle on finished soup
- ⅓ cup chopped onion
- ⅓ cup chopped red or green bell pepper
- 2 cloves garlic, minced
- 6 cups water
- ⅓ cup diced carrots
- 1 cup brown lentils
- ⅓ cup grano
- 1 (4-ounce) can unseasoned tomato sauce
- Sea salt and freshly ground black pepper
- ½ cup small shell uncooked macaroni (optional)
- Freshly grated Parmesan cheese

Heat the oil in a large saucepan over medium heat. Add the onion, bell pepper, and garlic and sauté for 5 to 10 minutes, until tender. Add water, carrots, lentils, and grano and simmer over medium heat for 30 minutes, or until tender. Add the tomato sauce and salt and pepper. Add the macaroni in the last 6 minutes. Sprinkle Parmesan cheese and drizzle olive oil over each serving.

"The heart of the Mediterranean diet is vegetarian—pasta in many forms, leaves sprinkled with olive oil, all kinds of vegetables in season, frequently washed down with wine, cheese along the way, all finished off with fruit. I say "leaves." Where we live in South Italy *sfogli* is the Italian word for all kinds of leaves that are an important part of the Mediterranean diet. This includes many kinds of lettuce, Swiss chard, purslane, and plants I can't identify with an English name. Leaves to eat are always at hand."

—ANCEL KEYS, PhD

"In spring and summer, the vegetables in Spain can be spectacular—rare white asparagus and tiny artichokes from Rioja, glowingly sweet red peppers from Murcia, tiny emerald green peppers from Galicia, and tasty fresh limas from Andalusia. In many areas, vegetables were rarely boiled; rather they were slowly sautéed in olive oil until tender or else quick fired."

—PENELOPE CASAS

FRUITS AND VEGETABLES

Some cars are lemons; Jesus was the fruit of his mother's womb; a daughter may be the apple of her daddy's eye (even if one of her out-of-favor suitors might be a bad apple); New York is the Big Apple; a friend who does a favor is a peach; and some dates grow on trees while other kinds of dates are taken to the movies.

Fruits do some heavy lifting in our etymological lives, as does the word *fruit* itself. Of course, most food words do (we eat pigs, for example, while people who

Fruits in Our Lives
K. DUN GIFFORD

pig out sometimes hog all the food), but fruits seem more freighted than most others. I think it has something to do with sweetness, because our first food is milk, sweet with lactose sugars, and the taste preference for sweetness is hardwired in our taste and smell organs. Mary Poppins immortalized this image with her song "A Spoonful of Sugar," which makes the medicine go down.

We often begin our days with orange juice and end it with apple pie. We add fruits to grains to make them taste better. We put strawberry jam on toast, orange marmalade on English muffins, grape jelly and peanut butter in sandwiches, raisins in scones, cranberries in muffins, and blueberries in pancakes.

We eat oranges with duck; cranberries with turkey; lemon with fish and also with chicken; tart fruit, cherries, and jellies with roast beef; prunes with pork; chutney with lamb; and pineapple and raisins with ham.

We regularly match fruits with dairy to make pairs: cherries jubilee, yogurt with fruit on the bottom, strawberry milkshake, cheese and quince paste, cream cheese and strawberry jam, cherry cheesecake, and all kinds of ice cream.

Fruits are the soul of many liqueurs: Cointreau, Nonino grappa, framboise, and many others.

We put lemon in tea, lemons and lime in Coke, strawberry and cherry in other sodas, we drink strawberry margaritas, lemon vodka, pineapple piña coladas, and apple martinis.

Where would we be without the flowers that come before the fruits with their nectar that bees use to make honey? Where would we be without grapes to make wine?

Grapes, of course, are wonder workers. They give us the pleasures of wines, a centerpiece of worship in some of the world's largest religions, the raisins that go to school with children and to work with adults all over the world, and natural sweetness in trail mixes and energy bars.

Fruits also give us the pleasures of fruitcakes, which are—depending upon your point of view—either gustatory or comical. They do their solid and soldierly holiday service year after year, providing pleasure for people who love their richness and symbolism. For others, they are the source of the annual ritual of fruitcake humor.

For some reason, fruits have acquired another meaning, too—describing someone who is "a bit off," sort of

strange, maybe, but amusingly so. More recently it is a term of endearment for pleasurable affectionate humor.

Whatever the meaning or whatever the pleasure, fruits will be forever a part of our lives.

Fruits and Vegetables: Thinking about What They Are

K. DUN GIFFORD

Somewhere along the timeline of my life I became a compulsive gatherer and planter of seeds; a manic grower of plants, trees, and bushes; a relentless hunter of very fresh vegetables; and a driven picker of fruits and berries. No doubt this makes me a bit odd in the eyes of some, but it also makes me a member of the noble army of frustrated gardeners for whom there is never enough time to have a really perfect garden.

I am also a sometime believer in the semi-outrageous notion that plants "hurt" in some way when they are cut or picked, which was popularized in a troubling short story by Roald Dahl about the wife who could hear her carrots screaming when her husband pulled them up from the earth of their garden.

And I know that we understand only a small fraction of the health benefits of eating the fruits, vegetables, and tubers that good mother earth offers up to us in her cupped hands.

DEFINITIONAL MADNESS

Each of us knows with certainty that some plants we eat are vegetables, while some are fruits. For example, we are fully confident that oranges, bananas, apples, and strawberries are fruits, but that cucumbers, lettuce, celery, and spinach are vegetables.

But what about potatoes? Asparagus? Corn? Rice? Oatmeal? Peanuts? Walnuts? Beets? Which are they, vegetables? Fruits? Neither? What makes one a fruit and one a vegetable?

Maybe thinking about the seeds of these plants gives us some clues.

It's pretty obvious that rice is a seed, and that a pea is, too. We know that apples and grapes have seeds, but wait—what's going on with seedless apples and grapes?

We know that peaches and olives and avocados have a single seed, and that it's a pretty good-sized one, too. We know that pumpkins and watermelons have lots of slippery seeds; we wrestle with a snarly mess of pumpkin seeds when we carve our Halloween icon; and we may spit or pinch-squirt watermelon seeds at each other at a Fourth of July picnic. We don't see onion or asparagus seeds, but know they must produce seeds somehow or they'd go extinct.

So, the presence or absence of seeds isn't much help in distinguishing fruits from vegetables.

Food markets don't much worry about making a distinction between them. In the produce section they display all together, fresh in blazing colored profusion. But if they're not fresh, they're stashed all over the store—frozen solid as bricks in freezer cases; pickled and sweetened in cans and jars; tucked into zucchini bread, blueberry muffins, raisin cookies, or cranberry cereals; slipped into candy or "energy" bars; squeezed as juices into bottles, cartons, and freezer containers; and added as flavoring to medicine, cola, gum, and tea.

We might also try to classify them as fruits and vegetables by how we eat them: raw fruits or cooked vegetables, for example. But this approach falls apart pretty quickly, too, because we eat a lot them both ways, and joyously—we eat strawberries fresh in desserts, cooked in jam, and frozen in ice cream. We eat spinach raw in salad, and cooked with olive oil or butter. We eat peanuts out of the shell, salted with a cocktail, as peanut butter, in candy as brittle, and as a satay sauce with chicken.

At least we know that beans are seeds, because we know about bean sprouts, which turns them into a vegetable. And black pepper ground from peppercorn, well, a peppercorn is a seed picked from a vegetative plant, but we call it a spice.

Out of all this we can see a few things clearly. Our grocers do not care much about the distinction between fruits and vegetables. We eat the seeds of some fruits but not others (banana yes, apple no); we also eat the seeds of some vegetables but not others (cucumber yes, carrot no).

Let's think about grains, because the three basic grains (wheat, corn, and rice) make up the foundation of eating patterns for the great part of the world's populations. Farmers who grow them know them as seed grains, because they plant them. Farmers who raise poultry and livestock know them as feed grains, because it's what they feed to their animals. We eaters know them as oatmeal, or rice pilaf, or cornmeal, or flour. We also know them as food that we've milled and ground, and boiled, baked, and fried—as pita pockets, corn dogs, sushi, and so on.

In fact, we humans literally live on grass seed.

Nature's Bounty

ROSIE SCHWARTZ, RD

Rosie Schwartz is a well-known Canadian nutritionist, food writer, healthy eating crusader, and television commentator. Her gift is reducing complex nutrition-speak into language that Canadian consumers can understand and absorb to help them with their daily food choices. The author of The Enlightened Eaters Guide, *Rosie is one expert we count on to explain important nutrition information about fruits and vegetables.*

Nature's offerings can be palate-pleasing indeed. Imagine the sheer enjoyment of having summer tomatoes strewn with fresh aromatic basil and splashed with a fruity olive oil, a bowl of luscious berries, or a perfectly ripe juicy peach. But there's much more to these foods than just their taste. Little did your mother know that when she told you to eat your fruits and vegetables that she was helping you to unleash a virtual arsenal of disease-fighters. Scientists are just beginning to discover the dazzling array of phytochemicals contained in assorted produce. The compounds from plant foods—called "phyto" as in plant—number in the thousands and appear to be key weapons in the battle against the common illnesses of our society, including heart disease, stroke, certain cancers, diabetes, cognitive decline, and rheumatoid arthritis, to name a few.

Fruits and vegetables—from A to Z—apples to zucchini—all provide an astounding cornucopia of health-promoting actions. They're chock-full of powerful antioxidants that protect against free radical damage—damage thought to be a major culprit both in the aging process as well as in the development of many diseases. The greater the intensity of color of fruits and vegetables, the higher the concentration of pigments, such as carotenoids or anthocyanins, phytochemicals with antioxidant activity. Dark leafy greens, avocados, and zucchini all contain lutein, the carotenoid linked to a decreased risk of colon cancer and macular degeneration, the leading cause of blindness in the elderly. The anthocyanins in blueberries, especially wild ones, may slow cognitive decline in the elderly. The list of the health perks provided by these foods is now seemingly endless.

DON'T JUDGE BY COLOR ALONE

While deeply colored fruits and vegetables may offer advantages, paler produce can also offer a powerful phytochemical punch. For instance, the allium family, with members such as garlic, onions, and leeks, has a stellar reputation for its beneficial effects in regulating blood pressure, protecting arteries, and preventing cancer.

Green cabbage, a paler member of the brassica family, contains higher amounts of the cancer-fighting compound flavonol than does its cousin broccoli. But broccoli's no slouch either, with more than one hundred isothiocyanates—some of which may detoxify cancer-causing agents, while others may stimulate enzymes in the body to fight cancer growth.

Variety, when it comes to fruits and vegetables, is more than just the spice of life. Choosing an assortment of each on a regular basis provides a diverse range of vitamins, minerals, and phytochemicals. Even varying preparation techniques can supply different weaponry against disease. Take tomatoes, for example. The pigment that gives tomatoes their red color is the carotenoid named lycopene, which is associated with protection against prostate cancer, artery disease, and macular degeneration. Research shows that the lycopene is better absorbed when tomatoes are cooked or processed and even more so, when consumed with olive oil. But raw tomatoes are more likely to contain the gel around the seeds. This gel had been shown to decrease the likelihood of developing blood clots that can lead to heart attacks or strokes. So savor a spicy salsa at one meal and a hearty ratatouille at another.

While having a combo meal at a fast-food eatery may not be an enlightened nutritional choice, when it comes to assorted fruits and veggies, it's a much different story. Research shows that lycopene and lutein together are more potent disease fighters than when each is consumed on its own. A Mexican tortilla soup—diced tomatoes, avocado, lime juice, and corn tortillas in a rich broth—is a mouthwatering example of how to make the most of a phytochemical mix. More studies looking at these complementary effects of various nutrients and phytochemicals in different combinations are currently under way. Stay tuned.

SUPPLEMENT SAVVY

Because of hectic lifestyles and marketing by supplement makers, do you opt for your lycopene in a pill form over a garlic-scented tomato sauce? Well, scientists recently compared the effects of a tomato powder, lycopene, or a placebo on laboratory animals with prostate cancer. Only the tomato powder provided a defense against tumor growth. Also contained in tomatoes are an assortment of lesser-known compounds called isoprenoids, substances with potent cancer-fighting qualities. It may be that all the various phytochemicals and nutrients in tomatoes are part of nature's complex anticancer chemical brew. Science doesn't yet have the answers. So while we await the verdict, part of the best prescription for good health may be just to eat your fruits and veggies.

A Word about Supplements

Nutritional epidemiology has suggested that dietary antioxidants are crucially involved in the prevention of degenerative diseases. Examining whether antioxidants taken as supplements are as effective as antioxidants eaten in foods, three recent human nutritional intervention trials tested whether the antioxidant beta carotene taken as a supplement could reduce lung cancer risks. The results showed no decrease—and even a modest increase—in lung cancer incidence and mortality with the supplements. Researchers Ames and Beckman conclude, "A complex animal like a human is unlikely to respond predictably to crude manipulations such as supplementation with one or a small number of compounds."

Many studies support this conclusion, including an important one by another leading researcher, Dr. James Joseph of Tufts University. He concludes that "if you take a supplement, you never get the benefit of fruits and vegetables that contain hundreds of compounds."

Color Your Palate

ANNE UNDERWOOD

Newsweek *magazine's Anne Underwood joined us for our 2002 symposium in Salerno, Italy, just prior to the publication of* The Color Code, *the book she wrote with Dr. James Joseph and Dr. Dan Nadeau about the healthfulness of foods (fruits and vegetables) with*

color. For us, she has graciously written a short, but very clear explanation about the importance of colorful foods.

To Chef Douglas Rodriguez of Miami's Ola Café, there is one essential truth about food. "People eat with their eyes," he says. "If food looks good, people reach for it." And to Rodriguez, it's no contest which is more alluring—a series of drab white entrées or an intriguingly colorful platter.

Rodriguez crafts colorful dishes for their eye appeal and flavor, but scientists say there's another reason to do so—health. That's why purveyors of nutritional advice, from the National Cancer Institute to the newly health-conscious writers of "Sesame Street," have begun touting a diet rich in colorful fruits and vegetables. They have good reason to do so.

For starters, you have the benefits of the pigments themselves, known technically as carotenoids and anthocyanins. These crimson, gold, orange, and purple-blue compounds serve as both antioxidants and anti-inflammatories. "Inflammation is the evil twin of oxidation," says neuroscientist James Joseph of Tufts University. Both are found in a growing list of chronic ailments ranging from heart disease to diabetes. You can fight back with colorful fruits and vegetables.

Pigments, though, are just one of many good things in brightly hued foods. Think of them as signposts pointing to other protective compounds called phytonutrients that detoxify the body, ward off tumor growth, keep arteries flexible, and switch on protective genes. As a rule of thumb, the most intensely colored fruits and vegetables have the highest levels of phytonutrients. And the more colors on your plate, the broader the spectrum of protection.

So as Kermit's creators are saying, "Eat Your Colors." It's healthy being green.

Are Antioxidants an Elixir for a Long and Healthy Life?

K. DUN GIFFORD

Oldways' early work with traditional diets and the traditional diet pyramids focused primarily on people's eating patterns and the macronutrients (fats, proteins, carbohydrates) consumed in these ways of eating. For example, the main source of fat in the Mediterranean diet is olive oil. But traditional diets are also rich in micronutrients, phytonutrients, and antioxidants that have important effects on health and longevity. Several Oldways initiatives in 2001 and 2002 focused on this subject. While we knew it was important to understand how and why these phytonutrients and antioxidants (or PAX) worked and why they were important, our overwhelming intent was to teach consumers that food choices are important, and that healthy food choices are just as delicious as they are healthy. 🖾

In order to produce the energy for life, chemical reactions in the cells of animals oxidize the nutrients in the food and drink they have consumed. By-products of these chemical reactions include "free radicals," some of which are dangerous and, unless neutralized, can cause fatal disease.

Scientific evidence is rapidly accumulating to show that most of the degenerative diseases that afflict humanity have their origins in the oxidizing actions of free radicals that attack millions of your body's billions of cells. These degenerative diseases include heart disease, cancer, diabetes, asthma, rheumatoid arthritis, Alzheimer's, senile dementia, urinary tract infections, malaria, and degenerative eye disease. There is strong evidence that early aging belongs on this grim list, too.

Fortunately, the body has a weapon to neutralize the poisonous power of these free radicals, which are called "free radical scavengers" and are among the other phytochemicals in fruits, vegetables, nuts, seeds, and whole grains. Most of the phytochemicals in these foods are in their skins or husks.

Each of us has the power to accelerate or slow down the oxidizing reactions of free radicals. We cannot stop them, but with consistent attention to our food and drink choices, we can slow them down and reduce our risks of falling prey to one of these terrible degenerative diseases. Best of all, we can do so while eating and drinking the best, most delicious food and drink. And it's why eating lots of fruits and vegetables truly matters.

Eat Your Vegetables

SARA BAER-SINNOTT

Mothers and fathers have sung the "eat your vegetables" refrain probably for as long as human history. Finish your peas! Eat that spinach! Just take little bites of those carrots! There were ancient tunes long before Clarence Birdseye started freezing vegetables.

Italian, Greek, Spanish, French, and Turkish parents have a way with vegetables that is, well, foreign to most Americans. In our travels for Oldways over the last fifteen years, we have been struck many times by how really simply the restaurant and home cooks fix a plate of vegetables that no one—not even the most finicky of eaters—can turn down. We have brought many recipes for these dishes back with us and hope you'll try these simple yet elegant and delicious dishes modeled after ones we enjoyed on the culinary road.

IN PARMA

At a time-pressured meeting at Barilla's headquarters in Parma, we stopped for a three-course, half-hour lunch. For the first course, the cooks carried in platters of paper-thin slices of prosciutto di Parma, beautiful chunks of Parmigiano-Reggiano, rich with bits of crystal, and a big bowl of sliced raw tomatoes, fennel, carrots, celery, and peppers. A small white bowl on a

Anti-O and the Rads!

To explain how antioxidants work, Dun created a series of children's fables. Our favorite is Anti-O and the Rads!

A never-ending, deadly war is fought every second of every day of your entire life in every corner of your body. This war is fought over your body's billions of cells, and the stakes are very high. If enough of your cells are overwhelmed by their enemies, your risks for cancer, heart disease, early aging, and a host of other miseries go up markedly.

The soldiers in the army of your body's defenders are antioxidants. The soldiers of the army attacking your body are oxidants, and their weapons are called free radicals. These are particularly nasty weapons, and they are the same ones that cause iron to rust and butter to go rancid. In your body, free radicals force cells to mutate and age—your body then "rusts and goes rancid."

General Anti-O commands your defending antioxidant army. She is a skilled tactician, and she is much loved as the army's first woman field general. Her soldiers are called Anti-Os. General Rad is the commander of the attacking free radical army. He is widely admired for his tenacity but feared for his cunning and ruthlessness. His soldiers are called Rads. The two generals are evenly matched, as the Anti-Os go up against the Rads.

General Rad deploys his attacking Rads in countless clever formations, but Anti-O's stout front-line defenders kill millions of them. But more millions of other Rads elude or fight their way past these defenders and are in position to forcefully attack your cells.

To mount its attack, each Rad zeros in on a stable pair of electrons and breaks up its union, binding with one of the separated electrons in order to form a new stable pair. The now-single remaining electron becomes a new Rad, and the process starts again. This lifelong cycle severely damages your cells (sometimes disrupting their linings, sometimes mangling their DNA), and stimulates the inexorable processes of cell mutations and breakdown.

But General Anti-O has a second weapon in her arsenal. She oversees an incredible array of repair tools that can fix much of this cellular damage. Some can even snip out mangled pieces of DNA before they can wreak their devastation by creating new but mutated cells.

This war in your body never ends while you are alive. It rages back and forth, with the Anti-Os sometimes holding the upper hand, and other times the Rads holding it.

All armies march on their stomachs; without food, they are not strong enough to fight. To keep her soldiers at full fighting strength, Anti-O needs a steady supply of plenty of food. If she gets it for them, then she can keep the army of Rads in check.

The foods Anti-O needs are those containing antioxidants, which she gets from fresh, dried, or frozen fruits and vegetables, nuts and peanuts, and juices and wine (in moderation). With enough of these every day, Anti-O has the weapons she needs to mount her good fight to keep your body healthy. If you do not eat enough of these foods, you take her weapons away and give General Rad's free radical army an easy victory.

What you eat and drink decides who wins the battle. With every swallow, you influence the war's outcome. So it's up to you—they're *your* food choices.

white dinner plate was set down in front of each of us, and since we weren't quite sure what to do with it, we watched and learned that we were to pour extra virgin olive oil and balsamic vinegar into the small bowl, take the veggies we wanted from the platter, and then dip the fresh veggies into the oil and vinegar mix. So simple, and so delicious!

We finished up the meal with a small plate of perfectly cooked pasta with diced fresh vegetables, and then fresh fruit for dessert. And then a glass of water, a glass of wine, and pungent espresso. Simple, delicious, healthy, and just the right amount of food.

BY THE LIGURIAN MEDITERRANEAN

Before an Oldways conference in Liguria, our friend and well-known scientist and medical doctor Attilio Giacosa invited us to his home for dinner, high on a slope looking down at the Mediterranean Sea, just north of Portofino. Giacosa is a cancer specialist, and he always ends his scientific presentations with a breathtaking photo taken from the rooftop of his home, of the red ball of sun settling down for the night over the Mediterranean Sea. We were so pleased to be invited to sit on the rooftop with him and his family and enjoy the same sunset with a glass of icy Prosecco. The dinner he and his wife served to us included vegetables from his rooftop and sideyard gardens—not just one vegetable as a side, but an entire course of vegetables, all cooked differently and topped with the sweet extra virgin olive oil that is uniquely Ligurian.

OLIVE OIL MAKES THE VEGGIES GO DOWN

Strangely enough (or perhaps not strangely!) it is another scientist we think of when we pair vegetables with olive oil. Professor Antonia Trichopoulou, from Athens and one of the real "mothers" of the Mediterranean diet, has said over and over again that "it's the olive oil which makes the vegetables taste so wonderful

in Greece." Together, olive oil and vegetables are the essential ingredients of the Mediterranean diet.

LET YOUR MIND BE BOLD

Over and over again we find a great affection expressed for the great tastes of fruits and vegetables in the Mediterranean and Asian and Latin American cuisines, particularly when contrasted with the apathy about it in America. We remember a well-known U.S. nutrition scientist saying after our vegetarian conference in 1997, "I'd eat this way every day if it would taste as good as it has for the last three days!"

Eating vegetables doesn't mean choking down soggy, limp, overcooked broccoli or canned, mushy, gray peas that your mother might have served, or the weird-smelling vegetables your college roommate cooked up on the hot plate. It can mean a new world of clean, simply prepared, fresh, frozen, or preserved vegetables. Let your mind be bold—your taste buds will reward you!

PRIORITIES, PERSEVERANCE, AND PATIENCE

Whether they admit it or not, parents can have control over the food their children eat. It's just a matter of the three Ps: priorities, perseverance, and patience.

It's easy to buy ready-made, salty, highly processed snacks for kids to eat with their friends after school or over the weekend. It's also very easy to buy the small packs of baby carrots and celery sticks, along with sauce or salad dressing for dipping, and leave them out for the kids.

And, it's not so difficult (10 minutes difficult, perhaps) to chop up fresh fruits and vegetables for your children. Mothers don't have to stop serving chips and dips, particularly now that trans fats are being taken out of snacks, but they can also take the time to cut up apples, and arrange them on a plate with peanut butter. Children will clean up whatever is put out—the apple slices with peanut butter on the side disappear as quickly as the bowl of chips and cookies!

Just One More Bite!

JANICE NEWELL BISSEX, MS, RD,
AND LIZ WEISS, MS, RD

Between them, Janice Bissex and Liz Weiss have been educating people about nutrition for almost half a century. Bissex has been a nutrition advisor to the U.S. Senate, worked at Boston Harbor Hotel with chef Daniel Bruce, and has been president of the Massachusetts Dietetic Association. Plus, she's a mother of two. Also a mother, Weiss was one of the CNN health correspondents who first covered Oldways and the Mediterranean diet. She spent two decades writing and reporting on nutrition and health for CNN and PBS, among others. They've teamed up as authors of The Mom's Guide to Meal Makeovers *and are founders of the free online Meal Makeover Moms' Club (www .mealmakeovermoms.com). Who better than Janice and Liz to offer advice about eating fruits and vegetables and beans?*

Getting young children to try new foods, especially vegetables, can be a challenge even in the best of times. One simple strategy to encourage healthy eating is to establish a rule whereby everyone at the table must take a "no-thank-you bite." By making this rule lighthearted and fun, everyone (grown-ups included) will happily agree to take at least one bite of everything that is served. They can then say, "Thanks, I love this and want more," or "No, thank you." Believe it or not, it can take up to twenty tries before a child learns to like a new food. The greater the variety of foods you're able to introduce, the better.

This may seem obvious, but it's important to make the vegetables taste good. One way to do that is to lightly season them with salt, herbs, spices, or even extra virgin olive oil or sesame oil. For example, with the help of a small amount of extra virgin olive oil, garlic, and kosher salt, you can transform plain spinach into mouthwatering garlicky sautéed spinach. Don't be afraid to add some fat! Fat imparts a lot of flavor and, if you choose the right kind of fat, it can bring good health to the table.

Setting a good example and not making a big issue about what a child does or does not eat is also critical. It's the parent's job to offer a variety of healthy foods, and it's the child's job to decide what and how much to eat. The harder you try to convince your kids to eat their vegetables, the more likely they are to reject them. If the vegetables are delicious and others at the table are enjoying them, the youngest members will eventually learn to love them, too.

Five Easy Ways to Get More Fruits and Vegetables in the Diet

1. Shred a Carrot: Peel and shred a carrot and mix it right in with your favorite tuna sandwich.
2. Make a Smoothie: Blend together 1 cup 100 percent fruit juice, 1/2 ripe banana, a handful of frozen strawberries (or any frozen fruit), and 1/2 cup vanilla or fruited low-fat yogurt.
3. Dice It Up: Sauté a finely diced red bell pepper with your lean ground beef in recipes such as sloppy Joes.
4. Kick Up the Flavor: Turn steamed broccoli from so-so to sensational by drizzling with extra virgin olive oil and a pinch of kosher salt.
5. Dip It: Dip strawberries in melted dark chocolate.

Chefs Collaborative 2000 Charter and Statement of Principles

In 1993 at the Oldways international symposium in Hawaii, called "Food Choices 2000," Oldways organized the Chefs Collaborative. The collaborative was and still is a group of chefs committed to sustainability. The Chefs Collaborative is now an independent organization, but the charter and statement of principles that we wrote in 1993 still ring true.

PREAMBLE: We, the undersigned, acknowledging our leadership in the celebration of the pleasures of food, and recognizing the impact of food choices on our collective personal health, on the vitality of cultures and on the integrity of the global environment, affirm the following principles:

STATEMENT OF PRINCIPLES

1. Good, safe, wholesome food is a basic human right.
2. Society has the obligation and responsibility to make good food affordable, available, and accessible to all.
3. Good food begins with unpolluted air, land and water, environmentally sustainable farming and fishing, and humane animal husbandry.
4. Sound food choices avoid unnecessarily processed foods and emphasize local, seasonal, and wholesome ingredients.
5. Cultural and biological diversity is essential for the health of people and the planet. Preserving and revitalizing sustainable food and agricultural traditions strengthen that diversity.
6. The healthy, traditional diets of many cultures offer abundant evidence that a variety of fruits, vegetables, beans, and grains is the foundation of good diets, and are often a feast for the senses.
7. Sharing the pleasures of the garden, the kitchen, and the table vitally enriches our lives, our families, and our communities.
8. As part of their education, our children deserve to be taught basic cooking skills and to learn the impact of their food choices on themselves, on their culture, and on their environment.

This draft charter and statement of principles was adopted on July 15, 1993, at a meeting following the international symposium, by the chefs listed below, with the restaurants they represented in 1993.

John Ash, Fetzer Vineyards
Paul Bartolotta, Spiaggia
Catherine Brandel, The Café at Chez Panisse
Rick Bayless, Frontera Grill
Kathleen Daelemans, Grand Wailea Resort Hotel and Spa
Gary Danko, The Dining Room at the Ritz Carlton
Robert Del Grande, Café Annie
Mark Ellman, Avalon
Susan Feniger, Border Grill
Amy Ferguson-Ota, Ritz-Carlton on the Big Island
Larry Forgione, An American Place
Joyce Goldstein, Square One
Madhur Jaffrey, Dawat Restaurant
Jean-Marie Josselin, A Pacific Café
Mo Kanner, Culinary Institute of America
Matthew Kenney, Matthew's
Deborah Madison, Café Escalera
Zarela Martinez, Zarela
Nobu Matsuhisa, Nobu
George Mavrothalassitis, La Mer, Halakulani Hotel
Peter Merriman, Merriman's
Mark Miller, Coyote Cafe and Red Sage
Mary Sue Milliken, Border Grill
Bradley Ogden, Lark Creek Inn and One Market Square
Philippe Padovani, Manele Bay Hotel
Nora Pouillon, Nora's
Michael Romano, Union Square Cafe
Oliver Saucy, Oliver's
Jimmy Schmidt, Rattlesnake Club
RoxSand Scocos, RoxSand's
Allen Susser, Chef Allen's
Alan Wong, Canoe House, Mauna Lani Bay Hotel
Roy Yamaguchi, Roy's and Roy's Bistro

Sustainable Cuisine

K. DUN GIFFORD

Dun wrote this essay for a 1996 dinner at the United Nations honoring sustainable cuisine, organized by Oldways, the Chefs Collaborative, and the Earth Pledge Foundation. Michael Romano, chef and partner at Union Square Cafe, was the organizing chef for this spectacular meal, and his team of chefs included Paul Bartolotta, Rick Bayless, Patrick Clark, Alan Hardin, Larry Hayden, Gray Kunz, Waldy Malouf, Anne Rosenzweig, Jimmy Schmidt, and Allen Susser. 🌿

Defining "sustainable cuisine" turns out to be oddly difficult, for the same reasons, probably, that defining "good government" is difficult.

This may be because each of the two words in these pairs is so very subjective, and that when they are paired, their very conjunction multiplies the definition's complexity exponentially.

Opening the lid on sustainable cuisine, then, lets loose thousands of pieces of our definitional puzzle, which suddenly looks a lot more complicated.

It's time for some help.

"Sustainability" is, in fact, a relatively new term, and it is suddenly all around us. We have sustainable agriculture, sustainable development, sustainable diets, sustainable cities, sustainable tourism, and now sustainable cuisine. Generally speaking, people who use sustainability as a modifier for all these nouns share a similar but vague sense of its meaning, a meaning akin to the "good earth" sense of sustainable yield.

The United Nations Conference on Environment and Development (the fancy name for the 1992 Earth Summit in Rio) offered up a definition of sustainability: the "capacity to meet the needs of the present without compromising the ability of future generations to meet their own needs."

This definition accords with our shared general understanding of what sustainable yield means. But if we want to remain with this United Nations formulation for sustainable cuisine, then "cooking" will have to reflect the "quality or style" of the "today-must-not-compromise-tomorrow" sense of the language of the Rio Summit definition.

Sadly, however, it is too restrictive for solving our sustainable cuisine definitional puzzle, because cuisine really has to do with the entire continuum of human survival. It's cooking, to be sure—but we cannot cook without food and fire, we can't have food without agriculture and transport and storage, and we can't satisfy our desires for food that tastes good and our innate instincts for nourishment unless we have learned kitchen skills. And so on.

At Oldways, we began trying to define sustainable diets more than a dozen years ago. We searched all the literature and talked to hundreds of resource people.

At midcourse in this search, we came up with a simple triangular graphic image that has worn well the tests of time and stern challenge. On one leg of the triangle is the legend "HEALTH," on the second leg is "ENVIRONMENT," and on the third leg is "TRADITION." In its center, we have sometimes put images of food and drink, and sometimes words such as "sustainable diets" or "sustainable cuisine" or "sustainability." To indicate that sustainability is a matter of personal choices, we have used the caption "VOTE WITH YOUR FORK FOR A SUSTAINABLE FUTURE" under or over the triangular image.

This word-and-picture "definition" of sustainable cuisine has stood up well against the shifting winds of changing attitudes. However, in trying to define sustainable cuisine, we've concluded that what's important is to keep on extending the search itself, and enlarging the circle of people making the search with us. We may never find the Holy Grail of a perfect definition, but by searching we will have spread a wider awareness of the importance of the concept and encouraged broader acceptance of its essential meaning for the health of this planet and its peoples.

The Farmers' Market and Its Web of Connection

DEBORAH MADISON

Deborah Madison has done it all. She was the original chef at San Francisco's famed Greens restaurant; she wrote Vegetarian Cooking for Everyone, *one of the most fun, interesting, and usable cookbooks for vegetarians (named Cookbook of the Year by the International Association of Culinary Professionals), and she is a wonderful teacher who shares her knowledge and experience with everyone. One of her recent projects and published books (Local Flavors, Cooking and Eating from America's Farmers' Markets) involved the farmers markets sprouting up all over America. We can think of no one better to talk about farms, fruits, and vegetables, and the communities that celebrate them.*

Today, wherever you live or travel, you aren't too far from a farmers' market. New markets appear each year. Small ones grow larger; old ones get permanent homes and structures, huge markets spin off smaller ones. It's an ever-evolving business in which one size doesn't fit all. In fact, one of the likable things about farmers' markets is that they are as far away from a chain as you can get. Each one has its own personality, and yet, there are some predictable elements to all.

Also called greenmarkets or growers' markets, what gives these markets their stamp is that the food sold is grown or produced by the person selling. It's all about direct marketing, the banner under which the whole movement began. Sometimes the name farmers' market gets corrupted, and unfortunately, there are hybrid markets that allow resellers to sell what they buy at the produce terminal, a practice that devalues the efforts of local farmers and sends the message that food should be cheap. But the real message that the farmers' market can send is that the true cost of growing food is reflected in the higher prices found there. The farmers' market

shopper may be paying more, but she's getting great value for her dollars.

What values? Starting with the food, since that's the product. Its quality is superior. It's truly fresh, and therefore vital and nutritious, having been picked just the day before. It's usually delicious, especially in the case of those foods that simply don't travel—apricots, peaches, and sweet corn. Often the food is organic. The farmers' market is likely to offer varieties of fruits and vegetables that are fragile but flavorful—those amazing tomatoes that overwhelm with taste but that are harder to grow than their industrial counterparts. And when it comes to meat, the shopper can find choices that even the super-natural food stores don't have—grass-finished beef and bison, lamb, elk, pheasant, big plump chickens, tastier breeds of turkeys, eggs that are just out of this world.

What especially excites me about these markets is that they are where one finds those foods that truly express regional cultures—shagbark hickory nuts and black walnuts in the midwestern markets, which are not found elsewhere. Or, wild huckleberries in Montana, Creole cream cheese in Louisiana, native green chiles and chicos in New Mexico, those great peaches in the Texas hill country. Every part of the country has something that's particular to its geography, culture, and history—its own local flavors. These are foods that have histories, and when you find them, you might well get a story from the person who grew, found, or otherwise produced what you're holding in your hand.

Farmers' markets have long served as a kind of proving ground. Many cheesemakers get their start there while they're still very small and developing their craft. Vietnamese and Hmong farmers both found a vital economic niches for their communities, which seem to be made up of great growers. At the same time, they've introduced new varieties of vegetables to America and inspired other farmers with their handsome displays and skillful growing.

More than just a way of doing business, these markets provide enriching links and connections over the fundamental act of procuring food. They're one of the few places where you can meet the person who makes (grows) something you use (food). Questions, feedback, stories, exchanges with nearby customers—dialogue, in short—have the opportunity of occurring with strangers in a setting that is essentially convivial. Thus the farmers' market is one of those few places where the roots of culture can get irrigated so that a good long growth is ensured. Not only are we enriched for the experience of eating well, shopping at a farmers' market is a good way to rub shoulders with people we don't normally meet, and to keep in touch with our rural neighbors. And rural communities can keep money working at home when there's a farmers' market to sell in.

A warm welcome always awaits you at your local market. Sure, it's a bit more trouble to carry all those bags, deal with all that cash and so forth, but there's nothing better in the end. Not only will you come home with your arms filled with the most inspiring food imaginable, but your heart might just come home fuller and happier than it was when you left the house.

The Enduring Aubergine

COLIN SPENCER

*Colin Spencer is a noted British food writer. He's written wonderful books on food and history, and vegetables and vegetarianism (*The History of Vegetarianism, The Heretics Feast, The Vegetable Book, Vegetarian Gourmet Dinner Party, The New Vegetarian, *and most recently, the prize-winning book,* British Food: An Extraordinary Thousand Years of History). *He also spent many years as a contributor to the UK newspaper, the* Guardian. *Colin has traveled with us—to Italy, Spain, Greece, Tunisia, and Turkey—and reported on the food and traditions in these countries. For the Oldways symposium in Istanbul, Turkey, in 1993, we asked Colin to give a presentation on the eggplant, the quintessential ingredient for Turkish cuisine. Neither he nor we have forgotten the title of the talk we asked him to give—"The Enduring Aubergine." Here, for space constraints, are a few enduring excerpts from his presentation about the aubergine, known in the United States as eggplant.*

The premise that I am offering is that traditional cuisine acquires its singular character from the particular foods indigenous to that region at the dawn of history. The range of ingredients is, of course, dictated by the geography: terrain, climate, soil composition, ratio of mountains to plains, the rivers, bodies of water. There is another highly important factor: where a region lies on the world trade routes.

We, the food gurus, tend to praise, indeed idolize, the traditional cuisines that have the richest and most variegated range of ingredients, not always realizing that a temperate climate, plenty of sun, and an adequate rainfall have made such fruits of the earth possible. Over the years, climates change, of course, fertile soil can turn arid, and desert can replace green pasture, but a people will tenaciously cling to their traditional foods even though they may have to be grown elsewhere.

You cannot settle down, build durable shelters, and begin to live in one place without two essentials, a supply of fresh water and a food that can be stored throughout the winter. Meat is a natural fresh food rich in the winter; if needs must, you could always kill an animal, though it would be well to remember that livestock animals were kept for what they gave you alive—not just their milk, eggs, fresh blood, and wool—but their manure, dried as fuel. Dead, every bit of carcass was used, the horns and hooves, the bristles, hides, and fleeces. But animals could not feed the majority of people. Livestock represented wealth and power in your society, and if you slaughtered them, you diminished both, so herds had to grow as the visible stocks and bonds of an entrepreneur.

The second essential for a community was a plant food that could be stored throughout the winter. Granaries, then, are the hallmark of the first civilizations. But other foods can be stored as well; we have found in caves in northern Israel pits cut out from the stone that were used to store acorns as early as 30,000 B.C. All kinds of nuts, dried fruit, seeds, and pulses can be stored throughout the winter, especially in a hot, dry climate. Think how large a part these grains, seeds, dried fruits, pulses, and nuts play in the cuisine of the Middle East. Here in Turkey we see them in the breads, bulgur, buckwheat, sesame, tahini, in many meat and dried fruit dishes, in the use of almonds, pistachios, walnuts, and pine nuts used in the sweet dishes. The pulses, the beans, chickpeas, and lentils are still part of everyday dishes for many people.

But let us leap forward to those first great civilizations and look at the garden of King Merodach-Baladan the Second, who was king of Babylon from 721 to 710 B.C. and managed to maintain Babylonian independence against Assyrian military supremacy. Like the Emperor Charlemagne fifteen hundred years later, Merodach-Baladan must have been keen on cultivating plants, for we have a record of what was grown in Babylon's royal kitchen garden.

There were peas, beans, onions, leeks, garlic, carrots, fennel, beets, chard, lettuce, gourds, melons, and pistachios. But only a few of these vegetables, I suspect, would we have recognized immediately. Take the carrot, for example. The reddish-orange carrot we know today was bred in the eighteenth century, while what grew in this garden was either a yellow or a small purple carrot, or it could have been a parsnip. Translations of ancient texts constantly confused the two; but on the evidence of the cuisine, I would plump without any doubt that for Babylonians it was a carrot. The beet would not have been the root, but the leaf. Pliny mentions a salad of white chard, lentils, and beans. The most commonly mentioned vegetables are the onion, garlic, leek, and radish, but the radish was grown mostly for its oil, used for lighting. When eaten, it was laborers' food and it would have been the white root they ate, similar to what we now call daikon. The alliums (onion, garlic, and leek) must have been greatly treasured for their fiery and stimulating qualities.

Geographically, the Middle East (or Asia Minor as it was called for a time) was blessed by its position; it was in the midst of all trade routes. To live there in those times it must have seemed that one resided at the center of the civilized world. Everyone came to you to get anywhere else. The only way of traveling from Europe to the Far East was through there, and many of the plants that grew in Asia Minor came either from southern Africa and Egypt, like okra and mallow, or from East India and China, like aubergine and rice. No food plants seemed to come from Europe; for one thing, the climate was colder, and plants that flourished there did not much care for a warmer climate.

But what of the aubergine, so much a basic now of Middle Eastern cuisine? It is interesting that though aubergines are a member of the potato (solanum) family, they were not discovered in the New World with the tomatoes, peppers, and chiles, which would make such a devastating change in world cuisines. Originally aubergines come from the tropical forests of Asia. In the Tang dynasty in China it was called the Malayan purple melon. As you know, aubergines come in all colors, sizes, and shapes, but were not selectively bred; they were certainly used as early as the fifth century B.C. as mentioned in a gardening manual. From the cherry-size green aubergine, to the creamy white egg-shaped one, to the larger lilac and white striped and dark purple sausage-shaped ones, these varieties in some guise grew in the rain forests of prehistory—smaller certainly, but I believe they would be very recognizable in shape and color by us today. They could have been among the fruits eaten by our primate ancestors and certainly were eaten when *Homo erectus* emigrated from Africa one million years ago and began to colonize Asia and China. The aubergine berries must have been one of the fruits eaten by these travelers.

Considering how poisonous some members of the solanum family are, we must be grateful that aubergines are not only harmless, but beneficial. Aubergines were certainly eaten in the Indus Valley civilization and from thence their popularity traveled into the whole of India. As trade and cultural connections with Asia Minor were close, the aubergine became a common food in the Persian Empire. Alexander must have eaten many aubergine dishes, and you would have thought that the Greeks might have taken the vegetable home, but after all, these were Macedonian soldiers and the subtleties of the table were not much appreciated. So the aubergine stayed firmly in the East. Its common name there, "poor man's caviar" or "poor man's meat," tells us that it was a common food, much enjoyed. Yet it was a classless food, enjoyed by the great and the good as well as the poor.

Middle Eastern literature is full of anecdotes about the delights of various aubergine dishes and many recipes carry the name of the tale. Surely no other vegetable, except for garlic, appears so often as part of folklore. The Arabs took the aubergine to all the Mediterranean countries that they conquered, but this delicious and flexible vegetable had to wait another thousand years to meet its one true love, its soul mate and most natural partner—the tomato.

A Potato Primer

MOLLY STEVENS

When we met Molly Stevens in 1997 Dun knew that he had found a candidate for Oldways chef. Now of course this position isn't real, it's just in Dun's imagination. Although not the Oldways chef, Molly has traveled with us on overseas Oldways symposiums, and she's helped us with cooking demonstrations during scientific conferences. She is also a teacher, a recipe developer, and most recently, a prize-winning cookbook author. But more than that, she's an inspired interpreter of the subliminal linkages among the garden, the stove, and the plate.

From the very first knobby, multicolored, bitter-tasting tubers cultivated in the Andes some two thousand years ago, to the monstrous russets grown in the midwestern United States today, potatoes have always come in many shapes, colors, and sizes—and still do. Through a well-traveled history (first to Europe with the conquistadors and then to Asia and eventually back to North America), the mighty spud has found its way into kitchens across the globe and has become second only to rice as a global food crop. Potatoes offer an amazing variety in taste, texture, and character that mean adventure for the cook and great enjoyment for the consumer.

With over a thousand varieties of potatoes grown worldwide, it seems senseless to catalog them all. A simpler and more useful approach is to classify them into low-, medium-, and high-starch varieties. Low-starch potatoes (many red and white skin varieties) have a creamy, waxy texture and are best for boiling, salads, and roasting. Medium-starch potatoes (look to yellow-fleshed varieties) are a bit less waxy in texture, closer to mealy, and are good for gratins, roasting, and some mashes. The high-starch potatoes (primarily russets) have a dry, fluffy interior and are the ultimate for mashed potatoes, gnocchi, french fries, and baked potatoes.

In the past few decades, we've seen the rise of many wonderful heirloom varieties of potatoes—everything from dark, rugged-skinned purple ones, to slender, knobby fingerlings, and plump, smooth round types with flavors ranging from delicate to earthy, sweet to pleasantly bitter, nutty to downright buttery. The best way to judge a new variety is to simply steam or braise it (recipe on page 68) and taste for yourself.

Artichoke 101

STEVE PETUSEVSKY

Steve Petusevsky, or Chef Steve as he's known across the country, is as versatile as a utility player: he's worked for a large grocery chain (Whole Foods), written cookbooks (The Whole Foods Market Cookbook), writes newspaper columns, is a gifted communicator, and used to own a restaurant/store (Steve's Carried Away Cuisine). He's also an expert on vegetables and grains of all kinds. We've asked him to tell us about one of his favorites.

Some foods are just downright intimidating. Calves' brains, sheep's eyes, and snake are pretty obvious examples of foods that some people shrink from while others reach for.

Artichokes, too, put some people off—but not Californians. They are very popular in that state, where endless fields of beautiful artichoke crowns grow as far as the eye can see. Italians love them too—they are sold from carts on street corners and shoppers carry whole fresh artichokes on long stems over their shoulders as they walk on Ligurian village streets.

But in our markets, poor artichokes often sit alone, slowly decomposing. I feel badly seeing this. To the inexperienced home cook, they seem like a lot of work for not much return. In reality, it is just the opposite. After boiling the artichoke, you eat the bits of flesh that cling to the leaves. Inside is the artichoke heart and the nutty mellow artichoke bottom, cradling the "choke" the small clump of bristle you discard. And most people don't realize that the stem, peeled and boiled, is probably the tastiest part.

Of course you can buy artichoke hearts and bottoms in cans, and sometimes frozen. But their flavor just can't compare to fresh.

So, get out your knives and pay attention to "Artichoke Preparation 101." Bring a large pot of water to a boil with plenty of salt and a sliced fresh lemon. The lemon prevents the cut artichoke from browning and flavors the water.

To prepare the artichoke, cut the stem off about $1/2$ inch from the base of the artichoke. Reserve the stem you cut off. Cut the very end off and peel the cut-off stem. Some of the outside leaves of the artichoke will fall off. Pull off the remaining loose leaves from the edges and cut the top inch from the artichoke as well. Rub top and bottom cut surfaces with a cut fresh lemon and place the artichoke in the boiling water. Cook the artichoke for 8 to 10 minutes, until a knife inserted in the base pierces easily. The stem pieces can be plunged into boiling water until tender. When cooked, place the artichoke in ice water to stop the cooking and preserve the color.

Now that your artichoke is cooked and tender, the fun begins. Stick your fingers into the center of the cooked artichoke and pinch the small, fibrous leaves, removing them. You will expose the fuzzy choke, which contains the nettles. Although these are beautiful to look at, you must scrape them out with a spoon, exposing the artichoke bottom. That was a bit of work, but now it's over, and you can enjoy the fruits of your labor.

Place each leaf between your teeth and pull to enjoy its delicate flavor. You will get a bit of delicate artichoke flesh in your mouth. You also have the cooked stem and artichoke bottom to enjoy.

You can serve the chokes cold or hot. Serve them with melted butter and lemon or a really good quality extra virgin olive oil and lemon. You don't have to add much to enhance their natural flavor.

Avocados: A Worldly Fruit

JOHN MERCURI DOOLEY

In October 1995, Oldways organized an international conference entitled "Traditional Diets as Models for Healthy Eating" to examine whether Mediterranean and traditional diets from other parts of the world are as beneficial for preventing cancer, obesity, and diabetes as they are for preventing heart disease. We included a case study of avocados within this conference, since avocados are historically an important part of the traditional diets of Americans and are now an ingredient of the diets of the people of the Mediterranean and Asia as well.

Most importantly, at the time, the avocado was terribly misunderstood and misrepresented. Conditioned by the U.S. government and low-fat product advertisers to be fat-phobic, consumers were afraid to eat avocados because they were thought to be (1) full of fat and (2) full of cholesterol. Looking back now, it's hard to imagine that avocado growers were putting stickers on avocados to remind consumers that there was no cholesterol in avocados (since they are a plant, they have no cholesterol!). This Oldways conference helped resurrect the avocado—for its healthful, "good," monounsaturated fat, for its fiber, for its satiety, for its versatility, and most of all, for its great taste. The essay below summarizes the conference presentations made by chefs and cookbook authors Maricel Presilla, Zarela Martinez, Martha Rose Shulman, and Rick Bayless, as well as Australian nutritionist Rosemary Stanton.

Avocados are a rich topic for case study. They are a fruit, a cousin of apples, pears, and bananas. They rank high among foods that "taste good," because they have a silky texture and a distinct flavor. In the words of food writer Suzanne Hamlin in the *New York Times,* "avocados are easy to love. Smooth, buttery, easy to digest, almost always available and needing nothing but a quick peel to eat, avocados are so good that they must be bad; our puritan ethic does not often equate pleasure and health. But the healthful benefits are irrefutable."

Unlike most fruits, however—but like olives—they contain fats along with their other nutrients. For years, this fact has discouraged many people from eating avocados. But it now turns out that the fat in avocados—again, like the fat in olives—is monounsaturated fat, which is "good fat."

Avocados are a simple, ancient food of the Americas. Almost alone among fruits, they lend a melting richness to meals. They are added at the last minute to soups. Chopped, the fruit is a mellow complement to a Mexican supper of hot tortillas, green-tomato salsa, and fresh cheese. Cut into long thin slices and laid on a plate alongside picadillo, or Latin hash, the avocado's texture and fleeting anise-hazelnut flavor calms the spice. And as Wilson Popenoe relayed in his 1920 *Manual of Tropical and Subtropical Fruits,* Guatemalan Indians had a saying that laid bare this fruit's place in their hearts: "Four or five tortillas, an avocado, and a cup of coffee—that is a good meal."

The avocado is indigenous to mainland tropical America. Noted Mayanist Sophie Coe reports in *America's First Cuisines* that wild avocado seeds found in southeastern Mexico have been dated at 8,000 to 7,000 BC, and the fruit was being cultivated in Tehuacán by 6,000 to 5,000 B.C. Probably soon thereafter, experts say, the fruit spread from Mexico through Central America and into Peru.

Historical records indicate that avocados were planted in Jamaica by the Spaniards in the mid-seventeenth century, and that they slowly spread through the rest of the Caribbean over the next century. There were no recorded plantings in Florida, however, until 1833, when Henry Perrine grew them south of Miami. In 1871, R. B. Ord planted three avocados in Santa Barbara, and from this small beginning, avocado orchards spread throughout large parts of Southern California.

There are hundreds of varieties. The large, smooth-skinned variety sold in small numbers in the United

States is of the West Indian race. Experts say the Fuerte variety—small, pear-shaped, and green—is possibly a natural hybrid of the Guatemalan and Mexican races. The Haas, with its small dark pebbly skin, is by far the predominant variety grown in the United States.

FROM ANCIENT TO MODERN KITCHEN

"We know little about how avocados, or paltas, as they are called in Peru, were eaten in pre–Columbian America," wrote Coe. "The one recipe we may be sure of is the Aztec 'ahuaca-mulli,' which, Anglicized, became the world-famous guacamole, or avocado sauce. This combination of mashed avocados, with or without a few chopped tomatoes and onions, is the pre-Columbian dish most accessible to us, because the Aztecs used familiar tastes of New World onions and coriander. Wrapped in a maize tortilla, preferably freshly made, or even on a tortilla chip, it might ever so distantly evoke the taste of Tenochtitlán, the Aztec capital."

Guacamole is served in many ways today in Mexico, often with tacos or at the start of a meal with hot tortillas and other snacks; or with rice dishes, refried beans, or beef, chicken, or fish. In northern Mexico, green tomatoes are added to it, and in Veracruz, it is made tart with lime juice to accompany fish. When Patricia Quintana, Mexican food authority and author of *Cuisine of the Water Gods,* visited Michoacan, on the central Pacific coast of Mexico, fishermen there prepared ceviche with lime and dried oregano, and, after curing, laid the drained fish on a bed of guacamole lightened with zucchini juice. In Oaxaca, Quintana was served guacamole flavored with tomatillos and garlic, as an accompaniment to fried empanadas stuffed with a mixture of shrimp, tomato, and chiles.

With or without a bowl of tomato salsa beside it, guacamole has become ubiquitous as a dip for tortilla chips in the United States. Chefs especially in the Southwest use guacamole in a number of ways. It is served as part of a salad, for example, sometimes with chopped radishes, cucumbers, or other vegetables added. At the other extreme, in the American tradition of taking a simple foreign dish and turning it into a fantasy of abundance, some restaurants include guacamole in multilayer tostadas that are the Tex-Mex equivalent of a Big Mac—with extra everything.

At their simplest, though, in the land of their origin and now wherever they are grown, avocados are eaten as a fruit. Food historian Maricel Presilla grew up in Cuba, where she remembers eating them "just as we ate green mango, with salt." Eaten on their own as a fruit, or mashed and mixed with tomatoes and onions, sliced and added at the last minute to salads and soups, or laid on a plate as an accompaniment, avocados are a no-fuss American food. And a very healthy, thoroughly sublime one.

CRETE'S MIXED GREENS AND TOMATOES WITH BLACK-EYED PEAS

PAULA WOLFERT

Paula Wolfert is one of a kind. She is as gentle and sharing as her books are interesting and thorough, and we love her intensity, focus, and, best of all, her sense of humor. She is a pioneer; she was among the first cookbook authors to travel to many of the places whose cuisines she studied, wrote eloquently about, and helped make popular. She learned her craft in the kitchens and homes of Morocco, southwest France, and Turkey, and then came home to figure out how Americans could approximate the tastes of those very local cuisines in the United States. This took years of research and testing, and it is one reason her cookbooks and writings have been such a powerful influence on America's leading food professionals.

This is Paula's favorite recipe for greens, adapted from her book Mediterranean Grains and Greens. *This recipe makes us recall fondly her trips with Oldways to Turkey, Greece, and southern Italy where she relentlessly pursued* horta, *or greens, and older ladies who would show her their "old ways" of cooking them.* 🌀

SERVES 6 TO 8

- 1³/₄ cups dried black-eyed peas
- 2¹/₂ packed cups mixed tender leafy greens (three or four of these sweet greens—beet greens, baby spinach, Swiss chard, miner's lettuce, pea shoots, mâche, orache, nettles, lamb's quarters, and green amaranth—with a sprig of cilantro added for fragrance)
- ¹/₄ cup extra virgin olive oil
- ³/₄ cup chopped onion
- 3 scallions, white and tender green parts, finely chopped
- 1 cup diced fennel bulb
- 1 sprig fresh cilantro, stemmed and coarsely chopped
- 1 cup grated tomatoes
- Pinch of fennel seeds, bruised in a mortar
- Sea salt and freshly ground black pepper
- Water (optional)

Soak the black-eyed peas for an hour. Drain and transfer to a pot and cover with fresh water. Bring to a boil over high heat. Decrease the heat to a simmer, then simmer for about 30 minutes, until tender.

While the beans are cooking, wash the greens and let them sit, dripping wet, on a plate.

In a 4-quart saucepan over medium heat, warm the olive oil. Add the onion, scallions, and the fennel and cook until soft, golden, and aromatic, about 10 minutes. Add the greens to the saucepan along with the cilantro, tomatoes, fennel seeds, and salt and pepper and cook for 10 minutes.

Drain the black-eyed peas; discard the water. Add the black-eyed peas to the saucepan along with a few tablespoons water, if necessary, to keep everything moist. Simmer for another 10 minutes and correct the seasoning. Serve warm or cool.

THICK-CRUSTED GREENS, ONION, AND FETA PIE

AGLAIA KREMEZI

During our travels and symposiums in Greece with cookbook author and food writer Aglaia Kremezi, we visited cooks, restaurants, and producers to learn about the Mediterranean diet on its home ground. For a symposium on Crete, Aglaia arranged for home cooks to demonstrate their family recipes for making those wonderful savory Greek pies filled with horta *(greens). These pies adorn family dinner tables and festival meals throughout Greece.*

This recipe is inspired by the "greens" pies of the Cyclades. If you like, you can make ten individual half-moon pies instead of one big one.

SERVES 8 TO 10

CRUST

> 4 cups unbleached all-purpose flour
> 1 tablespoon baking powder
> Pinch of sea salt
> ²/₃ cup extra virgin olive oil
> ²/₃ to 1 cup water

FILLING

> 1 cup finely chopped red onion
> 3 scallions (white and most of the green parts),
>   thinly sliced
> 2 cups firmly packed chopped mixed greens
>   (spinach, arugula, chard, etc.)
> ¹/₂ cup fennel tops (or dill), chopped
> Sea salt
> 10 ounces feta cheese, crumbled
> 1¹/₂ cups Greek or whole-milk yogurt
> ¹/₄ cup toasted bread crumbs
> Freshly ground black pepper
> 2 large eggs, lightly beaten
> ¹/₄ cup sesame seeds
> 3 to 4 tablespoons milk

To make the crust, mix together the flour, baking powder, and salt in a large bowl. Add the oil and rub the ingredients between your hands until the texture is like bread crumbs. Gradually add enough water to make soft, elastic dough. Cover with plastic wrap and let rest for about 10 minutes. Alternatively, you can make the dough in a food processor. Combine the dry ingredients and pulse to mix, then, with the motor running, add the liquids. (Let the dough rest in the food processor for 2 to 3 minutes.)

To make the filling, put the onion, scallions, greens, and fennel in a colander and sprinkle generously with salt. Knead with your hands for a few minutes to wilt, then rinse briefly under warm running water. Drain well and squeeze with your hands to extract as much liquid as possible.

In a large bowl, combine the greens mixture, feta cheese, yogurt, bread crumbs, and pepper to taste. Taste and add salt if necessary—feta is usually quite salty. Stir in the eggs.

Preheat the oven to 400°F. Oil the bottom and sides of a 13 by 9-inch baking dish and sprinkle with 2 tablespoons of the sesame seeds.

Divide the dough into three pieces. Take two of the pieces and cover the other. Briefly knead together the two pieces and roll them out on a lightly floured surface into a sheet large enough to cover the bottom and sides of the baking dish, with a ¹/₂-inch overhang. Fit the dough into the dish and add the filling. Roll out the remaining piece of dough into a rectangle just a little larger than the dish and place it over the filling. Fold the overhanging bottom crust inward. Pinch the two edges together, turn them inward, and press to seal, making a neat cord around the edge of the pan. Flatten the cord with the tines of a fork to prevent it from sticking out, because it will burn during baking. Prick the surface a few times with a fork, to let steam escape during baking, and if you like, score parallel lines on the top of the crust, with a pastry wheel, crossing them to make diamond-shaped patterns. Brush with the milk and sprinkle with the remaining 2 tablespoons sesame seeds.

Bake for 1 hour, or more, until the crust pulls away from the sides of the pan and is golden brown on top. If the top browns fast, cover loosely with aluminum foil.

Let cool before cutting. Serve warm or at room temperature.

OVEN-BAKED EGGPLANT WITH MOZZARELLA AND FRESH HERBS

CLIFFORD WRIGHT

In Sardinia and Sicily, eggplant is especially popular. This is a nice eggplant preparation that is not as heavy as recipes that call for frying. You first grill the eggplant slices, and then bake them in an aromatic tomato sauce heavily laced with herbs.

SERVES 6

   3 large eggplants (about 3½ pounds), trimmed
        and cut into ³/₈-inch slices
   Sea salt
   ½ cup extra virgin olive oil
   1 small onion, finely chopped
   2 cloves garlic, finely chopped
   2 pounds tomatoes, peeled, seeded, and chopped
   3 tablespoons finely chopped fresh mint leaves
   2 tablespoons fresh thyme leaves
   Freshly ground black pepper
   ½ cup coarsely chopped and loosely packed fresh
        basil leaves
   ³/₄ pound mozzarella cheese, sliced

Lay the eggplant on paper towels and sprinkle with salt. Leave them to release their bitter juices for 30 minutes, and then pat dry with paper towels. Prepare a charcoal fire, preheat a gas grill for 20 minutes on high, or heat a ridged cast-iron skillet over high heat for 10 minutes.

Brush each slice of eggplant with olive oil and cook on the grill or in the skillet until even black grid marks appear, about 4 minutes a side. Transfer the eggplant slices to a baking tray and continue cooking the rest.

In a large skillet or saucepan, heat 3 tablespoons olive oil over medium-low heat. Add the onion and garlic and sauté until translucent, about 8 minutes, stirring so the garlic doesn't burn. Add the tomatoes, mint, and thyme and season with salt and pepper. Cook until the sauce is thick, about 35 minutes, stirring occasionally.

Preheat the oven to 400°F. Arrange a layer of eggplant in a lightly oiled baking casserole and cover with a few ladlefuls of sauce, then a sprinkle of basil, and then a layer of mozzarella. Continue until the eggplant is used up. Arrange the mozzarella on top of the last layer of eggplant and cover with the remaining sauce. Bake until the cheese starts to bubble, about 35 minutes. Serve hot.

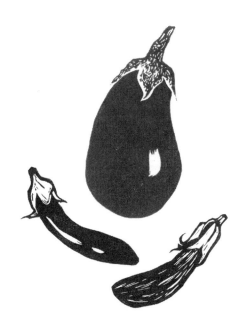

SPLIT PEA AND MELTED EGGPLANT SOUP

PENNY KRIS-ETHERTON, PhD

The "melted" eggplant adds a wonderful texture and takes on the flavor of the peas and other ingredients. This is a very versatile recipe and can be modified by changing the broth, vegetables, and/or herb and spice selection. Or, add meat, fish, or poultry, if desired.

Season to taste with marjoram, black pepper, basil, thyme, cumin, Italian seasoning, 2 bay leaves, parsley, and oregano. This recipe can be made in a slow-cooker by cooking on low all day.

SERVES 6 TO 8

5 tablespoons extra virgin olive oil
1 large onion, chopped
3 carrots, chopped
3 stalks celery, chopped
1 to 2 cloves garlic, crushed
2 (14-ounce) cans chicken broth
8 ounces split peas
2 baby eggplants, peeled and chopped
Splash of white wine (optional)
Dash of hot sauce (optional)
1 (14-ounce) can stewed tomatoes
Water
Fresh herbs of choice to taste

Heat the olive oil in a large saucepan over medium heat. Add the onion, carrots, celery, and garlic, and sauté for about 5 minutes, until the onions are translucent. Add the herbs and cook for 30 seconds. Add the broth, split peas, eggplants, wine, and hot sauce and cook over medium heat for about 1 hour, until the eggplant disappears or "melts." Add the stewed tomatoes and simmer for 1 hour more. During cooking, add water and herbs as needed. Serve hot.

GRILLED RATATOUILLE

ROBIN KLINE, MS, RD

People who won't look twice at eggplant gobble this up. Summer flavors of grilled vegetables and sweet tomatoes make it irresistible. Serve as a side dish to grilled meat or as a topping for grilled French bread.

MAKES 6 CUPS

1 large Italian eggplant, trimmed, sliced 1/2 inch thick
2 large bell peppers (at least one red), grilled, peeled, and diced
1 red onion, sliced 1/2 inch thick
1/3 cup extra virgin olive oil, plus additional oil for brushing eggplant
2 tablespoons fresh oregano
2 tablespoons fresh thyme
2 tablespoons balsamic vinegar
1 clove garlic, crushed
1 1/2 cups halved super-sweet cherry tomatoes
3/4 teaspoon sea salt
1/2 teaspoon freshly ground black pepper

Prepare a medium-hot fire in a grill. Brush the eggplant and peppers lightly with the olive oil. Grill the eggplant, peppers, and onion over direct heat until they are soft and lightly browned, 8 to 10 minutes, turning as needed. Remove the peppers from the heat, let cool, and dice. Remove the eggplant and onion from the grill and dice.

Toss the eggplant and onion in a large bowl with the diced peppers, 1/3 cup olive oil, oregano, thyme, vinegar, garlic, and tomatoes. Toss gently; season with salt and pepper. Serve slightly warm or at room temperature.

COSTA RICAN CABBAGE SLAW

HANNIA CAMPOS, PhD

Over the years we've collaborated with many faculty members of the Harvard School of Public Health and Harvard Medical School who represent different specialties, different research goals, and different nationalities. Dr. Hannia Campos is from Costa Rica, and her research interests include the health of the people of her native country. Based in Boston and married to another School of Public Health faculty member, Frank Sacks, Hannia returns to Costa Rica every couple of months to further her research projects. We're lucky she shares with us the spoils of her trips to Costa Rica; she often returns with special foods, like Christmas tamales, or with new recipes from her family's kitchen.

This slaw is traditionally served as a side dish with rice and beans or to make a "gallo" (a corn tortilla with shredded barbecued meat or chorizo).

SERVES 4 TO 6

1 cup seeded and diced tomatoes
1/2 cup firmly packed minced fresh cilantro
1 cup finely chopped red bell pepper (optional)
1 small head green cabbage, finely shredded
1/2 cup freshly squeezed lime juice
Sea salt

Mix the tomatoes, cilantro, and red pepper in a bowl. Add the cabbage and toss. Add the lime juice and salt to taste at the last minute before serving to avoid wilting of the cabbage.

PICADILLO DE CHAYOTE CON MAIZ

HANNIA CAMPOS, PhD

A picadillo consists of diced vegetables mixed together. Picadillo comes from the Spanish word picar *meaning "to chop." A picadillo could be compared to succotash, as the cubed vegetables are equal in size. Chayote is a type of squash that is available in Latino markets and other specialty stores. Achiote is a paste made from annatto seeds that can also be found in Latino markets. This dish is also known as* ajiaco *(chayote and corn medley). It can be served over brown rice or with corn tortillas.*

MAKES 2 CUPS

2 tablespoons extra virgin olive oil
1 medium white onion, finely chopped
2 tablespoons minced garlic
1 teaspoon achiote paste
2 tablespoons chopped fresh cilantro
1/2 cup chopped celery, including leaves
1 red bell pepper, finely chopped
1 tablespoon tomato paste
6 fresh chayotes, diced in 1-inch cubes
Water (optional)
1 1/2 cups fresh or frozen corn kernels

Heat the oil in a medium saucepan over medium heat. Add the onion and garlic and sauté for about 2 minutes, until transparent. Add achiote paste, cilantro, celery, and bell pepper. Cover and simmer for 5 minutes. Add the tomato paste and stir for 1 minute. Add the chayote and simmer, covered, for 15 minutes. Stir lightly and add water, if necessary (just enough to be able to move) to prevent sticking. Add the corn and stir for a few more minutes. Serve immediately.

LIME GUACAMOLE

SARA BAER-SINNOTT

As much as we love traditional guacamole, this is a wonderful, very fresh-tasting alternative. It's light and clean, and perfect for a summer lunch or cocktails. At Oldways we spread this avocado treat on toasted whole-grain pita wedges or tortillas for lunch, at least once a week! ▨

SERVES 2

I ripe Haas avocado

I lime, quartered

Sea salt

Tortilla chips, tortillas, or pita toasts, to serve

Open the avocado and scoop out the flesh. Mash with a fork or spoon. Squeeze the juice of the lime, quarter by quarter and add to the avocado. Add salt to taste. Serve with tortilla chips, tortillas, or pita toasts.

BRAISED POTATOES WITH GARLIC AND BAY LEAVES

MOLLY STEVENS

Look for small potatoes that you can braise whole, such as German butterball or French fingerlings. Regular small red potatoes are wonderful, too. Either way, the potatoes come out all creamy and delicately infused with the flavors of bay and garlic. ▨

SERVES 4 TO 6

1¹/₂ pounds small red, yellow, or white potatoes, scrubbed

3 tablespoons extra virgin olive oil

I cup water or chicken stock, or as needed

2 bay leaves, fresh if you can find them, torn in half

2 to 3 cloves garlic, peeled and bruised

Coarse sea salt and freshly ground black pepper

If the potatoes are larger than a golf ball, cut them in half. If you are leaving them whole, check to see if they have thick skins by scraping your thumbnail across the skin. If the skin doesn't tear, remove a strip of skin around the circumference of each potato with a vegetable peeler—this will allow the flavors of the braising liquid to penetrate the potato better. If the skins are relatively thin, leave them intact.

Put the potatoes in a saucepan large enough to hold them in a snug single layer without crowding. Add the olive oil and pour in enough water or stock to come halfway up the sides of the potatoes. Add the bay leaves and garlic. Season with salt and pepper. Cover and bring to a simmer over medium heat. When the water is simmering, lower the heat to medium-low so the liquid simmers gently. Braise, lifting the lid and turning the potatoes with a spoon once halfway through, until the potatoes are just tender when pierced with a thin skewer, about 20 minutes.

Remove the lid, increase the heat to high, and boil, gently shaking the pan back and forth, until the water evaporates and you can hear the oil sizzle, about 5 minutes. The braised garlic cloves will break down and coat the potatoes as you shake the pan. Serve hot.

VARIATION: Once you've braised small potatoes a few times, you'll see that the recipe is ripe for improvisation. Feel free to vary the herbs, substitute dry white wine for the chicken stock or water, or use butter in place of olive oil. One variation is to use 2 leafy sprigs of rosemary in place of the bay leaves and butter in place of the olive oil. Use chicken stock as the braising liquid and braise as directed.

MASHED POTATOES WITH
KALE AND OLIVE OIL

STEVE PETUSEVSKY

This is wonderful as a side dish or it can be stuffed into eggplant slices, peppers, or zucchini shells. Be sure to wash the kale leaves well as they can be gritty. You can substitute Swiss chard or spinach, if you prefer. If you are using either, 3 cups will substitute for 1 bunch trimmed kale. Be sure to trim the ends of the stems.

SERVES 4

> 3 pounds all-purpose potatoes, peeled and cut
> into large chunks
> Water
> Sea salt
> 4 tablespoons extra virgin olive oil
> 4 cloves garlic, minced
> 1 bunch kale, large stems stripped and discarded,
> leaves chopped
> 1/2 cup warm milk or light cream
> Freshly ground black pepper
> 5 scallions, white and tender green parts,
> chopped
> 1/4 cup freshly grated Parmesan cheese, for
> garnish (optional)

Put the potatoes in a large pot and cover with water. Add a pinch of salt. Bring the water to a boil and continue boiling for 20 minutes, or until the potatoes are tender. Drain and place in a large bowl.

Heat 2 tablespoons oil in a large sauté pan or skillet over medium heat. Add the garlic and chopped kale and sauté for 4 minutes, until softened. Add the sautéed kale to the bowl with the potatoes.

Mash the potatoes and kale together with a potato masher or fork. Slowly add the warm milk and combine.

Season with salt and pepper; mix just until creamy with a few chunks.

Place the potatoes in a serving bowl. Make a well in the center and pour the remaining 2 tablespoons of olive oil over the top. Sprinkle with scallions and Parmesan cheese. Serve immediately.

PARMESAN AND ROMANO
STUFFED ARTICHOKES

STEVE PETUSEVSKY

This simple recipe is a great way to introduce novices to the splendors of artichokes.

SERVES 2

> 2 trimmed and cooked artichokes (see page 60)
> 1/2 cup unseasoned dried bread crumbs
> 1/4 cup freshly grated Parmesan cheese
> 1 tablespoon freshly grated Romano cheese
> 1 teaspoon dried oregano
> 1 clove garlic, minced
> 1 tablespoon melted butter
> 1 tablespoon extra virgin olive oil
> 5 basil leaves, minced
> Freshly ground black pepper

Preheat the oven to 350°F. Place the artichokes upright in a nonreactive baking pan just large enough to hold them. Gently open up the leaves a bit, loosening them far enough to stuff.

Combine the bread crumbs, Parmesan cheese, Romano cheese, oregano, garlic, butter, olive oil, basil, and pepper to taste in a small bowl. With a spoon, place this stuffing between the layers of artichoke leaves. Use half the stuffing for each artichoke.

Bake, uncovered, for 20 minutes until golden brown and warm inside. Serve hot.

SPRINGTIME SOUP

ROBIN KLINE, MS, RD

This clever soup uses the asparagus spears for full flavor and saves the pretty tips for a salad or garnish. The lemon, spinach, and asparagus announce "Spring is here!" Serve this beautiful jade soup for dinner with crusty French bread.

SERVES 2

1 1/2 pounds asparagus, trimmed and peeled

1 tablespoon butter

1 medium onion, chopped

1/4 cup long-grain rice

1 teaspoon fresh thyme leaves

1/4 teaspoon freshly ground black pepper

3 cups chicken broth

1/4 cup freshly squeezed lemon juice

4 ounces baby spinach leaves, trimmed and torn

1/2 cup freshly grated pecorino Romano cheese

Break off asparagus tips and reserve for another use; chop the rest of spears into 1-inch pieces.

In a large saucepan over low heat, melt the butter. Add the onion and asparagus and sauté over medium heat until the onion is translucent and the vegetables soft, about 5 minutes. Stir in rice, thyme, and pepper. Add the broth and bring to a boil; cover and lower the heat to a simmer. Simmer until the rice is tender, about 12 minutes. Remove from heat and puree soup using an immersion blender or remove to a food processor.

Reheat the soup and stir in the lemon juice and spinach. Stir in the cheese, cover, and let rest for 2 to 3 minutes. Taste and adjust for salt. Serve hot.

FARMER CHRIS'S BRANDYWINES AND ARUGULA WITH MELON AND FETA SAUCE

ANA SORTUN

These three mouthwatering recipes are from Ana Sortun, the award-winning chef of Oleana Restaurant in Cambridge. Crossword puzzle fans will immediately spot the connection between "Oleana" and "Ana," the former lovely word being her full Norwegian name.

We pinch ourselves at the good luck of having Ana and Oleana in our neighborhood because she has brought creative, distinctive, and richly flavored recipes with a strong influence of Istanbul to her restaurant, some of them sprinkled throughout this book.

The salty taste of feta is a perfect match for the tomatoes and watermelon, especially mixed with the herbs and olive oil. If you can't find brandywine tomatoes, substitute any other large tomato.

SERVES 4

4 (1/4 inch thick) slices seedless watermelon

4 brandywine tomatoes, sliced 1/4 inch thick

6 ounces feta cheese

5 tablespoons extra virgin olive oil, plus more for drizzling

1/4 cup hot water

Sea salt and freshly ground black pepper

1 bunch arugula, trimmed, tough stems discarded

4 sprigs oregano

Using a round cookie cutter or the top of a glass, cut rounds from the watermelon slices. They should resemble the tomato slices but may be a little smaller. Lay out the melon and tomatoes on paper towels and season with salt.

Combine the feta, olive oil, and hot water in a blender and puree until smooth. Season with salt and a little freshly ground pepper (it may not need much salt depending on the saltiness of the feta).

On a large serving platter, arrange the tomatoes, melon rounds, and arugula overlapping slightly, and drizzle with the feta sauce. Roughly chop the oregano leaves and sprinkle over the top. Drizzle with a little more olive oil if desired and serve.

BEET TZATZIKI

ANA SORTUN

Ana's replacement of beets for cucumbers is an interesting take on the Greek tzatziki, traditionally used as a sauce or dip.

MAKES 2 CUPS

> 2 cloves garlic, chopped
> 1 tablespoon freshly squeezed lemon juice
> Sea salt
> 1 cup Greek or whole-milk yogurt, including cream on top
> 1 tablespoon extra virgin olive oil
> Freshly ground black pepper
> 1 cup shredded boiled Chioggia beets (about four the size of a golf ball)
> 1 tablespoon fresh dill

Combine the garlic in a mixing bowl with the lemon juice and salt to taste. Let stand for about 10 minutes.

Stir in the yogurt and its cream, olive oil, and pepper. Fold in the beets and dill and adjust the salt and pepper. Refrigerate until chilled and serve.

SMOKY EGGPLANT WITH PINE NUTS

ANA SORTUN

Be sure to use Greek yogurt or whole-milk yogurt with cream at the top, to make certain it's as creamy as possible.

SERVES 4

> Juice of $1/2$ lemon
> 2 fresh firm medium-sized eggplants, peeled and cut into chunks
> 2 tablespoons extra virgin olive oil
> 1 cup pine nuts
> $1/2$ cup Greek yogurt or whole-milk yogurt (with the cream on top)
> 1 teaspoon smoked salt (available by mail order from Aspen Cooking School)
> 1 clove garlic, chopped
> Sea salt and freshly ground black pepper to taste

Bring a large saucepan of water to a boil with the juice of half a lemon. Add the eggplant. There should be enough water to cover the eggplant. Simmer for about 15 minutes, or until eggplant is soft when squeezed with a pair of tongs.

Meanwhile, in a small skillet, heat 1 tablespoon of the olive oil over low heat. Add the pine nuts and carefully toast for about 6 minutes, until golden brown. Set aside.

Drain the eggplant well. While it's still hot, puree in a food processor until smooth. Add the yogurt, salt, garlic, and remaining 1 tablespoon olive oil and blend until white and creamy. Stir in pine nuts and add salt and pepper to taste.

Lidia and the Chefettes

In 1995, Oldways organized its first symposium in Puglia, the agricultural region that is the heel of Italy's boot. More olive oil is produced and more grapes are grown in Puglia than in any other region of Italy. With us for this weeklong symposium was a mix of more than one hundred journalists, cookbook authors, retailers, chefs, and scientists from around the world (United States, UK, Canada, Australia, Italy, Germany, and Japan).

As the week progressed—through sumptuous meals and tastings, market visits, cultural tours, and formal sessions—some of the chefs became "itchy" to get into a kitchen. Itchiest of all was Lidia Bastianich, chef and owner of Felidia in New York City, author of several cookbooks, and host of her own PBS cooking show.

Sitting on the bus, she plotted and planned with some other chefs, food writers, and cookbook authors for a dinner she would orchestrate in the kitchen of our home base in Lecce, the Hotel President.

Lidia had an all-star kitchen crew, which was quickly named Lidia and the Chefettes with Male Auxiliary. The Chefettes included Bonnie Lee Black, Catherine Brandel, Julia della Croce, Gillian Duffy, Sue Huffman, Dana Jacobi, Peggy Knickerbocker, Anne Lindsay, and Anna Nurse, with the advice and consent of the Chefettes' Male Auxiliary (Victor Broceaux and Waldy Malouf). Everyone pitched in and chopped, rolled, skimmed, boned, and everything else as Lidia directed. The end result was a magic meal of incredible spring vegetables and beans from the deep south of Italy.

Luckily, food writer Dana Jacobi spent less time in the kitchen shucking beans and chopping than she did compiling and recording the recipes created by Lidia and the Chefettes. After the symposium, by request, we sent these recipes to all the attendees. Now, more than a decade later, we're pleased to share one of them in this chapter, and a few others in the chapter devoted to beans (see page 92 through 94).

SHRIMP AND SWISS CHARD SOUP WITH ARBORIO RICE (*MINESTRA DI GAMBERETTI E BIETOLA*)

LIDIA AND THE CHEFETTES

Lidia Bastianich improvised this light yet hearty soup for us when she found the shrimp and Swiss chard remaining from another dish.

SERVES 6

- 3 tablespoons extra virgin olive oil
- 4 large Idaho or russet potatoes, peeled and diced into 1/4-inch cubes
- 1 large carrot, coarsely grated
- 2 teaspoons tomato paste
- 3 cups hot water
- 1 pound Swiss chard, stems removed, washed and cut into 1/2-inch strips
- 1 cup arborio rice
- Sea salt and freshly ground black pepper
- 1 pound medium shrimp, peeled, deveined, and cut in half lengthwise

Heat the oil in a Dutch oven or large casserole over medium-high heat. Add the potatoes and cook, turning frequently to prevent burning, for 5 to 7 minutes, until the potatoes are golden and there is a layer of potato starch caramelized on the bottom of the pot.

Stir in the carrot and cook until it has melted down and just started to color, about 8 minutes. Stir in the tomato paste and cook for 3 minutes more. Mix in the hot water. Bring the soup to a vigorous boil. Reduce the heat and simmer for 30 minutes. Add the chard to the soup and cook for 10 minutes. Add the rice and cook for 15 minutes, or until tender but not soft. Remove the soup from the heat. Season the soup to taste with salt and pepper. Stir in the shrimp and let them cook frm the residual heat until they are firm. Serve immediately.

MIXED CITRUS SALAD

K. DUN GIFFORD

Clementines, pink grapefruit, and other citrus can be substituted for any of the three basic fruits, or added to them. For serving the salad, choose either a salad bowl or a soup bowl. Large scallop shells are available in gourmet stores, and they, too, make for a good service. Another attractive option is ceramic bowls shaped as citrus, a half grapefruit, for example. A fresh flower on the side of the bowl adds a festive touch. If the fruit is covered and chilled in the refrigerator until just before serving it maintains its fresh appearance and textures. ✍

SERVES 8

> 3 oranges, peeled, seeded, and divided into segments
> 3 grapefruit, peeled, seeded, and divided into segments
> 3 tangerines, peeled, seeded, and divided into segments
> Dressing (recipes follow)

Place the sections in a small, shallow bowl, and move them around so they look arranged and not just dumped into the bowl.

Serve with any of the dressings in the following section poured over as indicated.

VARIATIONS: Add other fruits, among them sliced bananas, cubed cantaloupe, sliced strawberries, seedless grapes cut in half, sliced peaches, sliced plums (red or black), pitted cherries (red or yellow), chunks of pineapple, and diced apple if a crunch is desired. Other classic options include mint leaves, watercress, dill, slivered nuts, cubed dates, and shaved coconut.

Thoughts for Dressings

Dressings for citrus salads should contain fats for their mouth feel, flavor, texture, contrast, and familiarity. They set out nice contrasts with the crisp flavors of the citrus. A Mediterranean approach, for example, uses olive oil as its fat, for either sweet or salty dressings. The basic recipe combines 1/2 cup olive oil with 1/4 cup lemon juice, with variations from there, seemingly without gustatory limit.

Here are some of these variations added to the olive oil/lemon base. The oil choice need not be limited to olive oil; walnut oil, for example, adds a terrific nutty flavor to the citrus, and other oils do, too, such as avocado and macadamia nut oil. The trick is to figure out whether the citrus is sweet or tart, and then to use oil that contrasts with it.

1. Add 1/4 cup freshly squeezed orange juice, 2 teaspoons sugar, and 1/2 teaspoon sea salt.
2. Add 3 tablespoons sherry, brandy, or ouzo; 1/2 teaspoon sea salt, and 1/4 teaspoon cracked pepper.
3. Add two pinches of dry powdered mustard. It adds a nice bite, which contrasts well with the sweetness.
4. Add 1 tablespoon of finely grated zest from an orange or lemon.
5. Add 2 tablespoons of either a sweet liqueur (orange or cherry, for example) or something a bit more adventurous (ouzo, rum, limoncello).

The Four Seasons

Jesse Cool, author of *Your Organic Kitchen* and chef and owner of three restaurants in Palo Alto and Menlo Park, is often called an "Organic Queen." But we think this is too narrow a label—the more accurate one is "Queen of Local and Seasonal." Jesse's been buying and writing about local produce, and caring for and respecting the seasons and the land, as long as anyone else in California. The food at her restaurants—Flea Street Café, JZ Cool, and the Cool Café at Stanford's Cantor Art Gallery—is a testament to this passion and care. We asked Jesse to design a menu for each season, respecting the best of the best of each of them, and using harvests of the farms around Palo Alto and Menlo Park, California. A recipe for one dish from each season follows "The Four Seasons."

SPRING

Scallops Dusted in Cornmeal with Blood Orange
Vinaigrette and Asparagus

Marinated Grilled Lamb Chops with Rosemary
Blossoms, New Potatoes, Fava Beans, and
Spring Garlic

Old-Fashioned Vanilla Bean Custard with
First-of-the-Season Organic Strawberries
and Mexican Chocolate

SUMMER

Chilled Avocado Soup with Chile Rock Shrimp,
Cherry Tomatoes, and Cilantro

Salmon with Herbes de Provence, Sweet Corn and
Pepper Relish, and Saffron Rice with Pine Nuts
and Basil

Summer Fruit Compote with Chocolate Ice Cream
and Ginger Cookies

FALL

Tomato and Goat Cheese Stacks with Purple Basil
Pesto, Olives, and Edible Flowers

Chicken with Caramelized Onions, Glazed Figs,
and Pomegranate

Mashed Winter Squash with Marscapone

Apple Pie with Asiago Pepper Crust

WINTER

Salad of Bitter Greens and Chicory with Deviled
Eggs

Braised Short Ribs in Port and Spices, Winter
Root Vegetables, and Horseradish Cream

Mashed Smoky Cauliflower

Chocolate Tart with Cinnamon Poached Pears
and Crème Anglaise

NEW POTATOES, FAVA BEANS, AND SPRING GARLIC

JESSE COOL

This recipe is the epitome of springtime. Fava beans, freshly dug new potatoes, and not-yet-mature, fragrant-yet-mild garlic are first signs that winter is at its end. Garlic grows just like onions, with tender green leaves and a delicate, unformed slender bulb before the cloves begin to form. In her cooking, Jesse harvests some garlic plants early, using both greens and the bulb, just as she would a green onion. Serve with pasta, grilled meats, or roasted chicken. 🐚

SERVES 4 AS A GENEROUS SIDE DISH

2 cups or about ¾ pound new potatoes

About 2½ pounds fresh fava beans

¼ to ½ cup extra virgin olive oil

2 tablespoons chopped fresh rosemary

2 green garlic plants, whites and greens sliced into ¼-inch pieces

Sea salt and freshly ground black pepper

I cup chicken stock or water

Pinch of ground red pepper (optional)

Scrub the potatoes, cut into 1-inch pieces and set aside.

Cut open and remove the fava beans from the pod. You should end up with about 2 cups. Set aside.

In a medium pot of salted boiling water, cook the potatoes for 5 minutes, or until tender. Using a slotted spoon, transfer the potatoes to a medium bowl. Add the fava beans to the same pot of boiling water and cook for about 5 minutes, until tender. Transfer to a bowl and run under cold water to cool. Using a sharp knife, slice through the fava bean skins and remove the skin by popping out the tender bean. Set aside.

In a medium skillet over medium-low heat, warm the olive oil. Add the potatoes, fava beans, rosemary, and green garlic. Season with salt and pepper. Cook, stirring occasionally, for about 10 minutes, adding a little stock or water to moisten, if necessary. Remove from the heat and adjust the seasoning, adding cayenne if you choose. Serve warm or chilled.

CORN AND PEPPER RELISH

JESSE COOL

This versatile corn relish is great as a salsa with chips or spooned generously over grilled seafood or barbecued pork chops. 🐚

MAKES ABOUT 2 CUPS

Kernels from 2 ears sweet corn

¼ red bell pepper, finely chopped

2 tablespoons finely chopped red onion

2 tablespoons finely chopped fresh cilantro

I tablespoon seasoned rice wine vinegar

I teaspoon ground cumin

½ teaspoon chili powder

Sea salt

Bring a small pot of lightly salted water to a boil. Add the corn and cook for about 30 seconds. Drain and put in a medium bowl to cool. Add the red pepper, onion, cilantro, vinegar, cumin, and chili powder. Season with salt. Serve warm or chilled.

CHICKEN WITH CARAMELIZED ONIONS, GLAZED FIGS, AND POMEGRANATE

JESSE COOL

This wonderful autumn recipe can be served cold or room temperature and is also great the next day, served on top of a simple salad of tender lettuces and greens.

SERVES 4

- 4 medium-sized chicken breasts (free-range, organic if possible)
- Sea salt and freshly ground black pepper
- 2 tablespoons chopped fresh rosemary
- ¼ cup extra virgin olive oil
- 1 medium onion, thinly sliced
- 8 fresh figs, cut into quarters or halves depending upon size
- 2 tablespoons light or dark brown sugar
- 3 tablespoons balsamic vinegar
- ½ cup chicken stock or water
- ¼ teaspoon crushed red pepper flakes
- ½ cup pomegranate seeds

Rinse the chicken breasts under cold water and pat dry. Generously season with salt, pepper, and the rosemary.

In a large skillet over medium-high heat, warm 2 tablespoons of the olive oil. Put the chicken breasts into the pan and cook for about 5 minutes on each side to brown. Remove and set aside.

Decrease the heat to medium-low and add the remaining 2 tablespoons olive oil and onions to the skillet. Cover and cook for about 5 minutes, until the onions are very soft, stirring occasionally.

Add the figs, brown sugar, vinegar, and chicken stock. Stir, cover, and cook for 3 minutes. Add the red pepper flakes and put the chicken breasts on top. Sprinkle the pomegranate kernels over all. Cover and simmer for about 15 minutes, or until the chicken is cooked through and a meat thermometer registers 165°F when inserted into the meat.

Spoon the chicken and sauce onto plates and serve.

SALAD OF BITTER GREENS AND CHICORY WITH DEVILED EGGS

JESSE COOL

In the winter, hearty greens, like escaroles or chicories, when picked small, are lovely and tender in a salad. A bold dressing stands up well and a touch of sweetness makes the bitterness even more appealing. This recipe makes extra dressing, which keeps well in the refrigerator for weeks.

SERVES 4

- 1 cup extra virgin olive oil
- ¼ cup red wine vinegar
- 2 tablespoons balsamic vinegar
- 2 tablespoons sugar
- 1 to 2 cloves garlic, minced
- 2 tablespoons chopped fresh oregano
- 1½ teaspoons Dijon mustard
- 5 hard-cooked eggs
- 3 tablespoons mayonnaise, plus more as needed
- 1 tablespoon sweet pickle relish
- 1 tablespoon grated red onion
- Sea salt and freshly ground black pepper
- 1 pound bitter salad greens, cut into bite-size pieces
- ½ cup freshly grated Asiago or Parmesan cheese

In a small bowl, combine the olive oil, red wine and balsamic vinegars, sugar, garlic, oregano, and 1 teaspoon of the mustard. Set aside at room temperature.

Peel and cut the eggs in half lengthwise. Using a teaspoon, remove the yolks and put into a small bowl. Put the hollowed-out egg whites onto a plate. You will only be filling eight halves. Chop up the whites of one of the eggs and add to the yolks. Mash the yolks with a fork and add the remaining $1/2$ teaspoon of mustard, the mayonnaise, relish, and red onion. Season with salt and pepper. Add a little more mayonnaise to taste.

Using a spoon, mound the yolk filling into the cavity of the eight halves of egg whites.

Put the greens in a medium bowl. Add enough dressing to moisten the greens to your liking. Season with salt and pepper. Mound one fourth of the greens onto four plates or mound it all on one large platter. Sprinkle with the grated cheese. Put the deviled eggs on the plates or platter with the salad. Serve immediately.

"Vegetarian diets are winning converts rapidly in North America for reasons to do with health, animal welfare, the environment, family influence, religion, and ethics. Nearly 14 million Americans declare themselves vegetarians, and about a million additional people a year become vegetarians."

—K. DUN GIFFORD

SQUASH AND APPLE PUREE

MARIAN MORASH

As delicious as it is plain, winter squash also beautifully accepts herbs and essences. "Scenting" the squash adds a fragrant flavor: here Marian Morash uses apples, then adds orange and ginger, a lovely combination.

SERVES 4

3 pounds winter squash (Waltham butternut, buttercup, or other), peeled, seeded, and cut into 1- to 2-inch cubes
2 apples, peeled and quartered
Sea salt and freshly ground black pepper
1 to 2 tablespoons finely grated orange zest (optional)
Pinch of ground ginger or cinnamon (optional)
2 tablespoons butter (optional)

Bring 1 inch of water to a boil in a medium saucepan. Put the squash and apples in a steamer basket, cover, and steam until the squash is soft, 15 to 20 minutes. Transfer to a bowl and mash together to the consistency you prefer. Season with salt and pepper, and add the grated orange zest and ginger, if you like. Keep warm if serving shortly, or cool, cover, and refrigerate and reheat just before serving.

To reheat, preheat the oven to 350°F. Butter a $1^1/2$-quart baking dish. Spread the puree in the dish, dot the top with additional butter, if desired, and bake for 30 minutes.

Note: If you don't have a steamer, you can put the squash and apples right into the boiling water. Just keep an eye on it and add more water, if necessary. Drain well before pureeing.

Greek Schoolhouse Supper

In early January of 1997, we traveled to Iráklion, Crete, to finalize plans for an Oldways symposium there in April. As always in Greece, we traveled and worked with Aglaia Kremezi, an award-winning cookbook author, journalist, and an expert in Greek foods and wines. We reviewed all the details of the symposium: hotel, meals, cooking demonstrations, cultural tours, and more. It may be called work, but it is also pure pleasure, because we got to know the place, its people, and of course, its foods, wines, and cooking techniques.

While we were there, Aglaia introduced us to Mirsini Lampraki, a young food writer from Iráklion, the capital city of Crete. Mirsini invited us to her home for a traditional Cretan dinner, which lasted well into the night because we were mesmerized both by the splendid dinner and by the stories Mirsini and her husband Jorgo related. Jorgo was deeply involved in local politics, and he invited us to a celebration in his home village of Asites to commemorate the restoration and reopening of the local schoolhouse.

Late the next afternoon we drove inland from Iráklion toward Jorgo's village and wound our way up the mountain to find ourselves in a tiny town perched at its very top. We stopped in front of the beautiful old Asites schoolhouse, with white-washed walls turned a soft yellow-pink by the lowering sun. Inside we found simple furniture and traditional iconic images decorating the wall. We felt transported back in time.

We and the entire population of the town settled down at long tables, ready to enjoy the meal. It was like a Greek version of a Maine baked bean supper or a townwide 4th of July picnic in the Midwest. Each woman in the village brought food from her home, and these different dishes—greens of all sorts—were passed down the long tables.

But the evening didn't end with the meal. First, a chorus of children sang and danced a series of circle dances. And then, the real dancing began. It started with the men, who also danced circle dances. Then the women joined, rhythmically circling the men, and finally throwing plates to the ground as the music grew louder and the wine flowed longer. We were entranced, and danced, too.

We described our symposium to Mirsini and Jorgo, and our intense efforts to include elements of the "true local cultures." Seeing how much our evening in the schoolhouse had enchanted us, they arranged for it to be re-created in April for the symposium. As so it was. And, it was just as amazing as the original celebration. We even held a symposium session in the old schoolhouse, using an old white sheet instead of a screen to show slides and overhead projections.

The children of the village gave a special performance for us; the local beekeeper showed us his hives and gave us jars of sweet, dark, intensely flavored honey; the women invited us into their kitchens and showed us how they make bread and *horta* pies, and we danced in the schoolhouse and in the streets of the village, feeling like we were transported to a simpler, easier life.

Mirsini has graciously provided recipes for the dishes served by the women of Asites. *Efkaristo!*

CHICKEN WITH PURSLANE

MIRSINI LAMPRAKI

Chicken and green vegetables are not unfamiliar to American dinner tables—just think of chicken divan, or even a chicken Caesar salad. For something new, try this easy and healthy way to enjoy chicken. If you like, substitute spinach for purslane. ✏️

SERVES 6

I cup extra virgin olive oil

Shredded boneless meat from I medium-sized cooked chicken

I large onion, finely chopped

1/2 cup red wine

2 cups water, plus more as needed

2 medium-sized potatoes, peeled and quartered

IO to I2 baby zucchini, or any summer squash

2 pounds washed purslane or spinach

2 to 3 fresh tomatoes, finely chopped

Sea salt and freshly ground black pepper

In a large Dutch oven or casserole, heat the olive oil over high heat. Add the chicken and onion and sauté until slightly golden on all sides. Add the wine and water, cover, and simmer for 35 minutes. Add the potatoes and a little water (if the water has evaporated) and continue cooking, covered, for 15 more minutes. Add the zucchini, purslane, tomatoes, salt, and pepper and gently shake the pan to mix the vegetables with the chicken. Cover and simmer for 25 to 30 minutes until the sauce is thick. Serve warm or cold.

CHICORY CASSEROLE

MIRSINI LAMPRAKI

Rather than a pie, these greens are nestled in a casserole—a perfect dish for a midweek dinner for a busy family. ✏️

SERVES 6

1/2 cup extra virgin olive oil

3 large onions, finely chopped

2 pounds chicory or other greens of your choice

3 tomatoes, finely sliced

1/4 cup white wine vinegar

Pinch of sugar

Sea salt

2 cups water

Freshly ground black pepper

Heat the oil in a large skillet over medium heat. Add the onions and sauté for about 2 minutes, until slightly golden. Add the chicory, tomato, vinegar, sugar, salt, and water. Sauté, uncovered, for 5 to 15 minutes, until tender. Serve this dish warm, seasoned with ample freshly ground pepper.

"In the Italian south, beans are practically inseparable from pasta, and this tradition crossed the Atlantic with the Italian immigrants from those regions. Who in America hasn't dipped into a bowl of 'pasta fazool' (pasta e fagioli), as it came to be known in Brooklyn? The combination is as delicious as Sophia Loren and Marcello Mastroianni in an old Italian film."

—JULIA DELLA CROCE

"I use canned beans unless I have time to soak and simmer dried beans. Because I enjoy variety, I often use two kinds in the same dish."

—STEVE PETUSEVSKY

BEANS AND LEGUMES

T he definitional boundaries among beans, legumes, seeds, and pulses have traditionally been blurred, causing considerable confusion in writings and discussions about them. The United Nations charged into this breach in 1994, with its Food and Agricultural Organization (FAO) spelling out what words we should use to speak and write about our beans,

An Evolving Nomenclature

K. DUN GIFFORD

legumes, seeds, and pulses. It declared that henceforth all of these be termed *pulses*.

The FAO defines pulses as annual leguminous crops yielding from one to twelve grains or seeds of variable size, shape, and color within a pod. This applies only to crops harvested solely for the dry grain or seed, leaving out green beans and green peas, which are deemed vegetables.

As an example, fava beans are placed in the broad beans group (*Vicia fabaceae*) along with their brothers and sisters: broad beans, faba beans, horse beans, and field beans. This has upset some critics of this classification for whom fava beans are deemed the gold standard of beans, but the FAO scientific panels are listening to botanists and not gastronomes.

The term *pulses* excludes leguminous oilseeds, such as soybeans, which are used primarily for their high content of oil, extracted by industrial processes.

Because it is in the nature of things that the United Nation's nomenclature will gradually become the lingua franca, here is the list. The FAO classifies ten major pulse groups, and numerous minor pulses as follows:

MAJOR PULSES

Dry beans (*Phaseolus* spp.)
    Kidney bean, haricot bean, pinto bean, navy bean
      (*P. vulgaris*)
    Lima bean, butter bean (*Vigna lunatis*)
    Azuki bean, Adzuki bean (*V. angularis*)
    Mung bean, golden gram, green gram (*V. radiata*)
    Black gram, urd bean (*V. mungo*)
    Scarlet runner bean (*P. coccineus*)
    Rice bean (*V. umbellata*)
    Moth bean (*V. acontifolia*)
    Tepary bean (*P. acutifolius*)

Dry broad beans (*Vicia faba*)
    Horse bean (var. *equina*)
    Broad bean (var. *major*)
    Field bean (var. *minor*)

Dry peas (*Pisum sativum*)
    Garden peas (*P. sativum* var. *sativum*)
    Field pea (*P. sativum* var. *arvense*)

Chickpeas, garbanzo, Bengal gram (*Cicer arietinum*)
Dry cowpea, blackeyed pea, blackeye bean (*Vigna*
    unguiculata ssp. *Dekindtiana*)

Pigeon pea, Cajun pea, Congo bean (*Cajanus cajan*)
Lentils (*Lens culinaris*)
Bambara groundnut, Earth pea (*Vigna subterranea*)
Vetch, common vetch (*Vicia sativa*)
Lupins (*Lupinus* spp.)

MINOR PULSES

Lablab, hyacinth bean (*Lablab purpureus* spp.)
Jack bean (*Canavalia ensiformis*), sword bean
    (*Canavalia gladiata*)
Winged bean (*Psophocarpus tetragonolobus*)
Guar bean (*Cyamopsis tetragonoloba*)
Velvet bean, cowitch (*Mucuna pruriens* var. *utilis*)

Beans and Legumes: Protein Food

JULIA DELLA CROCE

Julia della Croce is a prolific cookbook author, and most of her books are about Italian cooking. Beans, pasta, and vegetables are essential ingredients for her, and her knowledge and experience with them are matched by her passion for teaching others about their great tastes and versatility.

Legumes are vegetables with the power of meat, and our ancestors couldn't have done without them. Not so long ago there were two kinds of food in the world, the food of the rich and the food of the poor. Variants of the common bean have been the mainstay of most poor people's diets since the plant was spread throughout our continent by migrating bands of Native Americans some seven thousand years ago. Traders carried them across the seas to Africa and Asia, and conquistadors brought them to Europe. Today, cultivated legumes are second only to grains in supplying protein and calories to the world's populations.

Although beans are one of the basic dishes of the world, they are up against the general ingrained snobbishness of many people. Consider the old saying that something without value is "not worth a hill of beans." My mother, for example, who grew up with a taste for meat and fine things, has used beans as a form of punishment. "I'm giving your father beans for dinner" meant that they were having a spat about something. Ironically, I always looked forward to these bean suppers because I loved beans, and my mother was such a good cook that even her bean retributions were delicious. I might add that my father has lived to the age of ninety-seven, probably with no small thanks to the large quantity of beans he was fed.

There is a growing appreciation for beans both from a culinary and a medical standpoint. In the wake of medical research about the folly of the meat-loaded Western diet, we opened our minds to all sorts of new bean ideas. Lentil soup, once the province of immigrants and Greek diners, actually became trendy two decades ago (I remember looking over a menu in a fashionable Madison Avenue restaurant with a friend and listening to him complain about how he'd had to eat lentil soup every day growing up a poor Italian immigrant and wasn't about to pay ten dollars a bowl for it now).

Thinking about what different cultures do with beans and lentils makes you realize that anyone who says they are inherently dull is giving them a bad rap:

- The French have always done wonderful things with beans and lentils—I am thinking in particular of cassoulet, a garlicky casserole of haricot beans and fresh pork rinds, preserved goose, sausages, and herbs.

- The Tuscans, who eat so many beans they were dubbed *mangiafagioli* ("bean eaters") long ago, showed us, among other things, how to cook cannellini beans to silky heights in a bottle with sage.

- On both sides of the Mediterranean border between France and Italy, people make a delicious hot flatbread called panissa, with chickpea flour, rosemary, and the local aromatic olive oil.

- The Latinos have blessed us with their cilantro-scented rice and beans, a dish of such importance that it is often preferred over meat.

- The Middle East makes a virtual art of bean and lentil cookery with the perfumes of cinnamon and angelica, the tints of turmeric and saffron, the flavorings of pomegranate and sour lime.

- The Caribbean islands marry kidney beans, root vegetables, pork chops, and ham all in one rib-sticking breakfast pot.

Now we eat edamame (fresh soybeans) as easily as Boston baked, and hummus instead of hamburgers. And when the "new" immigrations are stitched into the patchwork, Indian, Asian, and Latin bean dishes will continue to expand our bean horizons more and more.

I remember one bean dish that was a revelation, even for a group of two hundred international food journalists, chefs, and food experts on an Oldways trip to Puglia, in 1995. There we were in real bean-eating country (and, food for thought, my father's birthplace). A jaunt to Lecce's food market early one morning with restaurateur Lidia Bastianich turned up glorious fava beans at the height of their season. An hour later she was back in our hotel convincing the manager to relieve his kitchen staff for the night and let her take over with the Oldways gang—we would cook our own dinner using the beans, vegetables, and our other finds at the market. "What? You're asking to let a woman take over my kitchen?" was the last thing I heard from him. Later that afternoon, Lidia was giving orders in the kitchen while the rest of us shelled fava beans, chopped vegetables, and rolled pasta. You'll find the recipe for her braised fava beans and spring vegetables (*scaffata*) and her chicory and white bean salad in this chapter (page 93), and another recipe from this Lecce dinner made by Lidia and the Chefettes is included in the chapter on fruits and vegetables (see page 72). We're still talking about it.

Beautiful Beans

JULIA DELLA CROCE

Here's an overview of the diverse culinary uses for beans from a writer and cook who is well acquainted with preparing them. ▨

There are some 13,000 bean species. They grow on a bush (bush beans), or on a vine (pole beans or running types). For culinary purposes, there are two main categories, those with edible pods (like green beans or wax beans) and those in which only the seeds can be eaten (such as lima or fava beans).

Edible pod beans are eaten fresh, or thawed if frozen. Seed beans are eaten fresh or dried, depending on the variety. Fava beans are best when fresh, but when dried are wonderful as purées and in soups. Edamame beans are soybeans harvested just as they ripen but before they begin to harden.

Though beans are only beginning to make a serious debut on the culinary scene here, the United States leads the world in dry bean production. Government figures reveal that American farmers plant between 1.5 to 1.7 million acres of edible dry beans every year. About 60 percent are sold here, and the rest exported to overseas markets.

HOW PEOPLE EAT BEANS

Beans figure differently into traditional cuisines around the world. In Central America, beans are the be-all for protein, the macho mate in the rice-and-bean team, otherwise called *matrimonio,* so well matched is this duo. In India dal is the ubiquitous condiment that sauces so many dishes. In the carnivorous West, beans bolster the beef (think chile con carne) or cuddle side by side with ham or pork (think pork and beans), or play backseat to something else. For the vegetarian, beans are the lifesaver, with bean burgers, bean bacon, tofu, and tempeh masquerading as meat.

Beans can be boiled with a bay leaf and transported with no more elaboration than the dazzle of a drizzle of good olive oil. They can be made into tasty purees, like 'ncapriata, a regional dish of Puglia—creamy fava beans eaten side by side with a mess of tart and tasty cooked greens. They can be baked into a casserole with meat or not, bubbling away under a crust of bread crumbs or cheese. They can be stewed, fried, sautéed, or whipped up into quick soup.

Plant Protein Partners

K. DUN GIFFORD

Nutrition science research consistently warned over the last 40 years that an overconsumption of animal foods was unhealthy. These warnings triggered a gradual decline in the per capita consumption of meat in the United States, particularly red meat, and an increase in the number of people who describe themselves as vegetarians or part-time vegetarians.

Individuals and families considering cutting back on meat often worry that they will short-change their health if they don't eat enough animal protein. The fear is based on the fact that meats provide a complete supply of the amino acids, which human bodies transform into the proteins needed to sustain life. Plant foods do not provide complete proteins unless they are combined in specific ways.

Proteins do matter. They make up about half the dry weight of a human body, with fats making up the dry weight balance. As to the wet weight, water is about 60 percent, with protein and fat each at 20 percent.

The scientific reason behind the need for a steady supply of new proteins is well understood. Our bodies' proteins wear out as they fulfill their destinies, and so we must steadily build replacements. We can only do this with a continuing supply of the proper kinds of amino acid building blocks.

Because beef, chicken, and fish are animal foods,

they supply the necessary amino acids; they are "complete proteins." Plant foods (grains, fruits, and beans, for example) are "incomplete proteins," because they do not supply all the necessary amino acids.

The health of vegetarians flourishes on animal-free diets when they combine plant proteins from two different foods. Vegetarian eating pioneer Frances Moore Lappé called this pairing of the proteins in plants "protein complementarity," because the combinations of amino acids in a balance of plant foods can complement each other to produce the complete and balanced arsenal of amino acid building blocks.

Finding suitable plant protein food partner combinations is remarkably simple and inexpensive; a dish of rice and beans, for example, has perfect protein complementarity. So do Boston baked beans and brown bread. Or a peanut butter and jelly sandwich on whole-grain bread. The partnership works even by eating any one grain and any one legume some time during the day, not even at the same meal.

Soybeans are an exception to this rule because they contain the full range of amino acids that humans need to fabricate new proteins; they are a "complete protein" vegetable food.

Bean Basics

In case you're not a seasoned bean user, here are the basics of bean cuisine: cleaning, soaking, and cooking.

CLEANING DRIED BEANS

Cover the beans with cold water and pick them over to remove any foreign particles or dried skins that float to the surface. Drain in a colander and rinse under cold running water.

OVERNIGHT SOAKING METHOD

Soaking cuts cooking time by up to several hours. Place the beans in a large bowl and add enough water so the beans are about 3 inches below the surface; use cold water to prevent fermentation. Leave overnight. This is the best soaking method for beans to remain whole with a tender but firm texture, and a creamy consistency without mushiness once cooked.

ALTERNATE QUICK-SOAK METHOD

Put the beans in a pot with about 3 inches of cold water to cover. For each cup of beans, add $1/4$ teaspoon baking soda. Bring to a boil and boil for 5 minutes, then turn off the heat and allow them to soak for at least 1 hour or up to 3 hours, or until the beans have doubled in size. The baking soda will soften the beans and help break down the troublesome gas-producing oligosaccharides. It will also reduce the cooking time. Note that the quick-soak (or no-soak) method may cause beans to split or result in a slightly mushy texture.

It is not necessary to pre-soak beans, but beans that have not been presoaked overnight or quick-soaked may require more cooking water, about $1/4$ to $1/2$ cup per cup of beans, to replace the water that evaporates during their longer cooking time.

COOKING

Cover the beans with cold water according to recipe instructions. Cover the pan and bring the water to a gentle boil. Reduce the heat immediately and simmer, partially covered, until tender. The beans should cook without stirring to keep them intact and firm. Cooking time will depend on the type of bean and its freshness. Do not add salt or any acidic seasonings, such as vinegar, wine, citrus, or tomatoes, until after cooking; any of these will increase cooking time dramatically and toughen the skins of the beans.

BEAN FACTS

1 cup cooked beans = 210 to 240 calories

1 cup dried beans = 6 ounces

Beans and Legumes:
Protein for Vegetarians

K. DUN GIFFORD

When Oldways introduced its Vegetarian diet pyramid at a conference in Austin, Texas, in 1997, we were careful to address the issue of protein for vegetarians in some detail. Protein deficiency is one of the main criticisms of a vegetarian diet, usually made by meat advocates, and so we included a note accompanying the Vegetarian diet pyramid highlighting the foods that offer good sources of protein from plants.

Protein deficiency is a principal reason people cite for not following a vegetarian diet, but it is an unnecessary concern if foods from the vegetable kingdom that are high in plant protein are part of the regular eating pattern. The following are soy foods that also offer good sources of plant protein.

SOYBEANS

The soybean has been a principal source of protein in East Asia for more than two thousand years. Benjamin Franklin gets credit for bringing it to America in late 1770 after he discovered it in France. The following are some of the versatile foods that are derived from soybeans.

TOFU

Tofu, also known as soybean curd, is created when soy milk is separated into curds and whey. The curds are pressed into blocks and then packaged. A five-ounce serving of tofu has 86 calories and 10 grams of protein. It also contains about 8 to 9 grams of fat, primarily polyunsaturated fats.

There are basically two types of tofu: the type in water and refrigerated and the type aseptically sealed in cardboard without water and refrigeration. Tofu also comes in three varieties of firmness and texture. *Silken* and *soft tofu* can be used for making sauces, salad dressing, puddings, and shakes; *medium tofu* is excellent for cheesecakes, thicker puddings, pies, and any kind of filling; and *firm* and *extra-firm* can be used for stir-fries, in miso soups, grilled, and on kebabs (anywhere that meat would normally be served).

TEMPEH

Tempeh is cooked soybeans bound together by whitish threads called mycelium. Tempeh is made from spilt and hulled soybeans to which a tempeh starter is added, and then fermented in a process similar to that of cheese. It has a nutty aroma and a somewhat "meaty" taste. Tempeh can be purchased in the frozen food section of natural food stores and some supermarkets and is great marinated or grilled.

TVP

TVP is texturized soy protein. After soy oil has been extracted from cooked soybeans, soy flakes, which are about 50 percent protein by weight, are left behind and used to make the textured soy protein. TVP is used as one of the ingredients in vegetarian convenience foods. It is also available in plain pieces for home use in dishes such as chili and stews.

OKARA

Okara is the pulp that remains when soy milk is strained from soybeans. When baked, okara can be added to granola and baked goods, somewhat like shredded coconut. Okara patties can be found in the freezer section of natural food stores.

SOY YOGURT AND CHEESE

Soy yogurt is cultured from soy beverage using active cultures. Soy cheese is made in both soft and hard varieties. The soft cheese is made from aged tofu that is then whipped to a creamy consistency. Hard soy cheese is similar to mozzarella in both taste and texture. Both types use the milk protein casein to hold them together and make them melt, so many vegans do not use them.

SOY BEVERAGE

According to the USDA Standards of Identity, only lactational secretions from mammals can be called milk; it therefore requires beverages made from soy to be called soy beverage. This beverage is high in both protein and in calcium. It can be substituted for dairy milk in any recipe and has a good flavor.

SEITAN

Seitan is the Japanese name for seasoned wheat gluten. It has not received much attention in the United States except among vegetarians. The origin of seitan is not clear, but was probably developed by vegetarian Buddhists and has been in use in Asian countries for centuries.

Seitan is quite high in protein—4 ounces contain 70 calories, 15 grams of protein, 1 gram of fat, and, of course, no cholesterol.

Beans, Italian Style

JULIA DELLA CROCE

Italian cooking is not fancy. Its origins—like all Mediterranean cooking—are grounded on survival, sustenance, and availability. Meat was a special treat, served on Sundays or for special holidays or feast days, like weddings. Beans and legumes were everyday sources of protein, and Italian cooks created wonderful dishes with beans at the center of the plate.

In the Italian south, beans are practically inseparable from pasta, and this tradition crossed the Atlantic with the Italian immigrants from those regions. Who in America hasn't dipped into a bowl of "pasta fazool" (pasta e fagioli), as it came to be known in Brooklyn? The combination is as delicious as Sophia Loren and Marcello Mastroianni in an old Italian film.

Putting beans and pasta together goes back to the 1800s when pasta became the national dish of the cucina povera, "poor kitchen," as the Italians fondly call their simple, peasant-based cuisine. In 1895, Pellegrino Artusi, the author of the first national Italian cookbook, was calling beans "the meat of the poor." He wrote, "When the worker, having little in his pocket, sees with a melancholy eye that he can't even buy a piece of meat to make a good soup for his little family, he finds in beans a healing food, nutritious and economical."

The traditional Italian housewife, rich or poor, looked to heaven as well as to the purse when contemplating what to put on the dinner table. On Fridays, the Catholic religion forbade the consumption of animal flesh, so a meatless menu had to be devised. With typical panache, these inventive cooks created a whole world of quick, delicious, and nourishing dishes, and pasta and beans often found each other in the same pot. On other days of the week, a tasty piece of pork fat or a ham bone might be thrown in (see page 88 for the Sicilian variation of pasta e fagioli).

Canned Beans—A Compromise?

JULIA DELLA CROCE

If you're intimidated by dried beans—buying, soaking, cooking—there is a great alternative. Keep your mind open about the delicious possibilities of canned beans.

There is no question that fresh beans deliver flavor and texture lost in the drying process. When we can find fresh, tender cranberry or fava beans in the markets, we snap them up, thrilled to find the fledglings. But for the most part, what we know are packaged dried beans. They are dirt cheap and come in so many varieties. Yes, they need rehydrating, or soaking, before cooking, and in this day and age when we have so little time for forethought in the kitchen, we may not want to bother.

So what about canned beans? Dried beans usually retain their texture after cooking better than canned beans, but after many years of using both dried and canned varieties, I have come to the conclusion that canned beans are not necessarily a compromise—depending on the bean and depending on the brand. I find that chickpeas acquire a distinctively canned flavor in a tin, so I like their dried counterpart better. Some brands of canned beans are too mushy—beans should be whole and firm. And some companies add sugar (read the label), which alters the beans' flavor. If the beans have been packed with salt, rinse them before using. Because canned beans are mushier than rehydrated and cooked dried beans, they need only reheating. For salads, they can be used directly after rinsing.

FAVA BEAN AND PASTA SOUP FROM SICILY (*FAVE E PASTA ALLA SICILIANA*)

JULIA DELLA CROCE

The creamy, pleasantly bitter flesh of fava beans has a unique flavor in the bean family. Use only young, green-fleshed fava beans. The beans that nestle in the wooly interior of the long pods should be a clear green, not at all yellow.

SERVES 4 TO 5

- I pound fresh, young fava beans
- I¹/₂ tablespoons extra virgin olive oil
- I medium onion, chopped
- 2 ounces salt pork, chopped
- 6 cups cold water
- ¹/₄ pound linguine or spaghetti, broken into I¹/₂-inch lengths
- I tablespoon chopped fresh basil
- I tablespoon chopped fresh mint
- I tablespoon chopped fresh parsley
- 2 teaspoons sea salt
- Freshly ground black pepper

Remove the beans from the pods and pick off the little buds that appear on the side of the beans.

Place the oil and onion in a large saucepan over low heat, cover, and cook for about 5 minutes, until the onion sweats. Add the salt pork and sauté for 8 to 10 minutes, until it begins to color. Add the water and bring to a boil. Add the beans and partially cover. Cook over medium-low heat for 25 to 40 minutes, until the beans are tender. The timing depends on the freshness of the beans. When the favas are tender, stir in the pasta and cook until the texture is somewhat more firm than al dente (the pasta will continue to cook in the soup, so it is best to undercook it a bit), an additional 6 minutes or so, stirring now and then to prevent the pasta from sticking together. Remove from the heat, add basil, mint, parsley, and salt and pepper to taste. Serve.

VARIATION: If fresh fava beans are not to be found, you can use 5 ounces (3/4 cup) dried fava beans instead. Because dried fava beans can be very hard, they may have to be soaked, chilled, for two full days with baking soda, and you will have to change their soaking liquid several times during that period. To make this soup using dried fava beans, bring the drained, soaked beans and 8 cups water to a boil in a soup kettle; simmer until the beans are tender, about 45 minutes. Drain, reserving the bean cooking liquid; cool the beans. Remove and discard the tough outer skin from the fava beans. Follow the recipe instructions, adding the cooked fava beans and 6 cups of the bean cooking liquid just after adding the salt pork. Bring to a boil, add the pasta, and proceed with the recipe instructions.

EDAMAME BEANS WITH OLIVE OIL

K. DUN GIFFORD

This recipe offers a delicious East-meets-West combination, a great way to bring together good taste and nutrition.

SERVES 4

3/4 cup water
4 cups frozen shelled edamame beans
4 tablespoons extra virgin olive oil
2 teaspoons finely ground sea salt
Freshly ground black pepper

Pour the water into a medium cooking pot over medium-high heat. Bring to a boil, add the frozen beans, and cook, covered, for 6 minutes, until firm but tender. Remove from the heat, drain, and divide beans equally among four soup bowls. Spoon 1 tablespoon of the olive oil over the beans in each bowl, and sprinkle each with 1/2 teaspoon of sea salt and a generous pinch of pepper. Serve immediately.

VARIATIONS: This recipe has lots of room for improvisation, so play around. For example, when cooking the beans in the water, try adding 1 tablespoon dried minced onion, 1/4 teaspoon red pepper flakes, or other spices and seasonings of choice. Or, you can also use butter instead of olive oil: melt 1/8 pound of sweet butter in a small saucepan, add 1/4 teaspoon Worcestershire sauce, stir well, and pour over the beans just before serving; omit the pepper. Finally, you can sprinkle 1/4 teaspoon finely chopped herbs such as chives, mint, dill, fennel, sage, tarragon, or lemongrass over the beans just before serving.

BLACK BEAN TORTILLAS FROM GUATEMALA (*TORTILLAS DE FRIJOLES NEGROS*)

JULIA DELLA CROCE

Because Julia's children are vegetarians, she is always looking for new meatless recipes. Here's a simple and nourishing one for black bean tortillas she learned from her Guatemalan friend, Oswaldo Herrera. It's great for parties or mass feedings of kids because it's so quick and everyone can assemble their own. The trick here is to cook the beans until they are very soft, with just enough cooking liquid left in the pan to render a moist puree. Important: Because the skins need to be left out of the bean puree, the pureeing must be done in a food mill, not a blender.

SERVES 8

2 cups dried black beans, soaked overnight
    and drained
½ head garlic
1 small onion
½ small bunch of cilantro
6 cups cold water, plus more as needed
Sea salt
12 soft white corn tortillas
Olive oil or vegetable oil, for frying
1 pound queso blanco or other white cheese such
    as Monterey Jack, shredded

Rinse the beans and transfer to a large saucepan with the garlic, onion, three sprigs of the cilantro, and water. Bring to a boil, partially cover, and simmer until the beans are very tender, about 1 hour. If the beans begin to dry out before they are cooked, add more hot water as needed until the beans are thoroughly cooked. At the end of cooking time there should be a cup or so of bean liquid in the pan.

Remove the head of garlic, squeeze the soft cloves out into the pot with the beans and discard the garlic peels. Set the beans and their cooking liquid aside to cool, then pass the beans and enough of their liquid for a creamy consistency along with the cooked garlic and onion through a food mill. The puree should have the consistency of guacamole. Add salt to taste.

When you are ready to serve the tortillas, pour enough oil to cover the tortillas into a large frying pan and heat over high heat. When the oil is sizzling hot, slip in one or two tortillas, or as many as will comfortably fit without crowding and fry until crisp, about 3 minutes per side. Drain on paper towels.

When the tortillas are cool enough to handle, spoon a dollop of the warm bean puree on each tortilla, and top with a sprig of cilantro and the shredded cheese. Serve hot.

FRESH FAVA BEAN SOUP
(POTAGE AUX FÈVES FRAÎCHE)

K. DUN GIFFORD

When Fernand Point died in 1955, the noted food writer Joseph Wechsberg wrote that Point was widely "recognized as the master cuisinier of the twentieth century. No one challenged his supremacy." He characterized Point's style as "refined simplicity," describing an intense focus on presenting foods at the peak of their flavors. Point's recipe for fresh fava bean soup is my favorite example of his "refined simplicity," and this is the recipe in its entirety.

I have tried this recipe over and over, using fava beans, peas, lima beans, and edamame beans. Every time it produces an essence of the pea or bean itself, made silky by the butter. After a while I figured out that "some butter" meant less butter was better than more butter, and that sweet (or unsalted) butter gave a silkier result than salted butter. It's a nice presentation to float a pat of butter about half an inch thick on the soup at serving, but it's even better to make butterballs with small wooden paddles and float them in the soup.

Hulling fresh fava beans is not easy, but the result is worth it. An alternative to hulling is to press the cooked, hull-on beans in the sieve, but some of the bean flesh will get stuck in the hulls, so the yield is lower. I have tried using a blender to whiz hulls and flesh together, but the soups is never as silky. Frozen hulled fava beans are available in specialty stores, and they work just fine.

SERVES 4

1 pound fava beans or broad beans, freshly hulled
4 ounces lean bacon, chopped
1 sprig savory
8 cups water
4 tablespoons butter
1 cup toasted croutons

Place the fava beans, bacon, savory, and water in a large pot. Bring to a boil, decrease the heat to low, and cook for about 1 hour, or until the beans are al dente. Strain through a fine-mesh sieve. Divide the soup between 4 soup bowls and garnish each with 1 tablespoon butter and 1/4 cup croutons. Serve immediately.

"The health of vegetarians flourishes on animal-free diets when they combine plant proteins from two different foods. Vegetarian eating pioneer Frances Moore Lappé called this pairing of the proteins in plants 'protein complementarity,' because the combinations of amino acids in a balance of plant foods can complement each other to produce the complete and balanced arsenal of amino acid building blocks."

—K. DUN GIFFORD

BEANY BABIES

JANICE NEWELL BISSEX, MS, RD, AND
LIZ WEISS, MS, RD

When the USDA evaluated the antioxidant activity in one hundred of the most common foods, red beans came out on top. If you're not sure how to include more of this superfood into your diet, here's an easy and fun recipe to get you started, adapted from Janice Bissex and Liz Weiss's book, The Moms' Guide to Meal Makeovers.

SERVES 5

I (15¹/₂-ounce) can red beans, drained and rinsed

I cup frozen corn kernels, thawed

I cup dried bread crumbs

³/₄ cup shredded reduced- fat cheddar cheese

I large egg, beaten

¹/₄ cup light canola mayonnaise

I tablespoon freshly squeezed lime juice

¹/₂ to I teaspoon ground cumin

¹/₄ to ¹/₂ teaspoon chili powder

2 tablespoons canola oil

¹/₂ to I cup salsa (optional)

Mash the beans in a large bowl using a potato masher until not quite smooth; they should still be a bit chunky. Add the corn, ²/₃ cup of the bread crumbs, cheese, egg, mayonnaise, lime juice, cumin, and chili powder and mix well to combine. Shape the mixture into ten ¹/₂-inch-thick patties and coat with the remaining ¹/₃ cup bread crumbs.

Heat the oil in a large nonstick skillet over medium-high heat. Working in batches if necessary, cook the patties until golden brown, about 4 minutes per side. Serve with salsa for dipping, if desired.

CHICORY AND WHITE BEAN SALAD (*INSALATA DI CHICORIA E FAGIOLI BIANCHI*)

LIDIA BASTIANICH AND THE CHEFETTES

Beans are one of the stars of Pugliese cuisine, so when Lidia Bastianich and the Chefettes created their dinner in Lecce at the 1995 Oldways symposium, there were several dishes with beans at the center of the plate. Here's one of the scrumptious, typically Pugliese bean dishes.

A white wine vinegar was used when this dish was made in Lecce. Lidia remarked that it was surprisingly good for an industrially made product. Since you are unlikely to find such a mild white wine vinegar at home, red wine vinegar is suggested here. If you live in the United States and want to make this salad, Nichols Garden Nursery in Albany, Oregon, or the Cook's Garden in Londonderry, Vermont, sell the seeds for asparagus chicory. Otherwise use dandelion greens.

SERVES 6

8 ounces dried white beans (great Northern, cannellini, or navy)

2 bay leaves

2 pounds "asparagus" chicory or dandelion greens

3 cloves garlic, minced

¹/₃ cup extra virgin olive oil

¹/₄ cup red wine vinegar

Sea salt and freshly ground black pepper

Soak the beans overnight in enough water to cover by 3 inches. Drain. (Alternatively, cover the beans with cold water in a large saucepan over high heat. Bring to a boil and boil for 1 minute. Remove from the heat and let stand, covered, for 1 hour, until the beans have doubled in size. Drain.)

Add water to cover the bean by 3 inches, add the bay leaves, bring to a simmer, and gently simmer, with the pot partially covered, for about 1 hour, until the beans are tender but not soft. Drain the beans and discard the bay leaves. Let cool to room temperature.

To clean the chicory, cut off as much of the bottom as necessary to get rid of the woody part. Cut each stem in half crosswise. If you are using dandelion greens, trim off tough stems and cut the leaves crosswise into 4-inch pieces. Wash the greens carefully, using two changes of water. Drain.

Bring some lightly salted water to a boil in a large, non-reactive pot. Boil the greens until they are tender, 10 to 15 minutes, depending on their freshness and age. Drain well and set aside to cool. When the greens are cool enough to handle, squeeze out as much moisture as possible.

In a serving bowl, toss the beans and greens with the garlic, olive oil, and vinegar, being sure to distribute all the ingredients well. Season to taste with salt and pepper. Serve immediately.

BRAISED SHELLED FAVAS AND PEAS WITH ARTICHOKES (*SCAFFATA*)

LIDIA BASTIANICH AND THE CHEFETTES

"Scaffata" means "shelled," says Lidia Bastianich. For this dish, look for young artichokes, in which the choke has not yet formed.

SERVES 6

Freshly squeezed juice from ¹/₂ lemon

6 to 8 baby artichokes

6 large leaves romaine or Boston lettuce

¹/₄ cup extra virgin olive oil

I bunch scallions, white and green parts, sliced thinly

¹/₂ cup white wine vinegar

I pound green peas, shelled

2 pounds fava beans, hulled and peeled

¹/₄ cup chopped fresh mint

¹/₈ teaspoon red pepper flakes

Sea salt

Freshly ground black pepper

Place 4 to 5 cups cold water in a large bowl and add the lemon juice. Pull the tough outer leaves from one of the artichokes. Trim off the stem and any tough parts of the bottom. Cut the artichoke in half lengthwise. Cut each half lengthwise into thin slices. Toss the cut-up artichoke in the bowl of lemon water. Repeat with the remaining artichokes.

Stack the lettuce leaves one on top of the other. Roll the leaves together, starting with one side and rolling across to make a fat cigar shape. Cut the rolled leaves crosswise into ¹/₂-inch strips. Set aside.

In a large skillet, heat 3 tablespoons of the olive oil over medium heat. Add the scallions and sauté for about 5 minutes, until they are soft.

Drain the artichokes and add them to the scallions. Cover tightly and cook over medium heat, stirring occasionally, until the artichokes are soft, about 15 minutes. Add the vinegar and cook, uncovered, until the liquid has almost evaporated, about 10 minutes. Add the peas, cover, and continue cooking 5 minutes. Add the fava beans, cover, and cook another 10 minutes.

Stir in the lettuce, mint, pepper flakes, the remaining 1 tablespoon of olive oil, and salt and pepper to taste. If necessary to prevent sticking, add a bit of water. Cover and cook another 15 minutes, until the vegetables are very tender but the peas and beans still hold their shape. When the vegetables are cooked, check the seasoning and adjust if necessary. Serve immediately, drizzled with more extra virgin olive oil, if you wish.

BAKED LIMA BEANS
FROM BROOKLYN

ANNA NURSE

*Anna Nurse is an opera singer turned beloved cook-
ing teacher, and a friend of Oldways. She is famous
for this outrageous bean recipe, so we thought we
would include it here. Anna traveled to Puglia with
Oldways in 1995 and was a member of Lidia and the
Chefettes. Just to show you what she is made of—and
what these Oldways trips bring out in people—she
delighted everyone in the dining room by standing
up and singing opera at the table without so much
as taking a few minutes to go to her hotel room and
change her apron for dinner dress. Anna comes from
Pugliese stock, and as Puglia is a land of beans, it
shouldn't be surprising that she is good at cooking
them. As the recipe says, just be sure you don't drain
or rinse the beans before cooking them. By the way,
Anna serves these beans with a baked ham she's also
famous for, but she says you can substitute smothered pork chops. She adds to just make sure there are
biscuits and salad, too.*

SERVES 6

I pound dried large lima beans

6 cups water

I large onion, chopped

8 ounces slab bacon, diced

$^1\!/_2$ teaspoon dried mustard powder

$^1\!/_2$ cup chili sauce

$^1\!/_3$ cup molasses

I tablespoon cider vinegar

2 teaspoons sea salt

6 cups water

Put the beans in a stainless steel pot or heavy porcelain
casserole. Add the water and soak overnight in a cool
place or in the refrigerator, if you have room. The temperature must be cool enough to keep the beans from
fermenting. Do not drain or rinse the beans before
cooking.

Preheat the oven to 300°F. Place the pot of soaked beans
with their soaking liquid over medium heat and bring to
a boil. Turn the heat down to halt the boil, or the beans
will slip their skins. Simmer, covered, over medium-low
heat until the beans are almost tender, about 30 minutes.
There should be approximately 2 cups of cooking liquid
left. If not, add enough fresh water to equal 2 cups. Add
the onion, bacon, mustard powder, chili sauce, molasses, vinegar, and salt and stir. Cover and bake for 2
hours. Remove the cover and bake for an additional 30
minutes or until the beans are creamy. Serve hot.

AN EXPLOSION OF BEANS FROM THE CRETE EXPERIMENT

SARI ABUL-JUBEIN, AGLAIA KREMEZI, RICK MOONEN, AND JOE SIMONE

When a group of chefs got together to cook on the island of Crete, one of the creations was this explosion of beans.

SERVES 12

- 1 cup wheat berries
- 1 cup dried chickpeas
- 2 cups black-eyed peas
- 3 tablespoons extra virgin olive oil
- 2 Spanish onions, finely diced
- 3 scallions or 2 baby leeks, white and tender green parts, finely chopped
- 1 bunch fennel tops (choose young, fragrant greens), coarsely chopped
- Leaves from 1/2 bunch fresh mint, finely chopped
- 2 cups cold water
- Sea salt
- 5 to 6 medium tomatoes, peeled, seeded, and finely chopped
- Freshly ground black pepper

In separate containers, soak the chickpeas, wheat berries, and black-eyed peas in enough water to cover by 3 inches for 8 to 10 hours. Drain.

Bring 3 large pots of cold water to a boil. Salt the water in each pot. In separate covered pots, parboil the chickpeas for about 1 hour, the wheat berries for about 45 minutes, and the black-eyed peas for about 45 minutes, until slightly tender but still firm. Drain and set aside.

In a large saucepan, heat the olive oil over high heat. Add the onions and scallions and sauté until the onions are tender. Add fennel tops and mint. Add the cold water and a pinch of salt and stir to incorporate. Raise the heat to a simmer. Simmer until the greens are tender and the liquid has reduced somewhat, about 5 minutes. Stir in the tomatoes and cook for 1 minute. Add the chickpeas, wheat berries, and black-eyed peas, and simmer for about 15 minutes, until all beans are tender. Adjust the seasonings and serve.

> "Protein deficiency is one of the main reasons people give for not following a vegetarian diet, but it is an unnecessary concern if foods from the vegetable kingdom that are high in plant protein are part of the regular eating pattern."
>
> —K. DUN GIFFORD

"Traditional recipes using nuts are still prepared today throughout the Mediterranean. And in America, leading chefs and food
writers, inspired by Mediterranean and other healthy, traditional
cuisines, are using nuts in ways that will be reflected in
home cooking. Nuts add texture, and nuts lend a rich touch
to lean dishes. What's more, they are convenient."

—JOHN MERCURI DOOLEY

"The peanut has risen from its underground habitat to
become almost a symbol of American popular culture and
one of the world's favorite snacks—enjoyed on streets, in
amusement parks, and at sports events, and put to imaginative
uses in kitchens all over the world. Of all the New World
edible discoveries, only the chile, perhaps, has enjoyed such
stunning success in its travels around the globe."

—ANYA VON BREMZEN

NUTS AND PEANUTS

So, what are these friends, the nuts, peanuts, and seeds of the world's cuisines?

Technically, of course, they are members of the plant kingdom. More specifically, they are the children of their plant parents, because every year

the earth's trees, grasses, fruits, and vegetables bear and send forth countless numbers of their children as fertilized embryos—their inchoate children, in a way.

And just as animals put a huge amount of food energy into creating their offspring, so do plants. They wrap their seed children in hard coats to protect them from fearsome dangers—water that will rot them, bugs that will eat them, cold that will freeze them, sun that will oxidize them, and the powerful digestive acids of animals and birds that will destroy them if their hard coats are cracked.

These plant parents also put in the capsule of their seed children the stash of fat they need to grow, because plants, too, need fat for their journey through the neonatal and early postnatal stages of life, just as animals do.

The third parental gift is a package of carbohydrates, the principal source of the energy that the nascent plant needs to work its roots down into the earth to reach water and nutrients, and thrust its leaves up toward the sky to the life-giving, photosynthesizing sunlight.

The master commander of this remarkable capsule is a fertilized embryo packed into the capsule. It makes some of us uneasy to realize how similar plants are to the animal kingdom, particularly to its females—only when one of the eggs of plants or animals is fertilized can it become an embryo, poised to launch into life. Just as animals do, plants provide their embryos with stores of fats, carbohydrates, proteins, vitamins, and all the other essentials of life.

Only a tiny fraction of nuts, peanuts, and seeds survive long enough to grow to become a new plant, of course, because animals and birds and other creatures hunt them down relentlessly for food. We humans do, too, because just as for birds and animals, so it is for us: food is life; no food is death.

ESSENTIAL NUTS AND SEEDS

Nuts, peanuts, and seeds were essential foods for our hunter-gatherer ancestors—and also our farmer ancestors and their domesticated animals—because they were reliable and storable sources of the nutrient big three: fats, carbohydrates, and protein. The genomes and DNA of these ancestor-predecessors on our family trees were shaped over tens of thousands of years by what they ate, and our modern bodies need much this same nutrient profile even today; our genes differ from our scrounger ancestors only in small ways.

Scientific evidence is steadily growing for what until recently was a controversial hypothesis: that a central

reason for the steep recent increases of the killer chronic diseases in modern industrial societies (cancer, heart disease, and diabetes) is the rapid recent departure from classic eating patterns. As recently as the High Middle Ages, for example, low-born and high-born alike collected and ate acorns for acorn bread and soups. Some of the great treasures of human art history, the illuminated manuscripts of those times, contain gorgeous paintings of acorn gathering as one of the twelve "labors of the months." The nursery rhyme sings of "gathering nuts in May, nuts in May," but they probably couldn't make a rhyme with September, October, and November, when nuts are really harvested.

All kinds of other nuts and seeds were gathered and stored, too, among them walnuts and hickory in the cooler climates, and almonds in the warmer. But as human populations began to expand exponentially, our ancestors relentlessly cut down the glorious virgin forests for firewood, shelter, and boats. Over the centuries, the vast harvests of nuts and seeds—those pocket-sized storehouses of energy and nutrients—gradually fell to small fractions of what they once were.

Modern science is also unraveling a fascinating relationship between some kinds of nuts, peanuts, and seeds and certain types of nutritionally essential fatty acids—the omega-3 group of oils—that promote brain development and lifelong health. It is well known that fatty fish, such as salmon, are rich in these oils, but it has only recently become clear that some nuts contain large amounts of them too, along with a "parent" of these omega-3s.

Essential fatty acids are called "essential" because our bodies cannot fabricate them; to get them, we must eat them in our food. We can eat them in fatty fish; we can eat them in some greens, such as purslane and dark leafy greens; and we can eat them in some nuts and seeds. All of these have oils that our bodies are able to turn into the "essential" omega-3s.

Scientific evidence is clear now that this class of essential omega-3s is important not only for brain development, but also for reproductive health, for fending off Alzheimer's disease, for protection against heart disease and macular degeneration, and maybe for protection against some kinds of cancer. Happily, our old friends the nuts, peanuts, and seeds are terrific and reliable sources of omega-3s.

GOOD FRIENDS TO OUR MINDS AND BODIES

The reasons why we become fond friends with some people but not others are usually impenetrable—it always has seemed to me to have something to do with pheromones—but perhaps we can get an inkling from looking at why we are friendly with nuts, peanuts, and seeds.

As with people, usually we don't like some kinds of nuts, peanuts, and seeds, we are okay with others, and we really like other kinds. It's the same sort of thing about people—some we love, some we like, some we are indifferent to, and some we just cannot abide.

Behavioral scientists are beginning to understand that having and being with friends not only promotes a sense of well-being, but actually enhances emotional health. Nutrition scientists are now uncovering the solid health and genetic reasons why nuts, peanuts, and seeds can be very good friends to our minds and bodies.

This is very nice symmetry.

> "Nuts, peanuts, and seeds were essential foods for our hunter-gatherer ancestors because they were reliable and storable sources of the nutrient big three: fats, carbohydrates, and protein."
>
> —K. DUN GIFFORD

Nuts: Historical and Culinary Perspectives

JOHN MERCURI DOOLEY

In 1994 and 1995 Oldways organized two scientific conferences, one about tree nuts and health, and another one about peanuts and health. These conferences focused on the Oldways signature mix of history, science, and gastronomy. John Mercuri Dooley, then a Boston-based food writer, helped us by writing a brief history of nuts. We've taken excerpts to give a picture of the culture, history, and versatility of nuts. 🍂

Long before the development of any cuisine, in fact before agriculture or civilization, early humans gathered tree nuts for food. As cultures evolved, so, of course, did foodways, and nuts played a significant role in many cuisines. Cooks in the ancient Mediterranean, for example, relied on walnuts, hazelnuts, almonds, and pistachios to prepare savory sauces, stuffings, grain dishes, stews, drinks, and desserts.

Traditional recipes using nuts are still prepared today throughout the Mediterranean. And in America, leading chefs and food writers, inspired by Mediterranean and other healthy, traditional cuisines, are using nuts in ways that will be reflected in future home cooking. Nuts add texture, which Americans want in their food, and nuts lend a rich touch to lean dishes. What's more, they are convenient. Also, nuts are real food; they were not invented in a high-tech food lab. As such, nuts—high in healthful unsaturated fat, protein, fiber, and micronutrients—can be a part of an improved American diet that looks to traditional Mediterranean ways of eating as a model.

A nut, botanically speaking, is a one-seeded fruit, in a hard shell, with a tough dry fruit layer rather than a fleshy, succulent one. Under this restricted definition, explains Harold McGee in *On Food and Cooking*, hazelnuts and chestnuts are among those that qualify as true nuts. Practically speaking, however, a nut is simply an edible kernel in a hard shell. Almonds, for example, are kernels of a fruit related to peaches and plums. Cashews and pistachios are also seeds of drupe fruits, although they are not related to peaches and plums. Pecans and walnuts are members of the same family. Macadamia nuts are products of an evergreen tree. Peanuts are not really nuts, but rather are seeds of a leguminous bush and grow underground.

POUNDED NUT SAUCES

Catalan manuscript cookbooks from the early fourteenth century contain recipes for a number of sauces made with nuts. Elsewhere in Spain, in Andalusia, cooks for centuries have fried bread, almonds, and garlic and then pounded them in a mortar to make a sauce. The same pounded ingredients, unfried, form the base of *ajo blanco,* the exquisite Andalusian chilled soup that's a pre-Columbian precursor to gazpacho with tomatoes. Renaissance cookbooks are "full of recipes for sauces made from pounded almonds mixed with bread to make white sauces," says Nancy Harmon Jenkins, food writer and author of *The Mediterranean Diet Cookbook.*

NUTS IN BREADS AND DESSERTS

Italians, like many, many others, also enrich breads with nuts. An old-fashioned cornmeal flatbread from Tuscany, writes Carol Field in *Italy in Small Bites,* includes pancetta and walnuts. Casareccio, a rustic whole-wheat bread, can include walnuts, or pistachios. One of Field's favorites is a panettone, or Christmas bread, stuffed with dates and walnuts.

Nuts are a key ingredient in sweets throughout the Mediterranean. In Italy, there are numerous variations on biscotti studded with almonds or hazelnuts. Moroccans, writes Paula Wolfert in *Couscous and Other Good Food from Morocco,* serve platters of fresh, seasonal fruit with nuts as dessert in the summer, and bowls of mixed raisins, dates, dried figs, and nuts in winter. Nut-studded

nougat and other confections based on candied syrups are found from one end of the sea to the other, but it's at the eastern end that nuts are used most conspicuously in sweets. Turkey, Greece, Tunisia, and other countries have their own versions of baklava, stuffed with walnuts, pistachios, or almonds, and perfumed with ingredients such as lemon zest, orange blossom water, or cloves and cinnamon.

NUTS BEYOND THE MEDITERRANEAN

Some nuts—such as walnuts, hazelnuts, pine nuts, and chestnuts—existed in Asia, Europe, and America before Europe and America split into two continents sixty-five million years ago. Others, such as almonds and pistachios, are most likely native to Asia. Still others—cashews, peanuts, and pecans—originated in the Americas. Macadamia nuts are native to Australia, though are now thriving in Hawaii, Central America, and South America. Though there are no recorded nut recipes of the Aborigines of Australia, evidence indicates that they consumed macadamia nuts—or bush nuts—over many thousands of years.

In the Americas, Aztecs and other native peoples developed cuisines, incorporating nuts, long before Europeans traveled to their lands. "In the woodland areas of America—the Algonquin areas, the Iroquois areas—nuts provided a large amount of the winter sustenance, " says Mark Miller, of Coyote Cafe and Red Sage restaurants and the author of *The Great Chile Book.* In the southwestern United States, nuts have been an important part of the indigenous diet for about fourteen thousand years, Miller says. Native Americans depended on them while they made the transition from hunter-gatherers to living in settled agricultural communities. Nuts can be thought of, Miller says, "as one of the bases of southwestern civilization."

In Central Mexico, peanuts and other nuts became very important. They were ground with spices in stone metates as early as 1500 B.C., Miller says. The types of recipes that later became the pestos of Mexico started at that time. Much later, when Spaniards introduced the almond and other nuts, the dietary culture of Mexico became mixed. "We have the dishes that led to moles, for instance, which is probably the most complicated dish of Mexico," Miller says. "It always included nuts, usually pecans, almonds, sometimes peanuts, and usually some type of wild seed."

ASIA AND THE PACIFIC

Most Asian dishes are plant based, and many feature nuts. Indian and Southeast Asian cooks incorporate nuts, often cashews or almonds, into grain-based dishes, stews, and vegetable salads—called sambals in Indonesia and elsewhere—with carrots, cabbage, nuts, shrimp paste, lime juice, ginger, and chiles. Traditional Chinese cuisines also use nuts extensively, in dishes such as Sichuanese hot and spicy stir-fried chicken with almonds, cashews, and walnuts. Japan, too, is a large consumer of nuts, including almonds and walnuts.

MENU SIZZLE

"Texture" is a theme that comes up again and again when chefs speak of nuts. The crunchiness of nuts makes grains, as in pilafs, more palatable, says Deborah Madison, who likes to combine macadamia nuts with rice. Another traditional technique contemporary chefs use is to garnish chicken, fish, or vegetables with roasted or fried nuts. Nut coatings are also popular.

The richness of nuts, too, enhances leaner dishes, vegetarian or not, that are increasingly popular. Vegetables and grains, of course, contain little fat. "Augmenting them with a nut gives a sense of roundness in the mouth, which is something you're always after," Mark Miller says.

Peanuts: A View from the Peoples of the World

ANYA VON BREMZEN

At our 1995 conference about peanuts and health, Anya von Bremzen, the well-known cookbook author and food and travel writer, made a terrific keynote presentation on the origins of peanuts, excerpted here.

The peanut has risen from its underground habitat to become almost a symbol of American popular culture and one of the world's favorite snacks—enjoyed on streets, in amusement parks, and at sports events, and put to imaginative uses in kitchens all over the world. Of all the New World edible discoveries, only the chile, perhaps, has enjoyed such stunning success in its travels around the globe.

To me, the culinary and cultural allure of the peanut is how much of a common thread, a cultural link, if you will, it is between various food cultures as diverse as Malaysia, Ecuador, the United States, Africa, and Brazil. And unlike other, more chameleon ingredients that appear in cuisines across the world, the flavor of the peanut is so rich and unmistakable that any dish flavored with ground peanuts will carry a similarity in taste; hence, the surprising continuity in flavor between an Indonesian peanut sauce, a West African soup, Chinese noodles, a Peruvian stew, and an all-American sandwich.

There is common belief that the peanut originated in Africa, but, in fact, there is no evidence of a species of undomesticated peanut plants found anywhere except South America. Its first home was the Andean lowlands (as it can't sustain the cold of high altitudes), most probably Bolivia, from where it spread west to Peru to become an important pre-Columbian crop. Peruvian archaeologists have told me that excavations from some ceremonial sites as early as 3000 B.C. were covered with peanut shells.

No one knows how peanuts were cooked in ancient Peru, but one can suspect that they were used much as they are in indigenous cooking today; boiled and munched as a snack or toasted and sprinkled on various dishes. It was an agricultural economy based on the concept of storage, where anything that was rich in nutrients and that could be dried, stored, and reconstituted was very much in demand.

The Spanish colonists introduced nut-thickened sauces, as well as nut sweets and confections, which are very popular today throughout South America. With that blend of colonial and indigenous, so characteristic of present-day Andean food cultures, the use of peanuts often is what demarcates the division between the two. Whereas white upper-class Creole cooks use more expensive almonds and walnuts for sweet and savory dishes, peasant cooks use peanuts in exactly the same ways. In addition, the campesinos often serve chile-laden nut-thickened sauces over potatoes.

But centuries before the Europeans' arrival, the cultivated peanut plant spread to other parts of South America—including Mexico, where it was and still is referred to as "earth cacao." Though it never became a characteristic Mexican ingredient, it's used in pounded chile sauces and as a thickening agent for moles, together with pumpkin and sesame seeds.

It was from Brazil that the peanut traveled with the Portuguese to West Africa, along with other edible treasures, such as sweet potatoes and corn. The Africans, starved for nutrients, immediately recognized the incredible nutritional potential of the new food—26 percent of whose weight is protein. In addition the peanut plant enriches the soil in which it's grown with nitrogen. And of all the African crops, it became the one with the highest protein yield per acre. Besides being a major source of nutrition, the tastes of peanuts became central to West African cooking.

As in Brazil, the peanut traveled to the United States with African slaves who cultivated it and cooked with it in the plantations of the South. From the times of the Civil War, it spread around America. In 1925, an eccentric scientist named George Washington Carver became a passionate advocate of the peanut, producing a peanut cookbook and arranging multicourse banquets in which all dishes were made with the peanut. Peanut butter was popularized during the 1904 world's fair, and the nimble legume has been an American economic success story ever since, though most of the time it was a cheap snack, not taken seriously by gastronomes. It is only with the reinvention of American regional cuisines and the recent craze for exotic foreign food that the peanut has been put to extensive culinary use.

But to go back east, the peanut is first mentioned in China as early as the 1530s, only several decades after the discovery of the Americas. (The peanut was so welcomed all over Asia because of its ease of culture; it grows effortlessly in warm sandy soil, actually benefiting the soil by producing nitrogen.) How did it get there? Once again it came with the Spanish and Portuguese, now spice traders and missionaries. The Spanish took it to the Philippines and the Portuguese took it to India and Macao; from there it traveled to China via the returning Chinese traders.

Subsequently, New World crops, such as the peanut and the sweet potato, were brought to China en masse as famine relief crops. And while the Chinese abhorred the sweet potato, which was deemed the food of the desperate and the poor, the peanut got an excellent reception in the country with arguably the most sophisticated gastronomic tradition in the world. The Chinese already had a stunning abundance of various legumes and nuts.

"Clinical studies have changed what we think about nuts from a fattening snack food to a wholesome and heart-healthy food."

—FRANK HU, MD

The Chinese christened the peanut newcomer *lo hua sheng,* which means, "dropping flower gives birth," and put it to all sorts of imaginative uses in the kitchen, drawing on their rich experience of cooking with nuts. They made them into sauces, especially in Sichuan cookery; ate them boiled like beans, as they did in Africa; or deep fried in hot oil to give them a roast; and tossed into stir-fried dishes to add textural contrast. Peanuts pounded with sugar were a filling for sweet buns. Mixed with malt sugar, peanuts made a popular candy. Peanut cakes also were used as animal feed, and in hard times, eaten by humans.

But most important, the Chinese, who were master fryers, recognized peanuts as an invaluable source of oil. For centuries, they had extracted oil from soybeans, sesame seeds, and seeds of the plants of the mustard family. But the refined oil squeezed from peanuts was clear, flavorless, healthy, and inexpensive, because the peanut is 50 percent oil. It quickly became the oil of choice all throughout Asia, except India, where ghee was favored.

Gastronomically, the most interesting use of peanuts, and nuts in general, is to be found in the cuisines of Malaysia and Singapore where the cuisine is immensely varied, a creative blend of various ethnic Chinese and Indian cooking, native Malay, and European colonial influences. One of the best-known Asian dishes is satay, served with a spicy peanut sauce. In this country, satay is thought of as Thai, but its origins are in Java, Indonesia, where it arrived with Arab traders, essentially an adaptation of kebabs. The rich peanut sauce is a curry of sorts, based on a fragrant pounded mixture of aromatics, coconut milk, tamarind for sourness, and a touch of soy. In Indonesia, however, a dark syrupy soy sauce called ketchap manis is preferred.

In Indonesia peanut sauce goes beyond satay. Made according to different formulas, it can accompany a whole range of cold or warm vegetable dishes and meat dishes. Dishes in Thai cuisines where peanuts are a main flavor element, such as creamy peanut sauces and curries, are usually associated with Muslim influences from Penang (Malaysia), which came to southern Thai-

land via the narrow Isthmus of Kra that connects the two countries.

Finally, as we know from the activity of the early Spanish, the best way to market a new cuisine is by linking it with a familiar flavor. And so, the peanut plays a very important role in the popularization of Asian cuisines in this country. It's not surprising. One strong symbol of Southeast Asian cuisines in this country is satay with peanut sauce and wine. It is familiar; the peanut sauce tastes like all-American peanut butter!

Peanuts, Nuts, and Health

KATHY McMANUS, RD

Since the early 1990s and the start of the U.S. government's low-fat policy, communicating the role of peanuts and nuts in a healthy diet has been an uphill battle. Much of the confusion had to do with fat, and America's obsession with anything low-fat, which was launched by the 1988 Surgeon General's Report. The message—that peanuts and nuts are "bad foods" and should be avoided because they have fat—was and is patently wrong. One expert who has been a key player in developing clinical studies to prove that this message was and is wrong is Kathy McManus, RD, director of nutrition at Brigham and Women's Hospital. We asked her to give us a picture of the most up-to-date nutrition science about peanuts, nuts, and health.

Traditionally, peanuts and nuts have been perceived as "all fat" and something to avoid if trying to lose weight. However, recent research studies suggest that eating peanuts and nuts have beneficial effects and may reduce the incidence of some chronic diseases.

A growing body of evidence indicates that the type of fat in the diet is more important than the amount of fat. Numerous research studies have shown that diets high in monounsaturated and polyunsaturated fats, and low in trans and saturated fat, are heart-healthy. Peanuts and peanut butter also contribute other important nutrients to the diet such as fiber, folate, plant protein, resveratrol, and vitamin E, which may contribute to reducing the risk of diabetes, heart disease, and some cancers.

PEANUTS AND HEART DISEASE

Peanuts and peanut butter have been cited in a number of studies to reduce cardiovascular disease. In the Physicians Health Study, a large prospective trial of over 21,000 male physicians, results showed that men who ate peanuts and nuts two or more times each week have a 47 percent reduced risk of sudden cardiac death and a 30 percent reduced risk of coronary heart disease death compared to men who rarely or never eat them.

The Nurses Health Study examined eating habits and health outcomes in more than 86,000 nurses ages 34 to 59. Researchers at the Harvard School of Public Health found that women who ate more than five servings of peanuts and nuts each week decreased their risk of heart disease by about one-third compared to women who rarely or never ate nuts.

Results from the Iowa Women's Study showed similar findings. This study, conducted on more than 34,000 postmenopausal women with no known cardiovascular disease, found that higher levels of peanut and nut consumption were related to a lower risk of dying from heart disease.

A major study of approximately 27,000 Seventh-Day Adventists in California examined the relationship between 65 different foods and coronary heart disease. Of all the foods studied, nuts had the strongest protective effect on the risk of developing a heart attack or dying from heart disease. Further analysis on the diets showed that 32 percent of the nuts consumed in the study were peanuts. The researchers suggested the favorable fatty acid profile of peanuts and nuts—low in saturated fat and high in monounsaturated and polyunsaturated fats—is one explanation for their protective effect.

Studies in Australia and in the United States show that subjects who eat diets rich in monounsaturated fats, mainly from peanuts, have a greater decline in LDL (bad) cholesterol as compared to a low-fat diet. Instead of raising triglyceride levels as on the low-fat diet, the peanut-containing diets lowered triglyceride levels.

PEANUTS AND OTHER RESEARCH STUDIES

In the Nurses Health Study, women who were consuming a half serving (1 tablespoon) of peanut butter or a full serving of peanuts or other nuts (1 ounce) five or more times a week had a 21 to 27 percent reduced risk of developing diabetes, respectively. The study also showed that the higher consumption provided a greater protective effect.

In a weight loss trial conducted at Brigham and Women's Hospital and Harvard School of Public Health comparing a moderate-fat diet with a low-fat diet for weight loss, Dr. Frank Sacks and I found that those eating a moderate-fat diet lost more weight and stayed on the diet longer than those who were assigned to the low-fat diet. Study subjects on the moderate-fat diet replaced high-saturated-fat foods, such as butter, cheese, and red meat, with healthy unsaturated fat foods such as peanuts, peanut butter, nuts, and olive oil.

Populations in the Mediterranean and many Asian countries have been shown to have lower risk of chronic disease compared to those in the United States. There are many explanations for this trend. One is that their diets are more plant based. Plant-based diets are naturally low in saturated fat and cholesterol and contain a high level of fiber, and many vitamins, minerals, and phytochemicals. Resveratrol, the phytochemical found in red wine and grape skins, is also found in peanuts. Resveratrol has been associated with a reduced risk of some cancers and heart disease. Some researchers have shown a positive effect on cell adhesion molecules, thereby decreasing the risk of clogged arteries.

SUMMARY

The research to date from the population studies appears very strong that peanuts, peanut butter, and peanut products are healthful and can reduce risk of chronic disease. Some of the clinical intervention trials suggest mechanisms through which the beneficial nutrients that are found in peanuts interact.

The message that because peanuts contain fat they should be avoided is wrong. Research clearly demonstrates that unsaturated fats, found in peanuts and peanut butter, should be part of a healthy diet.

Family and Nuts

K. DUN GIFFORD

I wish the nutrition police hadn't sent their squads of scolds after nuts during the, well, the nuttiness of the low-fat diet fad craze of the 1990s, because it feels as if there are not as many of those great-tasting nuts around as there used to be. Too bad—nuts are a nearly perfect food, with lots of fiber, the healthy kinds of fat and protein, plenty of crunch, and terrific satiety power.

There were lots of nuts around when I was growing up. My mother and father loved walnuts, and a big bowl of them, still in their tough, tight shells, sat on a table in the living room, with sturdy old-fashioned nutcrackers and stout nut picks lying alongside. Mom and Dad had cocktails together each evening when Dad got home from work, and as they sat in the living room talking and looking at the evening paper, Dad would crack the tough-shelled walnuts and pick out the meats for Mom. He was really good with his hands and was intent on getting the meats out in full halves instead of broken pieces, as if it demeaned both of them unless he could give her a perfect piece of the walnut.

This was a shade of the past for them. Dad grew up in Kentucky, where walnut trees are native, and Mom's favorite aunt who lived in southeastern Ohio, just across the Ohio River from Kentucky, had native walnut trees on her farms. I was sure that the two of them had talked about this odd coincidence and that in some unspoken, ineffable way this walnut ritual was a string of their bonding. It rang as true for me as does the song "Two Different Worlds" from South Pacific, albeit with a happier ending.

English walnut trees rose sternly to the sky in the grounds of the Rhode Island Historical Society right across the street from our house, and in the fall we'd gather basketfuls of the walnuts when they ripened and fell to the ground. These were much tougher to crack open than the southern walnuts, their shells being thicker, and it was hardly worth the work because their meats were smaller. And they were not as sweet, either.

When Mom and Dad grew older, he switched from walnuts to pecans, and had bags and bags of them stashed in the back of the kitchen closet. He insisted on "the real ones," he said, which had to come from Georgia. So every year, when the two of them drove to Florida and back, they stopped at the roadside Stuckey shops to pick up a half-dozen or so big cloth bags of premium-grade pecans. When he ran short, Stuckey's parcel-posted them to him.

Pecans are thin-shelled, and you can put two of them into the palm of your hand, squeeze them really hard against each other, and crack them open. Pecans do not resist as strongly as walnuts; they're easy to crack with the nutcracker and the meats pop out more simply. Dad knew his nuts.

Stahmann Farms, a wonderful pecan farm outside El Paso, was a sponsor of our Oldways Latin American Diet Conference in 1996 in that Tex-Mex border city. I bought bags of top-quality "Number Ones" from Stahmann Farms to bring back to Nantucket for Dad and Mom, and he loved them. For a half-dozen Christmases afterwards, I had Stahmann Farms parcel-post him up a few bags. Around this time he had figured out a recipe for heating pecans in a black iron frying pan with butter and salt, which he stored in a plastic freezer container with a tight lid. They were wonderful, and, he said, it was the iron pan that made the difference. I told him it was not the pan, it was the pecans. It was always the same, good argument.

Later on, as his eyes grew weaker, even pecans got to be tough for him, and he switched seamlessly right over to peanuts. He loved the fancy Virginia peanuts—"they're the number ones," he'd say—and so he kept his larder stocked with them.

Mom loved chestnuts, which had found their way into her life when she spent a year in Rome and Siena. One of her great-uncles, a tall robust man with a white beard who wore capes, had been director of the American Academy of Rome, and he took her under his wing. He was a great gastronome, and she told us how they walked together through the streets of Rome and Siena, stopping here and there for a coffee for him and a juice for her, always with a sweet. In the fall it was roast chestnuts from street vendors, and she came to love them.

I remember vividly being in New York with Mom and Dad around Christmas, and for the first time smelling chestnuts roasting over the fires of street-corner carts, smells I'd never known before but that were somehow foreign and mysterious. Mom always bought a dozen, hot, some scorched, and wrapped in a newspaper cone. When they cooled a bit she peeled back the skin from where the vendor had made his "X" cuts, and broke the meat into pieces to share with us. "I learned about this in Rome and Siena," she told me. Street vendors still sell chestnuts in the winter in New York City, and I always stop to buy some. They smell and taste just as good now as they did fifty years ago, with Mom. And I have bought and roasted them at home, in the oven and over a roaring fire, but they do not taste as good as the ones in the streets of New York.

Walnuts are among the royalty in the crowded culinary kingdom of Perigord in the Dordogne, joining foie gras, truffles, Armagnac, confit, walnut oil, and Montbazillac wine in this royal court. To be there in the autumn, in the company of great producers of this royal larder, is the yeast of culinary daydreams.

While in this culinary kingdom we joined successful truffle hunts with unerring truffle-sniffing terriers; watched freshly peeled walnuts being stone-ground for their oil in a one-thousand-year-old water-powered mill; had one of those sybaritic four-hour, eight-course lunches in the Montbazilac castle with its proprietors; visited a dozen of the wineries that supplied King Henry IV and his wives, and provided Eleanor of Aquitaine's immense dowries; had a four-hour, five-course dinner with the mayor of Marmande at which every course featured fresh foie gras cooked in a different style; wandered the Marmande farms, which grow and ship to Paris the ne plus ultra tomatoes and strawberries sought out by the high-gastronome Parisians; visited the Lascaux cave in the company of its lead archaeologists; marveled and sampled at the autumn food festival in the streets of Periguex; and headquartered in a country chateau now operated as a fine country lodge.

The Chefs Nut Challenge

Nuts have a long history as key ingredients in Mediterranean cooking—from Spain to Turkey, from Italy to Morocco, from ancient times to the present—but most Americans still don't have a sense of nuts beyond beer nuts at bars.

We challenged forty chefs across the country and around the globe to develop a recipe, with an assigned nut and dish, for a Chefs Nut Challenge at the Oldways Tenth Anniversary Mediterranean Diet Conference (in Boston, in January 2003). We have chosen to reprint some of the mouthwatering recipes that use all kinds of tree nuts and peanuts in all kinds of sweet and savory ways (appetizers, salads, and main courses). Even though we can't include all, here is a sampling of the great imaginations and culinary skills of our wonderful friends—from soup to nuts (appetizers, salads, and main courses)!

ISLAND SKORDALIA (CAPER, ALMOND, AND WALNUT GARLIC DIP)

AGLAIA KREMEZI

This classic Greek dish is perfect as a spread, with mezes (small-dish appetizer), or as accompaniment to a fish or meat main course. 🖼

SERVES 6 TO 8

- I medium potato, peeled
- 2 cups cubed day-old whole-wheat bread, soaked in water until softened
- 3 to 5 garlic cloves, quartered
- $1/3$ cup extra virgin olive oil
- $1/4$ cup capers, preferably salt-packed, rinsed and drained
- 3 to 4 tablespoons freshly squeezed lemon juice
- $1/3$ cup blanched whole almonds, soaked overnight in water and drained
- $1/3$ cup shelled walnuts
- Freshly ground white pepper
- Sea salt (optional)

In a pot over high heat, cover the potato with water. Boil for 15 minutes, or until soft. Mash and set aside.

Squeeze the soaked bread to extract the excess water and place it in a food processor. Add the garlic and process into a smooth paste. With the motor running, add the oil, a little at a time. Add 3 tablespoons of the capers and 3 tablespoons of the lemon juice. Add the almonds and walnuts, and pulse a few times, until they are coarsely ground. Scrape the mixture into a medium bowl and fold in the potato. Season with white pepper. Taste and add salt, if needed (the capers are usually salty enough), and more pepper and/or lemon juice. Cover and refrigerate for at least 2 hours. Sprinkle the remaining 1 tablespoon capers over the skordalia before serving.

DUKKAH

CLAUDIA RODEN

Dukkah is a crumbly mixture of nuts, herbs, and seeds. Although its origin is Egyptian, we first encountered it in South Australia, at a riotous lunch hosted at St. Hallets winery. It was laid out in a dish in the middle of the table, and our Australian hosts instructed us to dip our bread into olive oil (also in a small dish on the table), and then into the dukkah. We've since served it at Oldways conferences and have given gifts of dukkah to our friends. You can use it as a dip, in cooking fish or chicken, or on salads or pasta dishes. The recipe we like best is from the renowned Mediterranean cookbook author Claudia Roden. 🖼

MAKES ALMOST 4 CUPS

- I cup sesame seeds
- $1^3/4$ cups coriander seeds
- $2/3$ cup blanched hazelnuts, skinned
- $1/2$ cup cumin seeds
- $1/2$ teaspoon sea salt
- $1/4$ teaspoon freshly ground black pepper

Preheat the oven to 350°F. Put each variety of seeds and nuts on a separate tray or a shallow oven dish and roast them all for 10 to 20 minutes, until they just begin to color and give off a slight aroma. As they take different times, you must keep an eye on them so that they do not become too brown, and take out each as it is ready. Alternatively, toast them in a large dry frying pan, stirring constantly.

Put the nuts and seeds together in the food processor with salt and pepper and grind them until they are finely crushed but not pulverized. Be careful not to over-blend, or the oil from the too-finely-ground seeds and nuts will form a paste. Dukkah should be a crushed dry mixture, not a paste. Taste and add salt if needed.

SPICED PECANS

STEVE JOHNSON

When Steve Johnson was chef of his Blue Room res-taurant in Cambridge, he used these nuts to make one of their most popular salads, which used Boston lettuce, cubes of Vermont cheddar cheese, dried cranberries, and a little thinly sliced red onion. He dressed the salad with a vinaigrette made with cider vinegar and a little fresh apple cider for sweetness.

This recipe for spiced pecans or other nuts can also be used to add spice to just about any nuts you like, and is wonderful for making your own home-made spiced mixed-nut combination for snacks with drinks.

MAKES 4 CUPS

2 tablespoons light or dark brown sugar
1 tablespoon sea salt
$^1/_2$ teaspoon sweet paprika
$^1/_2$ teaspoon chili powder
$^1/_4$ teaspoon ground red pepper
$^1/_2$ cup butter, melted
4 cups pecans, or any other nuts

Preheat the oven to 350°F. In a mixing bowl, blend the brown sugar, salt, paprika, chili powder, and red pepper. Pour in the melted butter and stir to mix. Add the nuts and toss to coat them evenly. Spread the seasoned nuts out on a baking sheet, and roast them for 15 minutes or so. Your nose will tell you when they are ready! Serve immediately, or let cool and store in a jar for later.

CRACKED GREEN OLIVE AND WALNUT SALAD

PAULA WOLFERT

Over the last fifteen years, Paula Wolfert has helped Oldways "crack the code" on many of the obscure in-gredients and dishes of the eastern Mediterranean. This accessibility to the region's spirited flavors and intense tastes has greatly enriched the under-standing of journalists, chefs, executives, and other Oldways friends about the region's great culinary traditions. This dish is delicious with a slice of mel-on or a brochette of grilled meat. Think Topkapi and caliphs!

SERVES 4

$7^1/_2$ to 8 ounces cracked green olives (preferably French Picholine or Greek Nafplion), rinsed, drained, and pitted
2 tablespoons extra virgin olive oil
$^3/_4$ cup walnuts, finely chopped by hand
2 scallions, white and tender green parts, minced
$^1/_4$ cup chopped fresh parsley
Pinch of Turkish or Aleppo red pepper
2 teaspoons pomegranate concentrate
1 tablespoon freshly squeezed lemon juice
Sea salt and freshly ground black pepper
$^1/_4$ cup fresh or defrosted pomegranate seeds

Combine all the ingredients in a mixing bowl; mix well. Cover and refrigerate overnight. Return to room temperature before serving. For best flavor, prepare the salad 1 to 2 days in advance.

AROMATIC SHRIMP SALAD WITH MANGO AND PEANUTS

CHRIS SCHLESINGER

This dish from Chris Schlesinger is inspired by his many trips to Southeast Asia and is a beautiful and healthy mix of seafood, fruit, and nuts. It embodies his signature boldness with intense flavors.

SERVES 4

- 1 pound large shrimp (12 to 16)
- 2 firm mangos, peeled and cut into medium dice
- 1 red bell pepper, cut into medium dice
- 1 cucumber, peeled, seeded, and cut into medium dice
- 1/4 cup fresh mint leaves
- 1/4 cup fresh cilantro leaves

DRESSING

- 3 tablespoons Asian fish sauce
- 3 tablespoons freshly squeezed lime juice
- 3 tablespoons soy sauce
- 3 tablespoons Asian sesame oil
- 3 tablespoons rice wine vinegar
- 2 tablespoons light or dark brown sugar
- 1 teaspoon ground coriander
- 1 teaspoon ground white pepper

GARNISH

- 1/4 cup roasted unsalted peanuts, minced
- 1/4 cup finely diced scallions, white and tender green parts
- 1 tablespoon minced fresh chiles
- 1 tablespoon minced fresh ginger

In a pan over medium-high heat, poach the shrimp for 4 to 5 minutes, until bright pink and firm. Drain and plunge into a bowl of ice water. Cool, peel, devein, and slice in half lengthwise.

In a large bowl, combine the poached shrimp with the mangos, red peppers, cucumbers, mint, and cilantro.

To make the dressing, combine the fish sauce, lime juice, soy sauce, sesame oil, vinegar, brown sugar, coriander, and white pepper. Whisk briefly. Pour the dressing over shrimp-mango mix. Toss gently.

To make the garnish, combine the peanuts, scallions, chiles, and ginger and toss briefly.

Divide the shrimp-mango mix among four plates and sprinkle the garnish mix over the top.

Nuts and Fruit

We have traveled to Liguria—the Italian Riviera—many times for Oldways activities. Food writer Fred Plotkin introduced us to it, and also to San Giorgio, a splendid restaurant in the small hilltop village of Cervo. We were there with him in the deep of winter, on a cold, windy, and overcast gray day. Tired and chilled at the end of the day, we drove up the steep hill for dinner with San Giorgio chef and owner Caterina, and as usual, her meal was exactly right. A hot chicken soup with mushrooms, braised beef with roast root vegetables, pureed squash, hot bread with fresh olive oil, and a green salad.

But it was the simple winter dessert we remember best, and one we duplicate every year at Christmastime. It was simple—a mix of at-perfect-ripeness clementines and peanuts in their shells arranged in a beautiful silver filigree candy dish. The artistry of fruit and peanuts was a beautiful addition to the table, and it is a clean, simple, elegant, and not-too-filling way to end any meal, even a special holiday meal. Of course in Italy we finished it with a glass of Moscato and a cup of espresso, but that's not hard to duplicate, even in New England!

CARROT, BEET, AND WATERCRESS SALAD WITH PECAN VINAIGRETTE

MICHAEL ROMANO

This aromatic salad has a double-barreled crunch—the vegetables and the nuts—and a wonderful balance of flavors, too.

SERVES 4

CRUNCHY SALAD

- 2 large carrots, peeled and cut into fine matchstick julienne (about I cup)
- I large beet, peeled and cut into matchstick julienne (about I cup)
- $1/2$ cup very thinly sliced red onion
- 6 cups watercress, large stems discarded

PECAN VINAIGRETTE

- $1/2$ cup pecans
- I tablespoon honey
- 2 tablespoons plus I teaspoon Dijon mustard
- I tablespoon plus I teaspoon sherry wine vinegar
- I teaspoon chopped shallot
- I teaspoon chopped fresh thyme leaves
- $1/4$ teaspoon kosher salt
- $1/8$ teaspoon freshly ground black pepper
- Pinch of ground red pepper
- I teaspoon plus $1/2$ cup grapeseed or vegetable oil
- I teaspoon mustard seeds

Preheat the oven to 350°F. Place the carrots, beet, and onion in a large bowl, cover with ice water, and let stand for 15 minutes. Drain well, and dry on a paper towel.

To make the vinaigrette, spread the pecans on a cookie sheet and roast until fragrant, about 10 minutes. Chop coarsely and allow them to cool.

Combine the honey, mustard, vinegar, shallot, thyme, salt, black pepper, and red pepper in a jar.

Heat 1 teaspoon of the oil in a small skillet over medium heat until very hot but not smoking. Remove the skillet from the heat, add the mustard seeds, and cover the pan. Shake the skillet, still off the heat, for 3 to 5 minutes, until the seeds sputter and darken somewhat. Add the seeds to the jar. Add the remaining $1/2$ cup oil and the toasted pecans and shake vigorously to combine.

Combine the julienned vegetables and watercress in a large bowl. Add the vinaigrette and toss. Serve immediately. The salad elements can be prepared in advance, kept separate, and combined just before serving.

PEANUT FIESTA VEGETABLE SALAD

KATHY McMANUS, RD

Straight from the kitchen of Brigham and Women's chief dietitian, this colorful and flavorful dish was also used in Kathy's and Dr. Frank Sacks's moderate-fat weight loss study (see page 103). It's a clear winner in terms of flavor and health.

SERVES 6 TO 8

- 2 large tomatoes, chopped
- I (15-ounce) can black beans, drained
- $1/2$ cup chopped red bell pepper
- $1/2$ cup chopped green bell pepper
- I cup corn kernels, fresh or canned
- $1/2$ cup chopped scallions, white and tender green parts
- $1/2$ cup thinly sliced carrot
- 2 tablespoons fresh cilantro
- $1/4$ cup extra virgin olive oil
- $1/8$ cup balsamic vinegar
- 2 tablespoons freshly squeezed lime juice
- I teaspoon ground cumin
- 3 cloves garlic, chopped
- I teaspoon chili powder
- $1/2$ cup unsalted peanuts

In a large bowl, combine the tomatoes, black beans, peppers, corn, scallions, carrots, and cilantro. Set aside.

In a small bowl, combine the olive oil, vinegar, lime juice, cumin, garlic, and $1/2$ teaspoon chili powder. Whisk thoroughly. Stir into the salad mixture and mix well. Refrigerate for 1 hour.

To serve, toss the peanuts with the remaining $1/2$ teaspoon chili powder and sprinkle the peanuts over the salad. Serve immediately.

SEARED SEA SCALLOPS WITH GARLIC AND BRAZIL NUTS

SAM HAYWARD

The menu at Sam Hayward's Fore Street restaurant in Portland features dishes with Maine-grown ingredients—seafood from Maine's cold waters and fruits and vegetables from its rocky soils. So we weren't surprised that he included local sea scallops in his recipe for the Chef's Nut Challenge!

SERVES 4

> 4 ounces whole raw Brazil nuts
>
> 6 cloves garlic, peeled
>
> 6 tablespoons grapeseed or safflower oil
>
> 6 tablespoons dry white wine
>
> 2 teaspoons natural cider vinegar
>
> $1^1/2$ pounds medium "dry" scallops, tough connective membrane removed (see Note)
>
> 1 cup loosely packed red orach leaves, washed and drained (spinach or another seasonal pot-herb may be substituted)
>
> $1/2$ teaspoon sea salt
>
> $1/8$ teaspoon freshly ground black pepper
>
> 2 tablespoons snipped fresh chives

Preheat the oven to 350°F. Spread the Brazil nuts on a baking sheet. Toast in the oven until aromatic and skins have darkened, about 8 minutes. Cool slightly, and rub off skins with a cloth towel. Dice the Brazil nuts into $1/4$-inch cubes, and set aside.

Combine the garlic cloves and oil in a nonreactive skillet. Over low flame, simmer the garlic in the oil for 5 minutes, or until light brown and very soft. Remove the pan from the heat. Remove the garlic with a slotted spoon, and crush to a paste by mashing with the side of a knife. Reserve the oil.

Bring the wine and cider vinegar to a boil in a nonreactive skillet. Boil until the volume is reduced by a third, and whisk in the mashed garlic. Remove from the heat.

Pat the scallops dry with a cloth towel. Season the scallops with sea salt and black pepper. Heat a nonreactive skillet over high heat, and add about 1 tablespoon of the reserved garlic cooking oil. Add the scallops, and sear on all sides until lightly browned, about 4 minutes. Add the red orach and the diced Brazil nuts, and toss to combine. When the scallops feel firm to the touch, add the wine-vinegar reduction, and up to 2 tablespoons of the garlic cooking oil. Toss well to combine. Season with the salt and pepper.

Divide among four dinner plates, generously sprinkling each with snipped fresh chives.

Note: Avoid chemically treated scallops. "Dry" indicates untreated scallops.

PEANUT-CRUSTED PORK LOIN

ED DOYLE

Chef Ed Doyle suggests serving this crunchy pork dish with mashed sweet potatoes and sautéed greens.

SERVES 4

  2-pound boneless pork loin, trimmed
  Sea salt and freshly ground black pepper
  3 tablespoons peanut oil
  1/2 cup molasses
  I egg yolk
  I tablespoon plus I teaspoon Pommery mustard
  2 teaspoons coarsely cracked black pepper
  1/2 pound peanuts, crushed
  I cup panko breadcrumbs (available in Asian markets)
  2 tablespoons chopped fresh cilantro
  I tablespoon diced shallots
  2 cups veal stock
  1/4 cup bourbon

Preheat the oven to 400°F. Season the pork loin liberally with salt and pepper. Heat 1 tablespoon of the peanut oil until very hot in a pan large enough to fit the pork loin. Sear pork, turning, for 5 to 10 minutes, until well browned on all sides. Set aside.

In a small bowl, combine the molasses, egg yolk, 1 tablespoon of the mustard, and cracked black pepper. Generously brush the mixture on the sides of the pork loin, leaving the ends plain. Put the crushed peanuts in a pie pan or plate. Mix the panko breadcrumbs and cilantro together in a separate pie pan or plate. Roll the pork first in the crushed peanuts and then in the panko mixture to coat. Place the pork loin on a roasting rack in a roasting pan.

Roast for 35 to 40 minutes, until the internal temperature registers 158°F on a meat thermometer.

Meanwhile, in a saucepan, heat the remaining 2 tablespoons peanut oil over medium heat. Add shallots and cook, stirring, for about 5 minutes, until translucent. Add the veal stock and remaining 1 teaspoon mustard. Cook to reduce by half. Add the bourbon and continue reducing to sauce consistency. Season to taste with salt and freshly ground black pepper.

To serve, slice the pork loin 1/4 inch thick. Drizzle the sauce over the pork and serve.

SWEET AND CRUNCHY HONEYED PEANUTS

THE PEANUT INSTITUTE

These roasted peanuts make a crunchy topping for ice cream or yogurt.

MAKES 1 1/2 CUPS

  1 1/2 cups water
  1/2 cup honey
  I cup sugar
  1 1/2 cups raw shelled peanuts
  I tablespoon peanut oil
  I tablespoon ground cinnamon

Preheat the oven to 350°F. In a saucepan, bring the water, honey, and sugar to a boil over high heat. Continue to boil until the volume is reduced by half. Remove from the heat. Add the peanuts and peanut oil.

Spread the peanuts in an even layer in a shallow baking pan and roast until the liquid is absorbed, approximately 40 minutes. Shake the pan occasionally to distribute the liquid. Once the liquid is absorbed, remove and toss the nuts with the cinnamon. Spread flat to cool. Store in a glass jar with a tight-fitting lid.

BASIC ROASTED PEANUTS

THE PEANUT INSTITUTE

MAKES 1 CUP

    1 cup raw shelled peanuts

Preheat the oven to 350°F. Spread the peanuts out in an even layer on a baking sheet and bake for about 20 minutes, until roasted. Let cool. Store in a glass jar with a tight-fitting lid.

Nuts and Peanuts for the Pantry

Here are tips for using nuts and peanuts and a few recipes to add a homemade touch to your kitchen pantry.

NUT FLOURS FOR COATING MEATS

For chicken, fish, or meat, mix equal parts seasoned breadcrumbs and finely chopped and toasted nuts (or even mixed nuts). For flavor and taste variations, try mixing different kinds of nuts, and/or adding herbs or spices that you like. Coat the chicken, fish, or meat with the mixture, and grill, bake, or broil. It sometimes helps if you press the coating with your fingertips or the heel of your hand, to make it cling more tightly.

SIMPLE HOMEMADE NUT OR PEANUT BUTTER

Place several handfuls of your favorite roasted nuts (almonds, walnuts, cashews, pistachios, pecans, hazelnuts, or others) or roasted peanuts in a food processor, blender, or juicer. Pulse and blend until creamy. Or, leave some chunks, if you prefer it chunky.

ROASTED PEANUTS

Roasted peanuts can pair up with just about any ingredient. Toss them on top of salads, cooked chicken or fish, barbecued meats, stews, in your favorite cookie recipe or . . . just place them in small bowls on a table and watch as they disappear.

ADDICTIVE SWEET-AND-HOT RUM-ROASTED PEANUTS

THE PEANUT INSTITUTE

Just as the name says, you can't eat enough of this sweet treat.

MAKES 1 CUP

    1 cup rum
    1/2 cup sugar
    2 tablespoons peanut oil
    1 tablespoon Worcestershire sauce
    1 tablespoon Tabasco sauce
    1 cup raw shelled peanuts
    2 teaspoons ground red pepper
    1 tablespoon ground cumin
    1 tablespoon ground ginger
    2 teaspoons sea salt
    2 teaspoons freshly ground black pepper

Preheat the oven to 350°F. Bring the rum to a boil in a small saucepan over medium heat. Add the sugar and continue to boil until the volume is reduced by half, stirring occasionally to dissolve sugar.

In a separate bowl, combine the oil, Worcestershire sauce, and Tabasco sauce. Add rum mixture and peanuts. Let stand for 8 to 10 minutes.

Spread the peanuts in an even layer in a shallow baking pan and roast until the liquid is absorbed, about 45 minutes. Give the pan an occasional shake to distribute the liquid.

Combine the red pepper, cumin, ginger, salt, and black pepper in a large bowl. When the peanuts are done, add to the bowl and toss to evenly coat. Lay flat to cool. Store in an airtight container.

"Quality originates at the source—with the people who work
the land and the pride they take in the yield."

—ALLISON HOOPER

"Until recently, and before the Oldways era, the value of olive oil
was mostly appreciated in the countries where it is produced, the
countries of the Mediterranean basin. We believed in it
and we honored it in our mythology and our traditions. There is
now considerable evidence that olive oil is beneficial to health
with respect to cardiovascular diseases, some forms of
cancer, and perhaps even osteoporosis."

—ANTONIA TRICHOPOULOU, MD

OLIVE OIL, BUTTER, AND OTHER FATS

Olive trees (*Olea europeaea sativa*) are cultivated on every continent except Antarctica, but 90 percent of the world's olive oil is produced in countries with a Mediterranean coastline. Olives are the fruit of these trees, and each fruit contains a single large seed, or "pit."

Olive Oil
K. DUN GIFFORD

Trees produce ripe olives each year, in the late fall and early winter months.

In many ways, olives are like apples. Both grow on trees, are pollinated by the wind and by insects, have many varieties, have many culinary uses, are eaten whole but for the seeds (pits or pips), are integral to a great many recipes and dishes, have spread all over the world from their origins, and are squeezed to make a juice (or oil). We do not eat olives straight from the tree, however, as we can with apples; olives must first be cured.

There are many different kinds of olives, with varying tastes and flavors, different grades and prices, and different processing methods. They grow equally well in elegant Tuscany, on vast Tunisian sand dunes, in windy Puglia, on broiling Andalusian rolling hillsides, in the vast reaches of western Australia, on hundreds of Greek islands, on stony Turkish mountains, in the dry hardscrabble of the Middle East, and in broad swaths of California. China is in the midst of planting 10 million olive trees, and the Thai royal family is planting olive plantations in that country's northern highlands.

Olives are harvested at different phases of ripeness. The less ripe olives are still green when picked, and the oil from these olives has a greenish cast. The riper olives are black when picked, and their oil has a yellowish cast. In either case, the harvested olives are crushed into a mash, and then pressed under heavy pressure so that the oil runs out of the mash and can be bottled and stored.

There is a difference between olive oil and olive pomace oil. Olive oil must be "natural," that is, not treated with solvents for extraction or purifying purposes. Olive pomace oil may be produced by using solvents, and it has no primary culinary uses. Olive pomace oil may not be called "olive oil."

Olive oil is, consequently, the category of our concern. It falls into three classes in descending order of quality: virgin olive oil, refined virgin olive oil, and olive oil. Of these three classes we are most concerned with the first, because it includes extra virgin olive oil and virgin olive oil, the highest-quality oils.

Two factors of quality determine whether or not an olive oil can be termed extra virgin or virgin: (1) a technical measurement of its levels of oleic fatty acids, and (2) an organoleptic assessment of its flavors (taste and smell).

Oleic acid is the principal monounsaturated fat in olive oil, and quality declines as oleic acid levels rise; lower is better. Technical assessment requires that for olive oil to be extra virgin, its oleic acids must measure 1 percent or less. To be a virgin oil, its oleic acids must measure 2 percent or less.

Organoleptic assessments are by definition personal judgments, and one person's great-tasting oil may be another's poor-tasting oil. As a result of the economic importance of determining which oils can be designated extra virgin (and priced expensively), the International Olive Oil Council has made great efforts to harmonize the range of sensory evaluations by establishing a kind of codex of standardized terminology and has organized training sessions for professional tasters.

Further along on the quality scale is olive oil, the term used for a blend of virgin olive oil and refined olive oil, so long as the refining process for the latter does not alter the structure of the glycerides in the fatty acids. Olive oil may be sold with the terms "pure" and "100% pure" on the labels of bottles and cans, but they cannot be used as modifiers for the words olive oil.

Olives are "squeezed" to give up their oil, either literally under great stone wheels and pressure mats, or in maceration tanks (which shred the olives) and centrifuges (which separate the oil and water squeezed from the olive). Heating is permitted at low levels for virgin olive oils to help release the oils from the macerated olives, so long as the heating does not alter the oils' structure.

"Cold-pressed" means that the olives gave up their oil and water without heat (or with very low heat.)

Extra virgin olive oils made from the same olive variety have distinctly different flavors, just as wines made from the same grape variety often have very different flavors. Among the well-known flavor and taste variations among extra virgin olive oils are the "peppery" oils from Tuscany, the "rounder and milder" oils from Puglia, the "sweet" oils from Liguria, the "robust" oils from Turkey and Greece, the "flowery" oils from Provence, and the "nuttier" oils from southern Spain. No one flavor is "better" than any other; like wines, it's all about personal preference.

Olive oil has been the principal dietary fat of Mediterranean peoples for millennia. In the last fifty years, epidemiological studies have revealed that Mediterranean people had healthier heart disease profiles than did populations with animal fats as their principal dietary fat. Clinical and metabolic studies are now determining the underlying scientific reasons for these differences.

Since olive trees are members of the plant kingdom, and their olives are fruits, olive oils contribute to the healthfulness of Mediterranean-type diets for two distinct reasons. The first, their fatty acid profile, which is monounsaturated, and the second, their numerous health-promoting micronutrients, such as phytonutrients and antioxidants, are the reasons olive oil contributes to the healthfulness of the Mediterranean diet.

Olive oil tastings are sometimes strange and even intimidating events. Professional tasters first look at the color of an oil, and then sniff it carefully. Then they take a small taste, and suddenly and sharply draw in a small breath or two or three, making a sharp noisy slurping sound, sometimes sounding like a gargle. It is always startling to watch them do this; it seems such a non-food and, frankly, silly way of going about it.

Professional wine tasters and cheese tasters carefully look, sniff, and taste; they do not slurp. Chefs who test their sauces and dishes also look, sniff, and taste, but do not slurp either. Perfume testers look and sniff; but obviously do not taste.

So my advice is (a) do not be intimidated by olive oil slurpers, and (b) do not slurp yourself. Look, sniff, and taste, as you would with the food itself. After all, you'd probably not invite back to your dinner table a guest who slurped a salad or soup dressed with one of your favorite peppery Tuscan olive oils, would you?

The Value of Olive Oil: Tradition and Health

ANTONIA TRICHOPOULOU, MD

With the Mediterranean diet, no one has been more passionate about olive oil and its importance in a healthy diet than Antonia Trichopoulou, a medical doctor and nutrition scientist at the University of Athens Medical School in Greece. As a scientist and as a Greek, she has a deeply passionate view about the real value of olive oil.

Until recently, and before the Oldways era, the value of olive oil was mostly appreciated in the countries where it is produced, the countries of the Mediterranean basin. We believed in it, and we honored it in our mythology and our traditions. There is now considerable evidence that olive oil is beneficial to health with respect to cardiovascular diseases, some forms of cancer, and perhaps even osteoporosis.

Over and beyond its intrinsic value, olive oil represents a vehicle (or delivery system) for high consumption of vegetables and legumes, plant foods that form the core of any healthy diet around the world.

Olive oil contains plenty of oleic acid, a lipid that in most studies has been found to be either beneficial or at least not detrimental with respect to health. It contains linolenic acid, which is now worshiped by many cardiologists. It can provide energy without imposing glycemic load. Not least, it can enrich foods with taste.

Interest is also now being focused on the microcomponents of olive oil. Their significance to health could be great. For the time being, the antioxidating activity of some of them has been studied, but research on this field is intensified and extended.

Be sure to look for extra virgin olive oil or virgin olive oil, which are produced without being submitted to high temperatures and have the highest concentration of potentially beneficial microcomponents.

On Choosing Olive Oil

ARI WEINZWEIG

Ann Arbor, Michigan, has been known for years as a great place to go to college and a great place to live. More recently, though, one of its claims to fame is that it's the home (and only home) of Zingerman's. Zingerman's delicatessen was started in the 1980s by a trio of college friends as a place to get great sandwiches. Twenty-some years later, Zingerman's is one of America's premier sources of high-quality ingredients from all over the world. It is also known as the Coolest Place to Work in America (so says Inc. magazine), and a company that chose to be great instead of big (so says Bo Burlingham's 2006 book, Small Giants). Ari Weinzweig, one of the co-founders of Zingerman's, has spoken at a number of Oldways symposiums, giving sensible, full-of-information talks about olive oil, cheese, and many other wonderful ingredients he's traveled around the world to learn about. He's an expert we count on, and we asked him to offer advice on choosing olive oils.

To choose an olive oil . . .

The first thing I'd think about is what I was going to do with the oil. For everyday frying or that sort of thing, I'd use an oil that's produced in larger quantity, blended from the olives of various farms. These oils usually lack complexity, but they're perfectly fine for dishes where the flavor of the oil will be of only minimal import, and they're certainly more affordable.

For more interesting dishes where I really want the flavor of the oil to be prominent in the finished food, I always seek out the most flavorful oils I can find. And I always work to match the flavor of the oil with that of the dish overall—lighter oils for fish; modestly fruity oils for more delicate lettuces and vegetables; peppery, green oils for mozzarella (where the oil is actually the highlight), meat, and spicier dishes. This is no different than pairing wines to foods to make a good match.

The key is understanding that different oils are appropriate for different dishes, and to that end I always have three or four different oils on hand at home so that I am ready for almost any sort of cooking I might do. I really encourage everyone to taste and compare oils for themselves so they can find the ones they like best.

Here are a few really important lessons I've learned about choosing and using great olive oil.

FLAVOR COMES FIRST

While in the United States we usually think of oil or fat as being something that is used in small quantities as a medium for frying or sautéing or dressing salads, in the Mediterranean the flavor of olive oil is an integral part of the flavor of the finished dish. I've learned not to dismiss olive oil as a sidelight but rather to view it as one of the featured flavors of what I'm cooking.

BETTER-TASTING OIL IS WORTH THE MONEY

With that in mind I've learned that you can never compensate for lack of complexity and character in a lower-end oil simply by using more of it. (It's akin to eating five regular chocolate bars rather than enjoying one really well-made varietal chocolate. Volume just doesn't replace flavor.) So I really work to use the best oils I can—you really can taste the difference.

THE MORE THE BETTER

Discovering these first two points has led me to a third discovery, courtesy of some of the great cooks I've met from the Mediterranean who taught me the importance of using good quantities of good olive oil. This runs counter to our American tendency to use fat and anything costly (like good olive oil) as sparingly as possible. My Mediterranean role models taught me to do the opposite—really pour on the olive oil so that its great flavor will enhance the flavor of the finished food.

EVERY REGION IS DIFFERENT

Like wine, every producing region (and actually every producer within each region) makes oil with a distinctive character. With that in mind I like to have a wide array of oils in my kitchen so that I can prepare all sorts of dishes and have the right flavor for each. At home I usually have a lot of olive oils on hand. At the least, though, I like to have a lighter oil from the Italian Riviera, a couple of really green, peppery oils either from Tuscany itself or made in the Tuscan style in one of the New World regions like California or New Zealand, a buttery oil from Provence, and maybe an interesting, modestly fruity oil made from Arbequina olives in Catalonia. Of course that's only a few of the many great oils that are out there—I encourage everyone who loves to cook to taste and compare and choose for themselves.

SIMPLE DISHES MAKE GREAT SHOW-CASES FOR OLIVE OIL

There are few better ways to eat than to simply enjoy a slice of toasted country bread topped with great olive oil and a little sea salt. It's a great showcase for a really great oil because the warmth of the bread brings out the aroma and flavor of the oil. Similarly, fine olive oil drizzled over simple broiled fish, just-cooked pasta, a great steak, or steamed new potatoes is a wonderful way to eat and to enjoy the rich complexity of the oil.

How (and Why) to Cook with Olive Oil

NANCY HARMON JENKINS

Nancy Harmon Jenkins is especially qualified to talk about olive oil. She lived in the Mediterranean while her children were growing up (Italy and Lebanon); she's traveled all over the Mediterranean; she worked closely with Dun during the founding of Oldways; and she wrote the very first cookbook with the Mediterranean diet pyramid in it (not surprisingly called The Mediterranean Diet Cookbook*).*

I sometimes hear American chefs claim that "You can't cook with extra virgin olive oil." Especially, they say, you can't fry with extra virgin olive oil. "Why?" I asked one notable Californian, who promptly replied, "The smoke point, of course—it's too low."

I don't know where he got his information but his confidence was misplaced, as thousands of cooks all over the Mediterranean world know well. From the most haute of haute cuisine restaurants to the humblest farmhouse kitchen, Mediterranean cooks happily use olive oil for all their cooking needs, from braising to roasting to deep-fat frying, and wouldn't dream of using anything else. Most of that oil is extra virgin simply because extra virgin olive oil was—and is—the only kind most Mediterranean cooks know.

The smoke point of any cooking fat, from butter to lard and including all the many different kinds of vegetable oils, is the point at which wisps of smoke start to rise from the pan, indicating the fat is beginning to degrade into undesirable, most probably carcinogenic, chemical compounds. If, like me, you have ever absent-mindedly left a pan on the fire by mistake, you will know that point well. (Incidentally, the next time this happens, don't even think about rescuing the smoking fat. Throw it out and start afresh. Burned fat of any kind has nothing to contribute to the flavor of a dish nor to the healthfulness of your diet.)

So what's the story with olive oil? In fact, because olive oils vary enormously in quality, depending on when the olives were harvested, how they were processed, and how they have been stored since processing, their smoke points also vary. But most commercially available extra virgin olive oils have smoke points in the range of 350 to 375°F, a perfect temperature for deep-fat frying, the highest-temperature cooking there is.

Of course, it would be folly indeed to use a fine, fresh, estate-bottled extra virgin, full of rich and complex flavors, in cooking, just as it makes no sense to use a bottle of Romanee Conti in your boeuf bourguignon. The very process of heating the oil drives off much of the intensity that makes it so precious—and so expensive. Save that kind of oil for dressing salads or drizzling over steamed fresh vegetables or baked potatoes (nothing finer!). But there are plenty of less expensive but still very good extra virgin olive oils, many from Greece or Spain, available in U.S. markets, and these should be your choice for all-around everyday cooking, whether braising, sautéing, or deep-fat frying.

> "The very process of heating the oil drives off much of the intensity that makes it so precious—and so expensive. Save that kind of oil for dressing salads or drizzling over steamed fresh vegetables or baked potatoes (nothing finer!)."
>
> —NANCY HARMON JENKINS

Better Butter

K. DUN GIFFORD AND SARA BAER-SINNOTT

Since so much of our early Oldways work was centered on the Mediterranean diet and its wonderful olive oils, many people (Julia Child included, at least for a while) thought we were dead set against butter. This was a bum rap and far from the truth; butter is beautiful, and we celebrate it.

As with eating most wonderful rich foods and dishes, there's much common sense behind the saying, "Forbidden fruits are the sweetest." Good butter is luscious and sweet, but there is no need either to forbid or demonize it.

What matters is understanding our foods and drinks, learning the skills of managing them wisely, and enjoying the ones we love. We need to understand that human bodies thrive in moderation and react badly to excess (hangovers being a vivid example).

Saturated fat is one of these things we need to understand and manage because it contributes the great tastes and textures to some favorite foods—butter and cheese, red and white meats, and some vegetable oils.

It's hard to imagine sitting down to breakfast in Paris without wonderful fresh French country butter and lush blackberry jam on a warm baguette. It's just as hard to think about passing up that BBQ burger, juicy steak house sirloin, ballpark hot dog, grilled cheese sandwich, holiday ham, Thanksgiving turkey or roast beef, smoked salmon, milk in the morning coffee, buttery Christmas cookies, and so on.

Close your eyes and try to remember the taste of butter melting on a hot-from-the-broiler English muffin or slice of toast or warm muffin; feel a buttery cookie melting on your tongue; picture a pat of butter slowing melting on a sizzling Delmonico steak, or on that stack of Sunday morning pancakes.

Butter is wonderful, and when you have some of Allison Hooper's, or some of other artisan creamery experts, you will know exactly why the butter banners are doomed to failure.

We met Allison through the Cheese of Choice Coalition, our campaign to prevent the government from banning unpasteurized milk cheeses in the absence of any scientific reason to do so.

We'd heard lots about Allison and her company, Vermont Butter & Cheese (it's based near Montpelier, only a few hours' drive from our office in Boston), and we'd tasted its superb products and listened to our chef friends rave about them. In our meetings about the Cheese of Choice Coalition we learned that we and Allison shared a passion about milk and great traditional foods made from it, staples for humans down through the eons of our evolution. And we think her story is a perfect pathway to talk about butter.

Allison went to France as an American college student in the late 1970s. Even though she had no farm experience, she wrote to organic farmers, offering her services for free room and board. A family in Brittany answered her letter, inviting her to join them on their farm and at their table. Allison was soon enjoying not only the satisfactions of working the land, but getting a full-fledged education in the European tradition of artisanal cheesemaking. ▨

Vermont Butter & Cheese was born when Allison met Bob Reese, a marketing director of the Vermont Department of Agriculture, in the early 1980s. He was organizing a special state dinner and the French chef he was working with wanted some American goat cheese. He called Allison, who was working as a state dairy lab technician. He knew she'd spent some time in France, and he convinced her to make some chèvre. Allison's chèvre was the buzz of the banquet, and by the time the tables were cleared, she and Bob were planning a cheesemaking partnership.

They launched the Vermont Butter & Cheese Company in 1984, and it still follows the path Bob and Allison took years ago. They developed a network of more than twenty family farms to provide them milk, from which they craft European-style artisan dairy products in the European manner at their creamery in Websterville.

They have earned worldwide recognition for the high quality of their products and the high standards of purity. The company is proudest of its contribution to the health of local agriculture. As Allison reminds her suppliers, workers, and customers, she learned her craft on a family farm in France, where the tradition insists that "quality originates at the source—with the people who work the land and the pride they take in the yield."

While working on the Brittany farm, Allison took careful note of the care with which the milk was handled. After each milking, she and the other farmhands separated out the cream and set it aside. Natural lactic bacteria then took over, ripening it into cultured cream, or crème fraîche. When the thick result was churned into butter, Allison knew she'd had a life-changing insight.

Inspired by it, Allison and Bob launched their creamery, and now culture the freshest Vermont cream and churn it to a European-style cultured butter. Higher in butterfat than standard U.S. butter, Vermont Cultured Butter is just plain exquisite—rich, silky, and sweet, with a wonderful mouth feel. They have a range of other wonderful creamery products, too, all based on traditions of fine raw materials, carefully crafted.

VERMONT BUTTER COOKIES

ALLISON HOOPER

Make a double batch of this recipe and enjoy a second batch later; the dough can be refrigerated for up to a week if wrapped tightly. The sea salt in the butter is a very nice touch; there's no iodine to mask the vanilla.

MAKES 3 DOZEN COOKIES

> 6 ounces Vermont Cultured Butter with Sea Salt Crystals, softened
> 1⅓ cups sugar, plus additional for topping
> 3 large egg yolks
> 1 teaspoon vanilla extract
> 1 teaspoon baking soda
> 1⅔ cups unbleached all-purpose flour

Cream together the butter and sugar until incorporated. Add the egg yolks and vanilla. Slowly add the baking soda and flour and mix just until the dough comes together.

Lightly flour a sheet of waxed paper or parchment. Place the dough on the paper and roll lightly to form a long cylinder shape about 2 inches in diameter. Wrap the paper around the dough and refrigerate for at least 2 hours.

Preheat the oven to 350°F. Slice the dough into 1/4-inch slices and place on an ungreased sheet pan. Sprinkle with sugar and bake for 8 to 10 minutes until still pale but light brown around the edges. Transfer to a wire rack to cool.

ALMOND AND BASIL PESTO FROM TRAPANI (*PESTO TRAPANESE*)

CAROL FIELD

Carol Field has written award-winning books about bread baking, Italian celebrations, and Italian food, and she's traveled all over Italy—exploring, tasting, and talking with Italy's great cooks (including the special nonas, the Italian grandmothers she featured in one of her books). She and her architect husband live in their north Tuscan house, close to Liguria (the "home" of pesto), several months a year. Carol's recipe for pesto is part Ligurian, part Sicilian, and a recipe that any nona would be proud of.

SERVES 6

> ¾ cup blanched almonds
> 1 teaspoon sea salt
> 6 large cloves garlic, roughly chopped
> 1 cup or 50 fresh basil leaves
> 5 sprigs flat-leaf parsley
> ⅛ teaspoon crushed red pepper flakes
> 6 small (1½ pounds) fresh tomatoes, peeled, seeded, and roughly chopped
> ½ cup extra virgin olive oil
> 1½ tablespoons coarse sea salt
> 1¼ pounds spaghetti
> Freshly grated Parmigiano-Reggiano or pecorino, for topping

If you are making the pesto in a food processor, combine the almonds and salt and grind together until they are so fine they are almost a flour. Add the garlic, basil, parsley, red pepper flakes, tomatoes, and olive oil. Process until you have a creamy sauce.

Bring a large pot with at least 5 quarts of water to a rolling boil, add the sea salt and the pasta and cook until al dente. Drain and toss with the pesto on a warmed serving platter. Serve immediately with grated cheese.

OLEANA TAPENADE

ANA SORTUN

Chef Ana Sortun credits her travels abroad as a major influence in her cooking. She apprenticed in Barcelona and worked in top kitchens in Turkey, Italy, and France. She serves this tapenade at her award-winning restaurant, Oleana, in Cambridge, Massachusetts. Serve it with crackers, pita bread, or bread sticks.

MAKES 1 CUP

1 cup pitted dry-cured black olives
2 cloves garlic, chopped
2 tablespoons capers, rinsed
2 anchovies, rinsed
2 teaspoons brandy or cognac
2 teaspoons freshly squeezed lemon juice
1/2 cup extra virgin olive oil
1 tablespoon chopped fresh parsley

Blend all ingredients coarsely in a food processor with a steel blade. Serve immediately or set aside for serving later.

"From the most haute of haute cuisine restaurants to the humblest farmhouse kitchen, Mediterranean cooks happily use olive oil for all their cooking needs, from braising to roasting to deep-fat frying, and wouldn't dream of using anything else."

—NANCY HARMON JENKINS

LEMON AND OLIVE OIL SALAD DRESSING

FAUSTO LUCHETTI

Freshly squeezed lemon juice is a perfect companion with olive oil, and together they are a wonderfully light and clean addition to any kind of salad. We learned this in Madrid, at lunches and dinners with Olive Oil Council Executive Director Fausto Luchetti and his wife, Mar; many of these meals were at Madrid's El Olivo Restaurant, a cathedral of Mediterranean olive oils.

MAKES 1 CUP

1 tablespoon sea salt
3 cloves garlic, minced
1/2 cup freshly squeezed lemon juice
1/2 cup best-quality extra virgin olive oil
Finely grated zest of 1 lemon

Mix together salt and minced garlic. Mix together lemon juice and olive oil.

Add the salt and garlic mixture to the lemon juice and olive oil in a tightly closed container. Shake and serve as a clean, fresh salad dressing. Sprinkle the zest on top of the salad just before serving.

NEW HAMPSHIRE AUTUMN ZUCCHINI BREAD

SARA BAER-SINNOTT

Each fall in New England it seems that there are zucchinis everywhere. It's impossible to escape a visit from friends and family without several giant zucchinis in tow. Here's one healthy and delicious way to put those giant zucchinis to use—a bread that's also made with healthy monounsaturated oil. You'll find this quick bread is perfect for breakfast, lunch, snacks, and even on the harvest dinner table. 🖏

MAKES 2 LOAVES

> I cup light olive oil or canola oil
> 3 medium zucchinis, grated
> I cup sugar, plus additional for topping
> I teaspoon vanilla extract
> 2 large eggs
> 2 cups unbleached white whole-wheat flour
> 1/4 teaspoon baking powder
> 2 teaspoons baking soda
> 2 teaspoons ground cinnamon
> 1/2 teaspoon freshly grated nutmeg

Preheat the oven to 350°F. Grease two 8 by 4-inch bread pans.

Mix together the oil, grated zucchini, 1 cup sugar, vanilla, and eggs until creamy. In a separate bowl, mix together the flour, baking powder, baking soda, cinnamon, and nutmeg. Slowly add the dry ingredients to the wet, creamy mixture. Divide the batter between the two bread pans.

Bake for 30 minutes, sprinkle each loaf with 1 tablespoon sugar. Bake for another 30 minutes, until the top is browned. Cool in pans for 10 minutes, then turn out onto wire racks to finish cooling.

GINGERBREAD

ELISABETH LUARD

A slice of gingerbread spread with sweet butter, a dram of whiskey in a cup of hot milky tea to wash it down—nothing better on a wet afternoon. For sun-starved northerners, ginger, the warmest of spices, delivers the taste of summer in the long dark winters. Traditionally used in baking in powdered form and unavailable fresh until recent years, it's the diagnostic ingredient in a Scottish gingerbread, a deliciously chewy, sticky cake eaten sliced and spread with butter for tea. 🖏

MAKES I CAKE

> 3 1/4 cups unbleached flour
> I tablespoon ground ginger
> I teaspoon ground allspice
> Pinch of sea salt
> Pinch of freshly ground black pepper
> I cup butter
> I cup light or dark brown sugar
> I cup black treacle or molasses
> I cup golden corn syrup
> 2 medium eggs
> 5 tablespoons Greek or whole-milk yogurt
> Splash milk

Preheat the oven to 325°F. Line an 8 by 4-inch loaf pan with wax or parchment paper.

Sift the flour with the ginger, allspice, salt, and pepper.

Melt the butter in a small saucepan over low heat with the brown sugar, treacle, and corn syrup. Mix well and leave to cool.

Mix the eggs with the yogurt in a small bowl.

Mix the butter mixture and egg mixture into the dry ingredients, stirring in enough milk to make a soft batter that drops easily from the spoon. Spread in the prepared loaf pan.

Bake for 1¼ hours, until the gingerbread is glossy and firm. You may need to cover it after the first hour, so it doesn't blacken. It doesn't matter if it sinks a little—it'll be nice and sticky. Turn it out onto a plate when it has cooled a little.

Butter-Centric?

In the mid-1980s, after an American Institute of Wine and Food conference in Santa Barbara, Richard and Thekla Sanford organized a pig roast on their ranch high in the Santa Barbara hills above the vineyards at their Sanford Winery.

This particular conference is fondly remembered by foodies for its "food fight" between Julia Child and Jane Brody of the *New York Times*. Julia took the position that nutritionists were ruining people's appreciation of good foods, and Jane took the position that gastronomes were encouraging people to eat too much rich and fatty food. Now both of these women were smart and quick-witted, brooked no nonsense, and knew their stuff. Julia scolded Jane for her "negativism," and Jane scolded Julia for being "butter-centric." Neither one gave the other an inch, and so it was just terrific theater because everyone in the audience knew they were both right. Everyone also ate the roast pig!

CHEZ HENRI'S CHIPOTLE AIOLI

PAUL O'CONNELL

Aioli is a great garnish for cold and hot soups, and a lively sauce for cold vegetables, eggs, and meats. It is traditionally served on cold poached fish. Paul O'Connell has provided a tangy version with cilantro, chipotles, and onion, but the basic recipe is a great plain aioli without them.

MAKES ABOUT 2 CUPS

1 egg
2 egg yolks
2 crushed garlic cloves
1 tablespoon mustard
¼ cup lemon juice
½ cup extra virgin olive oil
½ cup canola oil
½ bunch cilantro, finely chopped (optional)
1 small can chipotle chiles (optional)
1 red onion, finely chopped (optional)

In a food processor or blender, combine the egg, egg yolks, garlic, mustard, and lemon juice. Process until smooth. With the machine still running, add the olive oil and canola oil in a slow stream and blend until the mixture emulsifies to the consistency of mayonnaise. Add the cilantro and chiles and blend until smooth. For a chunky version, stir in the chopped onion.

"There really is no other foodstuff as perfect as cheese, neither fruits nor vegetables, meat nor seafood, beans nor grains, breads nor pastries. Not one of these foods comes close to cheese's perfection in terms of its intensity and nuance of flavor and fragrance, its remarkable gamut of textures, its ambassadorial regional specificity."

—STEVE JENKINS

"Cheese is a health-promoting safe food."

—CATHERINE DONNELLEY, PhD

CHEESE AND YOGURT

Cheese is preserved milk, and it is one of the first foods that early humans learned to make by transforming a "natural food" (milk) into a "preserved food" (cheese).

To transform their milk into cheese, cheesemakers ferment the milk to curdle it, and then separate the curds (cheese) from the whey (water). The curds are then formed in squares, rounds, loafs, or cakes. These cheeses are then cured, ripened, and/or flavored.

What Is Cheese, and How Is It Made?
K. DUN GIFFORD

All cheeses—be they artisan, farmstead, or processed industrial—are made in this time-honored way.

The discovery of cheesemaking was a magic accident of evolution. It meant that the valuable proteins and fats in the fresh, sweet milks of spring and summer could be saved for the harsh months of the winter, when they were sorely needed.

Archaeologists place the birth of cheese at about ten thousand years ago, with hard evidence dating to seven thousand years ago in the cradle of Western civilization, the Tigris and Euphrates Crescent. Much later, Egyptian, Greek, and Roman civilizations relied on the nourishment in cheese, honoring it in religious ceremonies, festivals, and the arts.

This ancient lineage is revealed in modern languages. For example, our word "cheese" has its root in the Latin word *caseus,* as does the German *kase,* Spanish *queso,* and Portuguese *queijo.* The French *fromage* and Italian *formaggio* find their root in the Greek word *formos.*

Cheeses were handmade from the milk of cows, sheep, goats, camels, horses, reindeer, yaks, caribou, water buffaloes, and other lactating animals. They were made by nomads, by herders, by farm families, and by residents of large noble and monastic estates. The milk was fresh—it had to be fresh—and the cheesemakers knew the source of their cheese milk.

"Farmstead" is the ancient word used to describe these cheeses, and recently another word—artisan—is also used, because they are handmade and not factory-made. These are the cheeses early humans ate through the millennia, and those who survived to become our ancestors gave us their genes and DNA, which welcomed our eating these cheeses.

The Industrial Revolution changed this equation forever, introducing homogenization, pasteurization, refrigeration, and freeze-drying to cheesemaking. These industrial processes offered entirely new ways to pre-

Cheesemaking: From Beginning to End

Fresh milk is brought to a cheesemaking place, tested for safety and quality, and cooled until the cheesemaker is ready.

Then, the milk is slowly heated to 85 to 92°F, and a bacterial "starter culture" is stirred in, triggering the first step in the transformation. For some cheeses, only one bacterial culture is added (cheddar, for example), while a second is added later for other cheeses (Gorgonzola, for example). These bacteria feed on the milk sugar (lactose), producing carbon dioxide and lactic acid. At this point, the milk has "soured" or "curdled," and if the whey is drained off, you have buttermilk or yogurt.

After the culture has been in the milk for about an hour, the cheesemaker stirs in rennet to accelerate the coagulation of the curds. Rennet contains rennin, an enzyme in the stomachs of young grass-fed animals that helps them digest their mother's milk.

Coagulation proceeds steadily over the next hour until the curd has "set" into a solid warm mass with the consistency of custard or cup yogurt. If the cheesemaker wants a soft cheese (such as Camembert or Brie), the curd is ladled into perforated molds, where the whey drains out. If the cheesemaker wants a hard cheese (such as cheddar or Parmigiano-Reggiano), the curd is heated for forty-five minutes and then drained.

This cheese is then shaped—cut into blocks, packed into molds for rectangles, squares, rounds, or large wheels, or rolled into balls or logs.

Salting, the next important step, plays many roles. It draws out even more water (whey), acts as a preservative, adds flavor and taste, inactivates enzymes, and deactivates any harmful bacteria. Salt is usually applied to the surface of cheese, but it is added to the curd for some few cheeses, notably cheddar.

The cheese is now ready to eat as a fresh cheese, or to be stored in an aging room, cellar, or "cave," where it gradually ripens and matures to be eaten in a week or a year or even longer.

The majesty of artisan cheeses—many of them revered for centuries—lies in the quality of the milk, the skills of the cheesemaker, and the fact that ripening cheeses remain living, breathing organisms as they ripen.

serve the nutritional values of milk. For example, in 1902, James Kraft invited "processed cheese food," which stays "fresh" for months either in the refrigerator or in a cardboard container on a kitchen shelf.

The industrial "process" for making processed cheese is first to make cheese in vast vats in factories. This cheese is then melted and a variety of additives are mixed with it: water, flavorings, coloring, fats, and preservatives. The mixture is then again made into cheese, and packaged in slices, shreds, wedges, rounds, and blocks or dried and crumbled for "shaker applications."

More than 95 percent of the cheese eaten in America is processed cheese.

Milk, the mother of cheese, is 15 percent solids and 85 percent water. Hard cheese is about 30 percent water, and a soft cheese is about 60 percent water. Milk and cheese have virtually identical nutrients, but those in cheese are more concentrated because cheese contains less water than milk.

A chunk of cheese about the size of two large eggs has one-third of the daily nutrients needed by an adult. Cheese is about 22 percent fat, unless it is made from skim milk. If it is a skim milk cheese, its fat content can vary from around 22 percent to zero.

> "Managing land, animals, cheese-
>
> making, and marketing is more than
>
> a job—it's a life."
>
> —JUDY SCHAD

Mozzarella di Bufala, the Traditional Way: Cheese at Vannulo's

EDUARDO NAPOLITANO

In 2002 Oldways organized an international symposium in Salerno—a province in the region of Campania, south of Naples, with landscapes as varied as the Amalfi coast, the plains of Paestum, inland mountains, and rocky coastline. Our travels throughout Salerno were helped by many, but especially Eduardo Napolitano, a young biochemist by training, but by passion a champion of entrepreneurial artisan food makers. Eduardo introduced us to several farmers and cheesemakers, including Vannulo, owner of an organic farm and dairy that breeds water buffaloes and produces extraordinary cheese, yogurt, and ice cream made from the milk of water buffaloes. To further understand how cheese is made, we asked Eduardo to explain how the cheese at Vannulo is made—and it's not just any cheese, it is the very special cheese, buffalo milk mozzarella (mozzarella di buffala).

At Vannulo's farm, water buffaloes are milked twice a day (morning and evening). The milk of the evening is placed in a refrigerated cooler and then mixed with the fresh milk of the morning, the following day.

The cheesemaker starts his job very early, about four in the morning. The raw milk mixture (evening and morning) is filtered and then heated in a stainless steel vat, and then the cheesemaker adds the right quantity of rennet and whey starter to aid in the coagulation and separation of milk and cream.

The milk clots into curds, and after an hour, a cross is cut into the clotted milk. This is a tradition cheesemakers share with traditional bread makers, which comes from the Christian symbol of the cross. After another one and a half hours, the clot is cut again, this time into nut-sized pieces. This cut clot is left in its whey (the watery part of the milk that is left after the curds form) for 2 to 3 hours, depending upon the environmental conditions. The whey is then drained and the clot is cut once again to smaller, rice-sized pieces.

The water buffalo milk clot is now ready to be added to hot water (90°C), a very unique process, which leads to *pasta filata* cheese, like *mozzarella di bufala*. The clot changes shape and gets stringy. The cheesemaker shapes the cheese by continuously mixing with wooden paddles. The cheese is then cut (in Italian "to cut" is *tagliare* or *mozzare*) and dipped in cold water to lower the temperature.

The "white water" produced when the clot is added to the hot water is rich in milk fats, proteins, and salts. This "white water" will be used to obtain a very important ingredient of traditional mozzarella cheese: the fermented brine, which is produced by the natural development of lactic acid bacteria when salt is added to the "white water."

The new cheese has a very light taste and is only lightly salted, and so it is cured in the fermented brine. This step salts it and makes the difference between a really good cheese and a not-so-good one.

"There are many types of cheeses, and many different ways to categorize cheese: raw or unpasteurized; pasteurized; hard, semisoft, and soft; smelly; blue; fresh and cured; smoked; and cheese made from the milk of goats, sheep, cows, buffaloes, and even camels!"

—K. DUN GIFFORD AND SARA BAER-SINNOTT

Cheese: Safe and Healthy

CATHERINE W. DONNELLY, PhD

When Oldways and the American Cheese Society challenged the United States Food & Drug Administration in 2000 on a proposed change of regulations regarding raw milk cheeses (see page 131 for information about the Cheese of Choice Coalition), we discovered the scientific studies of Catherine Donnelley. Catherine teaches food microbiology at the University of Vermont and is considered one of the world's experts on Listeria, *a feared bacterial pathogen in foods. But Catherine is also one of those scientists who loves food, who loves to explore and learn about food, and who teaches this love of food to her students (along with all they need to know about scary bacteria). Her work made a big difference to the Cheese of Choice Coalition, and we asked her to explain why cheese is both safe and healthy.* ▨

Cheeses are traditional foods that have been consumed for thousands of years; cheesemaking evolved centuries ago as a means of preserving raw milk via fermentation.

In the United States, the trend toward increased cheese consumption may be the result of recognition of both the healthfulness and safety of these foods (and, of course, the great taste). The characteristics of the specific cheese variety will dictate the potential for growth (and survival) of pathogens, with ripened soft cheeses presenting a higher risk.

Many hard cheeses, aged for sixty days or more, are made from raw milk, and these products enjoy an excellent food safety record. Included are Parmigiano-Reggiano, Grana Padano, Swiss cheese varieties, and cheddar cheese. The interactive effects of salt and acidity and loss of moisture during aging make these cheeses very safe.

Soft cheese varieties, such as Camembert, Brie, and Hispanic-style cheeses, such as *queso blanco*, present a higher risk from a microbiological safety perspective. These cheeses have a higher pH and higher moisture content, which can promote the growth of microbial pathogens. But although cheeses have been linked with documented outbreaks of foodborne illness, scientific evidence collected from around the world confirms that this occurs infrequently.

This is especially important because cheeses are highly nutritious foods that afford a number of well-documented health benefits. Cheese serves as an excellent source of vitamin D, proteins, peptides, and amino acids. Cheeses also provide an excellent source of calcium, which promotes bone health and helps prevent osteoporosis. Research has shown that calcium, when consumed via dairy products such as cheese, has weight control benefits including a decrease in body fat.

Emerging research evidence suggests that unique health benefits are offered by CLA, an essential fatty acid for which dairy products including cheese serve as the main dietary sources. Although only preliminary results are available, health benefits being ascribed to CLAs include anticarcinogenic effects (inhibition of the colorectal, prostate, and stomach cancers); cholesterol benefits (including the lowering of total and LDL cholesterol and triglycerides); body composition changes (reduction in body fat and increases in lean body mass); enhanced immune function; increased bone formation; and antidiabetic effects. Some cheeses even promote gastrointestinal health. Research studies have also shown cheeses to offer protection against development of dental caries.

Happily—cheese is a health-promoting, safe food.

The Right to Choose Your Cheese—the Cheese of Choice Coalition

ARI WEINZWEIG

In March 2000, Oldways and the American Cheese Society joined forces to assemble an international coalition to fight to preserve the rights of individuals to choose unpasteurized (raw milk) cheeses. The new coalition was called the Cheese of Choice Coalition, and Oldways, the American Cheese Society, and the Cheese Importers Association worked together to fight the proposed Food & Drug Administration ban on raw milk cheeses. To date, our collective work has been effective, but there are still regulatory threats that surface from time to time. And so we still continue to be vigilant to keep the right "to choose our cheese."

As part of this effort, Ari Weinzweig, cofounder and partner at Zingerman's, wrote the following essay, which was published in the April 2000 issue of the Oldways newsletter, The Oldways Exchange. *While written several years ago, the points remain relevant and illustrate the importance of the traditional old ways.*

For nearly eighteen years now, we at Zingerman's have gone to great lengths to locate, learn about, and sell the tastiest traditional foods we can get our hands on. In the process, we work hard to focus on the positive, to accentuate what we like about great food, and not to go off on the ill-conceived ideas of others. Personally, I'd far rather tell you what I made for dinner last night and why I liked it, than get off on some sociopolitical tangent about who's doing what to who. I'm not an alarmist, and I don't really like writing screeching tabloidesque headlines. But the threat to raw milk cheese is serious.

Full-flavored, traditionally made cheese as we know it may soon be banned in this country, unless we act now.

Despite the fact that there is almost no evidence to show any meaningful health threat, serious sources in Washington are telling us that the FDA is moving furtively to set the stage for banning all raw milk cheese from the United States. This could impact both imports and American-made cheeses. While a move of this sort would be almost invisible in the supermarket, it would have huge implications for lovers of traditionally made cheese. About 80 percent of what we sell at Zingerman's—including many of the world's great cheeses like Parmigiano-Reggiano, Swiss Gruyère, French Roquefort, Comte, and traditional English and Vermont cheddars, to name just a few—would no longer be available in the United States.

I suppose the fact that this issue is on the table isn't as shocking as I wish it were. In the postwar push by American science and industry to conquer nature, the United States government acted to ban the production and importation of all raw milk cheeses under the age of sixty days. So for the entire second half of the twentieth century we've not had access to some of France's best fresh goat cheese, Camembert, Brie, or other fine fresh cheeses. The fact that the government is considering extending this ban to ALL raw milk cheeses would make you think that there'd been a number of raw milk cheese–related health problems of late. Ironically, this has not been the case. Based on the evidence, there's really nothing to show that a well-made raw milk cheese carries any more health risk than any other cheese.

The fact that Europeans eat raw milk cheese in large quantities and live perfectly fine, healthy lives doesn't seem to have any impact on American government decision making. Today more than 20 percent of the cheese made in France remains raw milk. Thirty-five of the Certified Denomination of Origin cheeses in France are actually required by government regulations to be made from raw milk. Conclusion? If raw milk cheeses are banned, most of France's finest would become contraband in our country.

Now mind you, before anyone jumps on this health issue, I will tell you that there absolutely have been

instances of poorly pasteurized cheeses causing health problems. And, in the environment in which official Washington seems to operate sometimes, this evidence has been turned on its head and inside out to use as proof of the risk of eating raw milk cheese. In fact, it supports exactly the opposite conclusion. Carried to its truly logical end, what it should tell you is that when it comes to cheesemaking, pasteurization actually adds risk. How can this be? Well, it allows use of older milk with a higher bacteria count. It encourages big dairies to mix milks from different farms anonymously, which discourages farmers from producing the absolute best-quality milk they can. And it adds an unnatural, mechanical process to cheesemaking, which, by definition can malfunction or be misused.

So why pasteurize milk in the first place? Louis Pasteur pioneered the process in the second half of the nineteenth century. Working in his home region of the Franche-Comte, he discovered in 1879 that heating milk to high temperatures killed off the bacteria in the milk. Pasteur's process was a big boon for sanitation and health in an era where there was little to no refrigeration and folks frequently contracted diseases like tuberculosis from liquid milk. It also greatly extended the shelf life of liquid milk.

The question here, though, is what is the impact of milk pasteurization on cheese?

The problem with pasteurization, in the context of cheesemaking, is that it kills all bacteria in the milk, both desirable and undesirable. How can getting rid of bacteria possibly be bad? Because the desirable bacteria in the milk make such a big contribution to the flavor of the finished cheese. Without them, the cheesemaker is fighting an uphill battle, trying to make an exceptionally full-flavored cheese from less than full-flavored raw material. It can be done; but pasteurization is prone to removing much of the complexity and character that make great cheese great.

Can you tell the difference? Anyone who works with raw milk cheese will tell you they can. And in most cases I'd agree. Pascal Jacquin, who supplies a significant portion of the traditionally made French goat cheeses imported into the United States, adds: "It's like the difference between a free-range chicken and one that is caged."

Many cheesemakers also argue that pasteurized milk results in weaker curd in the cheesemaking, requiring longer maturing to get the big flavor that a good farmhouse cheese should have, altering the aging, and inhibiting texture and flavor development of more mature cheeses.

So how do raw milk cheesemakers make it work? Small dairy farms can control the sanitation of their herds and the milk much better than big ones, hence they have no need to rely on bacteria-killing pasteurization to ensure the quality of the milk. Instead farmers just do their job properly: traditional farmhouse cheeses—those made from the milk of the animals on a single farm—can be made with milk that is only hours old; they know the animals; they manage the entire process from field to finished cheese. Being forced to pasteurize would push these traditionalists down into a lower level of play, one where everyone plays with one hand tied behind their back, all in the interest of "protection."

Of course, the issue here isn't even whether the flavor of raw milk cheeses is better than those made from pasteurized milk. It is simply whether those of us who want to eat them will have the opportunity to do so without having to break the law or fly to Europe. It's about choice. It's all about the right to decide to eat a traditional cheese, made as it has been for centuries.

Sensory Stimuli

CATHY STRANGE

Cathy Strange, a national cheese buyer for Whole Foods Market, is one of America's most knowledgeable cheese experts, with many pointers on choosing cheese. 🍥

Cheese. Just thinking of the word sets off a world of sensory stimuli. I travel around the world to discover and purchase the highest-quality and most delicious cheese and specialty products for the Whole Foods Market shoppers. I love my job! Exploring and tasting cheese products infuses me with the energy of a young child. I wake up every day eager to learn and explore the nuances and tradition of the product, the philosophy of the cheesemaker, the beauty of the region, the history of the animals who supply the milk, and the lives of the dedicated farmers and producers.

In my unending search for the best-tasting cheeses, I hold onto key principles and my goals align with those of Whole Foods Market. My primary focus is finding the highest-quality natural and organic products available. I research farms and production facilities to determine what sustainable practices are in place to support the philosophy of environmental responsibility. I seek out products to satisfy and delight customers and the company team members I represent. I seek to establish partnerships with producers based on mutual respect, integrity, and trust. It is important that we share with our producers a principle of "shared fate," and our ultimate goal is to establish long-term partnerships based on a vision of success. When I discover a producer who makes a high-quality, great-tasting cheese, who shares our sense of environmental responsibility, and who seeks to build a relationship, I am able to introduce new products from around the world into our stores.

My personal favorite raw milk cheeses are the traditional, classic products, including Parmigiano-Reggiano, a taste of which transports me to the rolling hills and intersecting rivers of northern Italy. Cheesemakers stand over copper kettles filled with milk that produces only two wheels of the delicious product. The sight fills my mind, and the smell of heated milk excites my taste buds.

Le Gruyère, named for the elevated city on a hill in Switzerland, and Comte, representing the Jura Mountain district in France, are delightful cooked, pressed cheeses. I feel the chill in the air just thinking about these cheeses.

Stilton and cheddar from Britain are raw milk cheeses. Dessert never seemed so good! One of my new classic choices from the United States is Vermont Shepherd, a wonderful aged sheep's milk cheese with a complex, earthy flavor developed by Cynthia and David Major in Vermont. I can smell the caves where the product is aged, and the flavor takes me to the farm country. Another is Uplands Farms Pleasant Hill Reserve produced by Mike Gingrich in Wisconsin, a raw milk cheese that is modeled on traditional French washed rind cheese.

I could go on for hours about the delightful cheeses that all of us have the opportunity to enjoy through the local markets supporting quality cheeses. My hope is for all to enjoy the delights of wonderful cheese available from around the world.

Chèvre in Provence

ROB KAUFELT

Rob Kaufelt is owner of Murray's Cheese Shop in New York City. Here he unravels the mystery of choosing cheeses in his own personal way.

A cheese-monger is not what I set out to be, but it's what I am, and it's a satisfying life that suits me. Among its chief pleasures are discovering a new cheese and visiting the farm where it is made. There, the cheesemaker often has a great passion, and this is what I seek to share.

Late in the summer of 2003, I was staying with a friend in the Var region of Provence. It was a time of great heat and fires in that area. My friend Hervè, a French *affineur* (one who ages cheeses), had suggested a visit to François Borel, a young *chèvrier* (one who tends goats and makes goat cheese) whose farm was nearby.

François tends a small and special flock of rove goats, a magnificent and ancient breed of long-horned animals. They roam the surrounding forest eating brush and thus help to prevent fires. But they are a dying breed, with just a few thousand left, so their rich milk is not plentiful.

François milks his goats daily and makes fresh, unpasteurized cheese in small batches. He ladles the curds carefully by hand into molds for discs and cones, and then sets them in a little cave to age. After our tour, François gave us a few cheeses to take with us.

The sublime moment came an hour later. My friend Tamasin, a food writer from England, was driving. As the sun was setting, I opened the bag and took out a fresh disk sprinkled with powdered *sariette,* or summer savory. I held the cheese up to her mouth as she took a bite, then I took a bite. We looked at each other and smiled. The simplest cheese in the world, sprinkled with a tiny bit of local herb, and the most exquisite taste imaginable.

We gobbled it down and ate another, like kids with ice cream sandwiches, and acknowledged that nothing we had eaten at several of the region's finest restaurants had come close to matching the depth of flavor or sheer deliciousness of this small, fresh chèvre. In its simplicity lay its greatness. Of such moments are my work defined.

The Pleasures of Cheese

STEVE JENKINS

Steve Jenkins, master cheese-monger and partner at Fairway Markets in New York City, weighs in on the pleasures of cheese.

There really is no other foodstuff as perfect as cheese, neither fruits nor vegetables, meat or seafood, beans or grains, breads or pastries. Not one of these food groups comes close to cheese's perfection in terms of its intensity and nuance of flavor and fragrance, its remarkable gamut of textures, its ambassadorial regional specificity. I love the way cheese gives such a happy, welcoming halloo to these other foods, as if a cheese is on a mission, a stalwart fellow traveler perfectly content to ride alone but ever more ebullient with company. I love the way cheese always acts as the mediator between often quarrelsome tablemates, the whiny wine too young to be out this late, the sulkingly bitter olive or almond, the tarted-up and shameless piece of fruit that seems to know everything and is not shy about pointing the finger.

Cheese is low-maintenance. I value that it requires little more than one's knife and a sturdy surface. Nor is it so balefully evanescent like fruit and flesh. It will be there when you need it.

No foodstuff is so beckoningly sensuous. The texture of Vacherin Mont d'Or is voluptuous. The feminine fromage de chèvre Ste.-Maure de Touraine is transexually phallic, even pierced. A true Camembert smells of sex.

Numerous cheeses have been named for and made to resemble the female breast. The arousal of every cheese via brief exposure to higher temperature is evidenced by the cheese becoming moist and slippery.

Cheese as an elegant and traditional coda to haute cuisine? As you wish. As for me, I prefer it down and dirty, served at any juncture, served right alongside the first course, the main—certainly with the salad, served instead of a composed hot meal for heaven's sake.

MY PHILOSOPHY OF SELECTING CHEESE

My philosophy of selecting cheese is a simple matter, whether the cheese this philosophy is to be applied to is for my own personal enjoyment or that of my customers. The simplicity of this matter is borne out by the few questions I ask.

Is the cheese made more by a person or more by a machine? Tools are one thing. Even the most hands-on cheese recipe requires vats, hoses, rakes, colanders, and thermometers. But if the cheese is a product of mass production, a Henry Ford–like assembly line where very soon the few humans involved will be replaced by incorporeal robotic arms, then the cheese has been made by a machine, in which case I say, "No thanks." Mass-produced factory cheese is anathema to a memorable cheese experience. There is no character, no rusticity, no individuality to a factory cheese.

Has the cheese been made from raw milk? To use pasteurized milk in the creation of a cheese is unthinkable, illogical, if in fact the goal is to make a cheese that is as good as it can possibly be. And there can be no other goal for me, for all of us. Does the cheese taste good, look good, and does it give itself up nobly to the knife?

I will forever be in awe of the fact that cheese is one of the few things in this life that runs roughshod over the old saw, "You can't judge a book by its cover," because with cheese, you can. I don't need to taste a cheese to know whether it tastes good or not. If I behold a cheese that looks like it just stepped out of a limousine rather than a truck, a cheese wearing a three-piece suit rather than flannel and corduroy, a cheese sporting a label that is in some garish primary color within a logo crafted by committee, a cheese whose exterior is as flawless and glossy as the promise that its interior will be flabby and slabby, I say I will not select this cheese. It is not worthy of me.

If, on the other hand, the exterior of the cheese I behold is in some shade of an earth tone, from bone-white, to beige, to khaki, to straw-colored, through the russet-reds, rawhides and chocolatey browns, and sports a toadskin or a pebbly surface, or a deer antler's velvet, a surface that wants to be stroked, or is cloaked in gray gingham, or is stippled or tattooed over every square inch with its name and provenance, or is dusted or rouged or cobwebbed with some beneficent mold, or whose exterior, like that of fermier St.-Nectaire, like some expressionist painting or Hubble telescopic photo of a distant galaxy, reflects the colors white, yellow, red, green, and black, of five distinct and identifiable strains of bacteria, each a healthy, flavor-provoking substance, I then know the cheese is going to taste good. Heaven knows it looks good. As for that business about the knife, don't worry about it. It'll cut just fine.

With regard to my favorite cheese, I remain noncommittal. I've always found myself baffled by the question, exactly as I am when asked my favorite color or which of my children I love most. I'd have to say my favorite cheese is often the one presently before me.

Historical Traditional Sicilian Cheeses

GIUSEPPE LICITRA, PhD

Every two years a wondrous event takes place in Ragusa, in southeastern Sicily. The event–Cheese Art–celebrates traditional, high-quality agricultural products of Sicily, and in particular the raw milk cheese of Ragusa, called Ragusano. The organizer of the event, Giuseppe Licitra, is the director of CORFILAC, a Consorzio in Sicily. His passion is to keep alive Sicily's cheesemaking traditions and to promote and sell the traditional cheese of Sicily. Cheese Art was born out of Giuseppe's passion, and he and Ivana Piccotto and their colleagues at CORFILAC bring together cheesemakers, cheese sellers, research scientists, and journalists every two years to learn more about traditional raw milk cheeses around the world.

Traditional Sicilian cheeses are still produced today using raw whole milk and the old ways of cheesemaking. These old ways, handed down from generation to generation, are clear testimony of the durability of the cultural and artistic heritage deeply rooted in agricultural communities. Traditional cheeses are also tightly connected to the local conditions in which they are made. These include the breed of animal, soil, rainfall, climate, forage, biodiversity, and cheesemaking customs.

The Ragusano of Ragusa are made with raw milk from free-ranging Modicano cows, using natural rennet for coagulation, old-fashioned cheesemaking tools made from wood and copper, and natural caves for aging. Like all artisanal cheeses, no Ragusano cheese is exactly like any other, because each cheesemaker is an artist, herding his cows from pasture to pasture, milking them at the right time of day, making the cheese in his family's way, and aging it in his own caves with their own microclimate.

I love the complexities of Ragusano, with its spicy and fragrant tastes that linger long in the mouth and its aromatics that hint of the natural pastures of the Iblea plateau, where the cows graze under the hot Sicilian sun.

My Life As a Cheesemaker

JUDY SCHAD

Judy Schad left corporate life more than twenty years ago to raise goats. Along the way she's learned to make prize-winning goat cheese (Capriole) and instilled passion in many others as she's worked with the American Cheese Society. Most of all she's made her mark among cheese lovers with her spectacular goat cheese. We first heard about Judy from Sarah Fritschner, food editor of the Louisville Courier-Journal, *and then visited Judy, her farm, and her goats when the Chefs Collaborative had a conference in Louisville.*

My husband and I have raised goats and made cheese on our farm in southern Indiana for more than twenty years. There's been ample opportunity to grow, but we've always resisted. Managing land, animals, cheesemaking, and marketing is more than a job—it's a life, and we live right here.

Yesterday began at 4:30 A.M. with a pregnant doe having "kidding" problems. At 6:30, a hose broke on the milk line and the tractor wouldn't start. While my husband went to his real job and I grabbed coffee and waited on a vet call, I filled out a regulatory form on bioterrorism and milk safety—visions of locks on the barn door and the disaster of lost keys.

By early afternoon, we'd made cheese, rotated cheeses in the aging room, answered crucial e-mails ("do you have a cheese I ate in France called fromage?"), had a vet visit, feed delivery, UPS pickup, and an argument between two farm interns. Somewhere in between, I realized I hadn't visited my mother in a week, and the grandchildren were spending the night. Time to make a delivery in Louisville and get a bit of peace and quiet.

So why do I love this? Why, after a wonderful vacation, or even a trip to the post office, do I feel such elation when I come up that long drive through the woods? It's either a total connection with a place, or relief at not seeing two hundred sets of eyes reflected in the headlights—escaped goats, who've eaten another $1,400 worth in shrubbery.

PAXIMADIA

SARA BAER-SINNOTT

During our many visits to Greece over the last decade—in Athens, Crete, Chios, and Lesbos—we were always delighted to find paximadia on the menu. It's the Greeks' version of an open-faced tomato and cheese sandwich—traditionally it's made by piling up tomatoes and feta cheese on top of a barley rusk, and drizzling it with olive oil and a sprinkle of oregano. We included paximadia in the Oldways bread project, and also in our children's cooking and nutrition program, High Five! (see page 31). Its American version is perfect for the family table—lunch, dinner, or after-school snack.

SERVES 4 TO 6

6 whole-wheat bagels or rolls
1¹/₂ pounds ripe tomatoes or 1 (20-ounce) can tomatoes, drained
¹/₂ cup fresh oregano and/or marjoram
¹/₂ pound feta cheese, crumbled
Extra virgin olive oil

Toast the bagels. Pile the tomatoes, herbs, and feta cheese on the bagel, and finish by drizzling with the olive oil. Serve immediately.

FETA CHEESE SPREAD

SARA BAER-SINNOTT

Just imagine you're relaxing in a Greek taverna, looking out at the Aegean Sea, enjoying this tasty concoction with a glass of crisp wine or ouzo and club soda, if you're bold enough to try this licorice-flavored Greek national drink! 🌿

SERVES 4

   $1/2$ pound feta cheese
   Juice of $1/2$ lemon
   2 tablespoons chopped fresh oregano
   Sea salt and freshly ground black pepper
   Crackers or whole-grain toast

Preheat the oven to 400°F. Put the feta cheese in an ovenproof dish. Mix the lemon juice, oregano, salt, and pepper and spread over the feta cheese. Cover with aluminum foil.

Bake for 15 minutes. Serve hot out of the oven, spreading the melted feta-oregano mixture on crackers or whole-grain toast.

PASTA WITH CHEESE, GARDEN VEGETABLES, AND SFOGLIA

SARA BAER-SINNOTT

One of our favorite, easiest, and healthiest summer meals is pasta and cheese mixed with garden vegetables and sfoglia *(Ancel Keys, the "father" of the Mediterranean diet, describes* sfoglia *as Italian for "leaves"). This dish works with most cheeses—feta, Parmigiano-Reggiano, Grana Padano, cheddar, Gorgonzola—and each dish is special, with the taste dependent upon the cheese and vegetables used.*

For the greens and vegetables, borrowing generously from the meaning of sfoglia, *we like to use fresh basil, arugula, watercress, parsley, or any other fresh leafy herbs—along with fresh tomatoes, zucchini, peppers, or other fresh garden vegetables. This works well even in the darkest months of winter, with high-quality canned tomatoes and greenhouse-grown basil or arugula.* 🌿

SERVES 4

   $1/2$ pound of your favorite-shaped pasta
   $1/4$ cup extra virgin olive oil
   $1/2$ cup cubed or chunked or shaved cheese
       (of your choice)
   $1/2$ cup chopped tomatoes or bell peppers
   $1/2$ cup chopped leafy herbs or greens
   Sea salt and freshly ground black pepper

Bring a large pot of salted water to a boil. Add the pasta and cook until al dente. Drain and return to the pot. Pour the olive oil over the pasta. Mix in the cheese and chopped tomatoes and greens. Season with salt and pepper and serve immediately.

CHEESE FONDUE

CLAUDETTE NACAMULI

This recipe is from the kitchen of the mother of one of Oldways' former staff members, Nicole Nacamuli. Her mother spent her childhood in Switzerland, so, as you can imagine, a recipe for cheese fondue is second nature. Don't forget the fondue custom: if a lady loses her bread cube in the fondue, she owes a kiss to the nearest man; and if a man loses his bread, he provides the next round of drinks!

SERVES 4

3 tablespoons all-purpose flour
I pound imported Swiss cheese, grated
2 cups dry white wine
I clove fresh garlic, minced
I tablespoon kirsch or brandy (optional)
I loaf Italian or French bread, cut into cubes

Mix the flour with the grated cheese and set aside.

Pour the wine into a fondue pot and set over medium heat. When the wine is hot but not boiling, add the cheese and flour mixture, stirring constantly with a wooden spoon until the cheese is melted. Add the garlic and continue stirring. Bring the fondue to bubble briefly, and add the kirsch, stirring until blended.

Serve and keep hot over fondue pot burner. Immerse bread cubes in fondue using fondue forks, and enjoy with a good dry white wine.

Draining Yogurt

PAULA WOLFERT

A relative of cheese, yogurt is made from milk. And because its roots are in Bulgaria, cuisines from that part of the world feature many dishes using yogurt. Take Paula's advice and drain nonfat yogurt for a much better consistency. You'll be in for a very special taste treat, and you might even find that you can't live without it!

Yogurt, whether homemade or all-natural, low-fat commercial, consists of a delicate balance between curds and whey. Yogurt thins out when vigorously stirred, breaks down when heated without a stabilizer, and "weeps" when salty foods are added. For cooking purposes, I always drain low-fat yogurt to obtain a thicker consistency. (You can substitute nonfat yogurt, but the resulting texture is a little chalky.)

To drain yogurt, place lightly salted yogurt in a sieve lined with cheesecloth and leave it to drip for 30 minutes to 24 hours.

Within an hour from the time you begin to drain it, your yogurt will lose about 20 percent of its liquid, acquiring the consistency of light whipped cream. This is about right for use in salads. Within several hours, your yogurt will lose almost half its volume and acquire the consistency of sour cream. In this form it is perfect for dips, sauces, and soups, for thickening vegetable purees, as a basting medium for fish, poultry, and meats, as an accompaniment to rice and bulgur pilafs and stuffed vegetables, or as a substitute for butter in meat filling.

If you want your yogurt to obtain the very thick texture of cream cheese, allow it to drain even longer, after stirring in a few more pinches of fine salt.

Whenever you are draining yogurt, save the whey for cooking vegetables or for using as a drink. It's reputed to be good for the kidneys.

Drained yogurt, lightly salted, keeps longer in the refrigerator than commercial or homemade yogurt. Cover and store in plastic or glass containers and keep refrigerated for up to 2 weeks or until needed.

Goat's milk yogurt, available in fine food stores and health food stores, has a tangier flavor than cow's milk yogurt. You can use it drained for dips and salads. Sheep's milk yogurt, which is naturally rich and dense, needs less draining for dips and salads.

CHOPPED ROMAINE AND CUCUMBER SALAD WITH YOGURT DRESSING

ANA SORTUN

Use good yogurt for this recipe. It may sound ho-hum, but this salad is crunchy and layered with flavors. Consider the romaine more like a vegetable in this case. It will be thick and crunchy, and will need a little more dressing than a delicate lettuce would. The magic is the combination of the fresh parsley, dill, and mint.

To mince the garlic, use a garlic press or chop with the back of a chef's knife, then chop with the blade until it becomes really fine. When you use the back of a knife it smashes and chops at the same time. ◐

SERVES 4

SALAD

$1/2$ cup walnut halves

1 large head romaine, blemished outer leaves removed

1 cup chopped, clean arugula leaves

1 English cucumber

1 tablespoon chopped fresh flat-leaf parsley

2 tablespoons chopped fresh dill

1 tablespoon chopped fresh mint

Sea salt and fresh ground black pepper

$1/2$ teaspoon chopped Aleppo chiles (optional)

YOGURT DRESSING

2 large cloves garlic, finely minced

2 tablespoons freshly squeezed lemon juice

1 tablespoon good white vinegar, like champagne or other French white wine vinegar

$1^1/2$ teaspoons sugar

$1/2$ cup yogurt

5 tablespoons extra virgin olive oil

Sea salt and freshly ground black pepper

In a small skillet on low heat, roast the walnuts carefully until they lightly brown and you can smell them. Cool and set aside.

To make the dressing, in a small mixing bowl, combine the garlic with the lemon juice, vinegar, and sugar and let sit for at least 10 minutes so the garlic softens.

Meanwhile, wash and dry the romaine and arugula. The greens should be very dry or the dressing won't cling to them. Chop the romaine into fine shreds. Chop the arugula. Put both greens in a large salad bowl. Peel the cucumber and cut in half lengthwise. Spoon out the seeds. Cut in half so there are four pieces, and grate the cucumber on the large holes of a grater. Add to salad bowl with the parsley, dill, mint, and walnuts.

Finish the dressing by whisking the yogurt and olive oil into the garlic mixture. Season to taste with salt and pepper. Add half the dressing and another sprinkle of salt to the salad. Toss and taste for seasoning. If too light, spoon in more dressing. Sprinkle with the chiles, and serve immediately.

LINGUINE WITH GREENS, YOGURT, ALMONDS, AND BLUE CHEESE

AGLAIA KREMEZI

This dish is inspired by the traditional spanakoryzo (spinach risotto, served with yogurt) and the trahana (yogurt and cracked-wheat pasta) with greens. 🍃

SERVES 3 TO 4

Sea salt

1 pound linguine

1 pound mixed greens or spinach leaves, coarsely chopped

4 tablespoons extra virgin olive oil

2 cloves garlic, chopped

2 ounces Roquefort, Gorgonzola, or Stilton, mashed with a fork

1 cup creamy Greek or whole-milk yogurt

Freshly ground black pepper

$^2/_3$ cup coarsely ground, unskinned almonds

Fruity extra virgin olive oil, for drizzling (optional)

Bring a a large pot of water to a boil, add salt, and cook the pasta according to package directions. One minute before the end of cooking, drop the greens into the pot. Drain both the pasta and greens, reserving $^1/_2$ cup of the cooking liquid.

In the same pot, warm the olive oil over medium heat. Add the garlic and sauté for 1 minute. Add the pasta and greens, cheese, yogurt, and about $^1/_4$ cup or more of the cooking broth, enough to moisten pasta. Add the pepper and almonds and toss well.

Serve in a warm bowl or platter and take to the table at once. Drizzle with some fruity olive oil if you like.

YOGURT WITH SPICY QUINCE PRESERVES

AGLAIA KREMEZI

Homemade seasonal fruit preserves—or spoon-sweets as they are called in Greece—are a staple of every house. Spoon-sweets are served on a tiny glass plate, together with a small cup of coffee and a glass of water, to all guests. This recipe, adds an extra special touch of thick Greek yogurt. 🍃

SERVES 4

1$^1/_2$ cups grated quince preserves or quince jam

1 to 2 tablespoons grated fresh ginger

Pinch of grated allspice

Pinch of cinnamon

3 cups thick Greek or whole-milk yogurt

$^2/_3$ cup coarsely chopped unskinned almonds

4 sprigs fresh mint

Mix the preserves with the ginger and spices. Spoon about $^2/_3$ cup yogurt into each of four bowls, top with one-quarter of the preserves, sprinkle with almonds, and decorate with mint. Serve at once.

"The American Heart Association recommends two servings
of fish, preferably fatty fish, per week for healthy adults
to decrease risk of cardiovascular disease."

PENNY KRIS-ETHERTON, PhD

"I believe that we must manage our fisheries wisely, which means
fishing ground by fishing ground and fishery by fishery, because that's
how fishermen fish. Sweeping consumer publicity slogans, like
'Boycott Swordfish,' are superficial and inevitably short-lived. Only if
we focus on long-term realities will we save our fisheries."

—PAUL O'CONNELL

FISH

From oceans and seas, bays and estuaries, shallows and deeps, beaches and boats—we catch mackerel, tuna, sablefish, salmon, shad, swordfish, shark, sardines, bluefish, striped bass, anchovy, herring, mullet, monkfish, skate, sea robin, sea bream, sea bass, scup, hake, pollock, cod, haddock, smelt, whiting, redfish, snapper, orange roughy, grouper, mahi-mahi (dolphin fish), turbot, plaice, flounder, sole, halibut, octopus—among many others.

From ponds and lakes, rivers and streams, and from under the ice, we catch pickerel and pike; walleye and goldeye; rainbow, brown, golden, and blue trout; perch; bigmouth and small-mouth bass; catfish and crayfish; and white and yellow perch—also among many others.

> ## What Are These Sea Creatures, How Do We Catch Them, and How Do We Eat Them?
>
> K. DUN GIFFORD

FISHING TOOLS WE USE

We use bamboo rods, strung with twine and a worm on a hook; a fourteen-foot surf rod with a fiberglass plug and gang hooks; a very expensive fly rod outfit and intricately tied flies; or drop lines, or nets. But young and old, rich and poor, we catch these fish, and eat them proudly—roasted, grilled, boiled, poached, fried, baked, stewed, souped, and sandwiched.

LOBSTERS AND CRABS

Lots of sea creatures crawl around on the sea bottom, but the ones we prize most are lobsters and crabs. Once upon a time we caught huge ones: lobsters five feet long, crabs a foot across. But no more; we overfished them.

Lobsters and crabs are delicacies because their meat is tender and demand exceeds supply. We eat lobsters every which way; steamed, boiled, baked, stewed, chowdered, as lobster rolls and canapés. We do similarly with crabs, whether they be stone, king, spider, or blue.

IMPORTED TASTES

Sushi is an elegant way to eat fish and seafood raw. Bouillabaisse is a zesty stew of mixed trash fish and shellfish. Harry Belafonte taught us that "aki rice and fish are nice, and the rum is fine any time of day." We eat elegant British Dover sole and French sole meunière—same fish, different gastronomy. Squid masquerades as calamari, Patagonian toothfish as Chilean sea bass, and sablefish as black cod.

SALMON

There's something festive and soul-satisfying about salmon—maybe it's the bright color, maybe the velvet richness, or even the National Geographic image of these powerful swimmers flashing their sparkling silver flanks in the sun when they leap clear out of the water, struggling to vault over waterfalls and avoid the jaws of grizzly bears. But a crispy caramelized, broiled, grilled, or baked salmon steak, smeared with lemon or cucumber dressing; or velvety slices of smoked salmon, sprinkled with onions and capers—these are tastes and pleasures of the royals.

CLAMS AND SCALLOPS

Lots of things grow in shells sitting on, or buried in, harbor and ocean bottoms, including scallops, clams, conchs, and oysters. Mussels grow on rocks and poles (oysters do, too). Shellfish are caught wild, but increasingly they are farmed or sea ranched. Farms are more hands-on, as with shellfish raised in cages; sea ranches are more in nature's hands, which scatter the young, grow them, and have them ready for harvest when they mature. We eat shellfish raw, fried, baked, broiled, and boiled. We eat clam fritters, clam pies, fried clams, steamed clams, baked clams, clam stews, and clam chowders.

FLORIDA STONE CRABS

Stone crabs are peculiar characters—their claws are so strong they can easily crush a finger. But in one of nature's balancing acts, their powerful claws are easy to detach from the crab's body, without killing the crab.

The great stone crab craze of recent years does not—in theory—destroy the sustainability of the traditional stone crab fishery, because the stone crab fishery regulations mandate only twisting off a single claw, and then throwing the crab back with one of its sturdy claws still attached. Even with one claw, the crab can crush its food and defend itself while its new claw grows back.

For thirty years, my father and a few of his friends had stone crab licenses and ran a few lines of traps in Florida Bay. We kids were the labor force when we were down there, hauling the heavy traps (each carrying a cement block to keep it from drifting its "set" on the bottom) into the boat. The "grown-ups" usually took the crabs out of the traps with tongs, pulled off a claw (never both), and tossed the crab overboard to live another day and grow another claw. If we caught a crab with only one claw, we tossed it back to finish growing its other one.

Our other job was refilling the net bag with bait, which was the scraps from fish we had caught and cleaned (or scraps we collected from fish markets). This "gurry," rank with the stink of rotting fish, made terrific bait for attracting the crabs, but the men on the boat always stayed upwind of us as we wrestled the slimy mess into the bags and tied them to the inside of the traps.

But lest there be any misunderstanding—there's no crabmeat sweeter than stone crab, and to this day my family demolishes an impressive pile of them at our annual Christmas party.

SAUCES

Chefs of many cultures create a king's ransom of fish and shellfish sauces—Mornay, aurore, soubise, béchamel, Cardinal, poulette. mousseline, duxelle, diable, beurre noir, maitre d'hotel, beurre noisette, anchovy butter, aïoli, tartar, cucumber, cheese, cream, curry, dill, espangole, Louis, Newburg, velouté, and, of course, we all create the ubiquitous "cocktail sauce."

Fishing for a Healthy Diet

PENNY KRIS-ETHERTON, PhD

Penny Kris-Etherton, a driving force in developing clear explanations for consumers about the ingredients of a healthy diet, is a distinguished professor of nutrition at Penn State University. We first met Penny in 1997 at our Vegetarian Diet Conference and learned that she is not only a deeply respected researcher, but also has that rare ability to communicate the links between nutrition and love of food. She was a member of the 2005 Dietary Guidelines Advisory Committee, and here she explains why fish are important for lifelong good health.

Eating fish at least twice a week is associated with many health benefits, which appears to reflect its high-quality nutrient profile. Fish is low in calories and is an excellent source of protein, vitamins (including many B vitamins and, in fatty fish, fat-soluble vitamins such as vitamin E, D, and A), minerals (such as potassium, phosphorus, magnesium, and selenium), and omega-3 fatty acids.

Significant health benefits are associated with fish consumption and, specifically, the omega-3 fatty acids in fish. These benefits include decreased risk of heart disease (especially sudden death) and stroke, as well as favorable effects on inflammatory diseases, such as arthritis and dermatitis. In addition, omega-3 fatty acids play a key role in normal neurological development for preterm and full-term infants. Recent findings suggest that omega-3 fatty acids reduce risk of depression, including postpartum depression, and aggressive behavior. New research has also linked omega-3 fatty acids with improved bone health, specifically a reduction in bone loss in later years. The remarkable health effects identified for fish consumption have been the impetus for recent dietary recommendations.

The American Heart Association recommends two servings of fish, preferably fatty fish, per week for healthy adults to decrease risk of cardiovascular disease. For individuals with coronary disease, physicians recommend a high dose—about a six-ounce serving of fatty fish every other day. The American Diabetes Association recommends three servings of fish per week. To give perspective, the average per capita consumption in the United States is approximately only one serving per week.

Common sources of fatty fish are salmon, tuna, mackerel, and herring, although all fish contain long-chain omega-3 fatty acids. Farm-raised salmon and wild salmon have similar amounts of omega-3 fatty acids; however, farm-raised catfish have somewhat less omega-3 fatty acids than wild catfish. Commercially prepared fried fish tends to be lower in omega-3 fatty acids and higher in saturated fats and trans fatty acids. Therefore, for the most health benefits, grilling, broiling, baking, poaching, or pan-frying in liquid vegetable oil are the preferred ways to cook fish.

There is an ongoing concern about environmental contaminants in fish, especially methylmercury, and how they may impact the health benefits of fish. Fish consumption at levels recommended by the FDA and state health departments pose no increased health risk as the result of any environmental contaminants.

The important thing to remember is that the health benefits of fish are the reason why health professionals, health organizations, and government dietary guidelines recommend eating fish two times per week, especially fatty fish. And of course, eating fish is an enjoyable way to reap many health benefits.

"Significant health benefits are associated with fish consumption and, specifically, the omega-3 fatty acids in fish."

—PENNY KRIS-ETHERTON, PhD

Aquaculture:
The Environmental Choice

K. DUN GIFFORD

Environmental sustainability is integral to Oldways' programs. For example, Oldways is the "parent" of the Chefs Collaborative, the chefs' organization that in the early 1990s pioneered the promotion of seasonal, local foods (see page 54). But environmental sustainability is more complicated than many think. Thinking and acting environmentally means taking a deep breath and thinking about the long view.

The verities of fish farming, the most sustainable way to raise animal protein for human consumption, are a good example of this phenomenon. There is no serious scientific challenge to the fact that it is more sustainable and environmentally efficient to farm fish than it is to farm poultry and livestock. However, aquaculture is under siege from "clean ocean" advocacy groups for polluting oceans and producing seafood unsafe to eat. Curiously, none of the major health promotion organizations, no government bodies charged with overseeing public and ocean health, nor any major university research departments agree with these advocates. Sad to say, it's the consumers who suffer, because they are persuaded by "scare stories" to avoid eating seafood, and so miss out on its lifelong health-promoting qualities.

In response, Oldways launched its Water Farming Initiative at a conference in Baltimore in early 2002 by releasing a paper called "Heads or Tails," which compares and contrasts conflicting claims about a variety of aquaculture issues (fish feed, for example). It argues that farming fish is not a luxury; it is an environmental and public health necessity.

In an ideal future food world, everything will be in environmental balance—ocean fish stocks restored to full strength, sustainable aquaculture production at high levels, and intensive farming of land animals reduced.

Nutrition experts will be happy with this result: fish are healthier food than livestock. Environmentalists will be happy: aquaculture degrades the environment far less than agriculture. Fishermen will be happy: oceans will support robust and economically viable fisheries. And chefs and grocers will be happy: fresh and healthy seafood will be in steady supply.

This ideal future food world need not be a fantasy, as "big picture" environmentalists acknowledge. For example, Rebecca Goldburg, a leading critic of mangrove shrimp farming, says "aquaculture may be the only means to markedly increase seafood production, can be less detrimental to marine ecosystems than fishing, and may be a more desirable way to raise animal protein than terrestrial production." And WorldWatch founder Lester Brown predicts that "world aquaculture output is on track to overtake the production of beef by 2010."

"Big picture" environmentalists like these recognize agriculture's large pollution penalties: runoffs of fertilizers, nitrates, pesticides, herbicides, and manure that pollute aquifers, rivers, streams, lakes, and oceans. They also recognize that aquaculture is inherently more efficient than agriculture, as measured by the "food conversion ratios" that scientists use to compare the amount of feed eaten to the amount of edible flesh produced. Fish are highly efficient converters of feed, with a conversion ratio of about 1.5 to 1. This compares to ratios of 2.5 to 1 for poultry; 4 to 1 for hogs; and 10 to 1 for beef.

Fish are cold-blooded, so they do not burn energy to heat themselves in winter and cool themselves in summer. They are also nearly weightless and survive well with minimal skeletons of light bones. Because land animals are warm-blooded, they must burn significant energy to heat and cool themselves; and because they are not weightless, they must also burn food energy to grow and maintain their heavy bones and skeletons.

Both of these key environmental measures—pollution and feed conversion efficiencies—argue powerfully for expanding sustainable aquaculture.

This will be true even when ocean fishery catches are restored to maximum sustainable yield, because even then there will not be enough fish in the sea to satisfy the worldwide consumer demand for healthy seafood. Only a combination of wild-caught fish and farmed fish (and shellfish) will do the job.

Sustainable fish farming is a developing business, evolving and changing just as rapidly as computers and mobile phones. Unfortunately, its development is being disrupted by a small number of very wealthy "little picture" environmental groups. Because a significant percentage of their money is spent on public relations, these NGOs receive vast coverage in print and electronic media.

But to their credit, some leading U.S. newspapers are questioning these NGO claims and asking hard questions about their validity. This is heartening news for everyone—the catch industry; fish farmers who believe theirs is an environmentally clean business producing healthy, wholesome food more efficiently than land farms can; the penny-pinched scientists whose studies support the health benefits of eating fish and shellfish; and consumers who want healthy food.

For the Love of Fishing

K. DUN GIFFORD

I flat out love to fish, and I dream about it. I love fish markets and fish restaurants and aquariums. I love to cook fish and shellfish, and eat them. I love to dig clams and scoop scallops and jig for squid.

The gear we use to catch fish is beautiful. The seventy-five-year-old split bamboo fly rods that Charles Ritz gave me are astonishing, with craftsmanship the equal of fine Heppelwhite or Chippendale furniture. Reels have mechanisms that turn with the precision of fine watches but have the strength to overcome muscular two-hundred-pound fish and the durability to resist salt water and fierce sun.

The lures we use to draw fish to the hook are beautiful, too. We use exquisite small flies for insect eaters like trout, small silvery swimmers when salmon and tarpon and bluefish are feeding on minnows, live bait when the fish are lazy or reluctant feeders, heavy four- and six-inch plastic lures sprouting with gang hooks to fish for big bluefish and striped bass in the surf or tide rips, and bunched feathers for big tarpon and albacore and sailfish. The lore of lures has no end because the only limit to fiddling with old ones and inventing new ones is human imagination.

Then there's everything else: waders, hats, sunglasses, rain slickers, creels, boots, knives (very important), shirts, sun lotion, and lunch. And boats and radios and navigation gear and engines and fighting chairs and bait wells.

But for me it's probably a water thing, since I equally love big boats and small boats, sailboats and fishing boats, rowboats and speedboats. I love just being aboard boats. I have sailed in Alaska and Nova Scotia, the Hebrides and the Caribbean, Turkey, and Florida, across half the Atlantic to Bermuda, and raced small dinghies and large sailboats, including the America's Cup.

I learned real fishing by trial and error in the surf at the two sand spits marking the ends of Nantucket—Smiths Point at the west end, and Great Point at the north end (Nantucket island is shaped like a crescent moon). In the 1950s my father bought me a ten-foot bamboo surf rod with a level-wind reel, some wooden plugs with a couple of gang hooks on each, and also some lead drails, each with a single large fixed tail hook. My mother drove me out in our surplus World War II jeep late one beautiful afternoon to Smiths Point; we needed four-wheel drive because the point is a couple of miles of soft sand beach from the end of the dirt road. Casting was not a lot of fun for the first few trips to the point. Every time I tried to cast, I got a classic "rat's nest" backlash of tangles that thoroughly snarled the line and took fifteen minutes to straighten out. The damn level-wind reels were a plague in the years before the French invited the spinning reels that delivered us from this particular and devilish form of evil.

I watched the men lined up to my left and right along the edge of the surf—they cast with such smooth grace, seemingly without effort. They laid the rod and the plug out over their shoulders and behind them, then leaned back and stepped forward strongly bringing the rod smoothly but forcefully forward, and their plugs sailed off almost out of sight toward the lowering sun and out beyond the breaking surf. Then they cranked the handles of the reels like crazy, sometimes jerking the rod tip sharply to make the plug splash or the drail jump, so it would look like a frightened small fish that would make a good meal for the larger fish swimming around out there looking for dinner, which we were trying to catch for our dinner.

I was a failure for about an hour. My mother could not help; she was no surf caster. I got nothing but the dreaded backlash, time after time, and my plug futzed around in the foam at my feet. But I was not going to quit. I had read *The Old Man and the Sea*.

After a while, the best fisherman on the island, the legendary Gardiner Marsh, a truly eccentric crank, arrived in his four-wheel-drive panel truck and began to cast right next to me. I went cold; I was sure he was going to tell me to get the hell out of there, since I was in a good spot pretty near the end of the point where the current was most swift. My mother and I had gotten there early, before the big guys.

"Hey kid," he said, "use your thumb on the reel."

I did not know what he meant. "Can you show me?" I asked.

"Just put your thumb on the reel so it won't overspool and get you all tangled with a backlash. You don't have to press hard." Then he held his reel sideways toward me so I could see how he held his thumb against the spool.

"Go ahead," he said, "but throw it easy." Then he turned away and set up to cast, laid his fifteen-foot rod back and then with a beautiful, smooth, effortless motion threw his plug right into the sun, out of sight. Oh, it was nice.

After a while I got the hang of it, with no distance on my casts but with no backlashes, either. I hoped Mr. Marsh would look over and say something, maybe like, "Hey, nice work, kid," but he totally ignored me and while I struggled, he landed two or three big bluefish.

"OK, damn it," I thought, "I've got this figured out now. It's time to put my back into it and get some distance, or I'll just beat up on the water and never get a fish." So I laid my pole and plug back, took a big step forward and really heaved forward with the rod.

Disaster! The biggest backlash I had ever had, and the plug went out hardly twenty feet, splashing in the wash of the waves at the edge of the sand. I picked away at untangling the snarl for ten or fifteen minutes, my ears burning and afraid to look over at Mr. Marsh.

But I did get it clear, and started to reel in to cast again. Then—BINGO! I had a fish! I could feel it struggling against the rod.

"Hey Mom! Mom! I got a fish!"

The way it was surging around and bending my rod it had to be huge. I was sure it had to be the biggest bluefish anyone had ever caught. Man, oh man, then Mr. Marsh and I could talk about fishing! Sure enough, he stopped fishing and stood there watching me struggle.

Finally, I had my giant bluefish at the water's edge, and Mr. Marsh spiked his rod in the holder and trotted over to where my giant bluefish was thrashing. He set his feet against the surf, bent down to grab the wire leader, and dragged a two-foot-long brown, flat fish up onto the dry sand. It was not blue.

"Hey kid," he said, "you got yourself a big flounder! And damn, you hooked him right in the middle of his back!" Other fisherman spiked their rods and came over to see what all this commotion was about, laughing and joking about the flounder that hooked itself in the back while the kid was fooling with his backlash.

But then Mr. Marsh brought the fish over to me, and I watched how he held it under the gills and when he held it out to me I took it from him. The plug was still fixed to its back, both of its treble hooks stuck firmly in the fish's back.

"Kid," he said, "that's the biggest backlash fish of any I've seen caught anywhere. You did a good job. Now let's get this plug out of it so you can get back to fishing again before the sun goes down."

So it ended well. Mr. Marsh showed me how to work the hooks out; the rest of the men congratulated me on my "first blood" and went back to surfcasting again. I lugged the flounder back to the Jeep, where my mother was watching very warily since the fish was still thrashing weakly.

"Dear," she said, "that's not a bluefish, it's a flounder."

"I know, Mom," I said. "I'm leaving it here in the Jeep. I'm going to fish again and get you a bluefish."

I didn't that night, which was okay because I'd caught something. And before the summer was out I caught so many bluefish that even the neighbors asked me to stop bringing them around.

In the years that followed, Mr. Marsh was always cordial to me when I saw him at the surf's edge, giving me tips about what plugs and drails to use in which currents and wave conditions, and how to read the patterns of the diving gulls as they hovered over the heaving ocean surface, waiting for the powerful bluefish and striped bass to drive the bait fish to the surface. He loved the fish, and he was my teacher about tides and bait and lures and water.

I ran into Mr. Marsh at the tackle shop, too, where he loved to tell the story of my "great backlash flounder." In a few years it had grown into a much better and longer story than the original. After all, he was a fisherman.

"I flat out love to fish, and I dream

about it."

—K. DUN GIFFORD

Hunter-Gathering

MARIAN MORASH

Marian Morash is one of the best cooks we know, and as good a reason as any for her skill behind the range and ease in the kitchen is that she's seen it all, and done most of it, too. In the 1960s she was an assistant to Julia Child for her earliest black-and-white TV program, The French Chef *(Marian's husband, Russ, was Julia's producer and director), and continued as Julia's assistant as the TV world bloomed into vibrant color and big screens in the 1970s and 1980s. Marian was the original chef at Nantucket's Straight Wharf restaurant, remaining for fifteen years (the restaurant was founded by Dun's brother Jock and his former wife, Laine). Marian then was the* Victory Garden *chef on TV, a show for which Russ was the producer and director. Marian has written two very accessible and authoritative cookbooks,* The Victory Garden Cookbook *and* The Victory Garden Fish and Vegetable Cookbook. *Her easy grace in the kitchen is fortunate, because she often does not know what her husband will bring home from fishing, shellfishing, or harvesting.*

Twenty-five years ago we bought a little house in Nantucket; it stood alone on the moors overlooking the sea. The first thing my husband, Russ, did was to plant a garden. He is a frugal man and growing his own had long been his priority. What I didn't realize was that he was about to become a hunter-gatherer.

What was it that awakened this primitive urge? I think now that as he sat on his deck he began to visualize edible creatures under the sands of the harbor, and they were there for his consumption and free at that. Shellfish!

Well, not totally free because he had to buy a shellfish license and a few trappings, but cheap compared to outfitting himself with expensive rods and reels and charter fishing trips. There were steamers and littlenecks and cherrystones and quahogs and scallops in their time, all for the taking of brave men.

And so it came to pass that with our arrival on the island each spring the very first stop off the ferry is the shellfish warden's station on Washington Street. Armed with his new shiny round shellfish badge, Russ is totally legal and ready for the pursuit. We often arrive on Saturday, which is great timing because the next day, Sunday, is the only day of the week one can legally stalk steamers, those delicate soft-shell clams found during low tide in tidal flats. No equipment necessary, just good eyesight to find their squirt holes in the sand and no squeamishness about your hands digging in muck to retrieve them.

So, while I air out the house and make the beds, Russ forages with the contentment that Thoreau must have felt at Walden Pond—sublime peace in the most beautiful of natural settings. Over the years, gathering steamers (soft-shell clams) has become a must-do with the grandchildren, and the younger they are the more they love it—a job as messy and delightful as finger painting. They only eat the harvest when they grow older, which, in their early years, leaves the melt-in-your-mouth steamers for the adults.

When Russ comes back with a giant bucket of these delicate clams, more than we can manage, we call friends on the island. Russ's best hunter-gatherer buddy, Dun, usually goes out with him, but if he is delayed getting to the island he comes over for the feast. We always call him, because we know how much he appreciates these gifts from the sea.

Once the steamers arrive it's my turn to take over. I scrub them, gently, looking for ones that are "mudders," which means they are full of mud, not clam meat. Because they come from such murky depths and never close completely, they need to be purged. I do that by soaking them in saltwater and vinegar or a cornmeal bath. Then they are ready for the fire. Dun and I talk about recipes, but we always come back to basics: steamed soft-shell clams. A lovely white wine, steamers with melted butter, crunchy dipping bread for the broth, a spring salad from the garden, and our friend Joe Hyde's dessert "orange à l'Arabe," and we have feasted for little and enjoyed much.

Summer arrives and Russ and Dun set their sights on hard-shell clams. Russ checks the tide calendar for morning low tides—the haul will be supper. Now there is a bit more equipment necessary—a rake, a quarter-bushel wire basket, rope, and buoy. The basket is tied with the line to a buoy float. Once they arrive at their clamming location, the basket is placed in the sea with the buoy marking its spot. As the clams are collected they go into the basket under water, which keeps them alive and fresh. Hard-shell clams do not burrow as deeply into the muck as soft-shell steamers; they are closer to the surface. So Russ and Dun walk through the water with rakes in hand, aggressively hunting for the clams with both the touch of the rake and their feet. (May I add that no one, but no one, is allowed to know the location of the clam grounds; we are all told lies about the trip.)

"Over the years, gathering steamers (soft-shell clams) has become a must-do with the grandchildren, and the younger they are the more they love it—a job as messy and delightful as finger painting. They only eat the harvest when they grow older which, in their early years, leaves the melt-in-your-mouth steamers for the adults."

—MARIAN MORASH

Hours pass, and the men return. I can tell by the heft of the baskets as they come up the hill how well they have done. They are jubilant—they have provided once again!

Russ and Dun divide the clams and decide how many recipes we can get out of their haul. One must divide the clams by size. Littlenecks and topnecks, which are 2 to 2^1/$_2$ inches wide, are best for eating raw or for my favorite "Chili Clams" recipe. Cherrystones, which are 2^1/$_2$ to 3 inches wide, are perfect for grilling, broiling, or roasting. Quahogs over 3 inches wide have enough meat to make a tasty stuffing for the shells or for a hearty New England clam chowder.

Once the harvest has arrived, look at how the family gathers! I often think of the nursery story about the Little Red Hen. She asked the duck, the cat, and the dog, "Who will gather the wheat?" "Not I, not I, not I," they said. "Who will make the flour into bread?" "Not I, not I, not I," they said. "Who will help me eat the bread?" "I will, I will, I will," they cried.

Tonight's meal is one of two that have become staples on clamming day. We choose between Clams Cataplana—a wonderful Portuguese dish harking to the cuisine of the Portuguese fishermen of Cape Cod—or our traditional New England clam chowder.

We will have clam chowder, a garden salad with Boston lettuce, mesclun, and lambs lettuce from the garden, corn on the cob and, for dessert, hot berries with a dollop of ice cream.

Again, Russ gets away with a thrifty and gratifying meal.

With such an abundant harvest we set aside some littlenecks and quahogs for another day. They keep well refrigerated, and we'll call friends to join in. Dinner will begin with a raw bar, broiled chili clams, and roasted stuffed clams. If the children have gathered mussels off the jetties, they'll toss the mussels on the grill. The hot fire will pop them open and the fragrant meats inside are ready to be dipped into a melted lemon butter— what could be easier or more delicious? For the main course we will serve locally caught striped bass with a cucumber and dill sauce, sugar snap peas, and baby new potatoes. Of course, the cucumbers, dill, peas, and potatoes are from Russ's garden.

That makes him very happy.

October comes. Our schedule is written in stone. October 1st signals the first day of family scalloping. This is one month before commercial scalloping begins, and the treasure is the Nantucket Bay scallop—surely the most precious shellfish we know. Sublimely sweet and rare, this is the hunter-gatherer's ultimate challenge.

Russ must invest a bit more money—waders are necessary. These great rubber pants/boots with suspenders protect the home scalloper from frigid waters and allow him a few comfortable hours in the sea as he tracks down the elusive scallop. The smaller clam basket is replaced by a bushel-size wire basket to hold the catch. Russ mounts the wire basket in an inflated tire inner tube. This contraption is tied (with four-foot line) to his waist, floating behind him and ready to receive the scallops.

Russ is almost overtaken with joy as we arrive on the island for scalloping season. Of course Dun joins him, and I think of two little kids about to go off to the penny candy store with a fist full of coins. How happy they are as they suit up with waders, warm sweaters, hats, rakes, and floating wire baskets.

As they head out the driveway, I plan the meal. It will be very simple because the best preparation of scallops is simplicity itself. The scallops will be sautéed. Surely we will add a puree of Waltham butternut squash and for a green, Swiss chard; we have so much in the garden. A fine Chardonnay and perhaps a warm apple crisp for dessert. This is a meal that will be devoured by our family, grandchildren included. The kids may pass on clams, but never on Nantucket Bay scallops.

When the men bring back a full haul, the shucking takes all afternoon. After the scallops are shucked, I remove the small cartilage strip that is attached to the muscle meat and these amazing bivalves are ready to cook. (They are so sweet that it is hard, when shucking, not to pop a few raw ones into your mouth.) Into a hot pan with a bit of butter and olive oil and in less than three minutes the scallops have caramelized and are ready to eat.

We celebrate the harvest and the hunter-gatherers! They have provided a delicious and natural meal once again. We toast the gathering, bless the bounty of the sea and the soil, and look to the spring.

A Musgrove Oyster Roast

K. DUN GIFFORD

Oysters divide us—there's really no middle ground between people who like them and people who don't. It's truly awkward to eat half an oyster.

But there are a lot of ways to gussy oysters up so they don't have an oyster's briny taste or its silky texture—adding bacon or ham and broiling them, for example, or baking them in a pie, making oyster stew, and many others. Oysters Rockefeller (laying bacon and spinach and maybe hollandaise sauce on top and broiling them) is a way to make oysters "safe" to eat for people who are put off by the classic but often sharp and metallic taste of fresh ice-cold oysters on the half shell.

It helps that oysters and some wines are happy partners. A glass of crisp Sauvignon Blanc is wonderful with strong briny oysters, while a glass of oaky Chardonnay or even Sauternes or Muscat loves fat oysters.

My friend Bagley has a special way with oysters, and even people who cannot abide the slippery plump texture of raw oysters on the half shell seem to like his roast oysters. Bagley's place is called Musgrove and it is on the ocean coast in South Carolina, where he has an actual oyster roasting shed. This shed is about six feet wide and twelve feet long, with a sturdy roof supported by four brick corner columns but no walls. Under the roof is a fire pit about six feet long and four feet wide, with two-foot-high brick walls on three sides, in a rectangular "U" shape.

An oak wood fire is laid inside this "U," and a big iron plate is set down on iron pegs sticking out from the brick walls so that the plate sits about two feet above the firewood. The plate is tilted slightly from the horizontal, to set up a draft so that the smoke goes out the back end of the plate and doesn't swirl about, which if it did would suffocate the oyster roast guests.

After the fire is roaring and the iron plate has gotten very hot, great big burlap bags of South Carolina oysters are emptied onto the plate and spread around. The intense heat quickly causes them to open, releasing their juices to flow down onto the hot iron, where it turns to steam that rises up to bathe the oysters—now opening further—with all its briny ocean flavors. The oyster shells soon get hot, too, roasting the oyster meats nestled in them, turning the meats just a slight shade of mahogany and imparting a sweet smoky oak wood flavor.

Since the roast starts just as dusk turns to dark, it's a powerful scene—fire, smoke, sparks, and steam swirling in the breeze and rising into the night sky, firelight dancing on everyone's faces. Standing around drinking really good wine out of a paper cup, I always flash on an image of Vulcan, the Roman god of fire, doing a cookout for the other gods, with oysters and scallops supplied by Botticelli's Venus. I am damn sure we are about to eat as well as they would.

At some moment the roast master decides the oysters are done, and they are heaved with long-handled shovels onto an old oak shucking table that is worn smooth and scrubbed white from years of use. The oys-

> "There are a lot of ways to gussy oysters up so they don't have an oyster's briny taste or its silky texture—adding bacon or ham and broiling them, for example, or baking them in a pie, making oyster stew, and many others."
>
> —K. DUN GIFFORD

ter meats are knifed from their shells into large blue and white enamel mugs, and melted butter poured over the oysters from an enamel pitcher. The butter, too, smells smoky; it was melted in the pitchers set over the fire on edge of the iron plate.

We each take our mug to long wooden trestle tables on the grass near the shed, sit down on benches, and, under light from tall torches, we dig into our mug of oysters and side dishes of coleslaw, corn bread, maybe some potato salad, fruit pies, and plenty of adult beverages.

Even people who do not eat raw oysters try these roast oysters, and most end up eating the full mug. It may be because these evenings are enchanted and contagious, but it may also be that these roast oysters are transformed in the roasting—warm, buttery, sweet without their briny juices, and touched with Musgrove sauce, a "secret ancient recipe" (of course!) that I am sure is mostly Worcestershire sauce with some lemon, shallots, and a shot of Tabasco, even though Bagley won't confirm or deny.

We sit together at the tables laughing and talking, the moon hangs high over towering southern oaks, shining on the long gray beards of Spanish moss softly dripping from their branches and moving ethereally in the soft breezes, and the real world seems distant. Sometimes Bagley arranges for a local gospel group to come at the end of the roast and sing spirituals and other songs of the Carolina coastal lowlands, which always turns into a sing-along.

It's the magic of a Musgrove roast oyster enchanted evening. And the power of the oyster.

Shipboard Cooks

K. DUN GIFFORD

Cooking on a cruising yacht is a very different kettle of fish from cooking at home because of cramped spaces, a rocking boat, and limited refrigeration. But with the exceptionally fresh fish and shellfish usually available, stunningly good meals are a regular pleasure.

In 1990 I was the skipper of one of five sailing yachts our group chartered to cruise the Alaska shoreline. My crew was cookbook author and food writer Nancy Harmon Jenkins, and environmentalists Paul and Eileen Growald, and their two children.

Nancy is a great cook and food expert; she writes award-winning books and articles. She grew up in Camden, Maine, and though not an experienced sailor, she grew up with "wet feet," as is sometimes said about people who know a lot about the sea and have a feel for it.

We were determined to catch some really good eating fish as we sailed along out into the Pacific and around about Prince of Wales Island, threading through narrow twisting tidal channels or rollercoasting majestically over great rolling Pacific Ocean waves. Robert Frost wrote of them as "Great waves looking over others coming in," and when they reached shore, "The shattered water made a misty din."

We didn't catch any salmon (not for lack of trying), but bought some from a fisherman just coming in with his day's catch. We did catch halibut while fishing drop lines at anchor in protected harbors after the day's run.

Nancy did wondrous things with these fish, frying and sautéing and even baking on the tiny stovetop with foil over the top of a baking pan. And we grilled extravagant chunks of halibut on a charcoal grill contraption that we hung over the side of the boat.

We used all the normal seasonings for cooking fish and had great luck with the local juniper berries we picked from the shore. They were much more pungent than store-bought, and at first we used too many and they overwhelmed the oils in the fish. But Nancy got it

right quickly, and so we had wonderful bounties of the mighty Pacific married with tastes of the majestic virgin fir and pine forests running right to the water's edge.

Our Alaskan Native American friends along on the cruise taught us that what we thought was white froth stuck to pine branches that hung down over the rocks and into the water was actually herring eggs, and they showed us how to row close to shore in our dinghies and cut off some branches. Back on board our boat we cut these boughs into small pieces, dunked them into lightly boiling water in a big pot, and—surprise! The eggs floated to the surface. After a few minutes of dunking, there is enough roe to skim off in a serving spoon, and pretty soon there was a bowl full of the roe. A little butter, squeeze or two of lemon—Prince of Wales caviar!

SHIPBOARD ON THE OUTER HEBRIDES

Ten years later we organized another expedition, this time to the Outer Hebrides, the arm of islands that marks the very top edge of Scotland. For this voyage, Elisabeth Luard, another prolific, prize-winning food writer and expert on all manner of foods and drink of the United Kingdom and Latin countries, was on board. A second British friend and London bon vivant, Anna Bevan, was also aboard, and Sara Baer-Sinnott and her fourteen-year-old daughter Casey rounded out the crew.

Our yacht was the fifty-six-foot comfortable, broad-beamed (well, tubby) sloop Ninsar—not a speedster, but sure a pleasure to sail. To pick her up we flew into Stornoway, on the island of Lewis at the tip-top of the Hebrides, about as far northwest as you can get in Scotland.

On the day we took command of Ninsar, I went off to a long "captain's meeting" to discuss the course of sail for our five-boat flotilla, the protocols for communicating by radio among us, essential safety procedures, and an entire laundry list of other details.

The rest of my Ninsar crew went off to the Stornoway local grocer, butcher shop, and dockside fish market to provision our cruise—coffee, tea, milk, sugar, cereal, flour, butter, cocoa, cookies ("biscuits"), bread, potatoes, carrots, meat, soup, salt, pepper, spices, leeks, paper towels, lots of wine and spirits, and even some of the dreaded "haggis."

Ninsar's crew trundled all our provisions and duffel bags aboard (no hard-sided suitcases permitted) and when I got back we stowed everything away before going through a familiarization drill. How do you flush a sailboat toilet? Where are the fire extinguishers? How do life vests work? How do you light the stove? Start the engine? What's the man-overboard procedure? And so on, and on.

We set sail out of Stornoway at about one o'clock, sailing away under the gaze of a fine old castle that looked out over the harbor and leaving the comforting solidity of the pier behind to pick up the rhythms of the ocean swells at the mouth of the harbor. The northeast wind was brisk and cold but the sky clear, and off we went on a surging broad reach, five boats of hardy explorers strung out in a long line, the lead boat about three miles ahead of the rearguard, Ninsar.

We reached Loch Shell at dusk, and in a bit of a drizzle sailed all the way up to the head of this narrow fiord in the fading light, where we anchored within hailing distance of each other. We were alone together—no other boats were there. It was quiet and cold in our snug hideaway, sheltered from the wind's rushes by the broad shoulders of Benn Mohr Mountain looming over the fiord's head.

By the time we had the anchor down and set and all the lines and other gear all snugged away, Elisabeth had set out a great chunk of bright orange Scottish cheddar and some soda crackers, and opened a bottle of Spanish red wine from Rioja (she lived for many years in Spain) as we talked about dinner. Fresh cod? Kidney stew? Vegetable medley? Soup? Scrambled eggs?

She knew a quick and simple stovetop cod dish, she said, or could sauté some vegetables in the full-fat local butter for a stew, and toast some of the crusty country whole-wheat bread. We'd have fruit and biscuits for dessert.

Now, many boat crews are satisfied to be served a dinner even of warm canned beef stew—thrilled if it's not burned and happy if it's only burned a little so that a solid shot of ketchup can mask its acrid burned taste.

We decided to take it easy this first night aboard Ninsar: Elisabeth cooked up a zesty thick vegetable stew, and we followed it with some apples and local sheep cheeses. We opened another bottle of wine, our anchor was holding firm, the drizzle had stopped, the stars were out, and all was well in the world.

Elisabeth's best meal was a truly exciting fish stew. She had bought scallops and mussels and three kinds of firm white fish—haddock, cod, and pollock—and found exactly the right combination of leeks, onions, and root vegetables. She made a light stock from the edges and scraps of the fish and a mirepoix of the vegetables, and then added a mélange of the seafood. The result was a joyous, rich, deep golden broth, chunks of white fish of different textures, black-shelled mussels, scallops with their roe attached, and cracked black pepper, all overlaid with some mysterious smoky flavor.

"Aye," said Elisabeth, "that's the peat coming out."

"You mean you put that expensive Scotch in this soup?" I grumped.

"A girl's gotta keep some secrets, doncha know?" she replied, grinning happily as all of us attacked her stew. So I'm not 100 percent sure, but I'll bet a bottle of good Mull single malt that the mystery taste was Scotch from one of the famous whiskey islands of the Hebrides, and probably Mull.

Mussels Four Ways

K. DUN GIFFORD

The mid-July Saturday we had set for our beach picnic turned out as forecast—cloudless, temperature in the mid-eighties, a light southerly breeze—so we called around and set 10:30 as the time to meet at the dock. Each family would pack its own lunches and water and soda, and an hors d'oeuvre and a bottle of wine to be shared among the adults. I'd bring a beach grill and we'd collect driftwood for the fire, and we'd cook burgers and franks and whatever else communally.

We were headed to Muskeget, a small island lying off the west end of Nantucket, and would spend the day on the narrow sandy spit that fronted the Atlantic's rolling surf on its oceanside beach and sheltered a calm protected bay with its other. We'd swim and surf-cast in the Atlantic, water-ski and dig clams in the bay, play capture-the-flag and fly kites, cook and eat, and lounge around on the warm sand.

We were four families, we were all veterans of Robert Kennedy's last campaign in 1968, we all cooked well, knew our food and wines, and patronized good restaurants. None of our seven children were over ten.

It went without saying that we took great pains with our picnics, both because we cared about our food and also because we were competitive by nature. The key to coming out on top was not how expensive the cheese or prosciutto you brought was, but how artful the combinations you made from them—cracked pitted green olives with no pimentos and rich with cracked black peppercorns, for example. Or, slices of membrillo (Spanish quince paste) alternating with thin slices of buffalo mozzarella and cut into triangles and placed on water crackers; or cream cheese mixed with sweet red pepper relish and spread on rye bread cut into tiny squares and held in stacks with a toothpick—these were the kind of things we took from our coolers.

Then we found a huge bed of mussels at the mouth of the bay—big shells, shiny and black, with small beards.

They pulled away from the beds in great, heavy clumps, maybe fifty or so mussels in each clump. Now this was really exciting: it was hard to find mussels growing in clean ocean water so they'd be without grit, but here we had this surprise gift from the sea. So we pulled up a half-dozen clumps, and packed them in pails and buckets, by now emptied of their lunches, so we could take the mussels back with us.

Then came the inspiration: we'd have a Muskeget Mussel Feast! We all had vivid memories of wonderful mussel dishes we'd eaten somewhere, and jabbered away about them. "The best I ever had was a simple mussel soup with garlic and parsley in Paris." Or, "There was this mussel salad with a thin mustard dressing at that little place on 67th and Madison." Or, "Nothing ever beat the mussels and wild rice with a lot of vermouth that my father used to make." The memories poured out as we stood around looking at the shiny black mussels, getting ready to pack everything and everyone up for the trip back to the dock and the cars.

We ended up, inevitably, with a cooking competition. We divided into four teams and agreed to meet at my house at 6:30 to start cooking. Then we had to make up rules.

We agreed that each team would be limited to cooking with the same five ingredients: mussels, butter, onion, parsley, lemon, and, of course, salt and pepper, which did not count as ingredients. Each team could also incorporate two "wild card" ingredients of its choice, one of which had to be an alcohol (such as wine or vermouth) and the other of which could be anything at all. The judging would be by secret ballot, each team would cast a single ballot, and no team could vote for itself. The vote would be with stars, so each team would rank the other three teams from one star to four stars. No team would receive zero stars. The team with the most stars would win, and if there was a tie, then the teams would vote again, but just the tied teams would be scored. The prize for winning would be bragging rights, which we figured in this crowd was much more valuable than, say, a bottle of Dom Perignon split among four or five people.

We gathered at 6:30 and, like good politicians, immediately started arguing about changing the rules. We decided that each team had to cook with the same number of mussels (twenty); the children would count the ballots to minimize opportunities for ballot rigging; no dish could be cooked for more than twenty minutes; the mussels had to be in their shells during the cooking; all teams had to use the same bread, if any was called for in their recipe; a dish would be disqualified if it did not use each ingredient; we would use identical bowls and silverware for the judging to prevent design considerations from influencing gustatory judgments; all dishes would be presented simultaneously; the ingredients could not be changed once prep and cooking began; all cooking pots were to be steel or enamel; and cooking utensils could be wood or metal.

Once we were all agreed on the rules, the prep work and the cooking began, each team with its own prep station and with its own burner on the stove. Kibitzing and heckling were nonstop. Inevitably, quite a bit more wine was drunk than was added to the dishes.

Soon water was boiling furiously in each pot, ingredients were added, liquids were reducing, and the cooking smells were sensational. It was an island stove, and everyone crowded around. Two teams used wooden spoons for stirring, while the other two teams used stainless steel. The cooking alcohol ran the gamut—a white wine, a rosé, Pernod, and a half-and-half white wine/Pernod mixture (by a 2 to 1 vote this latter narrowly survived a disqualification challenge on the grounds that it exceeded the ingredients limitation).

The bread was broiling—baguettes split and spread with sweet butter. The dining table was set at its four corners with tasting spoons and napkins, awaiting the arrival of the tasting bowls.

Suddenly the timer rang its twenty minutes, marking the end of time allowed for cooking. "Polls are closed," someone shouted, "let the judging and the counting begin." The teams ladled their entries into the big serving bowls and carried them to the dining table.

Astonishingly, there was a clear winner with thirteen stars. The scores for the other dishes were ten, ten, and seven. The lowest-ranked had the mussel meat taken out of the shells.

The winning team chose mustard and pernod as their wild cards: it was Pommery mustard, and Ricard Pernod. They named it "Piquant Moules à Moulin Rouge" (this was also the best name). The dish concept as they explained it was simple: a classic French fish stock base, enough Pernod to call to mind (say) Picasso, Lautrec, Hemingway, Fitzgerald, and Stein, and enough mustard to suggest that the houses of Pommery and Dijon are not far away. (See page 167 for the winning recipe.)

Scallops—Little Eyes and Big Eyes

K. DUN GIFFORD

Scallops are evanescent, like morning dew—fresh, they are magical, reflecting in a single moment the secrets of the night just past while illuminating the kaleidoscope of the day just begun. But let scallops dry out and they are dull and lifeless; they cannot stand by themselves and need supports like cheese and ham and butter to give them life.

Too long out of the water, or out of their shells, and they go flaccid, and when put to the flame, turn tough and chewy. But if cooked soon after catching and shucking, they are silky, succulent, sweet, and kind of sexy, a true gift of the sea.

Sea scallops, the big-eyed ones, are large and smooth-shelled. They live in deep water and reach harvest size when their shells are five to ten inches in diameter. We eat the single muscle—the eye—that holds the shells together. This eye is often the size of a short stack of old-fashioned silver dollars, but usually somewhat smaller, like a fifty-cent piece.

Nearly all the sea scallops we eat are caught by fishermen who haul them up in dredges they tow behind their trawlers. These fishermen clean most of their catch on the way back to their home port from the fishing grounds, though they leave a small percentage of the scallops in their shells for sale to high-end restaurants.

There is also a new but very limited market for "diver-caught scallops," which are harvested by scuba divers in shallow waters and have the marketing cachet of not being dredged. In the 1970s I dove for sea scallops off tiny Johns Island in Maine with my friend, former California senator John Tunney; this was before overfishing and pollution, and the bottom in twenty-five feet of cold Maine seawater was quilted with scallops. We soon had a wonderful haul of perfectly gorgeous ones—our limit was what we could carry.

That night we gloried in sea scallops seviche as hors d'oeuvres, followed by scallops in a milky chowder, and finished with scallops quickly sautéed in country butter in a big black skillet with ground black pepper. Nothing fancy; the scallops were so fresh they needed no gussying up.

An Old Ways Clambake

K. DUN GIFFORD

During years of long, cold winter evenings, television producer Russell Morash and I talked about doing a "real old-fashioned clambake," but we never quite got around to it because it's such a fearsome amount of hard physical work. But then one wintry February evening he said he wanted to do a clambake as a special for his PBS television show, *The Victory Garden*.

He had only one condition: it had to be truly authentic—wooden benches and tables, wooden or wire baskets, seaweed, a fire pit, and all the rest, just like the movie *Carousel*. No plastic, no aluminum beach furniture, no propane. Could we pull it off?

Yes, we could, I told him, for in my younger years I'd been a member of clambake teams and so I knew the drill. The keys to a perfect clambake, I told him, were

a detailed schedule, clear assignments of responsibility, and lots of committed manpower—men, women, children, and especially energetic male teenagers to whom we could promise lots of beer and food. Twenty worker bees would do it, I said, ten for the bakemaster and ten for the chef, with as many eaters as he needed for the show. We'd figure out how to avoid plastic and aluminum and burn some sage leaves or something to encourage the weather gods to smile on us.

We set a tentative date for mid-July and began making lists. Russ would be clambake producer, I would be bakemaster, and Russ's wife, Marian, would be chef (she was also a restaurant chef and the *Victory Garden* chef). Marian's food assistants would be my wife, Pebble, our friend Susie Fine, and Marian's daughters, Vicki and Kate. My clambake assistants would be our friend Bud Enright and my sons, Dunny, Porter, and Chad, and Russ's nephew Jeff. Winemasters would be our friends Richard and Thekla Sanford, who brought their crackling Sauvignon Blanc and velvet Chardonnay wines from California.

We made a list of the additional family and friends we wanted to invite, and in a flash were up to about sixty people, of whom about half we could count on to be worker bees. That was plenty; it looked like we were in business!

So we gave the old ways clambake the green light, acknowledging that there's always something wishful (and wistful, too) about saying yes on a cold winter night to a project for a hot day in the middle of the summer. But we were determined.

Now, a true New England clambake means a couple of tons of large granite rocks, at least two pickup truck loads of hardwood logs, a pickup truck load of rockweed (it can't be any old seaweed, it has to be rockweed), a heavy canvas tarpaulin (in the old days they used worn-out sails), and lots of rakes and shovels.

So we wrote out a detailed action and responsibility plan, deciding that as a matter of principle we would scavenge rocks and wood and other stuff for the fire and buy only the food and drinks. We would collect silvery driftwood to make benches and tables; battery-powered screwdrivers had just hit the market, and they were an unimaginable joy to use in making furniture, random beach sculptures, and flagpoles.

We got our hardwood for the fire from the town dump. Split-rail oak fences line miles of Nantucket roads, and as the old ones are replaced with new ones, the old are discarded at the dump. Hardwood is essential because it burns very hot but slowly enough to heat the rocks all the way through; pine burns too rapidly, and it also leaves an oily scent and black smudges.

We also got our rocks from the dump—the town excavated sand for the landfill cover and left behind great piles of rocks, and so we had little trouble collecting the couple of hundred soccer-ball-sized rocks we needed. The canvas tarpaulin was easy—we got an old one from the boatyard, and, in fact, it was part of an old sail.

The seaweed is never easy. Rockweed only grows on rocks, and Nantucket is mostly sand. But the harbor mouth is protected by rock jetties two miles long, so early in the morning of the clambake our crew went over in my boat and pulled two boatloads of rockweed from these rocks and ferried them to the clambake site.

A couple of days before the clambake, Russ and I went over to "Clambake Beach" (it now has this name) and devised the layout—fire pit there, Marian's cooking setup over there, drinks just next to her, social area there against the dune, and so on. We staked out the fire pit, too, since it had to be dug eighteen inches deep, eight feet wide, and twelve feet long.

The day before the bake, we mobilized our crews and dug out the pit, fetched the rocks, and lined the bottom of the pit with them in two layers. We gathered the oak railings and laid them on top of the rocks, "cribbing" them in two layers at right angles to each other, while tucking kindling wood (small pieces of driftwood collected from the beach) in the nooks and crannies as fire starters.

The day of the bake was a bluebird day—dry air, bright blue clear sky, and a dying northerly wind that would turn southerly and warm by midafternoon. I picked up the lobsters and soft-shelled clams, Marian's crew brought an astonishing array of "clambake vittles," the Sanfords brought buckets of their great wines, Russ directed everything, and many hands brought water, beer, juice, and soda.

At 11:00 we lit the fire, because it must burn strongly for an hour or two in order to heat the rocks all the way through. It is traditional that the youngest child who can hold a match helps the bakemaster light the fire, and this person was my daughter, Apple, then eleven. Soon the oak was blazing away, with the gentle breeze carrying the sparks and smoke shooting up from it out over the harbor and away from land. Perfect!

From time to time we "raked down" the fire to get the red-hot embers down into the crevices of the rocks, and not let them remain stacked up and thus burn too quickly. We used long-handled rakes and also swept the rocks with "brooms" that we had made by tying green brush together with rope. This was very hot work; we wet down the rake handles, so they did not catch fire. And as it burned down we threw wood onto the fire to keep it blazing strongly.

The granite rocks change colors as they heat up—black first, then white, and finally red. They get so hot they splinter into pieces and their chemistry actually changes; they're no good to be used for another clambake.

Then it was time for Act 1 of the clambake choreography—putting the seaweed and then the food atop the blistering rocks and covering it all with the tarpaulin. Everyone was assigned specific tasks that had to be done in the correct sequence and as rapidly as possible so the rocks would not cool down.

Our Act 1 choreography proceeded as follows: We raked the fire down, pulled the ash and big burning chunks off to one side to expose the rocks, threw the rockweed onto the hot rocks and raked it out evenly, set all the food on top of the seaweed—lobsters, clams in little cheesecloth bags, a chicken leg and some butter and onion slices in brown sandwich-sized paper bags, corn on the cob still in its husks that had been soaked in the harbor, links of Portuguese sausages also in bags, and potatoes in net bags; threw more seaweed on top of the food and leveled it; wet it down with a couple of pails of seawater; pulled the very heavy tarpaulin (itself having soaked all morning in the harbor) over the top of the whole pile; and covered its outside edges with small rocks and sand to seal in the steam. All the while the steam swirled around our heads, giving us intense aromatic and sensory foretastes of the clambake pleasures to come.

As bakemaster, I watched carefully for a few minutes to see if the center of the tarpaulin would rise up a little bit from the pressure of the steam underneath. When that happened, it meant that all was well in clambake land: there was plenty of steam and the clambake would cook. What I really wanted to see was little puffs of steam escaping here and there along the edges; I could tamp these down, making the whole bake tighter and steamier.

Then, blessedly, it was time for a swim, a refreshing drink, or both. And while the bake cooked, Chef Marian and her team offered the first course: clam chowder, corn bread, and grilled Portuguese linguiça sausages.

After about an hour, I began to fret, since as bakemaster, it was my job to know ("guess" is a more accurate description) when the clambake was cooked and it was time to "break the bake." The worst fate is an undercooked bake, with all the heat gone out of the rocks, but a close second is an overcooked bake with dried-out stringy lobsters, tough clams, soggy corn and potatoes, and burned sausages and chicken. So as bakemaster, I walked around and around the steaming bake, poking here and there, and sweating.

Counting on all the stars being in alignment, after about an hour and a half, I decided it was time, and called loudly: "Time to break the bake!"

The frantic Act 2 of the clambake choreography began: The food helpers gathered up their baskets, and the bake helpers scraped the hot sand off the tarpaulin's edges, getting ready to peel it back.

"On my count," I said, "on three." So I counted, and on three, the tarpulin was peeled back and—wonderful!

The steam surged up with its dazzling smells of wood smoke and seaweed and clams and lobsters, swirled away in the breeze, and the top seaweed was raked gently aside—there! The lobsters were bright red, the corn not burned or droopy, the bags of chicken and potatoes still damp. Perfect! Everyone shouted and cheered.

The rakers pulled the food to the sides, where the food team (wearing barbecue mitts and using tongs) picked it up and put it into the wooden bushel baskets for its short trip to the driftwood tables, where Chef Marian and her team had set up their serving line and the bounty was all spread out.

Then she cried, "Let the clambake begin!"

And, as Rodgers and Hammerstein would say, this was a real nice (old ways) clambake!

"Consumers should pay no attention to the recent alarmist reports on PCBs in farmed salmon. They are based on hypothetical risk, whereas we have strong evidence from human studies that fish consumption twice a week can reduce risk of sudden cardiac death by about one-third."

—WALTER WILLETT, MD, DrPH

BROILED SALMON FILLETS WITH SOY AND BROWN SUGAR GLAZE

K. DUN GIFFORD

This is a simple, quick, and delicious way to cook fresh salmon. There is enough time while this is being prepared and cooked to boil some peas or edamame beans and toast a couple slices of whole-grain bread. A meal like this warms the hearts of gastronomes and nutritionists alike.

SERVES 4

- 4 (6-ounce) 1-inch-thick salmon fillets, center cut from a full fillet with skin and belly flaps removed
- 2 tablespoons extra virgin olive oil
- 1 cup soy sauce
- 1/2 cup dark brown sugar

Place the salmon fillets about 1 inch apart on a rimmed baking sheet lightly brushed with olive oil. Brush both sides of the salmon liberally with the soy sauce. Cover the fillets with waxed paper or foil. Let marinate for 30 minutes.

About 15 minutes before cooking, preheat the oven to 450°F. Set the rack in the oven so that the top of the fillets will be about 4 inches from the heat source.

Remove the waxed paper or foil from the salmon and brush their tops again liberally with soy sauce. Turn on the broiler and place the baking sheet in the oven.

After 3 minutes remove the pan, carefully turn the fillets over with a spatula, brush the tops with soy sauce again, and return to the oven.

In a small bowl, add the brown sugar to the remaining soy sauce and stir until the sugar is dissolved.

After 3 minutes, remove the pan, brush the tops of the fillets liberally with the soy and brown sugar mixture, return to the oven, and close the door.

After 3 minutes, remove the fillets and, using the tines of a fork, test to see if they are done. If the tines go through the steak easily, the salmon is cooked. If they do not, return to the oven and cook for another 2 minutes and check again. Repeat as necessary. Serve immediately.

CHILI CLAMS

MARIAN MORASH

This and the following recipe from Marian Morash can only add to the pleasures of the clambake.

Open the clams as close to serving time as possible. Or, if you like, you can open them a few hours earlier, put on the topping, cover them well, and refrigerate you are until ready to cook. The escargot butter needs to be chilled and can be prepared days ahead. The butter recipe will make more than you need so use any extra for more chili clams or place on top of grilled or broiled fish.

SERVES 4

ESCARGOT BUTTER

- 1 cup butter, at room temperature
- 2 cloves garlic, finely minced
- 2 tablespoons chopped shallots
- 2 tablespoons chopped fresh parsley

CHILI CLAMS

- 3 strips bacon
- 24 littleneck clams
- 6 small pickled hot cherry peppers, diced
- Lemon wedges (optional)

To make the escargot butter, beat the butter, garlic, shallots, and parsley together in a small bowl, cover, and refrigerate until you are ready to use it.

Cook the bacon in a small skillet over high heat until the strips are cooked halfway through. Cool and cut into 1/2-inch pieces. Set aside.

Preheat the broiler. Open the clams, discarding the top shells, and place them in individual au gratin dishes or on pie pans or on baking sheets, spreading rock salt, if necessary, to steady the clams and keep the juices from spilling out.

Top each clam with a small spoonful of chilled escargot butter, a piece of bacon, and a few pieces of hot peppers.

Broil until the bacon is crisp. Serve immediately, with lemon wedges.

NEW ENGLAND CLAM CHOWDER

MARIAN MORASH

There are as many absolutes to a New England clam chowder as there are New Englanders. Rhode Island traditionalists insist proper chowder must have carrots, but it is not necessary to this recipe's creator, Marian Morash, who has lived in Connecticut and Massachusetts. It's fine to add your favorite ingredients, but she makes one restriction: never use flour or arrowroot in a New England clam chowder. You can shuck the clams and chop the raw meats. This can be time-consuming so she likes to quickly steam them open. You can steam open the clams and prepare the meats the day before you make the chowder. You can also complete the chowder and reheat it gently the next day. Marian's husband, Russ, thinks it gets better with age. ✑

MAKES 3 1/2 TO 4 QUARTS

   4 ounces salt pork, cut into strips
   24 to 30 large quahog clams
   4 cups water
   2 to 3 tablespoons butter
   1 to 1 1/2 cups diced onions
   2 to 3 cups finely diced carrots (optional)
   1 1/2 pounds potatoes, peeled and diced (3 cups)
   4 cups half-and-half, or 3 cups milk and 1 cup
      heavy cream
   Freshly ground black pepper
   Pilot crackers (optional)

Blanch the salt pork in boiling water for 5 minutes to remove excess salt. Drain, cut into 1/4-inch dice, and set aside.

Scrub the clams and squeeze each open one to make sure it closes up when handled. Discard any that do not close. Place the clams in a large stockpot, add the water, cover, and bring to a boil. Cook just long enough to open the shells, 5 to 7 minutes. Using tongs, immediately remove the clams that have opened from the pot. Discard any clams that have not opened in 10 to 12 minutes. Remove the meats, taking care to save all the juices in the shells, and return those juices to the pot. Discard the shells.

Carefully and slowly pour the clam broth from the stockpot into a large bowl. Sand from the clams will have settled in the bottom of the pot; be careful not to let any of the sandy broth get into the bowl. Discard the sandy broth and set the reserved broth aside. You should have about 8 cups of clam broth.

Separate the soft clam bellies from the tougher muscle meat. Chop the soft belly meat into small chunks, place in a bowl, cover with a bit of the broth, and refrigerate until you are ready to use them. You will have approximately 2 cups chopped clams.

Mince the clam muscles until they are almost a puree. This is most easily done in a food processor fitted with a steel blade. Put the minced clams in the same bowl that holds the belly meat. Depending on the size of the clams, you will have 1 to 2 cups of minced clam meat.

Place the diced salt pork in a clean 4-quart pot. Cook over moderate heat, stirring often, until the pieces have rendered their fat and are browned and slightly crisp. Remove the crisped pieces and reserve.

Remove all but 2 tablespoons of the fat in the pot and add 1 tablespoon of the butter. Add the onions and carrots, and sauté for about 5 minutes, until the onions are golden and wilted. Add the reserved clam broth and the potatoes, bring to a boil, reduce the heat, skim off any foam, and cook gently for 20 minutes, or until the potatoes are tender.

Stir in the half-and-half and bring to a simmer. Add the minced clams and the chopped clams in their liquid, and cook gently for another 2 to 3 minutes to just heat through. Season with pepper and swirl in the 1 to 2 tablespoons remaining butter. Top each serving with the crisped salt pork pieces and serve with pilot crackers.

Note: If you like the chewy texture of the clam muscle meat, just chop the entire clam into small pieces and omit the mincing procedure.

Some folks like to leave some of the crisped salt pork in the pot and let it cook along with the potatoes. I find that the clam liquid usually is salty enough, so I add the salt pork as a final garnish.

If you prefer to omit the salt pork altogether, use 2 tablespoons butter and 1 tablespoon oil to cook the onions and carrots.

You can use half evaporated and half regular milk in place of the half-and-half.

Oysters on the Half Shell and Beyond

K. DUN GIFFORD

The thing to know about oysters is that, safely in their shells, they are quite tolerant of the human race. But take them out of their shells and they are quickly unforgiving. So the trick is to eat them quickly; after they're opened, don't let them sit around on a platter.

When first cracked open, oysters really do taste of the sea—or bay, or harbor, or estuary—where they lived. It's hard to believe, sometimes—they're such googly things—that experts can very quickly recognize where an oyster is from with just a quick taste. Wine experts can do the same for wine, of course—but oysters?

Many of us know oysters two ways—on the half shell and as oysters Rockefeller. The former offers the real flavors of an oyster; the latter camouflages them. This does not make one "better" than the other, just different, like wine and sangria, if you will.

It used to be that rich people had refined tastes—the Rockefellers, Morgans, Lehmans, Big Jim Brady, and, of course, the royals; they all ate oysters. They ate them all the time, dozens at a sitting.

Of course, there are not as many oysters now as there used to be; pollution killed off entire populations of them.

But entrepreneurs are learning how to cultivate them, anchoring rafts in areas where the waters are clear, and raising them from seed (baby oysters are called "seed" and "spat.") If all goes well, we may once again have the pleasures of good, plentiful oysters at reasonable prices.

I share with James Beard an intolerance of "cocktail sauce"—"my pet abomination," he called it, that "entirely destroys the delicate taste of the oyster." He was, of course, quite right about this, and his own favorite way to eat them—"a little squirt of lemon juice, and perhaps some freshly ground pepper"—finds full favor with people who know their oysters.

But this does not write off a hundred other ways to enjoy oysters: roasted, stewed, in stuffing for domestic and wild birds (turkey, duck, goose), in pies, under spinach, watercress, and ham—the list of oyster dance partners is a very long one.

My own favorites are these:

- Roast oysters: These are properly cooked over a wood fire, and since they open when heated, they end up with a hint of the wood smoke, which is never the same twice, or even from oyster to oyster. They can also be cooked in grill baskets, right over the flames, or on a cookie pan in an oven preheated to 450°F. They are done when they open. We eat them straight from the shell, or dipped in a roasting sauce, usually made from butter, Worcestershire sauce, and Tabasco sauce.

- Oysters on the half shell: They should be ice cold, served with just lemon juice and freshly cracked pepper.

- Broiled oysters: With a piece of ham on top. In the best of worlds, this ham will have some fat on it, which melts down onto the oyster during cooking. Pork and shellfish are one of those pairings the gods invented to enjoy at their luaus, cookouts, or picnics.

Cooked oysters can also be sublime, usually because a fat has been added (such as bacon or ham, cheese, or mayonnaise), along with a pungent vegetable (such as shallots, watercress, spinach, or green peppers). Here are some of the varieties of cooked oysters. It is well worth trying the ones that appeal to your own personal tastes.

- Oysters Rockefeller: Strange as it may seem, spinach is not the real thing for this dish; watercress is. And it makes all the difference in the world if the watercress has a zing and crispness that matches the steeliness of good oysters.

- Oysters Remick: With bacon, mayonnaise, and cayenne pepper.

- Oysters Kirkpatrick: With shallots and green peppers.

- Oysters Florentine: With spinach, cheese, and Mornay sauce, which is suspiciously close to oysters Rockefeller.

GIFFORD'S BAKED OYSTERS

K. DUN GIFFORD

If you love oysters on the half shell, you'll love these oysters hot from the oven. And if you think you don't like oysters, be sure to give this recipe a shot! 🦪

MAKES A DOZEN

12 oysters on the half shell
3 slices Canadian bacon
1/4 cup butter at room temperature
1/2 cup chopped shallots or onions
2 tablespoons freshly squeezed lemon juice

Preheat the oven to 450°F. Place the oysters on rock salt in a sheet pan.

Cook the bacon in a small skillet over high heat until the slices are cooked halfway through. Cool and cut each slice into four equal pieces. Set aside.

Mix the butter, shallots, and lemon juice together. Spoon the butter mixture on top of each oyster, and cover with a piece of bacon. Bake until the bacon turns brown, and the oysters are warm.

DIPPING SAUCE FOR ROAST OYSTERS

K. DUN GIFFORD

If you share with James Beard (and Dun Gifford) a distaste for cocktail sauce, this is a great alternative! 🖾

MAKES ENOUGH FOR 24 OYSTERS

1/4 cup Worcestershire sauce
1 (15-ounce) can beef consommé
1/4 teaspoon ground red pepper
1/4 cup freshly squeezed lemon juice

Mix together the Worcestershire sauce, consommé, red pepper, and lemon juice in a small saucepan. Heat until warm. Serve in cups or ramekins.

POACHED ALASKA HALIBUT WITH COURT BOUILLON

K. DUN GIFFORD

Halibut is bright white, lean, and firm, and usually sold in steak cuts. It is terrific broiled, grilled, or poached, and makes a nice mousse, too. On our Sail Alaska expedition in 1995 (see page 154), John Walton, on one of the other boats, caught a very large halibut one evening after we'd anchored in a snug harbor near Cape Chacon on the southern tip of Prince of Wales Island in Alaska. It had to weigh two hundred pounds and was very difficult to subdue.

I begged a steak from John and returned with one as a prize. Nancy Jenkins and I talked about how to cook it and decided to poach it with a juniper berry court bouillon and serve it up (of course) with lemon and butter and cracked pepper. Cloves are traditional in court bouillon and since we had none in our own spare ship's stores, why not try juniper berries?

Serve with melted butter and cracked pepper, or with any other sauces traditional with firm white fish—tomato, curry, or velouté (add cream to cooking liquid), for example. Halibut is excellent cold, too, with any of the mayonnaise variations, such as remoulade or Russian dressing. 🖾

SERVES 4

12 cups salted water
1/2 cup cider vinegar
1 cup juniper berries (or 8 cloves)
2 carrots, thinly sliced
2 onions, thinly sliced
1 cup white wine
1 bay leaf
1 to 2 pinches of dried thyme
1 to 2 pinches of fresh parsley
1 pound halibut steak
Melted butter, to serve
Freshly cracked black pepper, to serve

Combine the water, vinegar, juniper berries, carrots, onions, wine, bay leaf, thyme, and parsley in a skillet (or poaching pan) large enough to hold the halibut steak lying flat. Bring to a boil; simmer for 10 minutes. Carefully slide the halibut into the liquid and bring to a gentle boil. Cook for about 10 minutes per inch of thickness, and test with a fork. It is done when the fork goes right through easily.

Serve with melted butter and cracked black pepper.

HEBRIDES FISH CHOWDER

ELISABETH LUARD

A fish soup, or bree, can be made with any white fish—cod, haddock, and pollock are all suitable. You can also make it with the lesser parts of a salmon—tail and cheeks—though the bones and head are not suitable for a broth and you'll have to beg a cod head and bones from the fishmonger, or use plain water instead of fish broth. In the clean, clear waters of the Outer Hebrides, cookbook author and shipmate Elisabeth Luard salted the broth with a ladleful of seawater. Dairy products—butter and cream—are an important part of the traditional diet of the Western Isles: every household kept a cow, churned its own butter, and fed the whey to the pig, provider of the family's annual store of bacon. Serve with oatcakes (see page 42) and fresh cream cheese—soft, thick, and a little sour, known in the Highlands as Crowdie.

SERVES 4

I pound white-fleshed fish fillets (ask the fish-monger for the bones, skin, and heads, too)
Sea salt
4 cups water
I bay leaf
¼ teaspoon peppercorns
I small head celery
2 large carrots
2 large leeks
2 pounds yellow-fleshed potatoes, peeled and sliced
I tablespoon butter or vegetable oil
2 tablespoons diced lean bacon
Sour cream or crème fraîche
Chopped chives, for garnish

Dice the fish flesh, keeping an eye out for and removing any little bones, salt lightly, cover, and set aside.

Put the fish heads and bones into a large pot with the water and bring to a boil. Skim off any gray foam that rises. Add the bay leaf and peppercorns and salt lightly.

Remove the outer stalks of the celery, coarsely chop, and add them to the pot, reserving the heart. Scrape or peel the carrots and add the scrapings to the pot. Coarsely chop the green part of the leeks and add to the pot, reserving the white. Simmer for 20 minutes—no longer or the soup will taste bitter. Strain the broth and return it to the pot.

Bring the strained broth to a boil and add the potatoes. Turn down the heat, partially cover with the lid, and simmer for about 15 minutes, until the potatoes are nearly soft.

Meanwhile, dice the reserved celery heart, carrot, and leek. Melt the butter in a large skillet over medium heat and add the diced vegetables and bacon and sauté just long enough to soften the vegetables—don't let them take color. Add to the soup.

When the potatoes are tender, drop the fish on the top, cover, and simmer for 2 to 3 minutes, just until the flesh turns opaque.

Remove the soup from the heat, check the seasoning, and ladle into bowls. Drop a spoonful of sour cream into each bowl and finish with a generous sprinkle of chopped chives.

Note: If you don't have sour cream, use fresh light or heavy cream and sour it with a squeeze of lemon juice. If you don't have chopped chives, save a little of the leek green and use that instead.

PIQUANT MOULES À MOULIN ROUGE

K. DUN GIFFORD

This winning recipe of the Mussels Four Ways contest (see page 156) is a champion whether you're on Nantucket Island or Manhattan Island.

**SERVES 4 TO 6 FOR APPETIZERS, OR
1 OR 2 FOR A MAIN COURSE**

- 2 large white onions
- ¾ cup butter
- 3 tablespoons Dijon mustard, plus more as needed
- 3 cups Pernod, plus more as needed
- 3 tablespoons cracked black pepper
- 2 tablespoons flour dissolved in ½ cup cold water
- 1 lemon
- Bunch parsley
- 20 mussels

Very finely dice one large white onion, and coarsely chop the second onion.

Melt ½ cup of the butter in a large skillet over high heat. Cook the onions until browned, about 10 minutes.

Put 2 inches water, 2 tablespoons of the browned onion, the mustard, 1 cup Pernod, and 1 tablespoon of the cracked pepper into a stockpot, and bring it to a boil. Meanwhile, julienne the zest of the lemon and chop the parsley.

Allow the Pernod mixture to boil for 1 minute. Then add the mussels, the lemon zest, half the parsley, and the rest of the onion. When the mixture returns to a boil, cover, and set a timer for 4 minutes and 45 seconds.

Put the remaining 2 cups Pernod, 2 tablespoons cracked pepper, parsley, and ¼ cup butter in a large skillet and heat over high heat. With a ladle take 1 cup of the broth

from the mussel kettle and add to the skillet, which should be boiling hard. Stir the flour mixture into the soup to thicken. If you wish, adjust the sauce in the skillet, with additional mustard or Pernod.

When the timer goes off, pour the mussels' cooking liquid into a bowl, leaving the mussels in the stockpot.

The mussels will still be warm in their cooking pot, but not too hot to touch, and they will give off a whiff of Pernod (à Moulin Rouge).

To serve, put the mussels in a bowl or bowls and put the sauce in a pitcher. Pass the pitcher for each diner to pour the sauce into his or her bowl. The sauce will be the consistency of light cream, coating the mussel meats with flecks of green parsley and pale white onion.

SIMPLE BAY SCALLOPS

K. DUN GIFFORD

Bay scallops are the small ones, the size of marbles. Sea scallops are the big ones, about the size of a ping-pong ball. Not surprisingly, the bays have a much finer texture than the seas, but both are true gifts of the food gods in charge of delicacies. No one will be surprised to know that sea scallops are regularly cut into bay-sized pieces and sold as bays, because bays command higher prices, and it's not so easy to tell the difference when they are battered, fried, and smothered with tartar sauce; even experts are sometimes fooled.

With all scallop recipes, always favor undercooking rather than overcooking. Overcooked scallops may still taste good, but they have the texture of rubber bands.

SERVES **4**

> I pound bay scallops
> $^1/_2$ cup unsalted butter, plus more as needed
> Lemon wedges
> Freshly cracked black pepper

Heat a large cast-iron skillet over medium-high heat. Add the butter and move it around with a wooden spoon or spatula to help it melt quickly. When it is melted and hot, add the scallops all at once, and stir them around so that they are coated with the butter. Let them sit still for about 15 seconds, then move them around again and repeat for about 2 minutes, so they brown a bit all over. Remove the skillet from the heat and spoon the scallops onto plates. Squeeze lemon juice and shake the pepper over them, and eat them with toothpicks, one by wonderful one.

VARIATION: For floured bay scallops, dust the scallops with flour; wondra (instant flour) is good because it is less likely to clump. Proceed with the recipe as above.

Sprinkle with very finely chopped parsley after squeezing the lemon juice and the pepper over them.

SCALLOP SEVICHE

K. DUN GIFFORD

Tart and fresh, seviche is a perfect way to enjoy scallops. There are thousands of recipes for seviche. The basic ingredients are fish and citrus juice, to which any number of additional ingredients may be added, including an oil (olive oil, canola oil, or other vegetable oil), chopped onion, black pepper, sliced or diced avocado, herbs, and diced tomato. Optional additions include olives, tomato juice, peppers, lettuce (as a bed), garlic, parsley, capers, chopped cucumbers, and more, too. Papaya or mango cubes can be substituted for half (or even all) of the tomatoes; diced coconut (or cubes), which are sometimes browned lightly, can be added; and (sad to say) the ubiquitous cocktail sauce can be used as a base instead of fresh tomatoes. But done traditionally, with fresh ingredients, this is a terrific summer dish. Seviche is often served on large, tropical scallop shells.

SERVES **4**

> I pound bay or sea scallops
> Juice of 3 lemons
> Juice of 3 limes
> I cup extra virgin olive oil
> I pound tomatoes, peeled, seeded, and chopped
> I onion (Bermuda, if available), chopped
> $^1/_4$ cup chopped fresh parsley
> 3 tablespoons chopped fresh cilantro
> I teaspoon dried oregano
> $^1/_2$ teaspoon freshly cracked black pepper
> Lettuce leaves (Bibb, if available)
> I avocado, pitted and chopped

Put the scallops in a ceramic or other nonmetallic bowl, cover them with the lemon and lime juices, and then cover the bowl with plastic wrap, pricking a hole in it. Let rest in the refrigerator for 6 hours to overnight; for larger scallops, leave for 12 to 24 hours. The citric acids in the juice "cook" the scallops, and they are done when they have turned white all the way through.

In a large bowl, mix together the oil, tomatoes, onion, parsley, cilantro, oregano, and pepper. Drain the scallops, add them to the mixture, and combine well. Place a lettuce leaf on each plate, spoon 3 or 4 tablespoons of the mixture on top, and surround with avocado slices.

Classic Scallop Combinations

The happy company of scallops is cream, cheese, and frequently mushrooms. There are dozens of classic scallop dishes that bring these friends together in harmony, often in the companionship of sherry. This may be because the French love scallops, and recognize the appropriateness of these combinations. Coquille Saint-Jacques is probably the best-known dish, but there are dozens of other dishes. Many of them are based on adding scallops to basic sauces such as duxelles and Mornay. Scallops also show up regularly in chowder and seafood soups, where they add both texture and flavor.

The real trick always to keep in mind is that if scallops dry out during cooking, they are truly awful. So keep them moist—with fat in skillets; oiled on brochettes; in juice for seviche; and in milk, cream, and butter for creamy stews.

Grilling Sea Scallops

Here are some delicious ways you can grill scallops. If you want the smaller bay scallops, you'll need to plan on buying ten to fifteen per person; on the other hand, if you're buying the larger sea scallops, you'll need only four to five per person.

Grilled Sea Scallops en Brochette: The challenge is to cook the scallops all the way through without either charring the outside or drying them out. A restaurant technique is to boil them first in saltwater for a minute—no more—which seals them. Then thread them onto a skewer, and go to work. Those flat skewers (like swords instead of rods) are best so the scallops don't spin when you try to turn them. It's good to oil the skewers lightly, and if you use olive oil, use the yellow instead of the green (there are bits of olive in some green oils, and they impart a bitter taste when burnt).

Grilled Sea Scallops Plus, en Brochette: Almost anything goes here. Intersperse the scallops on the skewers with mushroom caps, ham, bacon, onion quarters, peppers, cherry tomatoes, zucchini, garlic cloves, and so on.

Grilled Sea Scallops Un-Brochette: Instead of skewers, use a hamburger grill, the kind with two parts that close and clamp the hamburger inside; or one of those "basket" grills. With these, there is almost no limit to what you can cook with your scallops. For example, you can put oiled zucchini or summer squash in the flat grill and grill them until they show a brown color, and then add the scallops. If using large sea scallops, cut them into disks horizontally across the grain and oil them lightly. Close the grill and return them to the heat for 2 to 3 minutes per side, until done. For the baskets, use cubed zucchini and summer squash, cherry tomatoes, and sliced green, red, or yellow bell peppers. Cook the vegetables until light brown, then add the scallops and cook for 4 to 6 minutes, shaking the basket gently from time to time.

"When we turned to look at protein, we found intense controversies about what kinds of protein are wisest to eat (plant or animal); how often and how much animal protein is healthy; how food animals are raised, slaughtered, and processed; and whether organic meats are sufficiently healthful to justify their higher costs."

–K. DUN GIFFORD AND SARA BAER-SINNOTT

"With animals raised for meat, there is more to processing than just picking the fruit!"

–JOHN AND SUKEY JAMISON

MEAT

For the length of the known history of food, most humans ate meat as the centerpiece of their daily rations, at least whenever they were fortunate enough to have it available and could afford it. Early humans got their meat by hunting down or catching, and then killing, four-footed land animals, two-footed land animals (such as birds), no-footed land animals (like snakes), and other no-footed creatures that live under water (such as fish and shellfish). And they got their grains, fruits, vegetables, and nuts by gathering them in the wild. These were hunter-gatherers.

Very, very slowly these hunter-gatherers and their descendants learned to domesticate and farm animals and fish, and to raise grains, fruits, vegetables, and nuts. In doing so, they became farmers, learned to build homes, developed

Meat in Our Lives
K. DUN GIFFORD

languages, lived in one place in a community, figured out how to store foods to tide them through the cold winters when food would not grow, and developed hierarchical structures and rules of governing behavior that are essential when humans live in close proximity with each other.

An Englishman named Colin Tudge wrote a book published in 1980 called *Future Food,* which has cult status among deep thinkers about, well, about the future of food. One of these deep thinkers is Joan Gussow, formerly a professor at Columbia University. Joan is responsible for turning a lot of us on to Tudge's book and for much of the careful theorizing on why the world needs "local and sustainable" agriculture now. Even better, she gets out of her academic robes and keeps an organic kitchen garden in back of her home on the east bank of the Hudson River.

Tudge and Gussow argue that if we do not get our agricultural act together, we're going to have unimaginably large nutrition and health problems. These will rise up from pollution, fresh water shortages, food-borne diseases from bad animal husbandry, and so on. Even the Central Intelligence Agency agrees with some of this, predicting that wars soon will be fought over access to fresh water supplies because of the huge amounts of it now being diverted to agricultural arid areas and industrial uses everywhere.

The wonderful thing about Tudge's writing is its accessibility. "The hunting and raising of beasts has determined, in large part, the course not only of cultural development but also of human evolution," he writes. "We are the kind of beasts we are, with deft

> "Nothing wrong with a good steak or
>
> BLT or ham and cheese or lamb chop or
>
> fried chicken—just not every day."
>
> —K. DUN GIFFORD

fingers and agile brains, partly because our ancestors pitted their wits against their fellow beasts, and partly because they succeeded." But, he argues, we have gone overboard today—we raise too much meat unsustainably, slaughter it inhumanely, and eat too much of it for our good health.

The scientific evidence for Tudge's argument is far more extensive today than it was in 1980, of course, but what's lovely about Tudge's book is his conclusion. "I see meat [in its proper role] as a scarce and precious thing," and not for "three meaty meals a day but as meat taken as a feast, the way that hunting people do." For an earth and its people burdened with the increasing demands of societies characterized more by consumption than subsistence, this sounds about right. Nothing wrong with a good steak or BLT or ham and cheese or lamb chop or fried chicken—just not every day.

SOME MEMORIES OF MEMORABLE MEAT

We humans evolved as omnivores; there's not much we don't eat, whether it be from the animal and plant kingdoms (or even the mineral, as with salt). Most other animals are either meat-eaters (lions, cats) or plant-eaters (cows, horses), but we humans are omnivorous crossovers.

If we are not vegetarians, it's meat that gets the respect and the place of honor at our tables, cookouts, and drive-throughs. Meat's at the center of the plate, the buffet, the tailgate, the grill, and the bun. And don't all of us have memories of memorable meat meals?

ROAST LAMB

At formal Sunday lunch after church at my grandparents' house, all three generations of us sat around the dining room table, and then a roast leg of lamb was set down in front of my grandfather. He stood to make the first few cuts into its fatty outer skin, now crackly crisp, and then into the pink juicy meat inside. Grampa was a great carver, and he laid down the slices neatly on the big platter ringed with the potatoes and carrots cooked in the roasting pan with the lamb in its "juices" (for which you can read "fat"). The gravy, too, was made with these juices, and we always had two kinds, a thin one, which was just the juices put through a fine strainer, and a thick one, which was thickened with flour. Grampa liked the flour gravy, and Granny liked the thin gravy. We also had mint sauce (not mint jelly), a condiment made by Crosse & Blackwell containing sugar, vinegar, and minced mint leaves.

ROAST BEEF

A big round of roast beef, wrapped with butcher's twine, lying on its side on the platter, oozing juices, the carving knife in my father's hand, whispering against the sharpening steel, the room filled with the rich aromas of roast meat. Dad was as good with the carving knife as Grampa, and soon the serving platter was layered with slices of juicy, medium-rare roast beef, with a couple of well-done ones off to the side for my youngest brother, who wanted his meat well done. The platter had onions, potatoes, and carrots on it, too, all roasted in the pan with the beef and its fats. We had gravy, too, without flour, and currant or beach plum jelly in silver bowls. It was just as luscious as the roast beef. Mom always asked the butcher to leave some fat on the outside of the roast, because it turned crisp in the roasting and basting, and we each got a bit of this "crispy" and loved it.

THANKSGIVING TURKEY

There was always a fat, proud, golden Thanksgiving turkey, stuffed with my mother's apple-and-breadcrumb stuffing, waiting for the carver to begin, surrounded by its supporting cast: giblet gravy gleaming in its silver gravy boat, green beans with shaved almonds, creamed squash with a simple sprinkling of nutmeg, sweet potatoes with marshmallows melting on top, creamed onions, cranberry sauce (both the jelly and the jam ver-

sion; some liked it smooth, some liked it rough). Mom actually cooked one twenty-four-pounder for the meal, and a second smaller one (say, eighteen pounds) for leftovers, sandwiches, and turkey soup with rice. We had Thanksgiving turkey for weeks, and this was a good thing.

FRIED CALF'S LIVER

Then there was liver. My dad liked it, and since he liked it, he was determined to make damn sure we did, too. His favorite way to cook it was very, very simple: dust the raw liver slices with flour, slip them into a very hot skillet with crackling Crisco thickly covering the bottom, and turn them a couple of times, dusting again with flour again if the juices ran out too heavily. The trouble with liver is that the time difference between edible and inedible is about 10 seconds—too long on the heat and the liver turns gray-brown in color and granular in texture; it's just awful, even gag-inducing. But if it's still a bit pink, it's, well, it's okay, especially if your father has his eyes fixed right on you. But try as hard as my father did, liver did not take root in any of us. You don't see liver around much anymore, at the meat counter or on restaurant menus. I don't know where it's all going these days, but I don't ask, either.

ROAST PORK AND PORK CHOPS

We ate a lot of roast pork and pork chops while my own children were growing up. Julia Child had something to do with this: she was a fan of pork, and in her books and on her TV shows she taught us all that pork is good roasted with fruit—think of pictures of a whole roast pig with an apple in its mouth. So we happily ate pan-fried or broiled pork chops with dollops of applesauce, roast of pork with prunes, whole hams cooked with pineapple slices draping over them and studded with cloves. The acids in fruits actually do tenderize meat, and make lean meat more palatable. Medieval and Renaissance cooks used fruits with abandon, particularly apples; meat in those days was very, very lean.

GRILLED STEAK

Steak was never a hard sell in our house. My dad was a steak freak, right to the end of his long life, and so were we. He really only wanted it grilled and had the fireplace in the kitchen rebuilt so that its hearth was waist-high, making it wonderfully convenient and friendly. I did the same in my kitchen, and it's a lot more sociable (and less susceptible to overcooking) than having to run in and out of the kitchen and into the backyard.

Dad was particular about his grill fires—charcoal briquettes were the absolute best, he insisted, and all the other ways were tied for last place. I'm not much for those briquettes; they're bonded with chemicals and sometimes with "starter fluids," which give the meat a petroleum flavor. It's hardwood charcoal for me, or better still, wood itself.

I am not a snooty epicure about steak. Some of the best steaks I've ever had were in great American steakhouses like Smith & Wollensky, or Morton's, or Peter Lugar Steak House. They use gas grills to cook thousands of steaks a day to perfection—a bit crisp on the outside, as-you-like-it doneness on the inside, and juicy, never dried out. So it doesn't have to be wood to be great; it may be that the steaks over wood fires just smell better.

It was a shock to learn that not all true gastronomes like corn-fed beef. "Too fatty, tastes like fat and not meat" say most Europeans. The Tuscans slice their lean steaks very thinly—say, a half inch thick—cook them rapidly over high heat, and then squeeze lemon juice over, spoon a little olive oil on top, and sprinkle on some sea salt. For Americans growing up in the cowboy tradition of great slabs of thick juicy steaks, it's startling to discover that those Tuscans eat thin steaks that taste absolutely wonderful, too.

FOIE GRAS, MANY WAYS

The strange thing about foie gras is that while I have eaten a lot of it, I cannot remember a single time when it was anything but just wonderful—smooth-textured but still thick and creamy, strangely exotic tasting, and luscious. That's not normal; everyone's got a favorite food that every once in a while is disagreeable.

I ate foie gras growing up, little dabs of pâté on a cracker at my parents' parties, often with a small bit of black truffle (or something masquerading as a black truffle). I've eaten fresh slabs of it on a goose and duck farm in France near Agen (which also houses a foie gras museum) deep in plum and prune country, sitting at trestle tables under flowering cherry trees listening to the geese gabbling, sitting with the farmer (and our mutual friend) François Pont, the former French foreign minister who happens to be a master of foie gras.

I've gorged during an afternoon meal of six courses each of which featured a different fresh foie gras preparation to celebrate the annual truffle festival and market in Perigueux in November. I've chosen it many times as an appetizer in New York restaurants, usually served icy cold on a plain white plate, with small cornichons and tiny ramps, or four perfect mustards, or a fan of small green apples and currant jam. I've savored it in a Nantucket kitchen on a dark and stormy night sautéed in a very hot skillet with a Sauternes reduction sauce and served with thin slices of broiled French bread.

Healthy Eating and
Animal Protein

K. DUN GIFFORD AND SARA BAER-SINNOTT

During the fifteen-year life of Oldways we have consistently challenged diet and nutrition fads that diverted consumers from the verities of eating wisely.

Most of the authors of these diets sell their books and products by scapegoating a food, or a food group—fats, carbs, sugars, and so on. Over time, these diets capture a small or even a modest percentage of the population, but after their brief moments of fame, fad diets generally drift off into the dustbin of history because people tire of them; they don't work; and medical and health professionals condemn them.

We challenged low-fat fad diets in the early 1990s because they fly in the face of the eating patterns of human evolution and virtually unanimous nutrition science. The soundest eating pattern, we discovered, was a moderate-fat approach, with about 30 percent of daily calories from fats. So, we developed an education campaign based on healthy, delicious, and traditional eating patterns like the Mediterranean diet, which included moderate consumption of "good fats" such as olive oil.

When we turned to look at protein, we found intense controversies about what kinds of protein are wisest to eat (plant or animal); how often and how much animal protein is healthy; how food animals are raised, slaughtered, and processed; and whether organic meats are sufficiently healthful to justify their higher costs.

We cut our teeth learning about protein with our traditional Mediterranean diet pyramid, which describes the optimal eating pattern in the Mediterranean in the 1960s. This was the cuisine of the middle class and the poor, and in Oldways' promotion of the healthfulness of this traditional Mediterranean diet, we reported that meat was eaten only several times a month. This sounded draconian to meat eaters, of course, but in southern Greece and Italy in the 1960s, meat was eaten as a treat, in the big Sunday meal after church. And when meat was a regular part of a meal, it was generally used as a flavoring, not as the central star of the meal. Fish and shellfish were probably eaten more frequently, particularly along the coastlines, but the data on this were not extensive.

Based on the evolving nutrition science, we've modified our thinking in the last several years to recommend meat several times a week, but always in modest quantities and with the fat well trimmed. The issue of concern is not the protein in meat—it's good for you—but the saturated fat that's part of virtually all animal products, which is not good for you.

We both love tastes of different kinds of meat—be it roasted, grilled, broiled, raw, braised, boiled, or steamed—and to provide a snapshot of the best meat products from cattle, pigs, lambs, and chicken, we've turned to some of the country's best sources for these meats. Bill Niman (pork, lamb, and beef), Mel Coleman (beef, pork, chicken, lamb, bison, and sausage), John Jamison (lamb), and Scott Sechler (chicken) represent the highest qualities of animal husbandry—respect for the environment and the land the animals graze on, awareness of barn and pen space, attention to properly balanced feed, and a focus on taste.

We hope their stories will make you stop and think about the meats you choose to eat, and that you will vote with your fork for meats from producers who respect these traditions of family farms.

For us at Oldways and our friends, these farmers symbolize the old ways: dedication to those ways that preserve sound farming practices, respect sustainability throughout the farming cycles, and produce natural meat with high nutritional values and outstanding flavor. Our estimable British food writer friend Philippa Davenport calls meats produced this way to be "of impeccable provenance," and we like this linkage of fine meats to fine works of art.

Niman Ranch Pork

BILL NIMAN

Bill Niman is a pioneer in sustainable ranching, and has raised cattle, pigs, and lambs for many years. The quality of the meats produced by his network of committed colleagues is so high that it appears on the tables of top-rated restaurants and is demanded by mail-order customers from coast to coast.

I started Niman Ranch thirty years ago in Marin County, just across the Golden Gate Bridge from San Francisco. We still raise cattle on the original ranch, but have expanded to sell pork and lamb, too. Today, Niman Ranch is a network of independent family farmers and ranchers who all raise livestock according to our strict protocols.

Niman Ranch's strict animal husbandry guidelines require that our animals be treated humanely, fed only all-natural feeds, and allowed to mature naturally, without using hormones. We offer beef, pork, and lamb to restaurants, retailers, and directly to consumers through an on-line market, and you'll see "Niman Ranch" on the menu at many restaurants these days.

Consumers don't think about it, but most meat in the United States goes through many distribution layers before it reaches them. At Niman, by working directly with a network of independent family farmers, we control our meat all the way from the farm until it reaches our customers. We know where and how each piece of meat is produced and provide direct feedback to our farmers and ranchers about quality.

REVIVING THE FAMILY FARM

Most hogs in the United States today are raised in confinement factories with liquid manure systems. (Liquid manure systems are ones where water is added to manure; typically lagoons are used to store animal wastes.) Because these confinement factories contain thousands of animals crowded into buildings, they are unhealthy environments for animals, making it necessary to feed them antibiotics as part of their daily diet. Weaning as early as two weeks of age also adds to the need for these continual doses of drugs. The liquid manure systems can cause pollution problems to nearby waters and can cause serious odor problems.

At Niman Ranch, we don't agree with this way of raising pigs. All of our hogs are raised on real family farms on open pasture and deeply bedded pens without the use of antibiotics or other drugs that promote artificial growth. And, none of our farmers use liquid manure systems. This old-fashioned way of raising hogs produces great-eating pork, is humane to the animals, and kind to the earth. In fact, we are the only meat company in America that can boast that all of our farmers follow guidelines for humane pig husbandry developed by the Animal Welfare Institute. Niman hogs are allowed to run, roam, and root. They are weaned at seven weeks, never given antibiotics, and are fed only the finest grains and natural ingredients.

And even better, this way of raising hogs produces the best-tasting meat. Because Niman hogs live most of their lives outdoors, they need an extra thick layer of back fat to regulate their body temperatures in the heat of the summer and cold of winter. This fat in turn produces superior marbling, flavor, tenderness, and palatability.

Most of our farmers raise their hogs on pasture that is used to grow soy, oats, and corn in other years. This rotational system allows the pigs to naturally fertilize crop fields with their manure. Although this traditional system is more labor-intensive than the modern confinement alternative, it produces little to no odor, poses no threat to water supplies, and sustains the land and community for future generations.

We process most of our pork in Iowa, then ship it fresh, never frozen, to our own butchering plant in Oakland. From there, the pork is distributed to restaurants and retail markets around the country as well as directly to homes from coast to coast (via our on-line market).

Our meat is a bit more expensive than industrially produced meat because it costs more to raise animals without using the shortcuts of drugs and confinement. More and more consumers understand that there is real value in buying meat that is raised without pharmaceuticals and hormones and by farmers who are treating the land and animals with respect.

Jamison Farm Lamb

JOHN AND SUKEY JAMISON

Although the Jamison Farm is in Latrobe, Pennsylvania, in the rolling Appalachian foothills near Sara's hometown of Pittsburgh, we first met John and Sukey Jamison through our development of the Chefs Collaborative (see page 54). John participated in Chefs Collaborative retreats as a member and a speaker, and the quality of his lamb helped to persuade chefs and journalists that sustainable ranching deserved strong support. 🐾

Jamison Farm began with a real estate deal.

We grew up in western Pennsylvania. Sukey and I were high school sweethearts, and we moved to Kansas City after we were married. After three years there, we moved back to Latrobe (near Pittsburgh) in 1976. We counted ourselves lucky when we found a spectacular stone farmhouse to buy, but the owner wouldn't sell it unless the surrounding farm was included. Since we wanted the house, we bought the sixty-five farm acres, too. After a year of splitting shares of the hay crop with our farmer, we decided we'd fare better economically with animals. Knowing absolutely nothing about raising animals, except that cows were too big for Sukey to handle, we made the decision to raise sheep.

We both had "day jobs," John as a coal salesman and Sukey as a caterer. Our kids were six and two years old, and Sukey took on the sheep farming as a 4H project with the kids. One day Sukey couldn't find lamb for a catering job, and she used our own lamb—which her customers found better than any other lamb they'd had.

At this time we were raising lambs and selling them through what's called the freezer trade. The way this worked was that when someone ordered a lamb, we sent it to a slaughtering plant, wrapped and froze it, and sold the whole lamb to the person who ordered it.

About this same time (early 1980s) grain prices were getting high, so we got interested in intensive rotational grazing. We really didn't know any better—we didn't know how people *should* farm, so this decision started us on the road to grass farming.

In 1985 we moved to a new farm with 108 acres, and right away disaster struck. John was laid off as a coal salesman, and we had three kids and two mortgages. We decided the lamb business was our best bet to stay afloat, and put advertisements in magazines like the *New Yorker* and started a mail-order lamb business. Sadly, the business was stagnant for two years but every day was a new learning experience.

Our luck changed in 1987 when we did a benefit for the Pittsburgh Children's Hospital and seven important chefs, including Jean-Louis Palladin, cooked for it. Jean-Louis was surprised to find that our lamb tasted almost exactly like the lamb he knew growing up in France, and we explained that lamb tastes like whatever it eats, and Jamison lambs eat grass like French lambs do.

We continue to feed our lambs on grass, using the intensive rotational grazing method that we have modified and improved over the years.

An intensive rotational grazing system divides pastures into sections; on our farm, we divided twenty acres into nine two-acre paddocks. Each paddock opens into the central corridor, which has a watering area at the end of it. The animals stay in the two-acre corridor for two days and eat the grass all the way down to two inches (from an original eight to twelve inches). After the two days they move on to the next paddock. The end result is great-tasting lamb and restored farmland. Without any fertilizer (we do use lime to adjust the pH), the animals have, in effect, renovated the pastures and restored the farm.

During their two-day grazing periods, the lambs eat the grass down to expose the soil, giving the white clover a chance to grow. Clover is a legume high in protein, so the animals eat a mixed pasture (legume/grass mix) that has the same nutrient value as alfalfa grass hay.

Because this mixture is so good, we have pastures where the lambs can graze year-round, as long as the snow isn't too heavy. In addition, they always have access, at their free choice, to hay.

With a commitment to taking care of our animals and our land, what started out as a disaster has "turned to clover." Today we have five hundred plus lambs on the farm and sell five thousand lambs per year to fine dining restaurants and consumers directly by mail order—and we still own and live in the beautiful farmhouse that started it all.

"More and more consumers understand that there is real value in buying meat that is raised without pharmaceuticals and hormones and by farmers who are treating the land and animals with respect."

—BILL NIMAN

Bell & Evans Chicken

SCOTT SECHLER

Scott Sechler is passionate about chickens, and is growing his company, Bell & Evans, with the same passion. Demand for his naturally raised chickens has soared as Whole Foods Market, Chipotle, and Panera Bread have recognized the quality of his chickens and his farming practices.

It all started with a dream.

Twenty years ago I had a vision that would set the standard for all chicken production facilities. I traveled the world visiting poultry plants and asking questions to realize my dream—which is now Bell & Evans chicken. Here's a very small snapshot of my vision.

We believe the best possible setting for raising chicks is a minimal-stress environment. Because it's humane and because it's much more healthful for the chickens and, in turn, for our customers. It's the right thing to do.

We keep our chickens comfortable at all times, in more than 150 spacious and environmentally controlled houses or chicken condos. Unlike some other growers, we don't subject our chickens to the stresses of overcrowding or wide variations in temperature. For example, our newest chicken house features windows that open and close automatically. The system provides year-round fresh air and climate control, and it lets the chickens bask in the warm light of the sun. We also clean out and disinfect every chicken house before each new flock arrives, which prevents many diseases and eliminates the need for antibiotics. The automated watering system dispenses as much fresh well water as the chicken wants. Again, it's not only humane, it's also healthful.

FREE RANGE? FREE TO ROAM?

Biologists have long understood that overcrowding of people or animals leads to stress, an assortment of health disorders, and aggressive behavior. We all need space, and chickens are no exception. Our chickens are free to roam. At our growers' farms you'll find calm, nonaggressive chickens with plenty of room to move about as they choose—getting all the exercise they need to grow up strong and healthy.

While these chickens are free to roam the houses, they're not "free-range"—and for good reasons. To assure the freshest, most tender meat, chickens are processed at seven to eight weeks of age. In order for these young chickens to develop healthfully, they are constantly monitored for temperature and diet in a strictly controlled environment and not exposed to bad weather or diseases.

ALL-NATURAL DIET

Chickens thrive on an all-natural, all-vegetable diet fortified with vitamins and minerals, without antibiotics. Chicken shouldn't be fed junk food like rendered meat scraps; bone, feather, or fish meal; or animal fats, oils, and grease. You wouldn't eat that stuff and chickens shouldn't either. What's more, chickens should never be fed growth hormones (federal law prohibits the use of artificial growth hormones in poultry), artificial preservatives, or unnecessary and non-nutritive coloring agents.

GETTING TO MARKET

Our chickens are individually graded. In the heart of Pennsylvania Dutch country, we've held onto their old-fashioned ideals about quality. We process our chickens in a modern, USDA-inspected plant, using only the latest technology.

The point of our process is we make sure our chickens eat better, so all our customers eat better, too.

Beef from Coleman Natural Meats

MEL COLEMAN, JR.

Mel Coleman, Sr., was a real western pioneer. A fourth-generation Colorado rancher, he founded Coleman Natural Meats in 1979 and pioneered the production and marketing of pure and natural beef raised humanely and with respect for the environment. When he died in 2002, his son, Mel Jr., took over, and continues to be a "quality visionary" in his father's footsteps. We asked Mel Jr. to write about the commitment he and his father have made, one that echoes the Oldways triangle of health and nutrition, environmental sustainability, and preservation of traditions.

Coleman Natural Meats, Inc., was the first national company to produce, market, and distribute natural beef and pioneered the U.S. Department of Agriculture (USDA) label describing our hormone- and antibiotic-free raising practices. In the United States, most commodity beef comes from cattle that have been given antibiotics and are implanted with hormones to accelerate growth and weight gain.

Through the years, as science and technology "advanced" and the demand for beef skyrocketed, so did the artificial nature of beef production. Growth hormones, not unlike the steroids used by some athletes, came into common use in order to make cattle market-ready faster. In addition, cattle were routinely fed antibiotics to improve production efficiency rather than treat disease. Today, the use of synthetic growth hormones and antibiotics in conventional cattle production is still common practice.

We've never cottoned to these new-fangled notions. Since our beginning, our cattle have been raised slowly and naturally from birth and never receive synthetic growth hormones or antibiotics. The mission of Coleman Natural Meats is to produce good-tasting, high-quality, wholesome food through sustainable methods.

Our goal is to produce foods that are great tasting, but good for you, safe, and raised naturally.

Several decades ago, my father pioneered the definition of what we believe "natural" should mean. My dad called it "staying ahead of the herd." Back in 1979 when we decided to sell natural beef by driving around Colorado and California in my dad's pickup truck, no one had yet coined the term "natural" in relationship to meat—even at natural food stores. In accordance with our strict protocol, Coleman Certified Cattle never receive antibiotics and are never fed animal by-products or animal fats from the day they are born. In addition, feeds are tested for antibiotics. If antibiotics are needed for a particular animal, that animal is treated and removed from our program.

Our family has ranched this way since 1875, and will remain "true to the trail" for as long as consumers demand the highest-quality, best-tasting beef available.

We use only "Coleman Certified" feedlots. Currently there are nine in three western states. All feedlots must adhere to our strict standards that we developed in tandem with some of the country's best experts in animal welfare and livestock management, including Dr. Temple Grandin, an associate professor of animal science at Colorado State University. As part of our animal wellness program, we have a consulting nutritionist, who has helped us to develop balanced rations for our cattle. Our guidelines specify that cattle are fed a well-balanced, vegetarian diet of natural grasses, grains, minerals, and amino acids. Animal by-products and animal fats are strictly forbidden, and feeds are tested for antibiotics.

We are not antiscience or antitechnology, but we do think utilizing antibiotics and hormones in cattle feeding for the sake of increased production is wrong. As part of our commitment to sound livestock management, we allow cattle in our program to grow at their natural pace, without added hormones or antibiotics. We also take precautionary measures to minimize undue hardship for our animals. It is well known that stress in the life of an animal can negatively affect the taste of beef. We intend to continue to consult with experts such as Dr. Grandin for ways to reduce the stress on livestock.

We also support family farms. Over the past several decades it has become increasingly difficult for small family farms and ranches to profitably market their products through the conventional channels. We developed a program whereby other small family farms and ranches could participate in our program and receive a greater value for their cattle. The majority of our cattle come from the western region of the United States, including our family's ranch in Saguache, Colorado.

Today, we are proud to say that we have provided more than seven hundred farmers and ranchers an opportunity to raise cattle "as nature intended," without the use of antibiotics and synthetic growth hormones, while at the same time receiving a greater value for their cattle. We've been involved in not only promoting the reduction of the use of chemicals in food production, but also advocating proper rangeland management, animal welfare, economic sustainability of family farms and ranches, and the preservation of the rural lifestyle that has been the hallmark of the American agricultural community. Most of all, we want our customers to enjoy beef that was raised right and tastes great.

First Blood

K. DUN GIFFORD

Everyone may not have the "hands-on" experiences Dun had as a child, so we include his recollections because they help us understand where meat comes from. ✏️

When my Dad went off to the Pacific in the Navy in World War II, I went to live with his father, whom we called Grampadad, in Katonah, New York. He and my grandmother lived in an old white farmhouse with a big lawn, and big trees.

He also had a "victory garden," which the War Department urged every American family to have "so our fighting men and women would have more to eat." Grampadad's victory garden was lush with vegetables and berries; they seemed to me to almost leap right out of the rich loamy Hudson River Valley soil, the color of chocolate pudding. He tended it to within an inch of its life, too—weeding, staking, pruning, replanting, and thinning all day long. It was a very large garden, the prewar heart of it enclosed by a waist-high stone wall with chicken wire to head height. His World War II extension was surrounded with rat wire to waist height and chicken wire above (he was worried about deer, too).

Too old to go to war against the Germans and Japanese, Grampadad waged his own private World War II against the rabbits that plundered his lettuce and carrots and everything else tender. These rabbits were the German and Japanese war machine for Grampadad, and he armed himself with fences to keep them out, whirligigs to frighten them, and dogs to terrify them. But the only thing that really worked was his double-barreled twelve-gauge shotgun.

Most mornings he'd get me up before dawn, and he'd sip his black coffee and I'd have my glass of milk, while we got ready to go out and stalk "those damn rabbits." We crept out of the kitchen in the dawn's half-light, careful not to bang the screen door, and snuck around the back of his work shed to peer around the corner and down onto the broad sweep of the garden.

He had some sort of sixth sense about these rabbits. "Try to smell them now, Dunny," he'd whisper. But I always thought he was making this up. I never smelled anything.

He remained quiet and stealthy as we crept down across the lawn to the garden and edged our way along its fence line, he with his double-barreled twelve-gauge shotgun at the ready, and me with my eyes wide.

Suddenly he'd tense and then BLAM! Or, BLAM! BLAM! when he fired both barrels. If I heard him hiss, "Son of a bitch," it meant he'd missed; but if I heard, "Got the bastard" (usually worse language than that; he was a creative curser), then I knew he'd nailed one. He was a very good shot, as old as he was; jump shooting like that in half-light is not easy. But every once in a while he'd bag a double, one rabbit with each barrel, and swear away happily. "Roosevelt should give me a big medal with ribbons!"

When we were done hunting, we carried the kill up to the shed and laid it out on the big workbench, where he skinned, cleaned, salted, and cut the meat up into kitchen-sized pieces. Then we rubbed clean the inside of the pelts and hung them from the rafters to dry, so they'd be ready for the man who bought them to make jackets and pillows. We took the meat inside and put it into the kitchen icebox, to be ready for lunch or dinner (or sometimes both). We ate a lot of rabbit—stewed, fried, baked, and fricasseed, always with the wonderful victory garden vegetables that we saved from those damn rabbits.

One particular morning Grampadad bagged only a single rabbit, and as usual we took it up to the shed and he laid it out on the workbench. It was not quite dead, and kind of twitched. Grampadad looked at me for a moment as he whetted his knife, and then held it out to me. "You've watched me do this twenty-five times, and you know what to do. It's time for you to be a man. I want you to skin this one," he said, and handed me the knife. I knew I had to take it.

So I did, and killed and skinned that rabbit. He made a big deal about telling my grandmother when we had breakfast, and she pan-fried it for dinner that night with garden vegetables and bacon fat and made my favorite gravy with flour and the drippings. It was really, really good.

At another time during World War II, I went with my mother on the train from Providence to Cincinnati; and then by car to Chillicothe, a small town in the lush farm country of southeast Ohio. My mother's maiden Aunt Mary lived there, on a farm inherited from her grandfather, who arrived there with his wife as settlers in 1826.

Aunt Mary lived in a solid brick Victorian house. I loved it because it was surrounded by flowers and had a vegetable garden out in the back, too, along with a chicken house and some ducks. Peter, who lived over the garage with his wife and children, was the keeper of the grounds and the birds.

At the end of breakfast every day Aunt Mary had a meeting with Peter about chores, and while she drank her second cup of tea they discussed "business," which included menus for meals.

"How are we doing with the chickens?" she asked Peter.

"Just fine," he said, which is what he said every day.

"Good," she said, "we'll have chicken for lunch, then. I think we'll need two. And Peter, Dun will come out to you after breakfast for an hour."

So after Aunt Mary finished her tea, out I went to look for Peter, and I found him in the chicken yard. "Well, Dun, let's get down to work. We don't want to get those women mad at us, now, do we?"

We swept out the chicken house, changed their bedding, refilled their water jars, and refreshed their feed. In the timeless pattern of senior and junior, "we" meant "me"; he supervised.

"Now," he said when we'd finished, "go catch me one of the hens."

This was not easy; chickens, even with clipped wings, are much quicker than you think. He'd taught me about moving slowly, shuffling my feet, and how to crowd a few of them into a corner. They are much calmer if there are a few crowded together than if there is only one chicken by itself. Once you get a bunch of them, maybe six, herded up to together into what I'd now call a critical mass, you take a breath, set your eyes on a particular one, and just lunge at it, going for a neck.

After a few pretty bad experiences (lying flat on your face in a chicken yard is no picnic in the park), I was reasonably competent at doing this and could catch one pretty much every time. So I caught one and brought it over to Peter, who was sitting on a big tree stump in another corner of the chicken yard.

He took it by the neck, and said, "Go get me one more. We want two." So I did, and carried it over to where he sat. "Now take this one and hold both of them. I'll be a minute, I have to get something."

He came back carrying a hatchet, which he laid down on the tree stump. He took one of the chickens from me and very quickly laid it down flat on the tree stump, trapping its feet under one of his boots, holding its head in one hand and the hatchet in the other.

Faster than you could blink, the hatchet came down WHACK! He cut the chicken's head off and he held the body up by its legs, blood pumping out from its severed neck. Before I could even flinch, Peter said in a cackle, "Look here, young man, this is your lunch. Now hand me that other chicken."

I did, and in a flash he had it stretched out on the tree stump, the hatchet in his hand, and another WHACK! But this time he quickly set the now-headless chicken on its feet on the ground, and it started to run, blood pumping out of its stump of a neck. It didn't run very far, but slowed down and then sort of keeled over.

"Better bring me that one that's down," said Peter. "Let's get 'em both plucked and into the kitchen while they're still warm. The women will know we're quick at our work that way."

During lunch, Aunt Mary said to my mother, "You know, Peter told me that young Dun seems to take to farming work quite well. He's been a great help around here."

I was sure that Peter had told Aunt Mary what happened out there in the chicken yard, but in one of those skin-prickling silent exchanges, Aunt Mary and I agreed that my mother would not really want to know about the chicken yard carnage, and so we didn't tell her.

It was quite delicious to share this "big secret" with Aunt Mary when my mother exclaimed at some length during lunch that she'd never had a chicken quite so tender and moist. Mothers are pretty smart, and I wondered if my mother really did know and was playing along. Years later, of course, I asked her, but she always smiled and insisted she knew nothing. Mothers are really, really smart.

Rabbit in Any Language

SARA BAER-SINNOTT

In our travels for Oldways throughout the Mediterranean over the years, Dun has, more often than not, ordered rabbit when it's on a restaurant menu. He's eaten and loved them all—French *lapin,* Greek *kooneli,* Spanish *conejo,* and Italian *coniglio.* He's tried rabbit with different sauces, with different vegetables and fruits, and prepared in many ways—grilled, baked, roasted, stewed, and so on.

I have to admit that I don't order rabbit myself, but often when we travel we're invited for glorious dinners at the homes of our friends and hosts. On those occasions, I happily eat all the wonderful food that's prepared especially for us, which means I've eaten a lot of rabbit.

My most enduring memory of rabbit (*coniglio* in this case) was in Italy, south of Naples, when we were on a winter planning trip to visit and select the sites for a spring symposium. My son Will—thirteen years old at the time and a very picky eater—was with us and he insisted on eating pasta at every meal.

After visiting Paestum and its ruins of Greek temples and magnificent museum (with the only known examples in the world of Greek fresco paintings, including the famous diver), we drove a mile or two to Maida Agroturismo, a producer of artisanal organic fruit and vegetable preserves, for more meetings and to spend the night.

The Agroturismo owners gave us a wonderful tour of their small shop and kitchen, and then led us into their dining room with fireplace for a cozy dinner. It had been a long, cold, and raw day, and it was splendid to be warm and enjoy the local wine. The dinner moved along as wonderful Italian dinners do—antipasti, pasta, primi, and a steady parade of dishes for us to sample. The final dish before the dolci was rabbit. It was simply prepared—baked with vegetables on the side—and absolutely delicious.

Will was horrified to learn what was on his plate—no way would he even think about trying what he imagined to be the Easter Bunny. But Dun cajoled and challenged him, of course, adding the usual, "It tastes just like chicken, and maybe when you're more mature you'll like it." Will fell for this, and in due course fell in love with the rabbit. Now, when he goes to an Italian restaurant he asks, "Do you have *coniglio?*"

Italian Meats

LOU DiPALO

We've spent many happy days, weeks, and months in Italy over the last fifteen years, and we've found—from north to south and especially in Emilia-Romagna— that wonderful cured meats are an important part of the cuisine in every region.

Few people understand the localized production of cured meats at which Italian artisans excel better or more firsthand than Lou DiPalo. His famous shop in Manhattan's Little Italy has brought in the best of Italian meats and other specialty products for four generations, often breaking new ground by introducing foods that haven't been sold here before.

Lou makes a wonderful point in his last paragraph. We have not necessarily lost the "old ways" with the advances in food science and technology, he argues, but are now able "to extend the season" so that we can enjoy the fruits of the old ways for more months of the year. Widespread refrigeration, better understandings of fermentation and oxidation, the workings of the bacteria that make cheeses, quality-testing sensors, and a host of other scientific and technical wonders have made the difference.

The heart of this corner of the meat industry is the passion of the people who produce it. Italians desire to give you the best product they can; for example, they take pride in the variety of pigs they have in each of their country's regions.

It all started with the Romans. In and around Tuscany and Umbria there were many wild pigs. Prosciutto and other cured meats were made from them, but little by little, the boars were fed a certain diet and eventually domesticated. For example, today Sicily has the black pig; Parma has the black parmigiana pig, which is extremely rare because in the 1960s the breed was hit with swine flu and it became nearly extinct. Tuscany has the brown and white Sienese pig.

Not very many years ago, wealth was measured by how many animals a family owned. The pig, in particular, is an all-giving animal—everything was used, from the head to the tail—and it was a valuable factor in the economy of rural families.

In Italy meat is eaten in modest portions when it is served as a course on its own. It is also used imaginatively with other ingredients in pasta, rice, soup, or appetizers. Probably the most important meats on the Italian table are *salumi,* air- and salt-cured or spiced and precooked hams, and *salame,* smoked meats and such.

Cured meats, *salumi,* are made differently in the various regions. For example, a prosciutto produced in Friuli has a different flavor, texture, and look than one from Emilia-Romagna or Tuscany; a *capocollo* produced in Calabria differs from one produced, for example, in Puglia. Some sausages are eaten fresh and others are dried, which intensifies their flavor. Once sliced, *salumi* are called *affettati,* which essentially means "cold cuts."

No doubt the most prized of the *affetati* is *prosciutto crudo,* meaning uncooked ham, which has become popular in America. With its popularity, however, has come a great deal of misunderstanding about the best ways to serve and to eat it. It's a shame to do anything more to the finest *prosciutto crudo* than to eat it raw, sliced as thin as paper (although not so thin that it falls apart), accompanied perhaps only by good *grissini,* Italian breadsticks. Despite the practice that persists of serving *prosciutto crudo* with figs or melon, it is best eaten on its own without sweet distractions. In the Parma and San Daniele areas where the best prosciutto in the world is made, asking for melon with your prosciutto would be the equivalent of asking for peaches to be served with your steak in Texas.

In Italy, the bone is seldom removed from the prosciutto because it keeps the ham moist and gives it flavor. *Prosciutti* that are exported to America are boned, which is convenient for slicing by machine. Skillful cutting with a knife results in slices that Italian culinary experts believe delivers more flavor, but this is rarely done in the twenty-first century. Most slicing, whether in *salumerie* (shops selling cured meats) or restaurants, is done by machine today. The preferred method is a specialized hand-driven slicer because the blade of an electric slicer generates heat, causing the texture of the paper-thin slices to change, even if slightly.

Cooking *prosciutto crudo* destroys its silky texture and remarkable delicacy, so it makes sense to use the ends for that purpose, which your prosciutto purveyor should be happy to sell to you for a discount. Prosciutto should be sliced thicker when used in cooking than when eaten raw.

Before there was refrigeration people had to find ways of preserving meat throughout the year. In and around the Mediterranean—in Italy, Spain, and Portugal—the method was to preserve through salting and air-curing. In Austria and Germany, where the climate is colder, it was through smoking. Somewhere in the middle, there was a bridge between the two, like around Alto Adige and Trentino in the Italian northeast, where Speck is made by a combination of curing through smoke, salt, and air. All this happened by accident, like everything else. In the cold weather, people had fires going constantly. They noticed that if meat was left in the fire room, it would be preserved. And they found that if they smoked it first they didn't have to cure it for so long.

The slaughtering process needed to begin in the winter, usually December, when the temperature was cold. By mid-June, the product was cured enough to withstand the heat of the summer. They used to cure in environments where there was clean, fresh air and fresh, flowing breezes. If there were no breezes many unwanted things would happen because air would help to evaporate the moisture and discourage bugs from setting on the meat. That's why certain areas are famous for certain products. Langhirano, a suburb of Parma in the region of Emilia-Romagna, and San Daniele situated midway between the Adriatic Sea and the Italian Alps in the region of Friuli-Venezia Giulia, are renowned for their *prosciutto crudo*.

Pork is the treasured meat for curing, but beef, donkey, horsemeat, goat, and goose are also used.

Curing meat is truly an art form in Italy. Even though temperature can be controlled now, the same traditions for making prosciutto and other artisanal food products continue, but with science now added. The old way is great but the new way also can be great because, in actuality, you now get a consistent product that will always be good. It used to be that people would say, "That was a good year" or "That was not a good year" for wine or prosciutto, or whatever. Now every year is a great year because they added science to the art.

Italian Specialty Meats in America

JULIA DELLA CROCE

Julia della Croce, Italian cookbook author and food expert, has traveled top-to-toe and sea-to-sea in Italy—shopping, sampling, and cooking great food in every region. Her books have taught many Americans the finer points of Italian cooking, and her vast knowledge of meats is a true case in point.

The word *salumi* comes from the Latin *salumen,* which means "salted food." Cured meats were widespread in the ancient world. In Rome, the artisans who produced them, the *cupedinari,* were respected craftsmen. The word prosciutto originates from the Latin *peresxuctus,* meaning "without liquid." A Roman cookbook entitled *De re rustica* ("On Farming"), by Marcus Porcius Cato, records the first recipe for making prosciutto. It is the same basic recipe that is used today throughout central and southern Italy.

As with cheeses and other artisanal Italian food products, the making of various *salumi* reflects local geography, climate, customs, and traditions with the result that countless variations exist from region to region. *Salumi* are sometimes produced at home, but even when manufactured in quantity for commercial consumption, they are made with a great deal of skill and concern for quality.

To appreciate and make full use of what Italian specialty meats are now available in America, here are some of the more universally known. Most of these can be served as an antipasto (appetizer) course, or even in other courses without any preparation.

BRESAOLA

Bresaola, a product of Valtellina in the region of Lombardy, is salted, air-cured beef haunch. Bresaola has a distinctive but delicate beef flavor. It is typically served as an antipasto alongside the local Grana Padano cheese with nothing more than a little extra virgin olive oil drizzled over it, or sliced over a bed of arugula and finished off with a little freshly squeezed lemon juice and a veil of freshly milled black pepper. Bresaola should be eaten soon after it is sliced—preferably within six hours, but certainly within twenty-four, as once cut it oxidizes and loses flavor quickly.

CAPOCOLLO

Capocollo, a cooked or cured shoulder ham, is fairly well known in America, but it is prepared differently throughout the Italian regions. The most famous versions come from Puglia and Calabria on the south of Italy, and Piacenza in the north, where it is called *coppa*. Capocollo is often flavored with salt, pepper, sugar, nutmeg, and white wine.

CULATELLO

Culatello is a ham made from the outside of the pig's haunch, unlike prosciutto, which is made from the entire leg. It is salted, seasoned, placed in a twine net, and air-cured for about a year. Adding white wine or other liquor and sometimes spices such as juniper and pepper makes culatello moist. The region of Emilia-Romagna, and the town of Zibello in particular, is famous for its sensational culatello.

GUANCIALE

Guanciale is salt pork from the jowl. Although used throughout Italy, it is a favorite cooking fat in and around Rome, where it is considered indispensable in the local specialty, spaghetti all'amatriciana. Guanciale is found in a very few Italian food specialty shops. It comes rolled up, like pancetta, but its flavor is distinctly stronger. Pancetta is usually substituted for guanciale where it cannot be found.

MORTADELLA

Mortadella resembles a very large American bologna with little white circles of fat throughout. It is a specialty of Emilia-Romagna, after whose capital city, Bologna, the American version is named. However, the resemblance stops there. Mortadella is made from very finely minced pork and high-quality pork fat. Whole peppercorns, pistachios, and spices are added before the mixture is formed into a huge sausage and cooked. Mortadella of fine quality is buttery, tender, and subtle, but immensely flavorful. Imported mortadella is not difficult to find in Italian food specialty markets in America.

PANCETTA

Pancetta is an Italian bacon (*pancia* is Italian for belly, in this case, pig's belly) cured with salt and mild spices, usually pepper and a hint of cloves. It is also lightly smoked, though this version hasn't caught on in America yet. In Italy, pancetta is produced in a slab or a roll, but here only the rolled variety is available. Many Italian specialty food markets carry it. The real flavor of pancetta is in the fat, so it is a mistake to look for lean meat here. Rather, look for a good balance of fat and lean. Pancetta is used in cooking.

PROSCIUTTO

Prosciutto is a general term for ham (*prosciugare* means "to dry"). *Prosciutto cotto,* or "cooked ham" is much like conventional boiled ham in America. *Prosciutto crudo,* on the other hand, is the remarkable, air-cured ham of Italy that is at once sweet and savory. The most famous *prosciutti crudi* are produced in the town of Langhirano in the region of Emilia-Romagna. Those of San Daniele, in the region of Friuli, famous for their superb quality in Italy, are exported to the United States in smaller numbers.

The first, called *prosciutto di Parma* after the province in which Langhirano is located, is made by some two hundred producers from a specified area. The secret of this ham lies in the feed and care given to some of the most pampered pigs in the world, the skill of the salt masters, the accumulated know-how of two thousand years of ham making in Langhirano, the clear air and not-too-humid breezes from the Parma hills, long and patient aging, the particular traditions, tastes, and palate of the Parmigiani, and—how else to say it? The love and passion of the ham masters. Imagine that along the Stirone River just south of the Apennines, this particular ham is made in such particular geographical and cultural conditions, and with such artistry and passion that nowhere else in the world can a ham be found that tastes or looks just like this one.

Prosciutto di San Daniele, on the other hand, comes from twenty-eight producers in the hills of San Daniele del Friuli, overlooking the Tagliamento River. The San Daniele people will tell you that this dreamy medieval town is the only place in the world where the particular combination of warm currents from the Adriatic Sea and fresh Alpine air from the nearby Dolomites collides to create their unique microclimate—a climate that contributes to the delicate flavor and fragrance of San Daniele prosciutto. The alternating cycle of dry mountain air and damp ocean breezes provides the ideal environment for making the raw-cured ham. Add the pampered pigs, two millennia of the ham maker's craft, a year or more

of curing under the supervision of ham masters who by now have prosciutto curing in their genes, love, and traditon, and you wind up with what the residents call a miracle, or at the very least, a gastronomic work of art.

Contributing to the sensational flavor of these hams is the exceptionally kind way the pigs are treated and fed, and the conditions in which they live. Lou DiPalo has many stories to tell about farmers whispering to their animals throughout the Emilia-Romagna, Lombardy, and Veneto countryside that could rival Robert Redford's mystical communion with horses in the film *The Horse Whisperer.* The farmers say that the secret ingredient is the surplus whey they feed the pigs from the Grana Padano cheese production, which has risen side by side with the prosciutto factories. In Parma, the pigs are fed on the whey from the Parmigiano-Reggiano cheese, which is a specialty of Emilia-Romagna.

The origins and every step of the manufacture of these hams (including size, shape, weight, aroma, and color) in the four-hundred-day curing process are strictly controlled, guaranteed, and protected by law, thus the D.O.P (*denominazione di origine protetta*) designation of each.

It should be noted that the superb prosciutto of the Colli Berici-Euganei Hills in the Veneto region is also exported to the United States, but in quite small quantity. No doubt, it, too, will someday become a household name among the ranks of food lovers outside the borders of Italy.

Lest the word "ham" conjure visions of clogged arteries to the uninitiated in matters of prosciutto, let me, here and now, dispel any fears: Because of the way they are produced, these hams contain little fat, a lot of digestible protein, and only natural, mineral-rich sea salt. Removing the fat from a slice of prosciutto is a big mistake because an integral part of the flavor and perfume in every slice resides there; the fat is actually low in cholesterol and high in beneficial oleic acid. Besides, you can only experience the whole flavor of prosciutto when you eat the ham and the thin rim of fat surrounding it together.

The *prosciutto crudo* produced today in Italy is a result of two thousand years of evolution in ham making. Its ancestors, made from wild boars that roamed the forests, were highly salted. Renaissance recipes suggest the addition of vinegar, wine, and such flavorings as coriander, fennel, and cloves. Today's prosciutto is made of only four ingredients: hand-selected legs of the most pampered pigs in the world, salt, air, and skill.

Today's premier prosciutto makers pride themselves on being able to produce the hams with as little salt as possible: the better the maker, the less salt used. The more fat the ham has, the sweeter it is, because fat absorbs less salt. Different parts of the ham have different colors and different flavors. Flavor is more intense near the bone, but the best part of all is in the center where the flesh is affected indirectly by the salt coating on the surface.

SPECK

Speck, from Alto Adige (or Südtirol, the German-speaking province of Bolzano), means "bacon" or "lard" in German. In fact, it is an artisanally made ham produced by combining techniques of air-curing, cold smoking with maple and beechwood, and brining in a blend of garlic, juniper berries, laurel leaves, and black pepper. The best part of the pork haunch is pressed into succulent rectangular blocks and aged for several months at which point they are firm, yet moist. Speck is an intrinsic part of country life in the Alto Adige area. Lou DiPalo talks about visiting an old farmhouse in the region where Speck has been made the same way for five hundred years. He asked the farmer why a mold must develop at a certain point in the process for proper Speck and was told, "This is the way my father did it."

"But," Lou adds, "if you go to places where they make Speck for commercial consumption, everything is controlled by technology. They weigh, they measure, they analyze . . . but the formula is the same, mold and all."

"It melts in the mouth like a cream puff," wrote someone about Speck in a travelogue. Speck has a subtle but zesty smoky flavor and can be eaten in paper-thin slices wrapped around breadsticks, like prosciutto, or placed atop whole-grain bread, or cut into thick dice or strips and added to a soffrito as a base for flavoring pasta, risotto, and other dishes. Lou brings in Speck from Alto Adige. No doubt it will soon be available in other U.S. markets.

The Skinny on Lardo

K. DUN GIFFORD

The first time someone starts talking to you about *lardo,* you think it's a practical joke, or you look over your shoulder for the hidden TV camera filming one of those shows on which people make fools of themselves. Just imagine, someone is actually trying to persuade you that the white fat from the backs of some special breed of Tuscan pigs is a rare delicacy, and when spread on warm toast is actually totally delicious.

Sure it is, you think, still looking around to see if this is a spoof.

But there we were, early one February morning on Tuscany's northern shoreline, leaving Pisa and Lucca behind and streaking north along the autostrada in the car with our friends from Massa. We were heading toward Carrara, a tiny town wedged in a tight valley on the steep road up to the white mountains of marble that Michelangelo haunted for years searching for the perfect blocks from which to carve *David,* the *Pieta,* the Vatican's altarpieces, and hundreds of his other masterpieces.

The autostrada runs right along the Mediterranean shoreline there, with the majestic peaks of the Apuan Alps looming over it on the land side, crowding the eastern skyline, looking at first glance to be covered with snow. But it's not snow, it's marble, vast miles of quarries, brilliant white against the undisturbed dark gray granite wrapping around them.

We wound uphill on a narrow, twisting road from

Carrara heading to Colonnata, the jumping-off place for the quarries, called the Cave di Marmo. Colonnata is a tiny village, perched literally on a ridge of rock outcroppings, with those brilliant-white mountaintop quarries surrounding it in a jagged circle. Every narrow cobbled street seems to end at the lip of a dramatic cliff, with magnificent vistas of the mountain quarries. It's very haunting.

But we were there to hunt down *lardo di Colonnata,* since Colonnata is the *lardo* epicenter for gourmands. We had not seen a single pig anywhere along the long steep road from Carrara up to where it ends in Colonnata's tiny central square, which was curious, since *lardo* is pig fat. So where were the pigs?

We went with this and a lot of other questions to one of the masters of *lardo di Colonnata.*

Lardo is, literally, salt-cured pork fat, which in itself is not unique; the white fat in bacon, hams, pork chops, and all sorts of sausages is salt-cured pork fat, too. Bacon, however, is made from the belly fat of pigs and has strips of meat in it, while *lardo* is from the back fat and is solid white, without meat. But what really makes *lardo* so distinctive is how it's cured.

From a block of white Carrara marble, the *lardo* makers carve a box about five feet long, two feet wide, and two feet deep, called a *conche,* and a more or less tight-fitting lid. These *conche* are lined up in the cellars of the buildings, where it is almost always cool and often cold, and to be honest the effect is more than a bit sepulchral. In this box they make their own special mixture of herbs, spices, peppercorns, salt, wine, and some other very secret ingredients, and the resulting bath is called the *salamoia.*

Salamoia has strong and pleasant herbal aromas, and they're all different from each other because each *lardo* maker has his or her own recipe. Into this *salamoia* bath they lay down full slabs of the fat, just the right number so the top one remains covered with the liquid.

They have deeply sliced these slabs in a crosshatch pattern to expose more of the fat to the *salamoia,* and rubbed them with sea salt, which draws the water out of the fat and adds to the salinity of the *salamoia.* They must remain in the bath for a minimum of six months, and the *colonnatesi* stir the *salamoia* from time to time, adding more water or wine if evaporation has dropped the level and perhaps refreshing the herbs and spices.

Our *lardo* maker lifted the lids of two or three *conches* so we could look at and smell his *salamoia* (it's not pleasant to look at)—and there was the *lardo,* whitish and spooky, just barely submerged, looking for all the world like a miniature Moby Dick. He poked it with a wooden stick and sort of jostled it, sloshing the liquid around to stir it up.

We asked him what herbs he uses in his *salamoia.* "Herbs of the mountain, very many, very many," he said, and rattled off a string of them in Italian. It certainly did smell like an herb mix, but the strong bracing smell of rosemary gave away the main ingredient's identity.

Then we went upstairs—a lot of them, since the building was built on a kind of ledge, with four floors above street level and four below, with windows on each floor of the side facing out so that air could circulate freely among the *conches.* The producer had laid out some slabs of *lardo* for us that had finished curing, and with a very sharp knife he sliced thin pieces the size of half a dollar bill; they were actually translucent from their transforming experience in their *salamoia* bath. He showed us how to lay the pieces on our tongues, and we did so.

The *lardo* very quickly melted, sending delicate aromas up to our noses and luxurious softened fat into our taste buds. If this sounds amazing, it was; you must suspend your disbelief and take my word for it that the stuff is wonderful.

He gave us pieces from different slabs of his *lardo,* explaining that the varying tastes were in the pigs (did they eat acorns or not, for example); in the character of the *salamoia* mix (what kinds of herbs in what proportions); in the temperature (higher up in the cellar was warmer than lower down except in the winter); and in how long the fat stayed in the *salamoia.* This made good sense.

The classic way to use *lardo* is as we use butter, spread on hot bread and toast, so it melts. This is actually sublime, because the aromas are more intense when the fat warms from the heat of the toast. Herbs can be sprinkled underneath the *lardo,* or on top of it, too—there do not seem to be any hard rules to discourage experimenting. *Lardo* makes beautiful omelets, too, and makes an especially beautiful herb omelet since *lardo* marries well with all kinds of herbs.

Some other ways to use *lardo:* smeared on dark bread cut into small squares or triangles as an hors d'oeuvre; spread on chicken breasts that are broiled with herbs in the oven; or melted over roast small chickens or other small birds. And a surprise—*lardo* is terrific on English muffins.

Summer Bachelor's Veal Scallopine

K. DUN GIFFORD

It was the summer of 1965, and while the shock and sadness of John Kennedy's assassination remained raw, the nation was moving on.

I had a summer job as a legislative intern for Rhode Island senator Claiborne Pell, and my wife and our two small children had fled Washington's blazing heat and dense humidity and gone to the seashore in southern Rhode Island and Nantucket for the duration, bunking in with our families, leaving me a summer bachelor. My lifelong friend John Wagley lived in Washington in a gorgeous Georgetown brick townhouse, and Worth Bingham was staying with Wagley for a few weeks. Worth was winning great notice as a hard-nosed investigative journalist and his wife was also on Nantucket.

So Wagley, Worth, and I spent a few evenings together each week as summer bachelors, playing highly competitive cards and backgammon for money. On most of these evenings, Wagley cooked amazing dinners while Worth and I dug around in his disorganized but top-of-the-line wine cellar for wines we wanted to drink. Wagley and Worth had traveled and caroused together in Europe many times during their college years and were fluent about good dishes and wines of France and the British Isles.

On this night of the heavenly veal scallopine, we'd played backgammon for a while in the cool library and drunk a lot of ice-cold blonde Lillet, a French aperitif from Wagley's cellar. Worth had unstoppable luck that night, so with a conniving glance, Wagley and I began agitating for dinner.

We went down to his kitchen, crowded with copper pots and pans of all shapes and sizes, crocks holding a forest of stirring spoons and whisks and mallets, and shallow drawers stuffed with a wonderful collection of kitchen knives and cleavers. The menu was simple: veal scallopine, roast potatoes, Bibb lettuce salad, French bread, and ice cream and raspberries for dessert. The wines were white and rosé; we decided that red was outrageous on such a blistering night.

The only help Wagley would ever accept in the kitchen was sink and cleanup duty; he did all the prep and all the cooking himself and brooked no assistance (this was okay with us, because he was such a great cook). So he set right to work, filled the sink with water, tore the lettuce leaves from the head, gently swished them all in the water, and left them to soak for fifteen minutes or so to refresh by absorbing water.

He then unwrapped the package of butcher's paper and examined the veal to assure that each slice was properly thin. "How thin is it supposed to be?" I asked him.

"Less than a quarter inch, more than an eighth, sort of depends, some slices feel like the meat is denser; they can be thinner than the ones where the meat is looser, like more floppy. Be sure never to get slices cut with the grain, they curl and fall apart. Always get ones that are cut across." He separated the slices into two stacks, one with the thicker slices and the other with the thinner ones, and then examined the thicker ones all over again, setting aside about half of them. "Gotta pound these thinner," he muttered.

He dusted the surface of his full-size butcher's block

table with flour ("It's French flour, you know, much better than American—the French grind it so it doesn't get so sticky"), took a heavy, well-used wooden kitchen mallet from one the drawers, moved the too-thick ones to the block, and began to pound the slices one by one. "Watch," he said, "this is really hard to do." He struck firmly but not hard, and when the mallet struck he kind of held it down and moved it firmly toward the edge of the slice. "If you hit it too hard it makes the meat mushy," he explained, pounding away. "It's called feathering."

When this was done he stacked all the veal again, and turned to rinse the small, red-skinned potatoes. Then he cut the potatoes into one-inch chunks, and dropped them, along with two or three pinches of sea salt, into water simmering on the stove in one of his well-shined copper pots. I noticed that he pinched with two fingers and a thumb, making it a bold pinch, not a timid one.

Next he took the lettuce from its bath in the sink, patted each leaf dry with a towel, put all of them in the salad bowl, and covered the bowl with the now-damp towel. He put a bottle of French olive oil and another of French red vinegar next to it.

Then he set up to cook the veal. He put a large sheet pan next to the stovetop and spread waxed paper on the bottom. Then he spooned about three cups of white flour into a small pile on one end of the pan, made a depression in the pile with the back of a spoon, ground a lot of black pepper into it, added two finely diced garlic cloves, and then turned the pile over onto itself with a spatula until it was thoroughly mixed. He cut three lemons into quarters, so he had twelve wedges.

"Okay," he said, "let's get the table set and have some more Lillet." Since the kitchen was on the ground floor, in the rear of the townhouse, it opened out directly onto a small bricked garden with a big camellia tree in the rear and an iron table and chairs next to the house. From the cabinets Wagley took placemats, silverware, candles, wine glasses, salt and pepper, and ash trays (we all smoked in the '60s), and we carried them outside and set the table. He brought out highball glasses for

Veal Preparations

Veal seems to embrace a variety of partners, in the same way that chicken does. The Italians are nuts for veal and have four classic preparations:

- **Veal Scallopine:** A thin slice of veal is dusted with seasoned flour and sautéed in butter or olive oil.

- **Veal Piccata:** A thin slice of veal is dusted with flour and sautéed in butter, after which a sauce is made from white wine and lemon reduced in the cooking pan with the browned bits scraped up as the liquid reduces. Butter is whisked into it before being spooned over the cooked veal.

- **Veal Marsala:** The same procedure is followed as for veal piccata, except Marsala wine (and sometimes chicken stock) is substituted for the white wine and lemon juice.

- **Veal Parmigiana:** The veal slices are coated with flour and dipped into a beaten egg and water mixture, sprinkled with grated Parmesan cheese, covered with tomato sauce, topped with crumbled or diced mozzarella and more grated Parmesan, and then baked.

The French have a version called veal Francese, which is basically the same as veal Parmigiana but without the mozzarella and with lemon juice. They have another version, too, veal scallops à la crème, which is made as above but with butter, chopped shallots, white wine, heavy cream, and lemon juice.

Wiener schnitzel is a related German recipe in which the veal is coated with breadcrumbs after it's been dredged in the flour and dipped in the egg and water mixture. The French call that version *escalopes de veau panées*, with variations like veal cordon bleu, veal scallops with cheese, and *escalopes de veau à la viennoise*, *à la milanaise*, and *à la holstein*.

the Lillet, and we sat down and had another drink and a smoke. Then Wagley was ready to cook, and we went back into the kitchen.

The potatoes were done, so he poured off the cooking water and left the potatoes in the pan, but off the heat.

He moved the stack of veal to one end of the sheet pan, and spread the pile of seasoned flour around so it was flat. He looked over his copper frying pans, took down a big skillet from its hook, and set it on the stove. Then he took down another and set it on a second burner. On the counter on the opposite side of the stove from the sheet pan he put a heavy white china oval serving platter. He opened the top of a wide-mouthed crock, scooped a big dollop of softened butter into both skillets, and turned on the heat to high under them, pushing the butter around with a flat-ended spatula.

When the butter was hot, he dumped the potatoes into the smaller skillet, pulled dried rosemary stems from a canister, and rubbed them vigorously between his palms over the potatoes, and ground a lot of pepper over them. Using a wooden spoon he stirred the potatoes gently, using a stroke that began at the outside of the skillet and turned them into the center. He did this until he was certain that all the potatoes were covered with melted butter, rosemary, and pepper.

He started in on the veal, lifting each slice from its stack, dredging it in the flour carefully so that there were, as he said, "no bald spots." He laid them carefully in the sizzling butter, turning each of them once before carefully transferring them to the serving platter, saying as much to himself as to us, "Don't want to knock off the damned crust." He also stirred the potatoes from time to time so they cooked evenly.

The aromas in the small kitchen grew in strength and richness: browning butter, rosemary, meat juices, garlic, potatoes, and then a mixture of all of them.

Wagley tore the Bibb leaves into small pieces with his hands, poured olive oil and vinegar over them straight from the bottles, added some three-finger pinches of sea salt and some vigorous twists of the pepper grinder, squeezed two or three lemons, and tossed it all using the two salad spoons. The first time I saw him do this, it was disconcerting, but now it had become spectacle, and I would have been disappointed if he'd foregone the show. "It tastes better when it's torn and not cut," he declared that first time, as if that would settle any of my qualms.

Then it was done, and we took everything outside to the garden and set it on the table—the potatoes in their cooking pan, the veal on the platter, the salad in its bowl. We lit the candles and sat down to eat.

We served ourselves from the platter, pan, and bowl on the big lazy Susan in the center of the table and filled our own wine glasses.

We talked politics, since that's the lingua franca of the city, and what's unusual about political talk is that it never ends but goes around and around, like a lazy Susan. For most citizens, politics is something that happens around election times, and then goes away until the next one. But not so in Washington: it's in the city's water and its hot air.

After dinner we cleaned up, and then drank some cognac and played cards. It was a perfect summer bachelors' evening.

The Crete Experiment

Since 1991, one essential ingredient of introducing the Mediterranean diet to American audiences has been overseas Old-ways symposiums, to which we've brought opinion leaders—American chefs, food writers, journalists, retailers and importers, scientists, and other experts—to Mediterranean countries for week-long explorations. Over the years we estimate we've traveled with more than 1,500 experts to different regions in Italy, Morocco, Tunisia, Turkey, Greece, and Spain.

We've learned that after three or four days in a new place, experiencing new tastes, ingredients, and preparations, chefs get itchy to get into a kitchen and put their own stamp on the things they've learned. Hearing the pleas of our chef friends, over the years we've found ways to get them back at a stove. Starting in 1994 at the famous and glamorous Hotel la Mamounia in Marrakech, Morocco, we invited the visiting American chefs to prepare several meals for the group. On the final night at la Mamounia, Gordon Hamersley of Hamersley's Bistro in Boston, led an amazing cast of American chefs—Jimmy Burke, Chris Schlesinger, Todd English, Bobby Flay, Jean-Louis Dumonet, Joyce Goldstein, Mark Kiffin, Evan Kleiman, Catherine Brandel, Deann Bayless, and Jesse Cool, along with a few food writers who wanted to help in the kitchen—who cooked an American-style Moroccan dinner in la Mamounia's kitchens, and served it poolside. The next year Lidia Bastianich organized and prepared a spectacular Pugliese dinner with about a dozen other attendees (see page 72). The crew was affectionately called Lidia and the Chefettes. We've had a number of dinners like this in subsequent years (in Chios, Liguria, Puglia, Salerno), but one we'll always remember is a night high up in the mountains of Crete, in a village called Anogia.

The group had already experienced Crete's version of the "Maine Baked Bean Supper"; we'd also watched a group of experienced cooks (all over the age of eighty) from Hania teach us the tricks of the *horta* pie; and we'd had splendid meals at our hotel and in restaurants in Heráklion. Our chef friends were ready to try their hands at cooking. We found a large restaurant willing to open its kitchen to our group, and with Greek food expert Aglaia Kremezi as chief cook, our group of chefs (Aglaia, Rick Moonen, Sari Abul-Jubein, Joe Simone, Jody Adams, Narsai David, Jay McCarthy, RoxSand Scocos, Jesse Cool, Deann Bayless, and Victor Broceaux) set to work preparing dinner while cheese expert Daphne Zepos gave us a primer on Greek cheeses. The chefs labored on in the kitchen while we held a small forum about the future of food, led by former *New York Times* restaurant critic Mimi Sheraton and Dun. Finally, the dinner was ready, and we were ready for our spectacular experiment!

The menu for our Crete Experiment included beans, greens, fish, bread, and vegetables, along with spectacular spring lamb and rabbit, and plenty of splendid Greek wines. The lamb and rabbit recipes follow; you'll find several of the other recipes sprinkled throughout the rest of the book.

SKEWERS OF MARINATED CRETE SPRING LAMB WITH ARTICHOKES AND LEMONS

JESSE COOL AND DEANN BAYLESS

This dish is simple and elegant, whether you use the fresh lamb of spring or you're grilling in the backyard on a hot summer evening. Be sure to marinate the lamb for at least 45 minutes, but the longer the lamb is marinated, the more tender and flavorful it will be. Serve over garlicky mashed potatoes. 🌿

SERVES 6 TO 8

2 pounds boneless lamb, cut into 1-inch chunks

1 head garlic, 4 cloves finely chopped

1 bunch fresh mint, coarsely chopped

1 bunch fresh parsley, coarsely chopped

$^{1}/_{2}$ cup extra virgin olive oil

Freshly ground black pepper

Chopped zest of 1 lemon

2 lemons, thinly sliced

2 baby artichokes, cut into quarters

Sea salt

Combine the lamb, chopped garlic, mint, parsley, olive oil, pepper, and lemon zest in a shallow bowl. Mix well. Let marinate for at least 45 minutes, or up to 8 hours, in the refrigerator.

Prepare a fire in a grill. Soak bamboo skewers in water for at least 30 minutes.

Leaving at least 1 inch on each end of the skewer free, alternate pieces of lamb, sliced lemon, and artichoke onto each skewer. Lightly season with salt.

Grill over medium-high heat until lamb is medium rare (about 4 minutes each side). Cut the remaining lemon (the one used for the zest) in half and squeeze juice over each skewer. Serve immediately.

OVEN-ROASTED RABBIT WITH LEMONS AND OLIVES

VICTOR BROCEAUX

Victor Broceaux is a long-time chef and an experienced restaurateur with Restaurant Associates, the New York City-based restaurant management company. His experience has taken him from the elegant Four Seasons restaurant in New York to corporate dining rooms and trendy restaurants across the United States. Our image of Victor, though, is of a hands-on chef, cooking up splendid Mediterranean meals in small restaurant or hotel kitchens, from Crete to Chios to Lecce. This dish from Crete is just as delicious stateside as it was in Greece. 🌿

SERVES 8

1 whole rabbit (about 1$^{1}/_{2}$ pounds total), cleaned

Sea salt and freshly ground black pepper

6 tablespoons extra virgin olive oil

3 lemons, julienne the zest of 2, and juice from all

8 cloves garlic, lightly crushed

$^{1}/_{2}$ cup white wine

3 sprigs rosemary

1 medium Spanish onion, cut to a medium-sized julienne

25 (about 1 cup) Kalamata olives, pitted

After unwrapping the rabbit, keep only the meat. Wash the meat in plenty of water. Dry with paper towels. Cut into eight portions. Dust the rabbit with salt and pepper and place in a large nonreactive pan or bowl.

In a medium-sized bowl, combine the olive oil, lemon, garlic, wine, rosemary, and onions. Pour over the rabbit and let marinate for at least 1 hour, up to 12 hours, in the refrigerator.

Preheat the oven to 375°F. Place the rabbit in a roasting pan and cover with the marinade. Roast for 15 minutes, basting often. Add the olives and reduce the oven temperature to 300°F. Continue to baste and turn the pieces as they begin to brown. Cover with aluminum foil if they are browning too much. Continue roasting until cooked through, about 90 minutes total. Discard the rosemary sprigs and serve.

MOM'S MAKEOVER MEATLOAF

JANICE NEWELL BISSEX, MS, RD,
AND LIZ WEISS, MS, RD

Family dinners can be heaven or they can be . . . difficult! Most of the recipes in The Oldways Table *are family-friendly, but the following recipes are ones we guarantee to be perfect for picky 8-year-olds, sophisticated 48-year-olds and coddled 78-year-olds.*

This recipe comes from Janice Bissex and Liz Weiss, who are both Boston-based registered dietitians with children and busy careers. They're also authors of The Mom's Guide to Meal Makeovers *and have some great ideas about helping families eat healthfully without a lot of fuss.*

Everyone loves meatloaf, but let's face it, some recipes serve up too much saturated fat and sodium. For this new and improved meatloaf recipe, Janice and Liz slimmed it down by using lean ground beef and added black beans, a shredded carrot, and ground flaxseed for a boost of fiber, vitamin A, and heart-healthy omega-3 fats.

SERVES 6

1 (15.5-ounce) can black beans, drained and rinsed
1 pound lean (90% or higher) ground beef
2 large omega-3 eggs, beaten
1 cup shredded carrot
$^1/_2$ cup seasoned breadcrumbs
$^1/_3$ cup ground flaxseed
6 tablespoons ketchup
$^1/_2$ teaspoon garlic powder
Sea salt and freshly ground black pepper

Preheat the oven to 375°F. Lightly oil or coat a 9 by 13-inch baking dish with nonstick cooking spray.

Mash the beans in a large bowl using a potato masher until mostly smooth but still a bit chunky. Add the beef, eggs, carrot, breadcrumbs, flaxseed, 4 tablespoons of the ketchup, and garlic powder. Season with salt and pepper and mix until combined.

Transfer the meat mixture to the baking dish. Shape into a 6 by 8-inch rectangle, about $1^1/_2$ inches high. Spread the remaining 2 tablespoons of ketchup evenly over the top and sides.

Bake until an instant-read meat thermometer registers 160°F, 50 to 60 minutes. Let stand for a couple of minutes before serving.

"If we are not vegetarians, it's meat

that gets the respect and the place

of honor at our tables, cookouts, and

drive-throughs."

—K. DUN GIFFORD

GRILLED STEAK FROM FLORENCE (*BISTECCA ALLA FIORENTINA*)

JULIA DELLA CROCE

One of the best meat dishes Italy has to offer is bistecca alla fiorentina, which has been one of the highlights of the Florentine table for a hundred years. In fact, the genuine dish is not a beefsteak at all, but really the rib of nine-month-old Chianina steers. In Italy, steaks are cut from the flavorful rib section, called costata or contracoste. The Chianina is an imposing breed of huge white cattle (a full-grown steer can weigh up to five thousand pounds), whose ancestry goes back to the times of the Etruscans. The meat of the adolescent steer is highly flavorful, tender, lower in cholesterol, and more digestible than other beef because it contains little marbling. Sadly, the breed is disappearing from Tuscany today, though in the United States and northern Europe, it is being bred with Herefords because of its lean, tender, and flavorful meat. Nevertheless, the dish survives, and it can be made using a good rib steak cut from prime-quality beef. Ideally, the steak should be grilled over the white embers of a hardwood (oak or olive) fire, which produce little smoke that affects the flavor of the meat. If these are not available, grill the steak over coals that have been started with kindling, not with chemical fire-starter, which affects the aroma and flavor of foods. 🗆

SERVES 4

    4 (6-ounce) rib-in beefsteaks, 1½ to 2 inches thick
    8 or more rosemary sprigs (optional)
    Sea salt and freshly ground black pepper
    High-quality extra virgin olive oil

Prepare a fire in an outdoor grill. The grill is ready when the embers or coals are at their hottest, that is, white and glowing. Position the grill rack about 2 inches from the glowing embers or coals and allow it to preheat well.

Meanwhile, bring the meat to room temperature and preheat a serving plate.

Place the steaks on the sizzling-hot grill rack. Cook them until they are well charred on one side, 2 to 3 minutes for medium to medium-rare. Turn the steaks immediately and cook them on the reverse side for another 2 to 3 minutes. Lay the rosemary on the heated plate and place each steak atop the sprigs. Sprinkle with salt and pepper to taste and drizzle with a little olive oil. Serve immediately.

CORIANDER-PEPPER CHOPS

ROBIN KLINE, MS, RD, CCP

Whenever we ask chefs, food writers, and cookbook authors about their favorite foods, or foods they couldn't live without, pork always comes out on top.

Robin Kline is now a food writer, but in her past lives she's been president of the International Association of Culinary Professionals (IACP) and executive director of the National Pork Council (she's the one responsible for the catchy slogan, "the other white meat!"). We thought it only fitting that we have a recipe from her for that "other white meat." Robin says she's never served these to anyone who hasn't subsequently asked her for the recipe. The seemingly disparate ingredients in this marinade come together for an amazing taste sensation, marrying perfectly with lean pork on the grill. 🗆

SERVES 4

    4 boneless pork chops, 1½ inches thick
    3 tablespoons soy sauce
    2 cloves garlic, crushed
    1 tablespoon ground coriander
    1 tablespoon coarsely ground black pepper
    1 tablespoon brown sugar

Place the pork chops in a shallow dish (or self-sealing bag). In a small bowl, stir together the soy sauce, garlic, coriander, pepper, and brown sugar. Pour over the chops and let marinate for 30 minutes.

Prepare a medium-hot fire in a grill. Remove the pork from the marinade and discard the marinade. Grill the chops over direct heat for 9 to 15 minutes, turning once, until the meat is no longer pink and the juice runs clear. Serve immediately.

MOMO'S PORK OSSO BUCO

ROBERT MARSH

Chef Robert Marsh prepares pork osso buco (meaning "hole in the bone") at Momo's restaurant, a popular spot in San Francisco located across the street from the PacBell Stadium. This recipe was chosen by Bill Niman, founder and CEO of Niman Ranch, as one of his favorite recipes using Niman Ranch pork. Serve over mashed potatoes or a substitute to your liking.

SERVES 2

Sea salt and freshly ground black pepper
12 ounces Niman Ranch pork osso bucco or
   1 piece pork shank
2 tablespoons extra virgin olive oil
1 large yellow onion, diced
2 carrots, diced
4 stalks celery, diced
2 tablespoons chopped garlic
3 tablespoons tomato paste
1 (28-ounce) can tomatoes
2 cups red wine
4 cups beef stock
2 teaspoons chopped fresh rosemary
2 bay leaves

Preheat the oven to 350°F. Salt and pepper both sides of the pork. Place the pork with the olive oil in a large skillet over medium heat. Brown for about 5 minutes on both sides, remove, and set aside. Add the onion, carrots, and celery and sauté until translucent, 5 minutes. Add the garlic and sauté for 2 minutes. Stir in the tomato paste and tomatoes and cook for 3 minutes. Add the red wine and cook for 2 minutes, then add the beef stock, rosemary, and bay leaves.

Place the pork in a roasting pan, cover with the wine mixture, cover the pan with aluminum foil, and roast for 2 hours, or until the meat is fork tender. Remove the pork from the pan and skim off the fat that has come to the top. Season the cooking juices with salt and pepper. Serve immediately.

FIVE-SPICE PORK RIBS WITH GINGER, SOY, AND SESAME

STEVE JOHNSON

Steve Johnson, formerly chef and co-owner of the Blue Room, and now chef and owner of Rendezvous, both in Cambridge, Massachusetts, recommends Niman Ranch St. Louis-style spareribs. This is another of Bill Niman's favorite pork recipes. 🍽

SERVES 4 TO 6

RUB AND RIBS

1/4 cup ground coriander

1/4 cup sea salt

3 tablespoons hot chili powder

2 tablespoons dark brown sugar

2 tablespoons crushed red pepper flakes

2 tablespoons Chinese five-spice powder

2 tablespoons ground star anise

1 teaspoon freshly ground black pepper

1 teaspoon ground cinnamon

1 teaspoon ground fennel seed

1 teaspoon ground ginger

1 teaspoon ground red pepper

2 racks St. Louis-style spareribs, 12 ribs each, about 2 1/2 pounds each

SAUCE

2 tablespoons minced fresh ginger

2 tablespoons minced garlic

1 cup Asian sesame oil

1/2 cup white wine

Juice of 2 oranges

1/2 teaspoon Chinese five-spice powder

1/2 teaspoon crushed red pepper flakes

1/2 teaspoon whole star anise

1/4 cup balsamic vinegar

1/4 cup soy sauce

2 tablespoons white sugar

To prepare the rub, mix together the coriander, salt, chili powder, brown sugar, red pepper flakes, five-spice powder, star anise, black pepper, cinnamon, fennel seed, ground ginger, and ground red pepper in a small bowl.

Apply a liberal amount of this spice mix to the ribs and rub it in.

Let the ribs stand while you prepare an indirect fire in a grill or preheat the oven to 275°F.

Grill over indirect heat for 2 to 3 hours, turning occasionally, until the ribs are mahogany brown all over and the meat is very tender. Or, roast for 2 to 2 1/2 hours.

Meanwhile, make the sauce. In a small sauté pan, gently simmer the ginger and garlic in the sesame oil for 1 minute. Add the wine and the orange juice and simmer again for about 5 minutes, until the liquid has reduced by about one-half. Then stir in five-spice powder, crushed red pepper flakes, whole star anise, balsamic vinegar, soy sauce, and white sugar. Remove from the heat. Serve the sauce alongside the ribs or generously spoon sauce over them.

VEAL SALTIMBOCA ALLA ROMANA E FEDERAL HILL

K. DUN GIFFORD

This recipe is adapted from one in Romeo Salta's 1962 cookbook, The Pleasures of Italian Cooking. *The adaptation is to accommodate the mozzarella cheese, which may have been an adaptation of Salta's, or something my dad and his restaurant friends in Federal Hill cooked up.* 🍽

SERVES 6

12 veal scallops

12 slices prosciutto

1/2 pound fresh mozzarella

1½ teaspoons sea salt

½ teaspoon freshly ground black pepper

12 fresh sage leaves, or ½ teaspoon dried
     sage leaves

4 tablespoons butter

½ cup Marsala wine

¼ cup chopped fresh parsley, for garnish

Cut the veal scallops into 5-inch squares, and do the same with the prosciutto until you have a number equal to the number of the veal squares. Cut the mozzarella into 4-inch sticks no more than a ¼ inch wide. Season the veal with the salt and pepper, and put a sage leaf (or a bit of dried sage) in the center of each one. Place four of the mozzarella sticks on each piece to surround the sage. Cover each piece with a square of prosciutto, and pin the veal and prosciutto together with two tooth-picks to make medallions.

Melt the butter in a skillet over high heat, add the medallions, and brown for about 3 minutes on both sides. Add the Marsala, and cook on low heat for about 5 minutes, or until the veal is tender. Remove to a warm serving platter with the prosciutto side up, remove the toothpicks, and pour the cooking liquid over the medallions. Garnish with a sprinkle of chopped fresh parsley, if desired.

WIENER SCHNITZEL

NORMA BAER

This German version of Viennese cutlet is from Sara's grandmother's kitchen. It was one of her childhood favorites, and it's become a top pick of her children, too. Serve it with angel hair pasta tossed with butter or olive oil and freshly grated Parmigiano-Reggiano or Grano Padano.

SERVES 6

6 veal cutlets (4 to 6 ounces each)

Sea salt and freshly ground black pepper

2 large eggs

2 teaspoons water

Flour, for dredging

Dried breadcrumbs, for breading

¼ cup butter

¼ cup extra virgin olive oil

Lemons, cut in quarters for garnish (optional)

Wrap the veal cutlets in waxed paper, and pound them with a wooden mallet or rolling pin to about ¼-inch thickness, and then season with salt and pepper.

Beat the eggs with the water in one flat dish or pie pan, put the flour in another dish, and the breadcrumbs in a third dish. Dip each of the cutlets in the flour, then the egg and water mixture, and finally the breadcrumbs.

Heat 2 tablespoons of the butter and 2 tablespoons of the oil in a large skillet until quite hot. Add three cutlets and cook for about 3 minutes on each side, until golden brown. Drain on a paper towel. Pour out the fat and wipe the pan clean with paper towels. Add the remaining 2 tablespoons of butter and 2 tablespoons of oil, heat the pan again, and brown the remaining cutlets. Drain on a paper towel. Garnish with lemons and serve.

"Sweetness is an innate and strong force in shaping human
evolution, and the biological preference for sweetness is universal."

–SCIENTIFIC CONSENSUS STATEMENT,
INTERNATIONAL OLDWAYS CONFERENCE ON SWEETNESS AND HEALTH,
OCTOBER 23, 2004, MEXICO CITY, MEXICO

"The energy that our brain cells need to fire, the energy that
our muscles burn so they can flex, and the energy that our organs
need to convert the chemicals in food and drink into the
chemical compounds that our bodies need for life—
this energy comes from glucose."

–K. DUN GIFFORD

SWEETS

Two images pop right up when I think of the word "sweetness": brown sugar and honey.

Brown sugar was a childhood affection: I spooned it on my hot cereal each winter morning and watched it turn soft and then melt into tiny glistening streams and ponds, or I spooned it onto summer's cold cereals and watched it dissolve into the creamy milk, turning it golden and tan. My grandmother had given each of us a silver porringer as a birth present, and for those many years of childhood we ate our hot and cold breakfast cereals from them every day except Sunday, when we had pancakes—with maple syrup.

Sweetness and Light
K. DUN GIFFORD

My mother kept brown sugar in a glass canister on the kitchen table where we ate most of our meals. Sometimes it was the dark brown sugar and sometimes the light brown. There seemed no particular pattern to the back-and-forth between them—such as dark for the dark winters, light for the bright summers—it was random. We used white sugar on our cereal only when we ran out of brown.

We also had cubes of light brown sugar, which she put in her coffee and tea. From time to time my mother had brown sugar crystals, too, which looked like little jewels. This was very fancy stuff; it came from England, and was usually a Christmas or birthday present from one of her friends. My father didn't have much use for brown sugar with his caffeine; he had a white sugar palate.

My mother put the heels of the bread loaves into the glass canister along with the brown sugar, because it kept the sugar moist. If you did not keep it moist, it got as hard as a sidewalk brick, so hard, in fact, that you needed a mallet or hammer to break it into small enough pieces. We children loved it when this happened, because we'd take a small chunk and with the spoon bury it deep in the hot cereal, where it would slowly melt. When we plumbed for this buried treasure with the spoon after a few minutes, we'd strike a rich, silky pool of sweetness, like a treasure, which would run out of the breach and trickle all around the bowl in small brown streams.

We would also sneak chunks of brown sugar from the canister to take to school, or out to play, hiding them in our pants pockets. Most of the time this was a great idea—we had a secret candy to suck on that our mother didn't know about! But it wasn't always so great, especially when we had water fights with our friends, got caught in a rain shower walking home from school, or got sweaty just plain running around. Of course, the chunk would melt, and not only was that a big sticky mess, there was no way to hide it from my mother.

My mother used brown sugar in a lot of other ways in addition to sweetening our cereal. We had brown sugar cookies, brown sugar and applesauce cakes, and many more delectable treats.

We invented stories about what was happening when the brown sugar and milk met each other in the cold

cereal. Most of them were about castles and beaches, because what happens in the cereal bowl is sort of like what happens to the sand castles on the beach. In summers we spent countless hours building sand castles near the ocean's edge, and on those days when the tide was rising, we knew that destruction was the castle's fate. So we made small "castles" of brown sugar in our cereal bowls, and watched the milk lap up against them, relentlessly reducing them to a delicious structural nothingness.

Those were the days when families started their days with a healthy breakfast, and there was a long shelf full of hot cereals to choose from, none of them instant. Among them were Wheatena, Quaker Oats, Irish oats, Scottish oats, Ralston, cream of wheat, cream of rice, and others. They were largely whole-grain cereals—chewy and toothy, and we did not have hunger pangs by midmorning.

A generation later I made hot breakfast cereal for my own four children, too, and on winter nights put the cereal and water into a stout pot with a tight lid and left it overnight on the stovetop, on top of the pilot light. It cooked slowly during the night and took only a couple of minutes in the morning to heat up, spoon it into their bowls, and watch them watch their own brown sugar melt and turn into their own little streams and ponds.

So I have a sense of brown sugar having been there "at the beginning" for me—of each day, of the day's meals, and of my remembered life.

HONEY

Honey, too, pops into my mind when I think about sweetness because I kept bees for many years, and gathered and bottled their honey. In those years I had urban bees in my backyard in Cambridge and rural bees in my summer backyard on Nantucket.

These wondrous bees worked furiously for me, flying sunup to sundown as far as a mile to suck nectar from flower blossoms. When they got back inside the hive, they pumped this nectar from their honey-stomachs into wax cells their sister worker bees had made, while other bees, their legs tightly gripping the edges of the cells, fanned their wings rapidly to blow air over the cells so the nectar would evaporate and gradually be reduced into honey. In fact, you can stand right outside the front of a hive while all this fanning is going on and the smell of the nectar from the moist air blowing out the hive is so sweet it's almost cloying—and it smells exactly like a bunch of the flowers from which they took the nectar.

The honey my bees made ranged in color from clear as water to nearly black. The clear was spring honey, when the blossoms are mostly white (fruit blossoms, for example), and the darkest was fall honey, when the blossoms are yellow (like goldenrod). The light honeys had delicate smells and tastes, while the dark honeys were much stronger. I loved my bees for the fifteen years I kept them, for their honey, of course, but also because of the extraordinary things they could do with their pinhead-sized brains, including communicating distance and direction of nectar sources to each other; deciding their queen, the only egg-layer in the hive, was getting on in years and must be replaced; feeding the male drones every day so they'd fly around a thousand feet above the hive in case a virgin queen needed to be fertilized; and pollinating my flowers, fruits, and vegetables so they, too, could reproduce.

But "advanced civilization" caught up with my urban and suburban bees toward the end of the 1980s, when a green lawn and ornamental bushes and trees became the mandatory icons of a well-kept home in the fast-spreading suburbs and vacation places. This brought a literal ocean of pesticides, herbicides, and fungicides with it, and sadly, in a few years, my wonderful bees succumbed along with other insects, the good ones and also the bad ones.

Along with my bees, later on in life, the pleasures of other not-fully-refined cane sugars joined these childhood delights, including molasses. I grew fascinated with molasses from thinking about the meals on whale ships and warships.

BLACKSTRAP MOLASSES AND THREE YEARS AT SEA

The conventional wisdom has it that the food served up to the wretches who crewed these vessels was putrid, inedible, nauseating, wormy, and even worse. No doubt some of it was—maggots in salted horsemeat and weevils in the hardtack biscuits.

But the conventional wisdom could not be true literally, because of the punishing physical labor needed to sail one of these ships, not to speak of catching, killing, and then rendering whales. And scurvy, the great killer of sailors in those centuries, was rampant. Why didn't they all die?

The answer lies in two places: the meticulous provisioning lists of supplies taken on board the ships, and the equally meticulous ships' log books that recorded each day's events.

The Nantucket Whaling Museum's outstanding collection of provisioning lists and ships' logs is a true mother lode, and it was there that I learned what sustained sailors and whalers whose voyages were frequently three years long.

They caught, cooked, and ate fish, of course, and no one doubts the healthfulness of fish. They stopped at Atlantic and Pacific islands and took on board fresh fruit and vegetables and live animals and poultry. And they carried in their holds enough barrels of molasses to last the full estimated length of the voyage, with enough for a daily ration of about a cup for each man on board.

Molasses is an amazing food. That single cup has about 560 calories, more than double the recommended amount of calcium, and triple the recommended amount of iron. Ship captains may have been cruel taskmasters, but without healthy crews their ships could not be sailed, so they fed their crews plenty of food when they had the rations.

Molasses, a byproduct of making sugar from sugar cane or sugar beets, is no longer in regular use for human consumption, although it is an important constituent of animal feed.

A FEW OTHER SWEET THINGS

Humans cannot live without sugars; there is no effective substitute for them. Every one of the trillion cells in a human body depends upon sugars not only for its life, but for the energy to do its jobs. The energy that our brain cells need to fire, the energy that our muscles burn so they can flex, and the energy that our organs need to convert the chemicals in food and drink into the chemicals that our bodies need for life—this energy comes from glucose.

This is one of those basic nutrition facts that finds its roots in evolution. Our ancestors chased down fruits for the sugar in them—fructose. They chased down vegetables and grains, too, and converted the carbohydrates in them to glucose (also known as blood sugar or dextrose). Just as important, all of those foods contained starches, which mammals convert to glucose. They stored excess glucose and glycogen, principally in the liver.

Well, you might ask, what about protein and fat? Don't our bodies burn them for energy? Yes they do. Proteins are broken down during digestion into animo acids; any excess amino acids are metabolized to glycogen or fat and available for further metabolism into energy. Fats can be converted to glucose in an absence of carbohydrates and other sugars, but the processes strain body systems and are not health-promoting in the long term.

> "We believed that making sugar the new diet devil not only was bad science and bad public policy, but would be yet another fad flame-out after its time in the media sun."
>
> —K. DUN GIFFORD AND SARA BAER-SINOTT

Managing Sweetness: Challenging Sweetness as a Culprit

K. DUN GIFFORD AND SARA BAER-SINNOTT

In the last few years, critics have singled out sugars and sweetness as one of the main culprits for overweight and obesity. It is clear that the consensus scientific evidence does not support this theory of a "single food culprit"; it supports instead the scientific principle that an excess of calories causes weight gain.

Focusing on sugar as the driver of overweight turns a blind eye to the real culprit (too many calories), distracts attention from this root cause of weight gain, diverts energy from developing effective solutions directed at excess calories, and prolongs the life of the overweight and obesity problem. For the same reasons that Oldways challenged the scapegoating of fats in the 1990s (see page 6) and the scapegoating of carbohydrates in the 2000s (see page 25), we determined in 2004 to challenge the looming scapegoating of sugars. We believed that making sugar the new diet devil not only was bad science and bad public policy, but would be yet another fad flame-out after its time in the media sun.

Our proposal: an international scientific conference and project on sweetness, and specifically on "Managing Sweetness."

WHY "MANAGING SWEETNESS"?

When addressing human behaviors that bring pleasure and comfort, such as eating and drinking, driving and sex, television and smoking, the goal of parents, educators, and public health specialists is not to forbid, because that's largely wasted effort. The goal is to impart skills that help people act wisely to avoid excesses, and these are the skills of managing.

We have many examples of successful public health campaigns based not on prohibiting, but on managing. Each of these campaigns identified a serious risk, developed solutions to reduce it, and organized successful education campaigns that persuaded consumers to change their behavior patterns. These campaigns include using seatbelts, promoting safe sex, using designated drivers, car seats for babies, life vests, bicycle helmets, and many more. They did not try to persuade the public to give up driving and boating, quit sex, or stop bicycling. These campaigns worked because they were based on teaching people how to manage risks, and not on prohibition.

We also have examples of how futile it is to seek outright bans of pleasurable activities even if they may be hurtful or dangerous to health. Prohibition, after all, was a failure and soon abandoned; it was truly dead on arrival. Teenage pregnancies are not susceptible to a single approach; a combination of educating about both contraception and abstinence seems the best we can do, even though the former has a higher success rate than the latter.

It is an uncomfortable truth that a half-century of programs to discourage overeating and overdrinking and to encourage exercise have not succeeded either, despite enormous expenditures and enormous effort.

The real reason for this failure is that the content and messages of dietary guidance have not kept pace with advances in how information is communicated today. Remarkably, they continue to mirror not only the content of the dietary guidance of the 1950s, but also the consumer messages.

There has been only one significant national effort to change the way Americans eat, and that was the food rationing programs during World War II. The content of these programs was developed by the national leaders in nutrition science, but the White House turned to the leaders of Madison Avenue advertising firms to develop the campaigns to sell them to the consuming public, over the objections of the nutrition establishment. These food-rationing programs were a huge success, helped along, of course, by patriotic fervor, but even from the perspective of sixty years, the professionally developed World War II advertising and public relations campaign were what sold them to a skeptical American public. It's a fascinating footnote that the famous sociologist, Margaret Mead, was the chair of the committee that recommended engaging the services of Madison Avenue.

Today's dietary messages stick out as horribly outdated, and so they flunk the competition for our attention (measured as "eyeball time and/or eardrum time") in our dense, relentless, message-rich radio, television, email, Internet, instant-messaging, and Blackberry environment. Even worse, the messages are largely negative—don't eat this, don't eat that, avoid this or that drink, exercise at least an hour a day, eat more/less carbs/fats/protein/sugars, and so on. Or, they're relentlessly positive: beta carotene fights cancer, fish oils fight irregular heartbeats, vitamin E helps cuts heal faster, echinacea's good for just about everything—but wait, we have new evidence and, well, maybe they don't do these things at all.

We looked into positive public education campaigns (do this) as well as negative campaigns (don't do this). We looked across a wide range of campaigns—buy my product, don't have unprotected sex, eat more whole grains, avoid foods containing trans fats, eat a good breakfast, exercise more, and so on. We sought to identify what kinds of messages pushed behavior change buttons, and also what kinds of messages failed to do so.

After extensive reviews of research into behavior changes, and much study of the soaring rates of overweight and obesity, we at Oldways and a large number of our long-term collaborators concluded that no success in countering worldwide weight gain was possible unless consumers were taught about incorporating the "Calorie Equation" into their lives. This equation is starkly simple: if calories taken in exceed calories burned off, the excess is stored as body fat, and weight goes up.

The "Calorie Equation" works for everyone: adults, children and teenagers, men and women, boys and girls, and people of all races and nationalities. It works for the people of the world's three great food cultures (wheat, rice, and corn) and all the minor ones, too.

A FOCUS ON SWEETNESS

Given the universal human "affection for confection," and the presence of sweet tastes in easily more than half of what we regularly eat and drink every day, we determined that a solid start toward realistic anti-overweight-and-obesity solutions would be an education program that taught consumers how, in the context of the "Calorie Equation," to manage sweetness. In keeping with our past successes, we turned to the leading scientific experts in overweight and obesity, as well as experts in the sweetness industry.

Farmers, after all, have known for millennia how to fatten cattle: they herd them into small pens and over-feed them. Too much food, and not enough exercise, inexorably equals weight gain. Like cattle, we humans are mammals and subject to the same thermodynamic rules of the "Calorie Equation." In addition, sugar is a safe food; no serious person, organization, or study has ever claimed sugar to be unsafe.

When born, our first food is sweet milk. And for the rest of our lives we eat sugars, too—in coffee, in cakes, on cereal, in colas, in candy, in fruits, in vegetables, in bread, and in fact, in most of our foods and drinks.

Managing Sweetness Scientific Consensus Statement

1. The acceptance of sweetness is innate and universal. Sweetness directs newborn mammals toward safe and nourishing foods and drinks, while bitterness signals potential harm.

2. Of the five most widely acknowledged tastes, three generally signal acceptance (sweet, salty, and umami), while two generally signal avoidance (sour and bitter). These early responses are modified by life experiences, producing adult tastes preferences.

3. Humans have sought sweet foods, sweet drinks, and sweeteners throughout their history, and sweetness continues as a strong force in food and drink selection, influencing large sectors of modern life.

4. There are many different sources of sugars in nature, in addition to sugar cane, sugar beet, and corn. These include fruits, vegetables, and milk.

5. The desire for sweetness is also satisfied by intense sweeteners, low-energy sweeteners (such as polyols), or combinations of these.

6. Sugars, intense sweeteners, and low energy sweeteners together offer useful options for managing sweetness.

7. Human digestion and metabolism do not distinguish between sugars found naturally in foods and those added to foods. All sugars are 4 calories per gram (4 kcals or 17 kJ/g).

8. Glucose is essential to life because it is the primary fuel that the body burns in metabolic processes to generate energy for its cells.

9. Maintenance of a healthy body weight depends on wise management of energy from all food and drink sources, coupled with wise lifestyle choices that include regular physical activity. This is particularly so in a society where energy and physical activity are not in balance.

10. A high frequency of consumption of sugars and other fermentable carbohydrates, combined with a lack of appropriate oral hygiene, has been linked to an increased risk of dental caries.

Agreed in Brussels on June 20, 2006, by France Bellisle, PhD (France); Flora Correia, PhD (Portugal); Adam Drewnowski, PhD (USA); John Foreyt, PhD (USA); Michael Gibney, PhD (Ireland); K. Dun Gifford, JD (USA); Ulrich Huehmer (Germany); Barbara Livingstone, PhD (Northern Ireland); Lluis Serra Majem (Spain); Dominique Parent-Massin, PhD (France); Patrick Pasquet, PhD (France); Sandrine Raffin (France); and Wim Wientjens, PhD (the Netherlands).

We have a hardwired "affection for confection," and we use hundreds of words and phrases of sweetness in our daily language. Sweetheart and my sweet love. Sweet spot and sweet tee shot. Sugar baby and sugar pie. How sweet it is and what a sweet kitty cat. "Sweet Baby Jane" and "Sweet Caroline." Vivid and comforting sweetness language and imagery are everywhere around us.

The first Managing Sweetness International Conference took place in Mexico City in October of 2004, with almost one hundred scientists, journalists, chefs, and industry representatives participating. After two days of presentations on historical, scientific, anthropologic, nutritional, and behavioral aspects surrounding sugar and sweetness, the Scientific Consensus Committee met on the third day to draft a scientific consensus statement on managing sweetness. A second meeting was held in San Diego in June 2005 at the American Diabetes Scientific Sessions, and a third was held in Brussels in June 2006. In Brussels, the Scientific Consensus Statement was updated and subsequently posted on the website of the European Union's Platform on Diet, Physical Activity, and Health. The new text of the statement (see sidebar) is the basis for the Managing Sweetness programs that Oldways is developing worldwide. Its premise is that humans have a genetic and evolutionary preference for sweetness and that learning to manage sweetness in the context of managing calories is the soundest strategy for success. It's "management, not banishment."

Babas and Lemons

MELISSA CLARK

Melissa Clark is a prolific cookbook author and food writer; she's written with chefs (Waldy Malouf and others), she's written about food and places (Nantucket and others), she's written with celebrities (Faith Ford and others). What she really loves is sweets. She traveled with us south of Naples to the province of Salerno, the land of lemons and limoncello. One of our first stops during our weeklong exploration was the Amalfi coast, where we spent a rainy downpour of a morning learning about the craft of limoncello and lemon pastries. Here, Melissa has graciously re-created the lemon babas she discovered in the beautiful, usually sun-kissed village of Minori, on the Amalfi Drive under Ravello on the way to Positano.

It wasn't that I was surprised to see babas in a pastry shop in Minori, in Salerno on the Amalfi coast of Italy. Ever since I stepped off the plane in Naples, babas were omnipresent: on menus at every little café; packed in dusty jars lining the shelves in touristy shops along the beaches; even mixed into gelato. Babas, it seemed, were as ubiquitous in Campanian pastry shops as molten chocolate cakes are in New York City restaurants.

It was the syrup the babas were soaking in that intrigued me. Instead of the usual dousing in rum, these babas were saturated in limoncello. True it was unusual, but it made sense given the context.

The Amalfi coast is justly famous for its particularly fragrant lemons, which come in several shapes, sizes, and colors. A drive along the edge of the deep blue Mediterranean Sea reveals acres and acres of sloping lemon groves, the trees covered in black nets to filter out the strong sunlight. While most of the lemons are shipped around Italy and beyond, commanding premium prices, many others are made locally into intense limoncello, a sugary, greenish-yellow liqueur.

Both babas and limoncello have been local staples for decades, but putting them together, it seems, is a fairly recent phenomenon.

"Traditionally, if you went into a café you'd see a bunch of old guys ordering pieces of plain cake and pouring shots of limoncello over the top," said Arthur Schwartz, the author of N☒☒les ☒ T☒ble (HarperCollins, 1998). But, he added, "babas soaked in limoncello is a new thing, though perfectly natural for the Campanians."

Although most Americans associate babas with the French, they are arguably even more popular in southern Italy, where they probably date back to the eighteenth century. This is when Marie Antoinette's sister Maria Carolina married King Ferdinand of Naples, said Mr. Schwartz, and there was much cultural and culinary exchange between the kingdoms.

Rum had always been part of the baba equation—until now. Limoncello, it seems, is quickly edging it out. Compared to those packed in rum, babas in limoncello are more perfumed and generally less sweet, with a welcomed tartness from lemon zest. See the recipe on page 212 for a lighter baba than most. Just don't try to substitute rum.

Cookies for All

SARA BAER-SINNOTT

In the world of baked desserts, some people are cake people and some are pie people (what do ☒☒ ask for on your birthday?), but I am a cookie person. The holiday I love more than any other is Christmas, and in part, it's because I love Christmas cookies.

The baking begins when Thanksgiving weekend is over. I do bake, but my mother is really in charge of Christmas cookies. When I was growing up in Pittsburgh she had an incredible repertoire: real sugar cookies in reindeer, bell, angel, Santa, and candy cane shapes (with and without sugar crystals and/or pink and green frosting); hazelnut crescents; green, pink,

and white meringues; rum balls; and jam-filled raspberry souvaroffs.

But the most memorable and scrumptious Christmas cookie of all was her special large-sized Santa cookie, individually decorated with raisins for eyes, a coconut frosting beard, red sugared hat, white frosted eyebrows and fur-trimmed hat, and cheery red cheeks and lips. To top it off, she individually wrapped each cookie in a crinkly cellophane with curly green and red ribbon and insisted that we savor these cookies, not gobble them. She restricted my father, my friends, and me to only one per day. My mother still makes baskets of Christmas cookies, and every year or so, makes the very special Santa cookies for my children.

Most important of all, these dreamy Christmas cookies gave me a lifetime love affair with cookies. They are my ultimate comfort food, and I often find myself whipping up a batch of my tried-and-true favorites—even though I'm always alert for new cookies to try, and maybe have a fling with. My favorites come in small and large sizes, have many flavors and tastes, and I savor them with milk, coffee, tea, juice; at my home and office and in jetliners six miles high; and in three dozen countries; but most especially, when I'm cozy at home with a plateful of my favorite sweet cookies still warm from the oven.

Cookies are just perfect (see page 214 and 215 for recipes to make your own).

Politics and Cookies

K. DUN GIFFORD

At an elegant dinner party for old friends one winter night in the early 1980s, John Kerry and I made the unlikely discovery that we shared a passion for "real" cookies—he for chocolate chip, me for butterscotch.

Others at the table joined our lamentation about the passing of "good, old-fashioned, authentic, traditional cookies," and a general sadness about their replacement in the marketplace with "standardized, assembly-line, factory, industrial, and pale imitations" spread around the table.

"Well," I said, "how about we try to pull together some recipes for everyone's favorite cookies and share them? My favorite is the fabulous butterscotch cookies my grandmother made—she used English butterscotch—and I can get the recipe from my Mom."

"You won't believe my recipe for chocolate chips," said John. "It's made with Swiss chocolate, Lindt probably, and I have the recipe. There's absolutely nothing like it."

Soon everyone was talking about his or her favorite cookies, and of cookie memories. To a person, we were absolutely sure that none of the cookies then sweeping across the country and popping up in the malls—Famous Amos, Mrs. Fields, David's—could hold a candle to cookies made with our recipes.

After dinner John and I were talking, mostly about politics, and we suddenly had the same brain wave—we could start a cookie company with our excellent cookies, and they'd be so popular we'd swamp the competition! We'd have my butterscotch and his chocolate chip, we'd name the business with our mothers' maiden names (Kilvert and Forbes) because they sounded sort of old-fashioned and authentic, and we'd get it going and then roll out franchises across the country.

There was a certain logic to this idea; it was not entirely a whimsy at the end of dinner with a lot of good food and wine. I was in the restaurant business at the time and had an excellent relationship with the owners of Faneuil Hall Marketplace, where we wanted to put our new cookie shop and where I was already involved with a couple of restaurants. John was very high-profile even then, and so that would help with the marketing. The stars were in alignment!

So we filed legal papers to establish the Kilvert & Forbes Company, raised the money to start up the business, signed a lease for a great location in the center of the central Faneuil Hall Marketplace building for our cookie store, bought equipment we needed to make the cookies and operate the store, and hired staff. Perhaps the best decision we made was to install the oven that made the cookies right in the store itself, so that glorious smell of our fabulous cookies baking spread through the building. We were dead certain that this would draw customers like honey draws bees, and we were right.

But the overriding consideration was getting the cookie recipes developed so they were the way we wanted them, and so they could be made over and over again with the same tastes and textures on a commercial scale.

For their authenticity and taste qualities (and despite the expense), we decided to use Swiss Lindt chocolate for the chocolate chip cookies, and British Callard & Bowser butterscotch for the butterscotch cookies. We used expensive high-butterfat Vermont butter, and the highest-quality King Arthur flour. We bought mixers that stood as tall as we did and an entire collection of industrial-strength stainless-steel spatulas, spoons, knives, whips, and a lot of cleaning equipment to clean the mixing bowls and implements.

We rented a storeroom/workroom in the basement of the adjoining building in the Marketplace, and we all gathered there one cold and damp gray Boston Saturday morning to make our first commercial-sized batch of cookie batter. We knew that simply "scaling up" proportionately the home-kitchen recipes that we'd carefully tested over the last few months would not work in commercial quantities, and that we would have to adjust them.

So we opened a 100-pound bag of King Arthur flour, a very cold 50-pound box of Vermont country butter, a 100-pound box of Lindt chocolate, and a 50-pound box of Callard & Bowser butterscotch. We had no idea what to do next, because the chocolate was not in bags of chocolate chips but in four 25-pound blocks, the butterscotch was also in 25-pound blocks, and the butter was in 5-pound blocks. There was no way the mixer could mix them!

We had no way to soften the butter in the workroom, and no grinder to reduce the chocolate to chip-sized chunks or the butterscotch to chips. So we improvised.

The butter was not complicated: we used knives to cut it into smaller pieces, and then mashed it to soften it.

But we were stumped by the chocolate and butterscotch; we had no mallets or even a length of 2 × 4 to smash it with. Then John remembered that he had a baseball bat in his car, and he hustled out to get it while the rest of started in on the butter. He returned with the baseball bat, and started banging away at the chocolate. It did break apart, of course, but pieces of it flew all over the place. This was not working. Someone remembered that there was a Williams-Sonoma store in the Marketplace, and so off she went to get some kitchen towels.

We draped them over the chocolate, and John started in on it again with the baseball bat. After a while he got it right, and we built up a big stash of chocolate chunks of just the right size.

Then it was my turn with the butterscotch. We set it out on the bench, draped a towel over it, and whacked away at it with the bat. It shattered just fine, but no matter what we tried, it did not want to be broken into anything approaching uniform-sized pieces. So I whacked at those butterscotch blocks for a long time, and from the resulting good-sized pile we picked out enough right-sized pieces to make our sample batch of cookie batter.

Only later did we learn that Lindt sells its chocolate as chunks and chips, and Callard & Bowser sells its butterscotch in chunks and chips, and we did not need to attack big blocks of the stuff with bats.

In a few days we found recipe formulations that satisfied us, did trial runs until we got all the production bugs worked out, and organized our grand opening. It was indeed grand, and from day one Kilvert & Forbes was a success.

After a few years of profitable operations, an excellent political door opened for John, and he decided to go for it. We decided then to sell our cookie company, and we did so at a nice profit. It is still in operation in Faneuil Hall Marketplace.

In his down-to-the-wire race for president in 2004, John could comfortably report that he had once been a businessman, and even better, a successful one.

Every time I was called by reporters during the campaign to confirm John's participation, I did so, but always smiled with the memory of whacking away at blocks of the world's best chocolate and butterscotch with a baseball bat.

Ice Cream: Like a Moth to a Flame

K. DUN GIFFORD

I am drawn irresistibly to ice cream and sorbet, and drawn equally to most of its close relatives, like sherbets and granité.

It all started in childhood (as it did with most of "my brothers and sisters in ice cream" with whom I share this passion), in summers toward the end of World War II. In twenty minutes, my mother, my brothers (the youngest in a carriage), and I, in company with my mother's sister and my cousins, could walk to the two-block Nantucket Main Street from the cottage we were all crammed into together.

For my mother and aunt, the targets of this after-the-children's supper stroll were the hanging out together with other women whose husbands and fathers were away in the war somewhere, and the sing-along of old favorites led by the blind accordionist, Herbie. But for us kids the target was our first stop, the Candy Kitchen, with its kaleidoscope of candy and ice cream.

The Candy Kitchen was every kid's magnificent, fantasy Sweet Mountain, of course—taffy, ice cream, soda pop, caramel, chewing gum, and the penny candy jar, with its mountain of unimaginable sweet treats. We each had a limit of a nickel to spend and were allowed to accumulate (we called it piggybacking) so we could spend, say, two cents on one day, meaning we'd have eight cents the next time. But ice cream wasn't candy, and so it did not count against our daily nickel limit, meaning we had ice cream and candy before we went to the singing.

There were twelve ice cream flavors, and they changed from day to day, except for the gold standards—vanilla, chocolate, coffee, and strawberry—which never changed. They had fruit flavors of ice cream and sherbet, regulars like orange and strawberry and cherry, and other regulars we never touched after trying them once, like frozen pudding. But the flavors that changed were spellbinding: licorice, caramel, peppermint, sweet lemon, banana, pineapple, chocolate pudding, and blends, such as orange-pineapple and caramel-vanilla. These people did a land-office business, because they had the early and late movie crowd (the movie house was just across the street) and we Main Street people in between.

One night I saw another kid with a two-scoop cone. Imagine! Two scoops! This was for me. The first scoop was ten cents (my mother paid) and the second scoop was a nickel. My mother made me pay for the second scoop out of my daily nickel, so most nights I went without the candy but had two scoops of luscious, sweet creamy ice cream.

Fast-forward with me about sixty years, to 2005. It's early August, and I am in my house in Nantucket with my son Porter, his wife Serena, and their kids, Suzannah, age seven, and Abbott, age five. "Dad," says Porter at breakfast, "how'd you like to come with the kids and me on the Ice Cream Harbor Cruise this afternoon?"

"The what?" I asked.

"It's a charter boat that cruises around the harbor, and they serve us ice cream. It costs ten bucks a head," he replied.

"Are you pulling my leg?" I asked.

"No, it's for real. We checked it out when we were down at the Boat Basin the other day."

"Yes, yes, Grampa, please come with us, please, please," said sweet Suzannah, and Abbott echoed her.

So at 3:00 we were down at the Boat Basin on a gorgeous afternoon, looking around at the assemblage of yachts, which ranged from little to big and everything in between. And there in her berth was the Anna W, our Ice Cream Harbor Cruise. She was an old boat I knew as a fishing boat in my childhood, with classic lines and an old straight-eight gasoline engine. She was fitted out with six tables and benches for four anchored to the deck in the cabin, with a roof overhead and open sides. She was painted white within an inch of her life and clean as a whistle. We were the first aboard and got the table we wanted, on the starboard side in the stern.

Once all the other passengers were settled, too, the captain yelled out, "Anyone want any ice cream?" We all yelled back in unison, "Yes!" So he and the mate served us each a great big bowl of vanilla ice cream, dotted with multicolor M&Ms, and once he'd done this, we cast off from the dock, and set out around the harbor on a beautiful midsummer afternoon, each of us, grown-ups and children, full of rich, creamy vanilla ice cream.

BUT ICE CREAM'S FATTENING!

The best ice cream in the world is made by the French, who unashamedly use eggs yolks and heavy cream to make it (actually, one-third heavy cream to two-thirds regular milk). This is real ice cream, not the generic stuff we serve here, which uniformly has gelatin, flour, whole eggs, and "stabilizers" in it. I think that's why Ben and Jerry's made such a big splash when they introduced their rich ice cream—it tasted like our memories and dreams of the "old-time real thing."

Do the French eat ice cream every day? No. Do they eat double and triple scoops when they do eat it? No; their ice cream is so rich and intensely flavored that a single small scoop is satisfying.

BABA LIMONCELLO WITH LEMON CREAM

MELISSA CLARK

We know and love our babas, traditionally saturated with rum soaking the pastry. This is a wonderful Italian variant—instead of with rum, these babas are saturated with limoncello, the wonderfully sweet lemon Italian liqueur.

SERVES 12

BABAS

1/2 cup milk

1/4 ounce (1 packet) active dry yeast

2 cups plus 3 tablespoons bread flour

3 large eggs

1 tablespoon sugar

1/2 teaspoon sea salt

1/2 cup (1 stick) unsalted butter, melted

LEMON CREAM

1 cup milk

5 tablespoons sugar

Grated zest of 1 lemon

Pinch of sea salt

3 tablespoons cornstarch

1 large egg, plus 1 large egg yolk

5 tablespoons unsalted butter

1/2 cup heavy cream

LIMONCELLO SYRUP

Grated zest of 10 lemons

2 cups water

3/4 cup sugar

5 tablespoons limoncello

Butter a 12-cup muffin tin and set aside.

To prepare the babas, in a saucepan over low heat, gently warm the milk. Pour it into the bowl of an electric mixer or other large bowl and sprinkle in the yeast. Stir until the yeast dissolves. Whisk in 1/2 cup plus 3 tablespoons of the flour and cover the bowl with plastic wrap. Let rise in a warm place until the mixture has doubled, 30 to 60 minutes.

Using an electric mixer with the paddle attachment or a food processor fitted with the dough blade, beat the eggs, sugar, salt, and the remaining 1 1/2 cups of flour into the yeast mixture until very smooth. Gradually mix in the melted butter and continue to mix until smooth.

Spoon the dough into the muffin tin, filling each cup halfway. Grease a piece of plastic wrap and cover the muffin tin. Let rise until the dough has risen just above the level of the muffin tin, about 1 hour.

Meanwhile, preheat the oven to 350°F. Remove the plastic wrap and bake the babas until they are dark golden brown on top and the bottoms sound hollow when tapped, about 20 minutes. Transfer the tin to a wire rack to cool.

To prepare the lemon cream, in a saucepan over medium heat, bring the milk, 3 tablespoons of the sugar, the lemon zest, and salt to a boil, stirring until the sugar dissolves. Meanwhile, in a bowl, whisk together the cornstarch, the remaining 2 tablespoons of sugar, the egg, and yolk. Whisking constantly, pour the hot milk mixture gradually into the egg mixture. Whisk to combine, then transfer the mixture back to the saucepan and warm over medium-low heat, whisking constantly, being sure to scrape the bottom and sides of the saucepan. As soon as the liquid reaches a boil, take the saucepan off the heat. Whisk in the butter, a tablespoon at a time. Transfer the mixture to a shallow bowl and lay a piece of plastic wrap directly on the surface of the lemon cream. Refrigerate until well chilled, about 2 hours.

To prepare the syrup, in a saucepan, combine the lemon zest, water, and sugar and bring to a boil, stirring to dissolve the sugar. Simmer until the liquid is yellow, 2 to 3 minutes. Strain the liquid through a fine sieve into a bowl. Stir in the limoncello. Let cool.

Just before serving, whip the heavy cream until it forms soft (not stiff) peaks. Whisk the chilled lemon cream well to loosen it, then gently fold in the whipped cream.

Slice the babas in half vertically. Submerge each baba in the limoncello syrup for 10 seconds. Arrange the babas on plates cut sides up, and drizzle them with more of the syrup. Top the babas with large dollops of lemon cream and serve immediately.

CREAMY VANILLA BREAD PUDDING WITH CHERRY COMPOTE

BARBARA LYNCH

No. 9 Park Restaurant chef and owner Barbara Lynch makes this simple and satisfying bread pudding, and it's incredibly versatile. Cherry compote is a perfect accompaniment for spring and early summer, but in other seasons, it can also be served with apricot or fig compote, or with caramel sauce.

SERVES 8

PUDDING

4 to 5 cups cubed white bread (enough to fill a 9 by 13-inch pan)

3 cups heavy cream

1/2 vanilla bean, split in half lengthwise, with the seeds scraped and reserved

1/2 teaspoon sea salt

4 medium eggs

1/2 cup sugar

2 teaspoons vanilla extract

COMPOTE

1 cinnamon stick

5 black peppercorns

1 bay leaf

1 cup water

1 cup sugar

2 cups cherries, pitted

Preheat the oven to 350°F. To prepare the pudding, spread the cubed bread in a greased 9 by 13-inch pan.

In a medium saucepan, combine the cream, vanilla bean and seeds, and salt. Heat over low heat until the mixture is just warm to the touch. Remove from the heat, set aside, and let steep for 1 hour.

In the bowl of an electric mixer fitted with a whisk, combine the eggs and the sugar and beat at high speed until the mixture is light yellow in color and falls from the beater in thick ribbons. Add the vanilla extract.

Rewarm the cream mixture until it is hot (do not let boil), remove from heat, and pour 1 cup of the hot cream into the egg mixture, whisking constantly. Pour the egg mixture into the remaining cream, whisk to combine, and then pour through a strainer over the baking dish filled with bread. Let rest until the bread has absorbed the custard, about 20 minutes.

Set the baking dish in a water bath filled with hot water. Bake in the center of the oven until firm, about 1 hour. Let cool.

To prepare the compote, tie the cinnamon, peppercorns, and bay leaf together in a small square of cheesecloth. In a small saucepan, combine the water and sugar, and add the cheesecloth sack of spices. Cook over medium heat without stirring until the sugar dissolves and the mixture becomes syrupy and begins to caramelize, about 8 minutes. When the mixture is light brown in color, add the cherries, cook for 1 minute, then remove from heat. Remove the spice bag and discard. Serve the compote warm alongside the bread pudding.

MOLASSES COOKIES

SARA BAER-SINNOTT

*After ten years of trying and reworking many differ-
ent recipes for molasses cookies, this one emerged
as Sara's hands-down favorite. The sorghum flour is
an option, and you'll be surprised by how smooth and
creamy the dough becomes with it. It's important to
undercook these cookies, making sure they stay soft
and gooey.*

MAKES 3 DOZEN COOKIES

3/4 cup softened butter
I cup packed brown sugar
2 large eggs
1/4 cup unsulfured molasses
1 3/4 cups sorghum flour, or 2 1/4 cups white whole-
   wheat flour, plus more as needed
I teaspoon baking soda
2 teaspoons ground cinnamon
1 1/2 teaspoons ground ginger
Raw, coarse, or sanding sugar (or substitute
   white sugar) for coating

Preheat the oven to 375°F. Oil or butter a large baking
sheet.

In a large bowl, cream the butter and brown sugar until
creamy. Add in the eggs and molasses and beat until
well blended.

In a separate bowl, mix together the flour, baking soda,
cinnamon, and ginger. Add the dry ingredients to the
butter mixture. Beat at medium speed until the mixture
doesn't stick to the bowl, adding more flour if necessary.

To form each cookie, make a golf-ball-sized ball, and
then flatten it between your hands. Dredge each flat-
tened ball in the raw sugar.

Place the cookies on the prepared baking sheet about
1 to 2 inches apart, and bake for 6 to 7 minutes. Don't
let the cookies get too brown on the bottom. Cool on
a rack.

HAZELNUT CRESCENTS

NORMA BAER

*These luscious, scrumptious, and traditional cres-
cent cookies never stay in the cookie tin very
long. They work well with any nut of your choice—
almonds, walnuts, pecans, or hazelnuts.*

MAKES 3 DOZEN COOKIES

I cup butter, at room temperature
1/4 cup white sugar
2 cups unbleached white flour
I cup ground hazelnuts (filberts)
I teaspoon vanilla extract
Confectioners' sugar for dipping

Preheat the oven to 300°F. Grease a large cookie sheet.

Cream the butter. Add the white sugar, flour, hazelnuts,
and vanilla and beat until well blended.

Shape the cookies into 3-inch-long logs, each about 1
inch in diameter. Then curve the ends to form a crescent
shape. Place on the baking sheet about 2 inches apart.
Bake for 35 minutes. Roll the cookies in confectioners'
sugar immediately after taking the cookies out of the
oven. Let them cool on a wire rack for about 30 minutes. Roll again in confectioners' sugar before serving.

EVERYONE'S FAVORITE CHRISTMAS COOKIES

NORMA BAER

Most everyone's mother makes sugar cookies or Christmas cookies, but Sara swears that her mother's are the best. There are two ways to handle the dough—one is easier and takes less time; the other results in more Christmas-like cookies. You'll love them both. ⬛

MAKES 3 DOZEN COOKIES

3/4 cup unsalted butter, at room temperature

1 1/2 cups sugar

1 large egg

3/4 teaspoon vanilla extract

2 cups unbleached white flour

1/2 teaspoon baking powder

1/2 teaspoon sea salt

Decorative sugar or Christmas sprinkles (optional)

Cream the butter with the sugar until creamy. Add the egg and vanilla and beat until well blended.

In another bowl, sift together the flour, baking powder, and salt. Slowly add to the butter mixture, beating until well blended.

To shape the cookies, using plastic wrap, roll the dough into logs about 3 inches in diameter. Slice the logs into manageable lengths. Refrigerate for at least 5 hours, or up to 1 day.

Preheat the oven to 375°F. Cut the logs into 1/2-inch slices. Place on an ungreased cookie sheet about 2 inches apart and sprinkle with sugar or Christmas sprinkles. Bake for 12 to 15 minutes, until they are golden brown. Let them cool on a wire rack.

VARIATION: ROLLED SUGAR COOKIES. Alternatively, if you wish to use cookie cutters, gather the dough into a ball, cover with plastic wrap or waxed paper, and refrigerate for at least 5 hours, or up to 1 day.

Preheat the oven to 375°F. On a lightly floured surface, use a rolling pin to roll out the dough until it is 1/4 inch thick. Using Christmas cookie cutters, cut the dough into shapes and place on an ungreased cookie sheet about 2 inches apart. Decorate the cookies with sugar or Christmas sprinkles. Bake for 12 to 15 minutes, until the cookies are golden brown. Let them cool on a wire rack.

HAZELNUT-COCOA BISCOTTI

SUSAN G. PURDY

Susan Purdy is one of this country's sweets experts. She has written thirty books, twelve about baking and pastry, including Have Your Cake & Eat It, Too; The Perfect Cake; The Perfect Pie; *and most recently,* Pie in the Sky. *We are fortunate to have her sweets smarts and hope you will (as we do) dunk her special biscotti in your favorite drink.*

Biscotti are classic Tuscan cookies, twice baked so they are firmly crisp. The original Tuscan biscotti di Prato were dipped into vin santo, a sweet dessert wine, and so a bit softened and sweetened. Today's biscotti are the ultimate dunking cookie—perfect when dipped into coffee, tea, hot cocoa, or (for that matter) sweet wine, a moda Tuscana.

For a touch of elegance, coat half of each crisp biscotto with melted semisweet chocolate and set on waxed paper to cool. Or, drizzle the melted chocolate in thin lines over a whole batch of cooled cookies spread out on a white serving dish—make swirls, grids, numbers, the initials of someone special, and whatever the Picasso and Jackson Pollack lurking within you dreams up. When you serve them your guests will separate a cookie or two from this work of art, and happily eat a part of your clever creation.

- 2$^1/_2$ cups sifted unbleached all-purpose flour, or as needed
- 1$^1/_2$ teaspoons baking powder
- $^1/_2$ teaspoon sea salt
- $^1/_4$ cup unsweetened cocoa, preferably Dutch-processed (Droste, for example)
- 3 tablespoons unsalted butter, at room temperature
- 1 cup sugar
- 3 large eggs
- 1 teaspoon vanilla extract
- 1$^1/_2$ teaspoons almond or hazelnut extract
- 3 tablespoons Frangelico (hazelnut liqueur) (optional)
- $^3/_4$ cup (about 4.5 ounces) coarsely chopped toasted hazelnuts (or substitute almonds or walnuts)
- $^1/_2$ cup (3 ounces) semisweet chocolate chips

Preheat the oven to 350°F. Lightly coat a cookie sheet with nonstick cooking spray or line with parchment paper.

In a bowl, sift together the flour, baking powder, salt, and cocoa. Set aside.

In the large bowl of an electric mixer, cream together the butter and sugar at medium speed until creamy. Then beat in the eggs, along with the vanilla, almond extract, and liqueur, if using. With the mixer on the lowest speed, gradually work in the dry ingredients, then the nuts and chips. Blend well. Scrape down the bowl and beaters. Gather the dough into a ball; if it feels very sticky, work in a little more flour, 1 tablespoon at a time.

On a lightly floured surface, divide the dough evenly in half. Shape each half into a log about 13 inches long, 1 inch high, and $1^1/_2$ inches wide. Place the logs about 2 inches apart on the prepared baking sheet, and gently flatten the top of each one until slightly domed; the finished log should measure $13^1/2$ to 14 inches long, $^3/_4$ inch high, about $1^3/_4$ inches wide.

Bake for 20 to 22 minutes, until logs are dry on top and firm to the touch; a wooden toothpick should come out nearly clean, with just a trace of batter showing. Remove the baking sheet from the oven and lower the oven temperature to 300°F. With a long spatula, transfer the logs to a cutting board and allow to cool for about 5 minutes.

With a serrated knife, cut the still-warm logs on the diagonal into $^1/_2$-inch-thick slices. Place the slices cut side down on the same baking sheet (don't regrease). If necessary, use a second pan.

Bake for 15 to 20 minutes, until the slices are dry and crisp. The longer they bake, the harder and crisper they will be; they crisp more as they cool. Let cool on a wire rack.

CHOCOLATE SAUCE ROYALE

K. DUN GIFFORD

It's rumored that post-Columbus British, French, Spanish, and papal monarchs craved a perfect chocolate fudge sauce for their perfect ice creams. This recipe is fit for royalty. And no wonder: it produces that chocolate fudge sauce of childhood memory, shiny and silky as it slides out of a silver pitcher and down over a double mound of light-yellow vanilla ice cream, hardening gradually but remaining soft and luscious.

MAKES 6 CUPS

> $^3/_4$ cup water
> $1^1/_4$ cups unsweetened cocoa powder
> 1 cup dark brown sugar
> 1 cup granulated white sugar
> $^1/_2$ teaspoon salt
> $1^3/_4$ cups heavy cream
> 3 sticks butter, softened
> 2 tablespoons vanilla
> 2 ounces cognac (optional)

Thoroughly combine the water, cocoa powder, brown sugar, white sugar, and salt in a large saucepan over high heat. Simmer, whisking steadily, for about 6 minutes, until smooth. Remove from the heat.

Place the cream, butter, and vanilla in a saucepan over medium heat. After the butter has melted, about 3 minutes, turn up the heat up to scalding for about 3 minutes. Lower the heat to low, and gradually whisk in the sugar and cocoa mixture for about 3 minutes, until the sugar has dissolved and the mixture is smooth. Add the cognac and combine.

Pour over ice cream immediately or serve warm (it becomes too thick when chilled or at room temperature).

"The ancient Romans loved all sorts of condiments and spices....
One undisputed success was the sweet-and-sour mixture [of] pepper,
mint, pine nuts, sultana grapes, carrots, honey, vinegar, oil, wine,
and musk. The family resemblance is still evident in
the various *agrodolce* sauces applied in Italy today."

—WAVERLY ROOT, *THE COOKING OF ITALY*

"Salsa, chutneys, dipping sauces, relishes, quick pickles, sambals,
flavored butters and mayonnaises, even barbecue sauces, spice rubs,
and glazes, all come under the heading of condiments."

—IRMA S. ROMBAUER, *THE JOY OF COOKING*

CONDIMENTS

The World of Condiments
K. DUN GIFFORD

Condiments are tricky. Often they're strange, not quite what you expect them to be. Their strong and startling tastes can be very sharp, very sweet, very tart, and even very bitter. Maybe this is why even a small amount can make such a big difference in the flavor of a dish.

They're a bit like a fun house at the carnival—kind of simple and tame at the beginning, but (as we anticipate) becoming scary and exotic as we plunge into it more deeply. But we don't turn back. Something about the unknown and exotic draws us on.

After all, we do eat some pretty strange things. Do you remember your first oyster? First steak tartare? First martini? First stuffed squid? Condiments help make these kinds of things go down.

WHAT IS A CONDIMENT?

Here's a good basic definition of condiments from the *The Food Lover's Companion*: "A savory, piquant, spicy or salty accompaniment to food, such as a relish, sauce, mixture of spices, etc. Ketchup and mustard are two of the most popular condiments."

Other condiments include spice rubs, barbecue sauces, chutneys, dipping sauces, salsas, mayonnaises, pickle relish, flavored butters, glazes, and chutneys. This makes it plain that condiments are generally not viewed as food at all, but as something we *add* to food to flavor it, to brighten its tastes, or even to mask a strong taste element. This is why we sour cream our baked potatoes, ketchup our burgers, mustard our hot dogs, dress our salads, dip our shrimp, and so on. Sometimes this masks the taste (spicy cocktail sauce dims the fishiness of shrimp) and sometimes it brightens it (steak sauce puts zip into lesser cuts of meat).

We all know ketchup—we pour oceans of it over hamburgers and hot dogs and French fries every day. This is commercial ketchup—sweet, predictable, familiar, and, blessedly, with always the same consistent taste and texture whether in round or square glass bottles, plastic squirt containers, little pots with little spoons, or plastic packets.

Mustard, too, is our lifelong friend, putting a bit more zip than ketchup into our burgers and hot dogs. Some people even put mustard on french fries. If you're one of those looking to kick your fries up a notch, splash them with a couple of dashes of vinegar, like the residents of the British Isles have always done. It's really refreshing.

Some of us use a lot of other condiments, too, such as horseradish, Worcestershire sauce, Tabasco sauce, Cajun rub, bourbon sauce, and, of course, the old standbys hollandaise and béarnaise. But our condiments are pale horses when they ride alongside the pintos, piebalds, chestnuts, and roans of the condiments of other cultures.

CONDIMENTI AROUND THE WORLD

Condiments can bring excitement and surprise to a dish or meal. Even if a meal is already excellent, it can be lifted to new heights with an artful deployment of a condiment.

The Italian word for condiment is *condimento,* which they say as "con-dee-MEN-toe," with the accent on the third syllable. It has a lovely round sound to it, and the plural is just as musical: *condimenti,* pronounced "con-dee-MEN-tee."

The parade of wonderful *condimenti* seems to have no end in Italy, but at its head are their glorious olive oils—some sweet, some pungent, some mild, some strong, and some in between. Italy, like France, has dozens of distinct regional cuisines, but each of Italy's is built on the strong foundation of olive oil. The cuisines of milk cultures like ours are built on butter (or on pale substitutes like margarine or vegetable oil).

For me, aged authentic balsamic vinegar from Modena tops the *condimento* totem. Its proper name is *aceto balsamico* (pronounced "ah-CHET-oh bal-SAM-ee-co"), a name that rolls off Italian tongues with a sense of affection, and maybe even with love. Our English word for it, with its hard "C" ending (bal-SAM-ic), is matter-of-fact and even businesslike, without any sense of pleasure or endearment.

The cuisines of the Indian subcontinent are built on fiery mustard seed oils, and the cuisines of Asia are based on sesame oils of vastly varying heat. These oils are staples of the diets, and in a literal sense are condiments since they are added to foods both as a cooking medium and also as a flavoring/texturing agent after cooking.

Measured by quantity, Americans are not condiment slackers. But measured by quality, we are.

We eat Thanksgiving turkey with gravy, stuffing, and cranberry jelly. We put A-1 and hickory-smoke and honey-barbecue sauce on steaks. We put all manner of odd barbecue sauces on our chicken so it doesn't dry out.

We put French, creamy Italian, blue cheese, green goddess, vinegar-and-oil, and ranch dressings on salads.

We put jam, jelly, and honey on bread, toast, and muffins. We put white and brown sugar on breakfast cereals. We stuff jelly into doughnuts, crullers, and sponge cake and coat their outsides with sugar icing.

We put ice cream on pies and in cakes. We put maple syrup, chocolate sauce, and caramel on ice cream, and fruit and nuts, too. We even put fruits and nuts into ice cream.

We coat fish with breadcrumbs and crushed nuts, and squeeze lemon on it. We eat lamb with mint sauce and mint jelly, pork with apples and applesauce, ham with mustard and with cheese, hot dogs with mustard and relish, and beef with horseradish or currant jelly.

We put hollandaise sauce on asparagus, dill on carrots, parsley on boiled potatoes, sour cream and chives on baked potatoes, butter on peas, vinegar on spinach, and slivered almonds on green beans.

And it sometimes seems as if we use mayonnaise on everything.

So, while we are not condiment slackers, there's a catch. Our condiments are dumbed down. We live in a condiment rut.

We are not satisfied with the tastes of top-notch traditional mustard. For some reason or another we seem compelled to flavor it: honey, poppy seed, country French, Catalina, horseradish, cranberry, jalapeño, and so on.

We don't just have soy sauce, we often flavor it as if we are adding a condiment to it: teriyaki, oriental, Thai, chili, hoisin, and so on.

We don't just have milk, we flavor it with chocolate, malt, coffee, and cocoa.

And we don't just have espresso or café au lait or Ceylon tea. We have to flavor it with vanilla and hazelnut and peppermint.

Steak sauces? The list of condiments added to basic steak sauce is a long one.

There are hundreds of these kinds of gussied-up "condiments" in supermarket aisles, and they can in fact elevate the flavors of bland food. Sad to say, however, the flavors are mostly artificial. We *condimentize* our condiments.

ACETO BALSAMICO

What we are missing is the wild variety and dense richness of *condimenti* that are real, true, authentic, traditional, time-tested, and valued as cultural icons. Instead, we have industrial versions, one-size-fits-all techno foods, dumbed-down editions of the real thing.

But *aceto balsamico* is the real thing, a real condiment, made the same way it has always been made. One single drop of it on a bite-size chunk of Parmigiano-Reggiano cheese, for example, transforms it into a unique sensory experience, and it does the same for a ripe strawberry. In both cases, the food (cheese or strawberry) is real food, and real *aceto balsamico* does not obliterate their tastes but, in the sense of a true condiment, elevates them, taking them to a new level. Believe me, the balsamic vinegar we know in our stores here is nothing like *aceto balsamico*, which is a real condiment, the real thing, and *really* good.

It may be heretical to say this, but good old-fashioned concession-stand yellow mustard on a Fenway frank is in the same class as balsamico on Parmigiano-Reggiano. Julia Child was never shy about speaking bluntly of her enthusiasms for real foods that she loved, and she taught millions of people to be equally enthusiastic about foods as lowly as cheap yellow mustard on Fenway franks. But she loved expensive *aceto balsamico* and a beautiful hollandaise sauce, too.

Aceto balsamico is syrupy, dense, lush, velvety. It is dark brown like dark chocolate but also deep purple-red like the skin of a ripe plum. It clings to the cheese and berries and your finger. It is sweet with a bit of a bite and has an intense aroma unlike anything else in the world.

Authentic *aceto balsamico* is permitted to be made only in the area around Modena in north central Italy, part of the region of Emilia-Romagna that runs east-west along the south bank of the Po River. This region is the home ground of other of the world's great food delicacies, too, including Parmigiano-Reggiano cheese, prosciutto hams, and a host of unique cured meats, salamis, bolognas, and culatello among them. It fascinates me that the people of Reggio-Emilia and Romagna are such an intensely gastronomic people.

There is, of course, an industrial version of *aceto balsamico,* called balsamic vinegar. Bottles of it are sold in supermarkets for home use and sold to restaurants for use on tables and salad bars. It's a lot better than those bottled dressings, such as honey mustard, ranch, creamy Italian, and so on, but it's a shadow of the real thing.

CHUTNEY

Chutneys are magical, dense, and very intense. The classic chutney is Major Grey's, which (so the story goes) he brought back to England with him from India, where it quickly became the rage and eventually a fixture of British cuisine. There is some mystery about whether, in fact, there ever was a Major Grey, as in this bit of doggerel:

> All things chickeny and mutt'ny
> Taste much better when served with chutney.
> So this is the mystery eternal:
> Why didn't Major Grey make colonel?

But no matter; over the years Crosse & Blackwell sold vast amounts of Major Grey's chutney all over the world. Thank goodness, because chutney is one of those true culinary treasures. It is wonderful with roasted meats, including poultry; it elevates them, much as *aceto balsamico* elevates hard cheeses. It has become a standard restaurant accompaniment for curries, which is wonderful if it gets more people to try curries, enjoy them, and come back for more (even if the people of India find this curry/chutney combination bizarre).

The base of classic Indian chutneys is mangoes, to which are added limes, tamarind, and a basket of spices, which may include any or all of the following: cloves, cinnamon, black (or red or green) pepper, onions, ground red pepper, garlic, mustard seeds, salt, orange and/or lemon rind, ginger, allspice, and turmeric.

Other fruits work very well in chutneys: pears, peaches, nectarines, kiwi, guava, apricots, dates, tomatoes, apples, raisins, bananas, and so on. The fruits can be combined, too, as in another classic, date and apricot chutney.

The cooking technique is that of preserving fruits: Clean the fruits and nuts (if any), cut them into small pieces, and put them into a kettle with a few cups of water to prevent any scorching, some sugar, and all the other ingredients. Simmer this on the stovetop over low heat for about two hours (or cook it in the oven in a covered casserole dish), and then spoon it into sterilized jars and cover tightly. If you recognize this as the way to make jam, you're right on the money. Chutneys are preserves.

MUSTARD

Some aficionados claim that all mustards are divided into two kingdoms, the smooth ones and the grainy ones. Others disagree, saying that the two kingdoms are the hot mustards and the mild mustards. So who knows, maybe there are actually four mustard kingdoms. (Some would argue that ballpark mustard is so unique and pervasive that it needs its own kingdom. . . .)

Smooth, yellow, and mild mustards are by far the most familiar in America, where they flavor ubiquitous hot dogs, burgers, cold-cut sandwiches, and a lot more, too. Be careful if you go to England, though, because yellow mustards there are often fiery.

The Greeks and the Romans knew mustard, and before them the Egyptians did; mustard seeds turn up in excavations of pharaohs' tombs. From this Mediterranean base, mustard migrated with traders to India and the Far East, and there became a fixture of those cuisines as well.

The French gave us the word "mustard," from *moutarde,* which appeared in the early Middle Ages. In those days the mustard seeds were mixed with grape must to make this *moutarde,* which was sweet (a bit like sweet-and-sour sauce in Chinese restaurants, but not so viscous and much better tasting). Over time *moutarde* morphed into unsweetened classic French Dijon and Grey Poupon mustards, which now hold places of honor in good kitchens.

Mustard and fire are a good match. My father slathered mustard on steaks, thick and thin alike, before laying them on a grill. He moved back and forth among smooth yellow mustards and grainy brown mustards, and often mixed the two more or less at random. I picked up this mustard and steak habit, and it's a good one, particularly if the steak is an expensive cut with not much fat.

We tried mustard on fish, too, and it's a big help with fine-fleshed saltwater fish without much fat, like snappers, grunt, and porgies. We would not use it on trout; for some reason bacon seems to work out best with freshwater fish. Of course, the mustard adds flavor, too, no matter if the fish is grilled, broiled, or pan-fried. It even works well with scallops.

Everyone knows that mustard is a felicitous companion for pork, whether it be in the form of chops, roast, or hot dogs. Try adding some brown grainy mustard with a little heat to your favorite yellow mustard for pork; it works well when fire has browned the meat.

Chicken is a traditional partner with mustard when the intent is to sharpen up chicken's normal passivity. In my sixty-some years I'll bet I've had a cream and mustard sauce on chicken five hundred times, because I never tire of it. The basic recipe is to bring equal amounts of heavy cream and meat or poultry stock to a boil; reduce it by about half; stir or whisk in about a third of a cup of mustard (any kind works); add some salt and pepper and any other herbs or spices, and you're ready to go. You can pour it over the cooked meat just before serving; dab it onto the roasting meat for its last five to ten minutes of cooking; or have it on the table in a pitcher or sauce boat for self-service. Since tarragon goes beautifully with chicken, mint with lamb, and rosemary with both, you can mince an herb or two and add it to the sauce just before service.

The main thing to know about mustard is that it is forgiving—you can experiment with it, be bold with it. It's your friend.

MAPLE SYRUP

There are three maple syrup hounds in my family, my father, me, and my second son, Porter. I am glad I caught this passion from my dad, and glad my son caught it from us. We think that Porter's son, Abbott, has caught this, too, but since he's only six we are not sure whether it's the real thing or just a childhood sweet tooth.

My earliest memory of maple syrup is eating it poured over johnnycakes at my grandparents' table in Providence during World War II. The rest of the world calls these fried cornmeal objects corn pone, but in Rhode Island they are johnnycakes.

You make them with stone-ground cornmeal (white or yellow), salt, and sugar mixed with boiling water and shaped into round cakes no more than three inches in diameter and about a half inch thick. Put these cakes into a very hot black skillet (we called this pan a "spider") with the butter sizzling, and mash them gently with a spatula. The reason is that when they are cooked, they are soft inside (like what I later learned was the texture of polenta), with a crispy crust on the top and bottom. The goal is to keep turning them so this crust is golden and not burned black.

Then comes the maple syrup, in those days from Vermont (always from Vermont, said my grandmother), sweet, viscous, and smoky. It came in a metal can shaped like, and decorated like, a wooden cabin in the deep snowy woods. We poured the syrup from a pitcher, which my Granny refilled from the cabin when we emptied it. She never scolded us for pouring too much syrup on the johnnycakes, but smiled in her gentle way; she knew we wanted extra to spoon up from our plates at the end, because maple syrup is just so good!

I learned much later that the mysterious smokiness in Granny's maple syrup came from actual smoke, because in those old days, sugarers boiled down the sap in their sugar shacks over roaring fires fueled with deadfall from maple trees and other hardwoods, avoiding pine because its smoke is resinous. Oil, gas, and electricity are used in boiling down the sap more frequently as concern for forest viability grows.

In the harsh winter of 2004–2005 my son Porter and his son, Abbott, discovered that a large maple tree next to their house in Cambridge is actually a sugar maple. Using the Internet, they figured out how to tap this tree (they made a tap and a contraption to hold a bucket below it to catch the drips), and bingo! It worked! Then they rigged up in their backyard a great big pot over an electric heater, and after a while (a long while), they had boiled it down to actual real authentic maple syrup. They also identified a lot more sugar maple trees within a quarter mile of their house. . . .

These days we get our maple syrup from friends who have farms in Vermont and New Hampshire and make it as a hobby. There is nothing like its bright sweet flavor on pancakes, vanilla bean ice cream, hot oatmeal, and in homemade cookies and cakes. If you buy some from your local gourmet shop, or from the Internet, you will know a true natural taste unlike any other. Authenticity is worth the extra few dollars.

GRAVY

I sometimes think that gravy is the quintessential American condiment. Every once in a while a family might make a real gravy—Thanksgiving giblet gravy comes to mind—but bottled industrial gravy (think Gravymaster) and powdered gravy mix in foil packets seem to be our new gravy norm. In fact, gravy is now so dumbed down that in grocery stores, the pet food aisles are crowded with squeeze bottles of gravy for cats and dogs!

Gravies are stalwarts of newspaper and magazine food pages, as in: "biscuits 'n' gravy," or "fried chicken and gravy," and it's fast becoming "[you fill in the blank] 'n' gravy." These faux gravies are poured over everything—poor-boys, beef, pork, lamb, chicken, potatoes, beans, even fish—with the specific purpose of providing the texture and taste that's missing without them.

This is too bad, because real gravies made from a reduction of stock are glorious. They are full of vibrancy without the metallic taste that gives factory gravies away. A shimmering sheen shines on the surface of real gravy made with a reduction of meat and vegetables (or from meat or vegetables alone), and it's the payoff for the hours of wonderful smells in the kitchen as the flavors gradually intensify. The clean richness of real gravies is just plain different from ready-mades and powdered mixes.

This dumbing down of gravies is another example of what really happens when food is industrialized with the goal of keeping it cheap: we lose a part of ourselves. Consider for a minute that in 2006, as we write this, federal regulations require that the ingredients for a school lunch meal must be kept to a total cost of eighty-six cents per child if federal funds are paying for part of it, as they are in most public schools. Faux gravies are widely used in these school lunches because they help to keep costs down. But is "cheap" a wise choice for growing minds and bodies?

Oldways Condiment Challenge: Smell the Taste

We invite you to go to the best gourmet food store you can find, and buy these three culinary gifts of the gods: balsamic vinegar, mustard, and chutney.

We want you to buy the top-of-the-line version of each: no cheap substitutes, no knockoffs, no pretenders to the Throne of Taste. Ask for help from someone who works in the store and who seems to care about the foods and is willing to spend some time with you on which of the condiment treasures to buy.

One unbreakable rule: you want the classic, traditional version of each condiment; do not let yourself be talked into a gussied-up "contemporary version." For example, get the smooth version of a good mustard, and not the version with the seeds. There is nothing wrong with mustards with seeds; it's just that you want the classic, smooth, brownish-yellow mustard from France.

When you get home, and have a half hour or so to play with your new culinary treasures, get three nice clean white plates, three teaspoons, and open up each jar or bottle. Scoop or pour out a dollop of each of the three condiments so that when you place it in the center of it own plate, it is about the size of the circle between your thumb and forefinger when you make the "OK" sign.

Look at each of the dollops carefully, trying to make a visual assessment of its colors and textures. Is it red? Brownish-red? Chocolate brown? Yellow? Tan? Cream?

Now touch each dollop with the tip of your finger, and draw out a smudge or stroke of it. You are trying here to get a tactile assessment of each one—is it thick, smooth, runny, sticky, oily, stiff? Something else?

Now sniff each one a few times, and try to put words around what you smell. Sharp? Musty? Pungent? If you closed your eyes and someone put a taste on your tongue, do you think you would know each one from the other?

Now, three quick steps.

First, stick out your tongue and take a taste of one of the condiments with the tip of your tongue, and hold it on your tongue for five seconds or so without taking your tongue back into your mouth. Think about what you are tasting, and try to put words around it. Sweet? Bitter? Bittersweet?

Second, pull your tongue back into your mouth, hold your nose, and draw in a breath or two through your mouth. Identify what you taste, and remember it.

Third, now close your mouth, and draw in a couple of breaths through your nose. Identify what you smell, and remember it.

You'll quickly realize that most of what you "taste" only becomes apparent when you are drawing in your breath. As counterintuitive as it is for most people, the taste buds on your tongue can differentiate only for taste qualities: sweet, salt, bitter, and sour. (A fifth taste quality—umami—has recently been discovered; it has to do with a "satisfaction" sensation.)

All the other "tastes," such as floral, vanilla, oak, apple, grassy, caramel, or herbaceous are "tastes of smell." Your olfactory senses can differentiate thousands and thousands of different such smells, many of which are not foods (gasoline, for example, or smoke, or sweat). They are not truly "tastes" at all.

You've now made friends with your *condimenti*, and even gotten to know them a bit.

The challenge is to figure out which of your food friends "they'll go well with." *Aceto balsamico* and Parmigiano-Reggiano are a well-known natural fit, as are strawberries and *aceto balsamico*. But mustard and raspberries would be terrible together. We know cheese omelets; would Parmigiano-Reggiano be a good companion for eggs? Chutney is terrific with meats, whether they be hot roast beef or cold roast beef sandwiches.

One of the greatest pleasures of the table is understanding how taste and smell complement each other, and using this understanding to put combinations on your table that exploit your absolutely incredible ability to smell the tastes!

Traditions, Tastes, and the Tables of Emilia-Romagna

LYNNE ROSSETTO KASPER

Lynne Rossetto Kasper is one of those people who, even if you have never met her, you feel like you do. Her silky smooth and friendly voice comes into millions of kitchens, living rooms, and cars with her nationally syndicated NPR show, The Splendid Table. *But before there was* The Splendid Table *on the radio, there was the book, also called* The Splendid Table. *It was the wonderful result of Lynne's multiyear exploration of Emilia-Romagna, the region of Italy that Italians call the food region, home to aceto balsamico, Parmigiano-Reggiano, prosciutto di Parma, lambrusco, Barilla pasta, culatello, spaghetti Bolognese, and more. It's no wonder her book received so many prizes.*

For many years Lynne has traveled with us and spoken at Oldways symposiums about the foods and wines of Emilia-Romagna and other regions of Italy. But in 1999 and 2000, we spent a week each year with Lynne in Emilia-Romagna, celebrating its splendid tables. Lynne wrote the essay that follows here after our second week together in this glorious part of Italy.

We may rave over Tuscany and rhapsodize about Puglia, but every serious student of Italy's foods and artisan culture must eventually come to the northern region of Emilia-Romagna. This is why the Oldways May 2000 trip was such an important step. This Oldways expedition focused on possibly the smallest piece of geography in the organization's history of travels and explorations and with good reason.

Emilia-Romagna sits between Venice and Florence on one of the most fertile plains in all of Europe. It is one of the two wealthiest regions in Italy. Emilia-Romagna is the only place in Italy where three of the country's most highly regarded foods can be produced—each a dramatic example of how microclimates and individual mentalities shape a traditional food. Each has maintained an international reputation for centuries.

Emilia-Romagna is home to the great artisan-made balsamic vinegars that can be sipped as liqueurs, (*aceto balsamico tradizionale di Modena* and *aceto balsamico tradizionale di Reggio-Emilia*), Parmigiano-Reggiano cheese, and *prosciutto di Parma.*

As the group of forty of us from America, England, France, and Japan learned over our week in the region, these foods are only the beginning. Emilia-Romagna's pasta is a paragon in Italy. Until only several years ago pasta in restaurants was usually handmade from the region's flour and eggs, and hand-rolled to achieve the perfect, pebbly, sauce-gripping texture. The *sfoglina,* or pasta maker, was a respected craftswoman. Everything that comes from the pig, even the fatback, can reach heights of succulence that can astonish.

Emilia-Romagna is the ideal place to study the effects on cuisine and artisanship of a long-term existence of four distinctive economic levels. For centuries Emilia-Romagna has had a thriving nobility, a strong city middle class, an equally successful rural middle class, and a peasant class.

Each has eaten differently and each has contributed to the region's seeming obsession with gastronomic excellence.

All these factors also made Emilia-Romagna a useful location for Oldways to examine the effects of the European Union's new food production laws on artisan traditions. In a forum entitled, "Will Traditional Artisan Foods Survive New Hygiene Rules?" we heard from Vincenzo Lavarra, president of the EU Agriculture Commission, Professor Carlo Cannella, director of the research center in Rome that determines sanitary standards, and representatives from the consortiums of producers of *aceto balsamico tradizionale di Modena, prosciutto di Parma,* and Parmigiano-Reggiano.

Representing points of view from outside Italy were Nancy Harmon Jenkins, Ari Weinzweig, Patricia Guy, David Rosengarten, and myself. One of Nancy's points explored the possibility that many of the new production laws might not be designed to serve and safeguard the consumer as much as they eliminate the small-scale artisan in favor of large-scale industry.

Ari Weinzweig, co-owner of Zingerman's, explored perceptions of U.S. consumers and explained how he seeks out artisan foods and educates his staff.

Wine writer Patricia Guy talked about bringing the region's lambrusco wine to foreign markets, with David Rosengarten of the Television Food Network adding that the quality of Lambrusco in Emilio has nothing to do with the soda pop–like beverage sold in the United States.

My own presentation focused on my concerns and observations of diminishing quality in traditional foods as they reach out to larger markets. Also I encouraged the Italian leaders to institute a program similar to Japan's protection of its gifted artisans: support and help talented artisans to continue producing; treat them as protected national treasures; and set up programs that make these trades attractive to young people.

As guests of the city of Modena and the consortium of families who make artisan-produced balsamic vinegar, *aceto balsamico tradizionale,* we ventured out each day to explore yet another culinary tradition. In the vinegar attics of Ermes Malpighi we learned something of the thousand-year-old process that takes between twelve years and a century to produce a bottle of traditional balsamic vinegar. In the countryside of Reggio province we saw the making of Parmigiano-Reggiano cheese, and learned that up until recently a cheese-maker apprenticed ten to fourteen years before being allowed to produce the cheese. Days were devoted to lambrusco wine, the art of the pig in Parma—*prosciutto di Parma,* Felino salami, and the culatello ham made only on Parma's province's plain.

Toward the end of the week we sought to bring these traditions together at the table in a setting that was perfectly appropriate—the organic farm of Paola Bini. Her Villa Gaidello was one of the first guest farms in Italy to gain recognition, and she is a pioneer in this now trendy movement, opening Villa Gaidello to guests more than twenty years ago. Equally important, at her table we experienced the essence of what is behind Emilia-Romagna's strong sense of quality and heritage—foods made by local farm women from strictly local ingredients. Everything we touched or saw was produced by local artisans.

Like much of Italy and other ancient cultures, Emilia-Romagna keeps inviting you to go deeper because its culture is like the layers discovered in restoring an old villa in the area. Remove the wallpapers and paint of the twentieth century to discover beneath them frescoes of the Baroque and Renaissance periods, bas-reliefs of the Romans beneath them, or the early drawings of the Etruscans.

This is the essence of Italy and of its foods. Little is what it appears to be on the surface. All is built on the foundation of what has come before. The great danger now lies in crumbling those foundations. When they are gone, the culture and its people will be rudderless.

"[Condiments are] aromatic substances which are added to food to improve its flavour. According to their dominant flavour one can class condiments in to salt, acid, bitter, aromatic, sweet, etc."

—PROSPER MONTAGNE, *LAROUSSE GASTRONOMIQUE*

"Great winemakers are definitely alchemists. They have
the ability to transform their own spirit, identity, imagination, and
place into liquid that survives for years in a bottle
and much longer in memory."

—JEANNIE ROGERS

"The [research] results have been amazingly similar: almost
uniformly, they have demonstrated that moderate drinkers
have much less coronary heart disease."

—R. CURTIS ELLISON, MD

WINE

All Gaul may have been divided into three parts two thousand years ago, as Caesar said it was, but that's all changed now, except for wine people, French and other, who remain divided but into just two groups, sensualists and measurists.

The first wine group, the sensualists, is peopled with individuals for whom wine is all about pleasure—tastes, smells, memories, companionship, meals, anticipation, mellowness, familiarity, things like that. They revel in the physical aspects of wine—color, viscosity, aromas, sweetness, tang, mouth-feel, acidity, things like this. They are not very focused on price and labels and point score or ratings. They are, so to speak, comfortable in their own skins about their taste

Wine: Thinking about It, Making It, Drinking It, and Talking about It
K. DUN GIFFORD

preferences for wine, since wine for them is all about sensory pleasure. They drink what tastes good to them, not worrying about its price or reputation.

The second group, the measurists, is peopled with individuals for whom wine is all about classification—Parker ratings, *Wine Spectator* point scores, Internet rankings, present cost and future value per bottle, reputation of winemaker, location of vineyard, whether the grapes grow on sunny slopes facing south or facing some other point of the compass, what soils the vines grow in (loamy, chalky, rocky, and other geologists' classifications), which chefs and wine stewards recommend it, who else likes it (movie stars, business titans, Food Network biggies), and other things like that. They want to know where the wine stands on a sort of pedigree scale.

Measurists seek safety in their wine choices, the safety that derives from recognizing that a fine Bordeaux is supposed to be just a bit tannic when young, that a fine red Burgundy has a smooth gentleness that must be stiffened with a spine of soft oak, that a big California Santa Ynez Chardonnay must have a bit of sweet oak but be touched with a whiff of vanilla, or that the "new" Australian blends wildly popular worldwide rely on a relatively high level of residual sugars. These are qualities that can be memorized.

You can have a lot of fun in the company of either sensualists or measurists, but keep in mind this piece of folk wisdom: Wine doesn't change people, it only allows them to be themselves, just more so. So it's a good idea not to provoke or challenge either one of these wine types, because some sensualists and most measurists can be terrible bores if they slide into a lecturing mode. You know the problem: someone across the table says to you, "The '99 Mouton will be drinkable before the '97 Lafite, doncha agree?" Or, "I'd sure take 5 points off the ratings of this Stags' Leap for its weak finish, wouldn't you?"

If this happens and, say, you're stuck close by this person at the table, try to change the subject to the hors d'oeuvres or the type of cheese melting over the organic leeks or even your grandchildren. Or just excuse yourself and say you've got to take an important cell phone call (take is more impressive than make), muttering under your breath as you leave the table that wine is supposed to be fun, isn't it?

HOW WINE IS MADE IN HOME KITCHENS

Buy some grapes, pick off any wrinkled or split ones, put a few bunches still attached to their stems into a large stainless-steel soup kettle, and crush them with a potato masher hard enough so they release their juices, but not hard enough to crack the seeds. Add another layer, mash again, and so on until the kettle is about three-quarters full of a mush of juice and crushed grapes, which are now called "must."

Add a cup of granulated sugar to help the fermentation, and cover with a cheesecloth to let air in and keep insects out. Temperature is important; too cool and it won't ferment properly; too hot, and it goes bad. Just right is somewhere around seventy degrees, which makes it "churn," allowing the skins to rise to the surface and form a "cake," which should be pushed back down at least once a day.

After another day or two, the fermentation will slow down, and it's now time to scoop out the cake with a sieve and toss it. Purists squeeze this cake for the juice still in it (just as some swear the sweetest meat is closest to the bone). Either way, now taste the juice and, while stirring well, add enough sugar to turn its sourness into a mild sweetness.

Fermentation will start up again, bubbling now rather than churning, and it goes on for a few days. When it quiets down, siphon the juice into a second container, leaving the sediment behind (which is called "the lees"). A useful container is the large glass jug used in water coolers, called a "carboy." Siphon the juice into this scrupulously clean carboy, taste it again, and add a little more sugar if it is again a little sour. *Important*: Put a gallon of this juice (it's "near-wine" in the same sort of way that low-alcohol beer is "near-beer") into a clean container and put it into your refrigerator (see below for why this is important). You can get siphon tubes from winemaking websites, or go to a local medical supply store and buy the most expensive tube they stock (it's likely to be the sturdiest one and the easiest to clean so you can use it again).

Now cork the carboy with one of those corks that has a spout running through it. Attach your siphon tube to this spout, and run it down into an empty wine bottle filled with water. The point of this Rube Goldberg setup is to let the final fermentation gases bubble off without letting any air back in, because at this stage air is the enemy: let it in, and it will spoil the wine. This process is called "racking." After another few days the bubbling will stop, and now top off the carboy using the "near-wine" in the refrigerator.

Cork the carboy, rig up the siphon tube to the wine bottle again (its real name is "fermentation lock" because it lets the fermentation gases escape without letting air in), and put the carboy in a dark corner for, say, four months. After a while the fermentation bubbles will stop, and once more you siphon this almost-wine into another clean carboy, taking care to leave the sediment behind. This clean carboy will not be filled to the top, and you must top it off using wine. It's a good idea to use wine of the same grape, but not necessary. But do use wine and not water.

And that's it. You've made wine!

Okay, so your wine is cloudy, and you want it clear. You can rack it two or three more times at three-month intervals, or buy "fining" materials from a winemaking website, which quickly make the sediment settle to the bottom.

Now you siphon your wine into clean wine bottles, cork the bottles with new clean corks, and lay them down on their sides to rest until you are ready to drink them. You should label them right away; do not trust to your memory. It's quick and simple to write directly on the glass with a child's yellow crayon, and worry later about a label.

That's it. You buy white grapes, you get white wine. You buy red grapes, you get either red or white wine.

This is strange, but true. To get red wine from red grapes, you have to leave the grape skins in with the juice for, say, ten days before you strain them out, so they will color the wine.

Will your wine be drinkable? Sure it will. All the great kings and queens and warriors and other great persons of history drank homemade wines—Henry V, Eleanor of Aquitaine, William the Conqueror, Louis XIV, popes, crusaders, all the lords and ladies. And our own historical big shots did, too—George Washington and Thomas Jefferson and Paul Revere.

It's also what the not-so-famous people drank, and they made it not only from grapes but also from honey and berries and apples and pears. In fact, they made it from just about anything that had enough sugar to make it ferment. Wine made from honey instead of grape juice is called mead, and even today mead is made and sold commercially in the United States and United Kingdom.

The illuminated manuscripts from the Middle Ages are full of gorgeous paintings and drawings of the "labors of the months," which include working the vineyards (pruning and harvesting) and crushing the grapes (peasants in bare feet standing in big wooden vats stamping on grapes to mash out the juices, and holding their pants or skirts up above their knees so the juices won't stain their clothes). If you look closely at some of these paintings you can see these grape stompers flirting with each other and just plain having a good time. There are also a great many fine illustrations of the lords and ladies at their elegant tables, quaffing theses wines along with their sumptuous meals.

Shakespeare's Falstaff is but one example of the hundreds in the literature of the times who took their wine seriously, and in his case, too seriously. He was fond of Spanish "sack," which was sherry to which distilled alcohol was added so that it wouldn't go off during its long sail from Spain to England. "Go fetch me a quart of sack, and put a toast in't," Falstaff said at one point to his drinking buddies in *The Merry Wives of Windsor.*

The Bayeux Tapestry (made about 1080 A.D.) pictures very clearly the enormous barrels of wine that William the Conqueror shipped across the English Channel with his army of men, horses, weapons, and food from Normandy to the south coast of England, on his way to the Battle of Hastings. William's Norman army defeated King Harold's English army at Hastings, and because Harold was killed there, William assumed the crown and became the founder of the British royal family.

Historians debate whether this French wine was added to William's army's drinking water (from springs and streams) in order to disinfect it, or whether it was poured into flagons for the troops on the morning of the battle to give them courage to go into a daylong battle with swords and axes. War was brutally face-to-face and hand-to-hand in those days, so I think the wine went for both purposes: soldiers with dysentery cannot fight, and soldiers "hot with wine" are more likely to throw caution to the winds in an all-out battle to chop the other fellow's head off before he chopped yours off.

MAKING WINE IN THE TWENTY-FIRST CENTURY

Making good wine for sale today is much less simple than it was in the good old days. Winemakers are confronted with thick books full of federal and state hygiene rules and quality-control regulations that must be followed to the letter if the winemaker wants to sell his or her wines to the public. Expensive computers and electronic sniffers and precise temperature controls put small- and middle-sized wineries under terrific financial pressures if they want to remain competitive with the huge corporations now the major forces in winemaking.

Multinational corporations are able to spend enormous sums on advertising and marketing, for example, and smaller wineries just cannot match them. The regularly published wine ratings of a handful of influential writers and publications cause large and rapid swings in the wines that consumers purchase. Grape hybrids and other kinds of genetic manipulations produce new grapes varieties tailored to specific "market profiles" that fit the profile of the wines that marketing surveys reveal to be the most sought after by an increasingly younger and wealthier wine-buying public.

These factors are drastically changing the wine world as we have known it. The shift is attitudinal: much less attention is now paid to wines we "should like" in favor of wines that we "do like." The foundation of this attitudinal shift is education—wine courses, glossy magazines, social mixers that use wine tastings as their milieu, television programs about wine, chefs' television shows with wine segments, big-screen movies that are all about wine or feature wine in the plot line (*Sideways*, for example), and nutrition science evidence that moderate wine drinking is heart-healthy for most people (the Mediterranean diet being the poster child for wine's solid place in a healthy eating and drinking pattern). The Internet will gradually assume a larger role, as well as the recent United States Supreme Court decision allowing interstate wine shipment to individuals.

This sort of tectonic shift in attitudes has happened in my own family.

My grandfather poured Spanish sherry before meals, French red wines (claret, he called them) at lunch and dinner, and Portuguese ports after dinner. That was it. I did not know there were others wines and fortified wines than these until much later.

My father (for reasons know only to him; his passion for them mystified all the rest of us) fell deeply in love with German white wines, but stayed with French reds. He was a martini man before dinner, a wine man during dinner, and a liqueur man after dinner. But he talked all the time about wines, and published a compendium of wine words and terminology.

And so, thank goodness, I became an omnivore about alcohol and, except for the inevitable few rolls off the log, have been a wise drinker who's focused more on flavors, tastes, and aromas than alcohol.

The Power of the Winemaker

JEANNIE ROGERS

Jeannie Rogers is the sommelier at Il Capriccio Restaurant outside of Boston, which is well known for its astonishing list of superb, small-production Italian wines. Jeannie is one of those people who share deep knowledge with boundless enthusiasm. She is truly excited about the wines on her list and talks rapid-fire about the wineries she likes and the winemakers she deals with. We knew she was the perfect person to explain the key role of the person who makes the wine. ◧

My idea about the role of the winemaker was directly influenced by an old Alfred Hitchcock story concerning the disappearance of Ambrose Bierce. It relates that Bierce was chosen by Aztec noblemen for his intelligence and spirit, who then captured him. Then they fattened him with only the best of foods and drink, bathed and rubbed him down with herbal infusions, and carefully roasted and joyously ate him, following their theory of transference of body, mind, and spirit through ingestion. The best winemakers treat their vineyards and cellars just like the Aztecs treated Ambrose Bierce.

These days the role of winemakers has even made it to the movies but it is far from romantic. The best winemakers have an eye on the future, not just what is in the bottle but in the ground. And being grounded isn't just about organic, biodynamic, and sustainable grape production, but about having a respect for the work of past and future generations. There will always be debates about cellar techniques, and ideas are always changing, but the best winemakers are always exploring, experimenting, and open to change. They are confident enough to follow their own path, though not closed to dialogue and information, and they learn from experience.

Great winemakers are definitely alchemists. They have the ability to transform their own spirit, identity, imagination, and place them into liquid that survives for years in a bottle and can survive much longer in memory. The snob factor of Lafite 1947 or Monfortino 1974 can intimidate and overshadow the fact that many great wines are not expensive, even if procuring them might just take a little more effort. For many of us, the ability to uncork a bottle (sorry, I still like the cork), and spend a little time in a different place with wine from a very particular winemaker is the best gift in this world.

Naming Wines: Grape, Region, or Exotic Animals?

K. DUN GIFFORD

Wine grapes come in two colors, red and white. Some of the red grapes are nearly black, but they are nonetheless still red; and some of the white grapes are nearly yellow or pink, but they are nonetheless still white. That's just the way it is with wine, because so much about wines is so subjective that unless everyone plays by some agreed-upon nomenclature rules, discussing wine would be as crazy as trying to understand a United Nations debate if everyone were talking in their native tongues at the same time.

Fortunately, wine people have agreed on more-or-less standard rules about the relationships between the name of a grape and the name of the wine made from it. The basic rule is that each wine takes the name of the grape variety from which it is made; the varietal name can be used if at least 75 percent of the wine is made from that grape.

Starting with white grapes: we drink Chardonnay wine made from Chardonnay grapes, Sauvignon Blanc wine made from Sauvignon Blanc grapes, Riesling wine made from Riesling grapes, Pinot Grigio wine made from Pinot Grigio grapes (which are called Pinot Gris grapes and Pinot Gris wines in the United States), and so on.

Moving to red grapes: we drink Pinot Noir made from Pinot Noir grapes, Cabernet Sauvignon and Cabernet Franc made from Cabernet Sauvignon and Cabernet Franc grapes; Merlot made from Merlot grapes; Zinfandel from Zinfandel grapes; and Italian wines like Nebbiolo and Sangiovese from Nebbiolo and Sangiovese grapes.

Naming wines for the grapes from which they are made is a quite uniform practice among the major wine-producing nations—United States, Australia, Chile, Spain, and South Africa. It's a powerful argument that a lingua franca for wines will bring more consumers to good wines and consequently lift all the wine boats.

The great winemaker and wine marketer Robert Mondavi opened a modern Pandora's box in the 1970s when he decided that Sauvignon Blanc was not a consumer-friendly phrase, and so he called his wines from those grapes Fumé Blanc. He told the story compellingly of his sudden inspiration about this: "How in the world will Americans buy my terrific Sauvignon Blanc if they can't even pronounce it? They will be too embarrassed to ask for it! But they can sure say Fumé Blanc, can't they?" And as with so many things about introducing American palates to premium wines, he was right about this, too, and creamed the market. Sauvignon Blanc and Fumé Blanc are sold today interchangeably.

This is simple. But winemakers also make wines by blending juices from different grape varieties. The great Bordeaux wines, for example, are blends of many grapes, Cabernet Sauvignon, Malbec, Merlot, Cabernet Franc, among them. The French claim that the greatness of these wines is due in part to the great skills of their winemakers in knowing the "perfect grape partners" for a given year's vintage.

Some of the greatest white and red wines in the world are made in the Burgundy region of France, in its central southeast. They are all called Burgundies, but are known by the names of their vineyard, which is how you know if they are red or white. There are hundreds of vineyards in Burgundy, so it is not simple to deal with the names of Burgundies; you really must do a lot of memorizing because it's about as complicated as learning the Latin declensions.

The great red wines from Burgundy are made from Pinot Noir grapes (as are a great many other wonderful burgundies elsewhere in the world). But there is a special distinctiveness about Burgundy burgundies, and there is general agreement that this has to do with *terroir*, a French word that has many meanings. The dictionary definition of *terroir* is "earth," but woe to the wine drinker who does not acknowledge the deep mysteries embedded in this word; deciphering the Mona Lisa's smile is easy compared to parsing *terroir*.

The most famous wines in the world are made in Bordeaux, in the southwest of France just inland from the Atlantic and along the Garonne River. Cabernet Sauvignon grapes are the heavyweight among Bordeaux grape plantings, but Bordeaux wines are blends incorporating other grapes, too, principally Merlot and Cabernet Franc (the California wine Meritage, another Mondavi innovation, is made from Cabernet Franc).

Bordeaux's wine grapes grow in rocky soil, cooled by the often damp prevailing westerly trade winds blowing in off the ocean. Because Bordeaux wines made from these grapes are so prestigious and so expensive, wine people have wonderful debates about whether they are "better" than other wines made from exactly the same grapes, but that are grown in loamy soil and far from an ocean's climatic influence. It's difficult to imagine a resolution to these intense and passionate debates, and this is not a bad thing, because it means wine people just have to force themselves to have more tastings, evaluations, discussions, and arguments—all the while drinking even more absolutely terrific wines.

Italian wine nomenclature is anarchy; it exists in a world of its own. It does have the merit of a long history, because Italians traditionally have different, regionally distinct names for identical grapes. This region-by-region nomenclature is fine for the Italians and for well-trained international wine experts, but bewildering for most of the rest of us. This is changing, as the European Union gradually imposes "terminology standardization" for wines marketed throughout Europe (another box checked by the international bureaucracies that want to standardize everything in sight). It is sad, of course, to see some of the old names disappear, but when all is said and done, a more rational nomenclature helps us all to make better choices when we're looking for "that perfect wine" for our favorite pasta al vongole.

Spain's wines, like those of Italy, are regionalized and have traditionally been named for their regions (for example, Ribera del Douro, Rioja, Penedes, or Jerez), and not by their grapes (for example, Tempranillo, Subirat, Garnacha, or Malvasia). But this is changing, too, as winemakers adopt contemporary marketing techniques.

In the last decade the Australians have vaulted to the front ranks of wine producers, principally because they make very good wines from very good grapes grown in very good agricultural and climatic conditions, and sell them at low prices. But in a bold marketing gamble, they promoted the fact that these Australian wines were blended, and in advertising claimed that this made them more drinkable. Consumers agreed, and sent sales of these varietal blends soaring—Shiraz-Merlot, Shiraz-Grenache, Cabernet Sauvignon-Merlot, and so on.

A single Australian wine brand, Yellow Tail, is the largest-selling imported wine brand in the United States, passing the long-time leader, the Italian wine brand Riunite. Yellow Tail's winemakers researched the American market and discovered a distinct preference for full-bodied and full-flavored red wines, and for slightly sweet, fruit-driven white wines. They made their wines to these profiles and the rest, as they like to say, is marketing history.

To convert consumers to their wines, the Australians broke conventional naming rules, too. Startling label names include Little Penguin, Jackaroo, Four Emus, Kanga, Laughing Magpie, Black Swan, and Mad Fish.

This Australian boom continues to change the world wine market, opening it up to fine wines made in Chile and South Africa, with wines from other regions following close behind. Like the Australian wines, many of them are blends, and are made to be drinkable by emphasizing tastes at the sweeter, milder end of the range, while de-emphasizing tastes at the bitter, astringent end of the range.

In the face of globalism's many combined forces, it's comfortable to predict that wine consumption will continue to expand. Part of the reason is the successful Australian experiment with "softer" wines, because it opens huge new markets to individuals—and women in particular, who often prefer softer tastes to astringent tastes. Rising levels of disposable income in the developed world, along with lowering freight costs with containerization, also drive increased sales of wine.

It's not a bad thing, consequently, to spend a little time learning about wines. They are the future of the alcoholic beverages that the human race has always enjoyed.

"Alcohol, initially as wine and beer, but eventually to include spirits, has been an ingredient of human life for as long as recorded history—at least eight thousand years—and undoubtedly for much longer. When wine is wisely embraced as an elemental part of a healthy lifestyle, it is a steady source of joy and pleasure."

—K. DUN GIFFORD

The Paradox's Bottom Line: Moderate Alcohol Intake Is Part of a "Healthy Lifestyle"

R. CURTIS ELLISON, MD

Serge Renaud and Curtis Ellison, the "Fathers of the French Paradox," like all good fathers, are still watching after their child. They continue to research, publish, and make presentations about their continuing French Paradox investigations. We've asked our Boston neighbor Curt Ellison to summarize the science behind the paradox's bottom line: "wine is part of a healthy diet."

While wine has always been considered by physicians to be the "healthiest of beverages," it was not until the 1970s that epidemiologists began to report that moderate drinkers had much lower risk of coronary heart disease than did abstainers. The number of publications on moderate drinking increased markedly after the *60 Minutes* program on the "French Paradox" in 1991: after this program, scientists apparently believed that it was "politically correct" to report data demonstrating beneficial health effects of alcohol, and not focus just on adverse effects of abuse. The results have been amazingly similar: almost uniformly, they have demonstrated that moderate drinkers have less coronary heart disease.

Scientists have identified many mechanisms by which alcoholic beverages reduce the risk of coronory heart disease. The most important effects are on the levels of HDL cholesterol, the "good cholesterol," which is markedly increased by any type of alcoholic beverage. Perhaps equally important are effects on coagulation: moderate drinkers are much less likely to form clots within the arteries to the heart (leading to a myocardial infarction), to the brain (leading to stroke), and to other organs. The decrease in clotting is related somewhat to alcohol, but also to other (nonalcoholic) substances present in beverages, especially in red wine. Many of the effects on clotting are transient effects, and the beneficial effects may last only for twenty-four to thirty-six hours after someone has consumed alcohol. The healthiest approach is for the regular (preferably daily) intake of small amounts of an alcoholic beverage.

Based primarily on data from large prospective studies from Harvard over recent years, a "healthy lifestyle" has been defined as one that results in 80 percent fewer heart attacks and 92 percent fewer cases of diabetes. This healthy lifestyle is shown in the list below, based on Meir Stampfer's (2000) and Frank Hu's (2001) studies reported in the *New England Journal of Medicine*.

DEFINITION OF A HEALTHY LIFESTYLE

1. Avoid obesity (body mass index 25).

2. Consume a healthy diet (high in fiber and unsaturated fat and low in trans fat) (for example, a Mediterranean-type diet).

3. Engage in moderate to vigorous physical activity (for at least half an hour each day).

4. Avoid smoking.

5. Consume $1/2$ to 2 typical drinks of an alcoholic beverage per day.

In addition to reducing risks of coronary heart disease and diabetes, moderate alcohol intake reduces the risk of most of the other "diseases of aging," including stroke and congestive heart failure, osteoporosis, dementia, and Alzheimer's disease. Of course, there are still many adverse health effects of abusive drinking (for example, certain alcohol-related cancers and cirrhosis of the liver). With the possible exception of a slight increase in the risk of female breast cancer, however, all of the other adverse effects of alcohol are related only to excessive or inappropriate drinking (as just before driving).

The bottom line: the risk of dying of any cause has repeatedly been shown to be about 20 percent lower for moderate drinkers than for abstainers.

There are certain people who should not drink at all (former alcoholics, people with certain medical conditions, people with religious or moral proscriptions against alcohol, etc.), and there cannot be a general recommendation for everybody to drink. On the other hand, I believe that it is unethical to withhold from the public sound advice on drinking and health. Accurate and balanced information on health needs to be presented to all. And the message from scientists is now very clear: for most individuals in Western societies, moderate drinking can be an important component of a healthy lifestyle.

Oldways Sensible Wine Drinking Guidelines

K. DUN GIFFORD AND SARA BAER-SINNOTT

Oldways has always included alcoholic beverages—in moderation—as part of a healthy diet. We were the first to put alcohol on an eating pyramid: the 1993 Mediterranean Diet Conference introduced the preliminary Mediterranean diet pyramid, with moderate wine drinking and exercise depicted next to the pyramid. We cemented this in stone with the official Mediterranean diet pyramid in 1994 (with the imprimatur of the Harvard School of Public Health and the World Health Organization). The Asian, Latin American, and Vegetarian pyramids followed in 1995, 1996, and 1997, respectively, all with wine and/or alcohol alongside the pyramid.

In all of this, the words moderation and moderate are integral to even thinking about wine drinking as part of a healthy diet. To make this point clear, and to provide further education materials, we developed the "Sensible Wine Drinking Guidelines." Working with nutrition and social scientists, the guidelines (see page 238)

were introduced in 1996. With almost a decade to look back, we believe they are even more relevant in today's not-so-moderate world.

These guidelines were developed by Oldways and R. Curtis Ellison, MD, Boston University School of Medicine; Dwight Health, PhD, Brown University; Stanton Peele, PhD, independent social science researcher; David Pittman, PhD, Washington University; Archie Brodsky, Massachusetts Mental Health Center at Harvard Medical School; and Meir Stampfer, MD, DrPH, Harvard School of Public Health.

STATEMENT OF PRINCIPLES

Throughout human history, wine drinking has been an important part of religious rituals, social relationships, family gatherings, and celebrations of the pleasures of living.

- A worldwide medical and nutrition science consensus now exists that sensible, moderate drinking of wine can be part of a healthy diet.

- Moderate, sensible wine and alcohol consumption can contribute to a healthy lifestyle.

- Sensible wine drinking improves social interaction and other of life's pleasures.

- Education about sensible wine drinking helps to prevent alcohol abuse.

- Wine has played a positive role in many cultures as a mealtime beverage and as an enhancement to a variety of foods.

- In regions of the world where wine is an integral part of everyday living, alcohol abuse problems are minimal.

- Society has a responsibility to teach all people, especially young people, about sensible drinking.

- Intense international interest in the benefits of wine gives cause to prepare and widely circulate a set of guidelines for sensible wine drinking.

GUIDELINES FOR SENSIBLE WINE DRINKING

1. Wine should be consumed by healthy adults only in moderation. (Moderate drinking is defined by the U.S. Dietary Guidelines as two 5-ounce glasses of wine a day for men and one glass for women.)

2. Wine should be consumed as a part of social, family, celebratory, or other occasions, but not as their central focus.

3. Wine should be consumed with food or around mealtimes.

4. Wine drinkers should know the distinction between moderate use and abuse.

5. Parents who drink should drink sensibly, presenting themselves as examples of moderation.

6. Moderate, nondisruptive drinking is socially acceptable, while excessive drinking and any resulting behavior that violates legal or social standards is unacceptable.

7. Wine drinking should follow clear, consistent, and sensible customs that emphasize moderation and discourage binge drinking.

8. The choice of abstinence for any religious or health reason must be respected.

9. Drinking must be avoided in situations where it puts the individual or others at risk. (Drinking is not recommended for people who are at risk for alcohol abuse, for people who take certain medications, for pregnant women, or for people where consumption of wine may put themselves or others at risk.)

10. Wine should be consumed slowly to enhance the taste of food and to add to the enjoyment of everyday living.

These guidelines acknowledge that consumption is not for everyone, and that the legal purchase and possession age in the United States is twenty-one. At the same time, the guidelines urge society and parents to take a more active role in teaching young people about responsible drinking customs so they are prepared to make informed choices.

> "It is our opportunity to embrace this national treasure, serve these wines at our family table, holiday celebrations, and religious services, as well as enjoy them while dining out. We are, in this, the American pioneer settling this reclaimed frontier."
>
> —KERRY DOWNEY ROMANIELLO

The Connection of Wine and Community

KERRY DOWNEY ROMANIELLO

The town of Westport is a Massachusetts and New England gem—"between the landscape and the wines, we were nearly convinced we were in Europe," reported The New York Times recently. It is the home of Westport Rivers Vineyard and Winery, owned by Carol and Bill Russell. Their executive chef is Kerry Downey Romaniello; with their talents and enthusiasm for wine and food, the owners and the chef are perfect matches for one another. Each has a "big picture" take on wine, and they execute it together seamlessly every day.

Wine has been part of the community of mankind for a very long time. The discussion of just how and how long is for another place. My profession keeps me in daily contact with the reality that the majority of American wine drinkers are disconnected from their own national "community" of wine. Wine was woven into the religious, agricultural, familial, and economic fabric of the earliest European explorers and settlers of the United States. Winemaking from native grapes and the planting of Old World vines began on arrival. The plan was to bring the "whole" of wine into their new regional community. The current mind-set and buying habits of Americans does not reflect this same inclination. Why do we not have the same connection to the growing, making, and enjoying of wine within our own communities?

Let's travel back first, to about 1000 A.D. Leif Ericson lands somewhere around Cape Cod, sees thick trees draped with clinging grapevines laden with fruit, and names this new land "Vinland the Good."

Step into the seventeenth and eighteenth centuries with Governor Winthrop, Thomas Jefferson, William Penn, and Benjamin Franklin. These men were among many who committed their resources and thousands of east coast acreage to hundreds of thousands of *vitis vinifera* vines brought from European cuttings. (The plentiful native grapes, *vitis labrusca,* they felt, produced an inferior wine.) These wine-producing vines had adapted to the heat of southern France or to the cold of the Moselle in Germany, so they could adapt to the varying climates of the New World. The vines did not succeed, however. American soil was home to a plant lice, phylloxera, that caused galls on the vines' roots. The nonnative vines weakened, and then died a slow death.

At the same time, the Spaniards were planting Franciscan missions and vineyards of the "Mission" grape up the coast of California. Monasteries and nunneries spread the gospel as well as their vineyards and sacred wines throughout Europe, North Africa, and Australia; so, too, the missions in California. The patient friars knew the adaptation of vines would take time, and their careful growing and winemaking techniques made great wines. These were some of the roots of the state's success with vineyards and wineries.

By the mid-nineteenth century, Ohio had become the "Rhine of America" making twice as much wine, from native hybrids, as California, including sparkling wine. Sparkling wine also found a home up in the Finger Lakes of New York. By now the solution to the phylloxera problem was developed; the *vinifera* varietals were grafted onto Native American rootstock. America was on her way to making fine wine.

At this time, the temperance movement was growing state by state. By 1919, the Eighteenth Amendment to the Constitution instituted national Prohibition. American wine hit a wall, shattering into sacramental wines, home production, and bootleg. The repeal came at the end of 1933. By then, America had weakened her relationship to the agriculture and culture of wine as a beverage of community and civility. Jug wines pleased the popular palate.

It wasn't until the 1950s and 1960s that winemakers in California began producing some fine wines from their Cabernet Sauvignon, Pinot Noir, and Chardonnay grapes at wineries like Mondavi, Heitz, and Buena Vista. At the same time, wineries were planting Pinot Noir and Riesling in Oregon and Washington. Winemakers in Maryland, Pennsylvania, and Virginia were also planting vines, and growers in Rhode Island, Connecticut, Long Island, and Massachusetts were close behind. Certain wine houses in upstate New York, California, and the Midwest held on through Prohibition.

Let's take a peek at what the United States looks like only a few decades later. There are more than three thousand wineries located in all fifty states; forty states have vineyards with 140+ Approved American Viticultural Areas. This means that like European appellations, we have areas across the country recognized as having a certain climate and topography for grape growing. Each area has unique growing conditions, like a cool or warm climate, that influence the choice of grapes grown and the style of the resulting wine. The United States produces about 7 percent of the world's wine, claiming only 3 percent of the export market. At a minimum, one of four bottles of wine bought in the States is an import; about 90 percent of the rest comes from one state.

Most foreign wine-producing countries treat their wines as a regional and national agricultural product, with the United States as one of their top export customers. They buy mostly from within their borders, especially from their own area. To them, wine has a value beyond varietals or price. Wine represents a taste of their home.

Does this all answer why we remain a bit detached from the growing and making of American wines in our communities? There are many other factors, of course. But this raises an interesting point. We, at this moment in time, are living in the "first generation" of regional American viticulture. We are the ones who can adapt the enjoyment of these wonderful wines into our lives to pass on to those who follow us. It is our opportunity to embrace this national treasure, and serve these wines at our family table, holiday celebrations, and religious services, as well as enjoy them while dining out. We are, in this, the American pioneer settling this reclaimed frontier.

In Love with Sweet Wine: Vin de Paille before Breakfast

ALICE FEIRING

We have fallen head over heels in love with sweet wines, those perennially misunderstood and under-appreciated wines from some of the greatest wine regions in the world, and we're planning to organize the perfect World Sweet Wine Tour. To help prepare, we asked Time *magazine's wine writer, Alice Feiring, to explain a little bit about sweet wine, particularly why she loves it.* 🖂

After a stellar tasting in their deep stone cellar, Jean Louis Chave, the younger generation of the most revered domaine in Hermitage, Domaine Chave, handed me a bottle of Vin de Paille. This is a sweet wine made from grapes raisined on straw mats—hence the *paille*. It was a 1996 and the first vintage his father and mentor, Gerard, allowed him to vinify. He explained the wine took five whole years to stop fermenting. Modern wine producers would never have the patience for such a lazy wine. They would have fed the wine yeast and presto—the wine would have finished fermenting in a matter of a few days, not years. But this is not the way winemaking happens with the Chaves. If the wine goes slow, then it goes slow.

Well, Jean Louis asked me to share that bottle with "George the Greek," an infamous character in Tain Hermitage. George's store changes into an impromptu wine bar on sultry summer nights. And that night, with winemakers swapping many bottles with each other (and me), the Paille was overlooked. At three in the morning, I called it a night. George insisted on making me breakfast in the morning.

I was still bleary when I stumbled into George's store, now transformed into a café. There were fresh-picked apricots, yogurt, pain seigle, espresso, and . . . a chilled 1996 Chave Vin de Paille. He insisted I taste it—before coffee. "Just think of it as your morning juice," he said.

The wine was a brilliant and nervous wine, an exotic nectar of apricots and peaches in one sip, gooseberries and pineapples and perhaps a bit salty. This was one of the freshest of the genre of "raisined grape" wines I've ever tasted. Even though I was about to get on the road again, I had to have a wee bit more.

Sweet wine is best when it is made the way the Chaves do it, in a completely natural manner. During fermentation the yeast eats up all of the sugars in the wine it can stomach. If the yeast is vigorous it wants to digest it all until the wine is left dry. However, if there is still sugar left, the wine stays sweet. You can stop the fermentation by adding neutral spirit—as with Port or the category of wines called *vin doux naturel* (such as the French Maury or Beaume de Venise). However, if the grapes are superconcentrated and supersweet to start with, fermentation will "stick" at some point.

The world's most famous sweet wines concentrate their sweetness with "the noble rot." Botrytis is a rot that sweetens the inside grape. This is the way with the golden Sauternes from Bordeaux, Monbazillac from the Dordogne, Azsu from Hungary, Beerenausleses of Germany, and in some years some gorgeous Loire whites made from Chenin Blanc.

Freezing is an option. This technique can make the most romantic of all sweet wines. While many "modern" winemakers very unromantically shove their ripe grapes into a freezer, there are still brave winemakers who gear up, steal out in the middle of the night of the first deep freeze, and pick frozen grapes off of the vine. They press those extremely concentrated fruits into precious and extremely expensive nectar—ice wine.

Another option is the raisin technique, probably the most ancient of all. Some say it debuted in Crete, when winemakers twisted stems of the grape bunch to cut off its nutrition. The grapes shriveled on the vine. This method is used in many areas of the world, most notably in France and in Italy. Some famed examples of these are Italy's Passitos (love the dark cinnamony Sagrantino di Montefalco from Umbria) and the seductive Amarones from the Veneto.

And then there's that honeyed Vin De Paille. The trick to making any top-notch sweet wine is to maintain the balance between the wine's lemony acidity and its sweetness. And this wine had it. In the end, it was a great match with the exquisite sun-blushed apricots. Sure, sweet wine is such a perfect way to end dinner, but before breakfast really isn't so bad either.

Sweet Wines Arising

Most of us who look forward to the supple tastes and subtle aromas of good wines believed that the Thunderbirds and Mogan Davids and Bartles & Jameses forever poisoned any chance that good sweet wines could stand in the front rank of popularity.

Fortunately most of us were wrong.

Even a cursory look at menus from interesting restaurants from all parts of the United States reveals a population explosion of sweet wines—not just in the dessert section, either, but as accompaniments to suitable dishes in all parts of the meal. This tracks with patterns in Europe, for the Europeans share none of our false pride in avoiding sweet wines—before, during, and after meals. These include the French Sauternes, Barsac, and Monbazillac, the German Eiswein, and the Italian Moscato.

Randall Graham of the Bonny Doon in California has never feared to tread in this arena, and so we have from him and other winemakers really wonderful homegrown sweet wines, too.

Sweet wines are an entirely new sensory experience for many wine drinkers, but as the "snob factor" about sweet wines heads toward extinction, sweet wines will ride up to their rightful place alongside dry wines.

Cognac Magic

EDOUARD COINTREAU

We have traveled north, south, east, and west in France with our friend Edouard Cointreau, and he never fails to introduce us to some of the most incredible culinary delights that France has to offer: truffles, walnuts, and walnut oil in Périgord; tomatoes in Marmande; Michelin-starred restaurants in Paris; foie gras on the table and at the Marché au Gras in Perigueux; incredible sweet wines in Monbazillac; and of course, a flight of cognacs with his parents at their chateau in Cognac. Our experience at home with his family was so magical that we asked Edouard to write about his family and cognac. Although not a wine, cognac can be savored in the same way, as Edouard shows us. Try cognac and water and maybe you will find the magic, too.

Cognac was once the drink of mature and wise men reaching for the knowledge of the old ways. Now it is cool and fashionable with the younger generation in China, the United States, France, and elsewhere. Increasingly, women are the champions of mixed cognac cocktails for parties or drinking cognac during meals.

My family has owned vineyards in the Cognac area since 1270. Born in Cognac in 1494, King François I had a favorite writer, Rabelais, the author of *Gargantua and Pantagruel*. Rabelais married his sister to Jehan Frapin, first sommelier of the King, a direct ancestor to my mother, Genevieve Frapin. We still own Cognac Frapin, with the largest vineyard in the Cognac region, three hundred hectares around our Chateau de Font Pinot.

My grandparents and my parents used to have a small glass of cognac at every lunch or dinner. They claimed that their excellent health came from cognac: my two great-grandmothers lived to be one hundred, and all my grandparents lived to be quite old, too. Whenever we had a serious cold, we would drink warm cognac, a remedy for everything. I started when I was ten or eleven. Actually when I was born, they gave my name "Edouard" to a cocktail made half of cognac (my mother) and half of Cointreau (my father).

Most French people in wine areas believe that they have a genetic heredity giving them a higher tolerance to process alcohol in their liver. There is a much-rumored study saying that 25 percent of the French population can drink twice as much as the other 75 percent, thanks to their genes. This is close to dogma for some in the Cognac area.

Cognac was one of the five cities that remained officially Protestant in Catholic France in the sixteenth century, and the Protestant culture dominates the region even today. People work very hard, are secretive, and are very careful with French strangers and the powers from Paris. They feel comfortable with foreigners and are more open to English-speaking visitors from the north of Europe, the United States, and Asia than the rest of France. Over 90 percent of cognac is exported, which is real business magic.

Learning about drinking cognac is easy. The best way is to actually go to the Cognac area and visit one big company (open to the public) and a small winery (always by appointment). Cognac Frapin has a unique comparative tasting for its visitors, with the VSOP and XO bottles of the largest brands: Hennessy, Martell, Courvoisier, Rémy Martin, Delamain, Camus, and Frapin. You can duplicate this tasting at home to find the brand that suits your taste. You will also quickly understand the brand differences.

Recently I have been enjoying cognac as a drink with water ("fine à l'eau" in French). It used to be the most popular drink in cafés in the nineteenth century, even ahead of absinthe. I often drink it with dinner, instead of wine, with the added benefit that a good bottle of cognac will last several more days than a good bottle of wine, keeping better without getting oxidized.

The Wines of California

NARSAI DAVID

Narsai David is one of those people with vast knowledge about foods and wines who enjoys sharing his love and appreciation for them with others. Before our 1994 Mediterranean Diet Conference in San Francisco, Narsai invited us to dinner at his home in Berkeley. We arrived to find a large crowd (about twenty people), most of them deeply knowledgeable about food and wine, and leaders of the U.S. and California wine businesses. They included wine public relations guru Pam Hunter, Stags' Leap winemaker Carl Doumani, and Charles and Doris Muscatine.

For each course, Narsai served several wines (all of them decanted so we wouldn't see the wine label), and asked that for each we were to try to identify the year and the type of grape, and if we could, the winemaker. Sara found this an impossible task. To her astonishment Dun actually identified several of the wines, and other guests identified other ones.

When we mentioned this recently to Narsai, we were just as astonished when he sent us the list of wines he'd served that wonderful evening (see sidebar). Since Narsai is part of the California wine story, we asked him to explain the development and changes in the California wine industry, especially how it became what it is today.

California cuisine did not grow out of a vacuum. Long before we started presenting our new ideas with food, and simplifying classic French cuisine, California wine was well established. The San Francisco Bay Area is surrounded by the premium wine-growing regions of Napa, Sonoma, Mendocino, and Livermore. So the influence of the wine presence was palpable.

I'm reminded of a tasting I organized in 1965 at the Potluck Restaurant in Berkeley. We tasted the 1962 vintage of five great Montrachets of France and a Heitz Chardonnay. The Heitz did not come in first, but more importantly, none of us was able to identify it in the blind tasting. A California Chardonnay . . . the equal of the greatest Chardonnay produced in France.

In 1976, the British wine merchant Steven Spurrier conducted a tasting in Paris to judge California wine. Five Chardonnays against five white Burgundies and five Cabernets against five red Bordeaux. To the amazement of the panel of nine prominent wine and food people, California wines had taken the day: 1973 Chateau Montelena Chardonnay and 1973 Stags' Leap Wine Cellars Cabernet Sauvignon were judged the best. *Time* magazine dubbed it the "Judgment of Paris."

Finally the world had to take notice. No longer were the "provincial" Americans touting their own wines. French investment in California wineries grew apace. Names like Chandon, Mumm, Roederer, Piper, and Taittinger appeared on sparkling wines. Christian Mouiex of Château Pétrus and Baron Phillippe de Rothschild of Château Mouton were producing wine in the Napa Valley.

In the early 1980s a new strain of phylloxera was discovered in the Napa Valley. A century earlier an ancestor of this insidious root louse had destroyed the vines of Europe as well as California. Untold millions were spent to replant vineyards. But that tragedy had a beneficial side effect. Individual clones of grapes were

---

Wine-Tasting Dinner at Narsai's

June 19, 1994, Berkeley, California

1989 Domaine Chandon Etoile (sparkling wine)

1986 Domaine Chandon Etoile (sparkling wine)

1986 Montreaux (sparkling wine)

1976 Schramsberg (sparkling wine)

1983 Stony Hill Chardonnay

1974 Spring Mountain Cabernet Sauvignon

1974 Charles Krug, Cabernet Sauvignon, Vintage Selection, Lot F-1

1983 Navarro Cluster Select Johannisberg Riesling

Pre-WW II Beaulieu Vineyard Muscat de Frontignon, decanted from a gallon jug

selected for specific locations, and the rootstocks were similarly selected.

Vines were planted much closer together. From a minimum of 363 vines per acre, new plantings increased to as many as 4,000 per acre (emulating the one meter grid used traditionally in France).

Pruning and thinning techniques were implemented. Growers were committed to producing the highest-quality grapes: vintners were no longer satisfied just with making fine wine. The goal was to make the finest wine possible to compete in the global marketplace. California in general, and Napa Valley in particular, have established their prominence in the world of wine.

"California cuisine did not grow out

of a vacuum. Long before we started

presenting our new ideas with food,

and simplifying classic French cuisine,

California wine was well established."

—NARSAI DAVID

Wine Appreciation in Restaurants

CAT SILIRIE

Cat Silirie, the wine director at No. 9 Park, Barbara Lynch's award-winning restaurant near the State House in Boston, is always full of information and enthusiasm about new wines, and about her latest wine travels. To complete the wine circle, I asked her to talk about how she advises customers about choosing a wine, and asked her to go through No. 9's Spring 2005 menu and recommend a wine for each dish. Then I asked Dun to add his own comments and choices to go alongside Cat's, but without showing him what Cat would recommend (see pages 248 and 249). We'll let you be the judge.

First and foremost, when choosing wines, I believe strongly in developing a point of view, an aesthetic. As a professional wine buyer for restaurants, I also feel that along with creating this aesthetic, my job is to communicate that point of view, so that our staff and especially our guests can see the "personal signature" of the wine list.

In a restaurant setting, many elements contribute to defining and communicating the wine list's point of view: the cuisine, of course, but also the design of the room, its location, style of service, and even the character and passions of the chef/owner.

Look for these clues in each of your visits to restaurants to guide your selections.

Yet when I go to a restaurant for the first time, I find it very helpful to have a sense of the chef's food. So I ask the sommelier and server (hopefully well-trained!) about the wines they think are appropriate for the restaurant's cuisine. Perhaps there is a specialization, or particular enthusiasm in the wine selection. It is always most interesting to be guided by a talented server, maître d', or sommelier. In other words, engage the staff!

For instance at No. 9 Park, chef and owner Barbara Lynch is deeply interested in and inspired by the regional and classic cuisines of France and Italy. Barbara favors elegance and understatement in both cuisine and ambiance. These tenets also define my aesthetic in selecting wine.

I believe that this editorial approach actually serves the consumer.

As a guest in a restaurant, one should feel free to ask about any specialties or motivating passions for their creations, both in food and wine. Of course, if the restaurant is a good one, these will be expressed without having to ask—it will be evident in the signatures I described above.

For the many people who enjoy wine and wish to improve their skills in choosing wines, I suggest the following.

Search for a taste of place. Wine is an incredible beverage in that it can express where it is grown!

Think about progression. It's fun to think about a progression of wines throughout the meal. There's no hard and fast rule, but I think it's best to move from delicate to medium to fuller-bodied as the meal progresses.

Specialize. Finally, it's hard to get to know the whole world of wine. There are many possibilities so work to learn about the wines you really love. For instance, learn about sparkling wines, or wines from Burgundy, or Pinot Noirs from around the world, or Syrah/Shiraz wines, or sweet wines. Have fun learning a lot about the wines you really enjoy.

Cheers!

Wine Snobs

K. DUN GIFFORD

We all know "wine snobs," those people who insist on demonstrating how much they know about wines, and insist on telling you what they know whether you want to listen or not.

These people are different from wine experts, who almost certainly know a lot more than wine snobs do,

but are not insistent on displaying how much they know.

What is most offensive about wine snobs is their absolutism—their certainty, for example, that a certain Pinot Noir of a certain year has a certain (fill in the blank) nose and certain (fill in the blank) tastes. It'll be blackberry with overtones of cherry, and have a creaminess on the tongue that is typical, say, of Pinots grown on sunny south slopes in loamy soil.

This absolutism is a little silly, because the great experts often find themselves in disagreement about the attributes of the same wine. If you doubt me, try this: go to your bookstore, pick up a wine book that rates wines and offers sensory descriptions of them, and pick out a red wine at random. Then pick up a second book that also does this, and read its description.

Odds are strong that both the ratings and the sensory descriptions will be quite different. How, you may wonder, can this be? One taster praises the hints of blackberry, while the other raves about the overtones of vanilla. One rates the wine a 78, and the other scores it a 93.

Is one right and one wrong? Are they both right? Both wrong? What does this say about that wine snob who insists—from his or her reading—that it's blackberry and 93?

IMAGINEERING TASTES

Now imagine you're sitting at your kitchen table with some Mozart or Miles Davis or soft rock playing on the stereo.

In front of you is a bottle of your favorite red wine, another bottle of your favorite white wine, two wine glasses, a bottle of still spring water, a water glass, a soft napkin, and a spitting pot. My wines for this will be a Sanford Pinot Noir and a Sancerre, maybe the Vacheron.

Also spread out in front of you are six small ramekins, one each of table salt, sea salt, ground black pepper, a sweet olive oil (Liguria or Puglia), a peppery olive oil (Tuscany), chopped fresh tomato, and diced cold chicken breast.

To start with a clean palate, rinse out your mouth with the water, and swallow or spit. Pour a half-glass of each of the red and the white wine. Sniff the red carefully, and take a sip, rolling it around in your mouth, and swallow or spit. Try hard to remember the aromas and tastes, the organoleptics. If you'd like, you can write notes on a pad, instead of trying to remember. I love this word, organoleptics. It's a round word, with a nice roll off your tongue. It means: "Relating to perception by a sensory organ, or involving the use of sense organs: organoleptic tests. Relating to the senses (taste, color, odor, feel)."

Now do the same with the white wine, and try to remember its aromas and tastes.

Now do the red again, and note how different its aromas and tastes are from the first time.

And guess what, when you do the white the second time, it, too, does not have the same organoleptics as it did the first time.

The point is this: I do not think that there are absolutes about the organoleptics of wines (except for the "off" ones when the wine has gone bad). And people who say that there are, are wine bores.

What has happened, of course, is that each taste of the wine modifies what comes after: it actually changes the way your taste and smell receptors (mouth and nasal passages) register the organaleptic chemicals, and it also prejudices the brain cells that register tastes and smells. It is also likely that the alcohol has an impact as well. And, we all know at the end of a long evening, that everything tastes the same!

Now let's work on the ramekins.

Wet your forefinger, dip it in the table salt ramekin, and lick the salt off your finger. Take a sip of the white wine, and note whether it tastes different now than how it did in your first tasting. Actually stop and think (or look at your pad if you wrote) and see if you register the same flavor tones. Now do the same thing with the red. Once again, we see that the salt (in this case)

has changed the wine's organoleptics. Now do the same thing with the sea salt. You'll note that the wines taste different than they did after the table salt. The reason for this is that nearly all table salt is iodized, and iodine has a strong influence over taste properties. And, of course, in addition to the iodine, all the other tastes that have preceded this one have an influence over the wine's organoleptics.

Now follow the same procedure with each of the other ramekins in turn, keeping notes on your pad as you go along. Actually, it's even better if you use file cards instead of a pad, and turn them over after you've made your entry, so that you can't see what you've written before.

Now that we have finished the tasting part of this, let's think about what's happened:

1. We know that two different kinds of salts changed the taste of both wines, and changed them differently. This means, of course, that if the chef has used iodized salt for our dinner, the wine will have a different taste than if he or she has used sea salt.

2. We also have learned that each of the foods in the ramekins has caused us to report a different organoleptic profile of both wines. If we had been drinking these wines with a meal, we might have had a soup as the first course. This soup might have been a broth, a cream soup, or a rich stock soup. The soups would have had vegetables, dairy, spices, and certainly salt and pepper. And they would have changed the tastes of the wines in different ways yet again.

So here's the gravamen of the charge. Let's assume we buy a nice bottle of white wine and another nice bottle of red wine for our dinner party. We're going to have hors d'oeuvres, a soup course, a main course, a dessert, and some cheese. We bought the wines thinking about how they would go with the main course, and we read in one of our wine guides and one of the famous wine magazines to find a white wine to go with the shrimp bisque, and a nice red wine to go with the flank steak with béarnaise sauce.

Our guests probably had an hors d'oeuvre or two (or maybe even a cocktail or two) before dinner. And so all of us have already begun to load our sensory banks with flavors, tastes, and aromas. So it's almost impossible to imagine that the organoleptic qualities that we anticipated for our white wine would be what we expected them to be with the shrimp bisque, because of the cocktails and the hors d'oeuvres. Just so, by the time we get to the flank steak, the wine notes we expected with it are also out of whack.

I hasten to say that this does not mean the wines are "bad" with these dishes. It's just that the organoleptic qualities of a wine tasted with a clear and clean palate, flushed with distilled water, and in a room clear of other smells, will not match those of the sensory richness of what's going on at our dinner party.

A further note: It usually shocks people to collect tasting notes from different sources (magazines, books, Internet) on the same wines, and to discover that they're not identical, and sometimes they're not even close to each other.

What I take away from all this is how silly some people are when they make—and defend—declarative and absolute statements that this wine has (say) "overtones of blackberry with wild cherry and hints of vanilla, and with a slight suggestion of road tar." This in fact may be what they have personally tasted or read in a reputable wine guide or magazine, and memorized. But most people at the table will know from their own senses of taste and smell that the wine does not in fact taste that way to them. So, we need to acknowledge that wine tasting is not a matter of absolutes, but of relativity. And be more tolerant of each other's tastes so that real dialogues open up. Wine can be a lot of fun if everyone checks their didactic views at the door!

Matched Pairings

Here are Cat and Dun's wine choices to match Barbara Lynch's No. 9 Park's spring 2005 menu. Cat and Dun chose these wines independently, without knowing what matches the other had made. Any duplicates are just a matter of taste, preference, and coincidence!

APPETIZERS

Oysters on the half shell with Prosecco mignonette

Cat says: This is a perfect example of a wine-pairing opportunity. There is no greater expression of terroir than a perfect subtle Muscadet.

Dun says: Muscadet is my choice.

Spring vegetable salad with potato crisps, saffron vinaigrette

Cat says: An Austrian Gruner Veltliner is just right; Gruner Veltliner loves green things like artichokes, salad, or asparagus, and pairs beautifully with them.

Dun says: Sauvignon Blanc from New Zealand, because the backbone of the New Zealand Sauvignon will stands up to the strengths of the saffron, artichokes, and asparagus.

Beet salad with Great Hill blue cheese, black olive croutons

Cat says: In winter, I would choose a nontannic red; but in spring, I think a really robust rosé from the Languedoc is perfect.

Dun says: A Gigondas. I love this wine with black olives, and I'd pick a strong one because of the strong cheese.

Asparagus velouté with morel mushrooms, truffle essence, quail egg

Cat says: I would recommend a Loire Valley Sauvignon Blanc like a Sancerre.

Dun says: The question is whether to have a big wine to match the mountains of those tastes, or something lighter, more subtle to offset them. Either an Oregon Pinot Noir or a white Bergerac. (When we told Dun about Cat's selection, he exclaimed, "You don't know how close I came to saying Sancerre!")

Insalata di mare with Blue Sky arugula, radicchio, stuffed piquillo

Cat says: A northern Italian white, like something from Lugana or a beautiful, classic Soave fits perfectly with this seafood salad.

Dun says: How about some nice Italian white wine, one near Venice—Silvio Jermann or Livio Felluga.

California squab brochette with country bread, confit, and rhubarb gastrique

Cat says: This is perfect for a Cru Beaujolais, a Beaujolais from Morgan.

Dun says: Sanford Pinot Noir is just right.

Butter-poached Maine lobster with Knoll Farm artichokes, cardoon, and green almonds

Cat says: This is definitely a great opportunity for a full Chardonnay from California.

Dun says: I'd like a Prosecco, a bubbly celebration wine with the lobster.

Hudson Valley foie gras with tropical fruit salad and brioche croquette

Cat says: At No. 9 we are pairing sweet wine with foie gras and fruit, especially sweet wine from Austria, like Alois Kracker.

Dun says: I love any kind of sweet wine from Aquitaine with foie gras, like a Barsac or a Monbazillac.

Prune-stuffed gnocchi seared with foie gras and vin santo glaze

Cat says: Entirely perfect for demi-sec Champagne.

Dun says: I'd go with a French Burgundy, perhaps a really wonderful Pouilly-Fuissé.

Roasted cod with spring-dug parsnip, endive tarte tatin, citrus beurre blanc

Cat says: This goes with so many wines, but I suggest a Chenin Blanc from the Loire Valley, like Vouvray. Loire Valley wines I associate with spring—floral, delicate, medium white wines go well with the freshness and delicate cod and spring root vegetables. Also, the honeyed sweet tone of Vouvray is much better with this dish than an acidic steely white wine.

Dun says: I think we want a Chardonnay, a Chalone Vineyard. They have a particular way of making Chardonnay, way down there in Monterrey in that limestone soil.

Roasted black bass with asparagus, peas, favas, morels, truffle jus

Cat says: Another way to choose wine is to consider the protein first, and associate it with wine, then think about the accompaniments. White wine goes with fish, so in thinking about these spring vegetable accompaniments, I think an Austrian Riesling is perfect. The Riesling loves green things, and is a nervy, energetic wine with a bone-dry finish.

Dun says: I'd like something woodsy to go with the morels. I'd like a high-end Chateau Ste. Michele, maybe their Pinot Gris.

Giannone Farms chicken, herbed gnocchi, mushroom fricassee, braised greens

Cat says: This is a wonderful dish for a light red, medium Pinot Noir from Côte de Beaune, a classic wine to serve with mushrooms and chicken.

Dun says: To loosen it up, we'll do a little bubbly. I'd like a sparkling Vouvray.

Vermont rabbit with parsley root, spinach sauté, Dijon cream

Cat says: This is another irresistible time for a red Burgundy, like Nuits Saint George or a Côte de Beaune.

Dun says: This is one of my favorite kinds of winter dishes, so I'd like a winter wine like Penfolds Grange Cabernet.

Bacon-wrapped rainbow trout with pickled ramps, baby red potatoes, Swiss chard

Cat says: The trout is delicate but the rest of the dish, especially the pickled ramps, need something with backbone. I like something Italian, like the Vernaccia di San Gigmignano. It's of medium texture, delicious with trout, and also pairs well with the bacon and ramps.

Dun says: To match the bigness of this dish, I'd like a big Stags' Leap Vineyard Cabernet Sauvignon. I know it's always risky to go red with fish, but you never get a big reward without a big risk.

Crispy duck confit with pommes boulangère, bok choy, rhubarb confiture

Cat says: Duck confit is a great excuse for a really rich red wine; the rhubarb has bright acidity and the confit is so intense. I like a Barbera: it has an inky purple color, with beautiful fruit acidity, and always performs well with a sweet-and-sour dish.

Dun says: I'd choose a Miguel Torres wine from Chile, because the wine's intensity will hold up to all that's going on in that dish.

Baby lamb with fava beans, eggplant relish, labna

Cat says: I like a Rhône Valley Syrah. Rhône reds usually have great warmth, intensity, and black pepper notes that goes well with the lamb and all the accompaniments.

Dun says: I like a Bandol rosé, from Provence in the south of France because when I think of baby lamb, I think pink. I like my lamb pink, and with two perfect pinks, it's a wonderful marriage.

Prime rib-eye with tarentaise and chard gratin, bone marrow, red wine glaze

Cat says: A classic beef dish that is perfect with a red Bordeaux, particularly a Cabernet Sauvignon–based Bordeaux from the left bank, like St. Julien or Pauillac.

Dun says: We want a strong red, and prime rib makes me think of bullfights, and so I'd go with a Rioja or Ribera del Duero from Spain.

ACKNOWLEDGMENTS

K. DUN GIFFORD AND SARA BAER-SINNOTT

The Oldways Table, and Oldways itself, could not have flourished without the generous help and contributions of a great many friends in food, wine, health, restaurants, media, nutrition, and agriculture. There are too many to mention by name, and we apologize if we have missed someone.

We very much want to thank those who contributed the essays and recipes that make up this book, who are listed in "About the Contributors" (page 252).

Many thanks also to Lisa Ekus, our agent, who has been such a valuable help as we found our way through this often puzzling world of publishing. At Ten Speed Press, we want to thank Phil Wood, Lorena Jones, Kathy Hashimoto, and Brie Mazurek, as well as others who helped make this book possible. Our longtime friend Edouard Cointreau was another guiding hand.

In addition, there are individuals, some of whom did not contribute directly to the book but who have been instrumental to Oldways, we would also like to thank.

In 1991 and 1992, Dun and others worked with a group of scientists to define the Mediterranean diet. The group includes Elisabet Helsing, Marion Nestle, Frank Sacks, Dimitrios Trichopoulos, Antonia Trichopoulou, and Walter Willett. They were the core group that helped us get the science right as Oldways spread "Mediterranean Madness" across the United States. We thank them for sharing their knowledge and expertise, and for the many years of wonderful collaborations.

We also want to thank other scientists who worked with us over the years, helping ensure that Oldways' programs have a foundation of solid nutrition science, especially: Hannia Campos, Michael Crawford, R. Curtis Ellison, John Foreyt, Attilio Giacosa, Joan Gussow, Eric Hentges, Frank Hu, David Hunter, David Jenkins, Julie Miller Jones, Cyril Kendall, Penny Kris-Etherton, Len Marquart, Kathy McManus, Jose Maria Ordovas, Chris Pelkman, Serge Renaud, Gabriele Riccardi, Eric Rimm, Irwin Rosenberg, Luis Serra-Majem, Gene Spiller, Meir Stampfer, Rosemary Stanton, and Andy Waterhouse. Thanks also to the late Ancel Keys and his wife, Margaret; without their groundbreaking research and work on the Mediterranean way of eating, there would be no Mediterranean diet pyramid.

As Oldways has grown and evolved, we've been fortunate to have a number of talented, dedicated, and fun-loving individuals in our offices, who for more than fifteen years have helped us transform our mission into programs, conferences, and publications. Many thanks and much appreciation go to Oldways employees, past and present, and especially: Annie Bonney, Aimee Murdock Burke, Annie Copps, Birthe Creutz, Courtney Davis, Greg Drescher, Catherine Dry, Cynthia Harriman, Robin Insley, Francie King, Lauren McGuire, Liz Mintz, Jessica Musikar, Nicole Nacamuli, Sarah Powers, and Christine Smith.

Oldways could not exist without the individuals, organizations, associations, and companies that have supported and attended our educational programs since 1990. We give special thanks to the individuals below, who, in addition to all the contributors to the book, have been truly instrumental in making the book and Oldways what it is.

Fausto Luchetti, formerly Executive Director of the International Olive Oil Council in Madrid, was an early supporter of Oldways, and worked closely with Dun for more than a decade as we developed our programs around the Mediterranean.

Jody Adams, Jesse Cool, Nancy Harmon Jenkins, Aglaia Kremezi, Chris Kurth, Elizabeth Minchilli Claudia Roden, Michael Romano, Ana Sortun, Patricia Wells, and Paula Wolfert have helped us improve the quality of our programs with their talents, ideas, comments, and imagination.

The following individuals around the world have also contributed.

Australia: David Evans, Marina Libia, Jane Lomax-Smith, Ian Parmenter, Mike Rann and Sasha Carrruozzo, Cherry Ripe, Jon Sainken, Jen Skiff, and Bill Spurr.

Belgium: Fabio Gencarelli, Mike Knowles, Steve Leroy, Hannu Loven, and Joan Prats.

Brazil: Yara Roberts.

China: Junshi Chen, Keyou Ge, and Li Zhu.

France: The Cointreau family, the late Mireille Johnston, Susan Hermann Loomis, and Jean François-Poncet.

Greece: The Boutari family, the Carras family, John Kelidis, Diane Kochilas, Ioannis Kosmidis, Aglaia Kremezi, Mirsini Lampraki, Yannis Mandalas, Orestes Manousos, Panagiotis Mathiellis, Christina and Dimitrios Panteleimonitis, and Claire and Vangelis Xyda.

Italy: Corrado Assenza, Caterina Barla, Guido, Luca and Paolo Barilla, Mauro Battaglia, Raffaele Beata, Leo Bertozzi, Franco and Rossella Boeri, Elia Bois, Luca Bolla, Francesco Bonfio, Andrea Cozzolino, Gian Guido D'Amico, Rosanna D'Antona, Paola DeDonno and family, Michele Errico, Giusepee Ferro, the Forcella family, Gennaro Limone, Domenico Maggi, Massimino Magliocchi, Maria Manfredini, Felice Merola, Rosanna Muolo, Serena Pederiva, Onofrio Pepe, Ivana Picciotto, Maria Paola Profumo, Raffaelle Ragaglini, Renzo Rizzo, Francesca Ronca, Luciano Sardelli, Rossella Speranza and family, the Stucchi family, the Taibi family, Benedetta Vitali, and Gianluigi Zenti.

Mexico: Hector Bourges, Rodrigo Calderon, Eduardo Cervantes, Adolfo and (the late) Miriam Chavez, and Patricia Quintana.

Morocco: Moulay Messaoud Agouzal and Driss Brittel.

Spain: Clara Maria de Amezua, Pepa Aymami, Begona and Pedro Ferrer, Norberto and Carmen Garcia, Juan Vicente Gomez Moya, Pau Roca, Paco Sensat, and the Torres family.

Turkey: Engin Akin, Vedat Basaran, Musa Dagdeviren, Ferda Erdinc, Filiz Hosukoglu, the late Tugrul Savkay, and Ayfer Unsal.

The United Kingdom: Anna Bevan, Nino Binns, Claire Clifton, Philippa Davenport, Anna del Conte, Randolph Hodgson, Elisabeth Luard, Simon Parkes, Maria Jose Sevilla, and Colin Spencer.

The United States and Canada: Sari Abul-Jubein, Rick and Deann Bayless, Amy Binder, Dixie Blake, Ed Blonz, Terrance Brennan, Kari Bretschger, Cinnamon and Victor Broceaux, Jane Brody, Maxime Buyckx, Linda Chaves, Deb and Ken Coons, Narsai David, Robert and Mimi Del Grande, Julia della Croce, Debra Dickerson, Naomi Duguid and Jeffrey Alford, Carol Field, Ruth Flore, Mark Furstenberg, Joyce Goldstein, Paolo Grandjaquet, Maria Guarnaschelli, Elisabeth Holmgren, Ihsan and Valerie Gurdal, Steve Jenkins, Pat Kearney, Corby Kummer, John LaPuma, Karen MacNeil, Tony May, Giovanni Mafodda, Augusto Marchini, Kiesha Marusa, Linda McCashion, Chuck and Jill McCauley, Jeanne McKnight, Phil Meldrum, Nancy Moss, Aniello Musella, Carolyn O'Neil, Kyle Potvin, Fred Plotkin, Maricel Presilla, Nancy Radke, David Rosengarten, the Rowley family, Lorna Sass, Kim Sayid, Joel Schaefer, Sally Schneider, Rosie and Earl Schwartz, Mimi Sheraton, Donna Shields, Don Short, Nina Simonds, Don Soetaert, Jeffrey Steingarten, Paul Sullivan, Asima Syed, Maureen Ternus, Phil Teverow, Judith Weinraub, Ari Weinzweig, Jasper White, Charley Wolk, and Daphne Zepos.

And finally, and especially, many thanks to our families and close friends. They have understood our dedication to Oldways and its mission, and have generously given us the freedom and encouragement to help us make a difference in how people around the world make their food and drink choices.

ABOUT THE CONTRIBUTORS

Sari Abul-Jubein is the owner of Casablanca Restaurant in Cambridge, Massachusetts.

Engin Akin is a Turkish newspaper columnist, radio show host, cookbook author, and a much-in-demand speaker on Turkish food. She lives in Istanbul.

Norma Baer is a home cook living in Exeter, New Hampshire.

Sara Baer-Sinnott is executive vice president of Oldways, joining in 1992 after working on special editorial projects at *Inc.* magazine. She was previously an environmental resources, business, and education consultant.

Anne Banville travels around the world for the USA Rice Federation, but she calls Washington, D.C., her home.

Lidia Bastianich is the chef and owner of Felidia and Becco in New York City, and Lidia's Kansas City, and Lidia's Pittsburgh. She is the author of four cookbooks, including *Lidia's Family Table* and *Lidia's Italian Table*, and host of her own PBS cooking show, *Lidia's Family Table*.

Deann Bayless and her husband, Rick, are chefs and owners of the internationally known Mexican restaurants Frontera Grill and Topolobampo in Chicago. They are authors of a number of cookbooks, including *Mexico: One Plate at a Time*.

Janice Newell Bissex, MS, RD, has been a nutrition advisor to the U.S. Senate, worked at Boston Harbor Hotel with chef Daniel Bruce, and has been president of the Massachusetts Dietetic Association. With Liz Weiss, she coauthored *The Moms' Guide to Meal Makeovers* and cofounded the free online Meal Makeover Moms' Club (www.mealmakeovermoms.com).

Jenny Brand-Miller, **PhD,** is Professor of Human Nutrition at the University of Sydney, Australia, and the author of *The Low GI Diet*.

Victor Broceaux is a longtime chef and an experienced restaurateur with Restaurant Associates, the New York City–based restaurant management company. His expertise has taken him from the elegant Four Seasons restaurant in New York to corporate dining rooms and trendy restaurants across the United States.

Hannia Campos, PhD, is a professor at the Harvard School of Public Health. Her research interests include the health of the people of her native country, Costa Rica.

Penelope Casas, one of the most knowledgeable experts in the United States about Spanish cooking, is the author of six books about the subject, most notably *Tapas* and *The Foods and Wines of Spain.*

Melissa Clark is a prolific cookbook author and food writer. She's written with chefs (Waldy Malouf and others), she's written about food and places (Nantucket and others), and she's written with celebrities (Faith

Ford and others). Her latest book, *Chef Interrupted*, features recipes from famous chefs, pared down for home cooks.

Edouard Cointreau is president of the Gourmand World Cookbook Awards, and when he isn't traveling around the world searching out the best cookbooks in the world, he divides his time between his home country of France and his adopted home in Spain.

Mel Coleman, Jr., is head of Coleman Natural Meats in Golden, Colorado, which was founded by his father, Mel Coleman, Sr., in 1979. The company pioneered the production and marketing of pure and natural beef, raised humanely and with respect for the environment.

Jesse Cool is the author of six books, including *Your Organic Kitchen*, and is the chef and owner of three restaurants in Palo Alto and Menlo Park: Flea Street Café, JZ Cool, and Cool Café at the Cantor Art Gallery at Stanford University.

Jeff Dahlberg, PhD, is an agronomist and director of research for the National Sorghum Producers. He is also chairman of the Whole Grains Council.

Narsai David has done it all in the food world: restaurant owner (Narsai's Restaurant in Berkeley, California), retailer (Narsai's Market, also in Berkeley), cookbook author (*Monday Night at Narsai's*), television host (PBS series *Over Easy*), and newspaper columnist (*San Francisco Chronicle*). He is now the food and wine editor for KCBS radio in San Francisco.

Julia della Croce is a prolific cookbook author, mostly of books on Italian cooking, including *Pasta Classica* and *Salse di Pomodoro*. She also writes about food, cooking, and traveling for newspapers and magazines, and teaches cooking classes.

Lou DiPalo is a third-generation purveyor of Italian specialty foods at DiPalo Fine Foods in New York City. The shop prides itself on selling foods from all areas of Italy, including oils, cheeses, honeys, chocolates, artisanal pastas, preserves, and cured meats from the Alps to Sicily.

Catherine Donnelley, PhD, is a professor of food microbiology at the University of Vermont and is considered one of the world's experts on *listeria,* a feared bacterial pathogen in foods. She has guided Oldways on the safety of traditional raw milk cheeses.

John Mercuri Dooley is a writer and poet who lives in Cambridge, Massachusetts.

Ed Doyle was formerly chef of Aura at the Seaport Hotel in Boston, and is now a consulting chef and a member of the board of the Chefs Collaborative.

Naomi Duguid and **Jeffrey Alford** are cookbook authors and photographers based in Toronto. Their prize-winning books include *Flatbreads and Flavors* and *Hot, Sour, Salty, Sweet*.

Curtis Ellison, MD, is a professor at Boston University School of Medicine and one of the original researchers of what has been termed "the French Paradox," the studies concluding that "wine is part of a healthy diet."

Alice Feiring lives in New York City and is a wine/travel columnist for *Time* magazine. She also organizes wine tastings and classes.

Carol Field is a prize-winning cookbook author and novelist who lives in San Francisco and Tuscany. She's best known for *The Italian Baker* and *In Nonna's Kitchen*.

John Foreyt, PhD, is one of the leading authorities in the United States on obesity, dieting, and behavior. He is director of the Nutrition Research Clinic and a professor in the Department of Medicine at Baylor College of Medicine in Houston.

K. Dun Gifford is the founder and president of Oldways. Previously, he has also owned and managed a number of restaurants in Boston and Cambridge, Massachusetts, and was a legislative assistant to Senator Edward F. Kennedy and national campaign coordinator for Senator Robert F. Kennedy's 1968 presidential campaign.

Cynthia Harriman is the director of food and nutrition strategies for Oldways and the Whole Grains Council. She is also the author of *Take Your Kids to Europe.*

Sam Hayward is the chef-owner of Fore Street Restaurant in Portland, Maine, and is a longtime supporter of local foods and sustainable agriculture.

Allison Hooper is the cofounder of the Vermont Butter & Cheese Company in Montpelier, Vermont. With a network of more than twenty family farms to provide them milk, the company crafts European-style artisan dairy products.

Frank Hu, MD, PhD, is an associate professor of nutrition and epidemiology in the Department of Nutrition at the Harvard School of Public Health. His main research interest is epidemiology and the prevention of type 2 diabetes.

John and Sukey Jamison raise lamb at Jamison Farm in Latrobe, Pennsylvania, in the rolling Appalachian foothills.

Nancy Harmon Jenkins is a Mediterranean cookbook author and food writer. She is the author of *The Mediterranean Diet Cookbook* and *The Flavors of Puglia,* among

others. She lives in Camden, Maine, and Cortona, Italy, and helped found Oldways.

Steve Jenkins is a cheese expert and the author of *The Cheese Primer*. He is also a partner at Fairway Markets in New York City and is responsible for the many specialty food products sold at Fairway.

Steve Johnson, formerly chef and co-owner of the Blue Room, is now chef and owner of Rendezvous, both in Cambridge, Massachusetts.

Lynne Rossetto Kasper is host of the NPR show *The Splendid Table* and also the author of the award-winning book of the same name (the only book to be named Cookbook of the Year by both the IACP and the James Beard Foundation in the same year). Lynne has also written for a number of newspapers and magazines.

Rob Kaufelt is a cheese-monger and owner of Murray's Cheese Shop in New York.

Ancel Keys, PhD, "Father of the Mediterranean Diet," was a professor at the University of Minnesota. He was the inventor of K-rations and the coauthor of *How to Eat Well and Stay Well the Mediterranean Way* with his wife, Margaret. Dr. Keys died in 2004 at the age of one hundred.

Robin Kline, MS, RD, is a writer with Savvy Food Communications. In her past lives she's been president of the International Association of Culinary Professionals (IACP) and executive director of the National Pork Council (she's the one responsible for the catchy slogan, "the other white meat!").

Aglaia Kremezi is a Greek cookbook author, food writer, photographer, and an expert in Greek foods and wines. Aglaia and her husband Costas live on the island of Kea, where Aglaia runs a cooking school and continues to write for the Sunday Athens paper *Kryiakatiki*

Eleftherotypia. Her most recent book is *The Foods of the Greek Islands.*

Penny Kris-Etherton, PhD, teaches nutrition at Pennsylvania State University and served as a member of the 2005 U.S. Dietary Guidelines Committee.

Susan Kron is managing editor of *CFO Magazine* and a home cook living in Boston, Massachusetts.

Mirsini Lampraki is from Crete and is a cookbook author and food writer. She has written several books on Greek cooking, edible greens, and olive oil, as well as one entitled *Greece/Turkey at the Same Table,* co-authored by Engin Akin.

Giuseppe Licitra, is the director of CORFILAC, a Consorzio in Ragusa, Sicily. His passion is to keep alive Sicily's cheesemaking traditions, and to promote and sell the traditional cheese of Sicily, particularly Ragusano cheese.

Elisabeth Luard is a cookbook author and food writer who lives in London and Wales. Books she has written range from *European Peasant Cookery* to *Sacred Food* to *Family Life,* an autobiography. She won the 2001 Glen Fiddich Award for her food writing.

Fausto Luchetti is the former executive director of the International Olive Oil Council in Madrid.

Barbara Lynch is the chef-owner of two award-winning Boston restaurants (No. 9 Park and B&G Oyster).

Deborah Madison was the original chef at San Francisco's famed Greens restaurant and is a cookbook writer and cooking teacher. Her books include *Vegetarian Cooking for Everyone* and *Local Flavors, Cooking and Eating from America's Farmers' Markets* (Broadway Books).

Robert Marsh is the chef at Momo's restaurant, a popular spot in San Francisco located across the street from the PacBell Stadium.

Zarela Martinez is a pioneering chef who introduced true and traditional Mexican foods to American tables at Zarela, her restaurant in midtown Manhattan, and through her three highly accessible cookbooks, including *The Food and Life of Oaxaca* (MacMillan) and *Zarela's Veracruz,* a companion volume to her television series.

Kathy McManus, RD, is the director of nutrition for Brigham & Women's Hospital in Boston, Massachusetts.

Rick Moonen is the chef-owner of RM Restaurant in New York City.

Marian Morash was the founding chef of the superb Straight Wharf Restaurant in Nantucket, is the author of two longtime best-selling cookbooks, *The Victory Garden Cookbook* and *The Victory Garden Fish & Vegetable Cookbook,* and was the television chef of *The Victory Garden.*

Claudette Nacamuli, a home cook in Winchester, Massachusetts, was raised in Switzerland.

Eduardo Napolitano is by training a biochemist, but by passion a champion of entrepreneurial artisan food makers in Salerno, Italy.

Bill Niman is a pioneer in sustainable ranching, raising cattle, pigs, and lambs for many years. Today, Niman Ranch is a network of independent family farmers and ranchers who all raise livestock according to strict protocols. The quality of the meats grown by his network of committed colleagues is so high that it appears on leading restaurant tables and in grocery stores from coast to coast.

Anna Nurse is an opera singer turned beloved cooking teacher in New York City.

Paul O'Connell is the chef and owner of Chez Henri in Cambridge, Massachusetts.

Ellen Ecker Ogden was a cofounder and co-owner of the Cook's Garden, a catalogue full of seeds, plants, and garden and kitchen supplies. She is now the chef of the Cook's Garden, directs the test kitchen program, and gives cooking lessons. She is the author of *From the Cook's Garden*.

Mike Orlando is chairman of Fresno-based Sunnyland Mills and founding chair of the Whole Grains Council.

The Peanut Institute is a nonprofit organization that is dedicated to research and educational programs about peanuts and nutrition.

Steve Petusevsky is a chef, cookbook author, and journalist who writes a syndicated newspaper column for the Chicago Tribune News Service. He was for many years a corporate chef for Whole Foods Market, and is the author of *The Whole Foods Market Cookbook*. He is now a consulting chef and journalist in southern Florida.

Susan Purdy has written thirty books, twelve about baking and pastry, including *Have Your Cake & Eat It, Too; The Perfect Cake; The Perfect Pie;* and most recently, *Pie in the Sky*.

Renzo Rizzo is chief of research and development at Barilla. His wife, Margherita Rizzo, is a home cook, and they live with their children in Parma, Italy.

Claudia Roden, is a prize-winning cookbook writer who was born in Egypt, grew up in Paris, and now lives in London. She is the author of many cookbooks, including *A Book of Middle Eastern Food, The Food of Italy*, and *The Book of Jewish Food*. In the 1980s, she was

the host of the BBC television series *Mediterranean Cooking.*

Jeannie Rogers is the sommelier at Il Capriccio Restaurant in Waltham, Massachusetts, well known for its astonishing list of superb, small-production Italian wines.

Kerry Downey Romaniello is the chef at Westport Rivers Vineyard & Winery in Westport, Massachusetts.

Michael Romano is the chef and partner at Union Square Cafe in New York City. He is also the coauthor of several cookbooks, including *The Union Square Cookbook*.

Judy Schad raises goats and makes a prize-winning goat cheese (Capriole) at her farm in southern Indiana.

Chris Schlesinger is executive chef and owner of the East Coast Grill in Cambridge, Massachusetts, and the author, along with John Willoughby, of several award-winning cookbooks, including *License to Grill*, and of *New York Times* newspaper food columns.

Rosie Schwartz, RD, is a well-known Canadian nutritionist, magazine and newspaper columnist, healthy eating crusader, and television commentator. She is author of *The Enlightened Eater's Guide*.

Scott Sechler is passionate about chickens and is growing his company, Pennsylvania-based Bell & Evans, with the same passion.

Robert Serrano is a grain miller from Grain Millers, Inc., in Portland, Oregon.

Cat Silirie is the wine director at No. 9 Park, Barbara Lynch's award-winning restaurant in Boston.

Joe Simone is now a private chef in San Francisco, California, but was formerly executive chef at Papa Razzi in Boston, Massachusetts, and was one of the chefs of the PBS show *Cucina Amore.*

Ana Sortun is the award-winning chef of Oleana Restaurant in Cambridge, Massachusetts. She is also the author of *Spice.*

Colin Spencer is a noted British food writer. He's the author of *The History of Vegetarianism, The Heretics Feast, The Vegetable Book, Vegetarian Gourmet Dinner Party, The New Vegetarian,* and the prize-winning *British Food: An Extraordinary Thousand Years of History.*

Rossella Speranza is the managing director of Natura & Cucina in Bari, Italy, and works closely with Oldways on projects in southern Italy, particularly in her home region of Puglia.

Molly Stevens won a James Beard Award and an IACP Award for *All About Braising: The Art of Uncomplicated Cooking* (Norton). She was named the IACP Cooking Teacher of the Year in 2006. She is a contributing editor for *Fine Cooking* magazine and coauthor of several cookbooks, including *One Potato, Two Potato.*

Cathy Strange is the National Team Leader for cheese for Whole Foods Market.

Antonia Trichopoulou, MD, is a medical doctor and nutrition scientist at the University of Athens Medical School, Department of Hygiene and Epidemiology, in Athens, Greece. She is also editorial board director of the W.H.O. Collaborating Center for Nutrition in Greece.

Anne Underwood writes for *Newsweek* magazine. She is the coauthor of *The Color Code,* a book she wrote with Dr. James Joseph and Dr. Dan Nadeau about the healthfulness of foods (fruits and vegetables) with color.

Anya von Bremzen is a cookbook author and food and travel writer for *Travel & Leisure* and *Food & Wine.* She has written a number of books, including *The New Spanish Table* and *Fiesta! A Celebration of Latin Hospitality.*

Ari Weinzweig is a cofounder of Zingerman's, one of America's premier sources of high-quality ingredients from all over the world, and also known as "The Coolest Place to Work in America," according to *Inc.* magazine. He is also the author of *Zingerman's Guide to Good Eating.*

Liz Weiss, MS, RD, has spent two decades writing and reporting on nutrition and health for CNN and PBS, among others. With Janice Newell Bissex, she is coauthor of *The Moms' Guide to Meal Makeovers* and cofounder of the free online Meal Makeover Moms' Club (www.mealmakeovermoms.com).

Walter Willett, MD, DrPH, is the Fredrick John Stare professor of epidemiology and nutrition, Departments of Nutrition and Epidemiology, and chair of the Department of Nutrition at the Harvard School of Public Health. He assisted Oldways in the development of the Mediterranean diet pyramid and is also the author of *Eat, Drink and Be Healthy* and *Eat, Drink and Lose Weight.*

Paula Wolfert is the author of several acclaimed Mediterranean cookbooks, including *Couscous and Other Good Food from Morocco, Mediterranean Cooking, Paula Wolfert's World of Food, The Cooking of Southwest France,* and *Mediterranean Grains and Greens.*

Clifford Wright is a culinary historian and food writer. He is the author of *A Mediterranean Feast,* a James Beard Cookbook of the Year, and *Mediterranean Vegetables.*

INDEX

Keys, Ancel, 8–9, 254
Kiffin, Mark, 193
Kilvert & Forbes Company, 209–10
Kleiman, Evan, 193
Kline, Robin, 66, 70, 196–97, 254
Knickerbocker, Peggy, 72
Kraft, James, 129
Kremezi, Aglaia
    about, 78, 193, 254–55
    recipes of, 64–65, 95, 107, 141
Kris-Etherton, Penny, 21, 66, 145–46, 255
Kron, Susan, 33, 255
Kurth, Chris, 40

L

Lamb
    Jamison Farm, 177–78
    roast, 172–73
    Skewers of Marinated Crete Spring Lamb with Artichokes and Lemons, 194
Lampraki, Mirsini, 78, 79, 255
Lappé, Frances Moore, 85, 91
Lardo, 188–90
Latin American diet pyramid, 11
Legumes
    nomenclature for, 81–82
    protein in, 82–83
Lemons. *See also* Limoncello
    Lemon and Olive Oil Salad Dressing, 123
    Lemon Cream, 212–13
    Oven-Roasted Rabbit with Lemons and Olives, 194–95
    Skewers of Marinated Crete Spring Lamb with Artichokes and Lemons, 194
Lentils
    Lentil Soup with Grano, 43
    Wild Rice and Lentil Salad, 39–40
Lettuce
    Chopped Romaine and Cucumber Salad with Yogurt Dressing, 140
    Vietnamese Rice Paper Roll-Ups, 32
Licitra, Giuseppe, 136–37, 255

Lidia and the Chefettes, 72, 92–94, 193
Liguria, 52
Lime Guacamole, 68
Limoncello
    Baba Limoncello with Lemon Cream, 212–13
    babas in, 207–8
Lindsay, Anne, 72
Linguine with Greens, Yogurt, Almonds, and Blue Cheese, 141
Liver, fried calf's, 173
Lobster, 144
Luard, Elisabeth
    about, 154, 155, 255
    recipes of, 41–42, 124–25, 166
Luchetti, Fausto, 123, 255
Lutein, 48
Lycopene, 48
Lynch, Barbara, 35, 213, 244, 248, 255

M

Macadamia nuts, 100
Madison, Deborah, 56–57, 101, 255
Maido Agroturismo, 183
Major, Cynthia and David, 134
Major Grey's chutney, 222
Malouf, Waldy, 72
Malpighi, Ermes, 227
Managing Sweetness International Conference and programs, 204–7
Mango, Aromatic Shrimp Salad with Peanuts and, 109
Maple syrup, 223–24
Marsh, Gardiner, 148–49
Marsh, Robert, 197, 255
Martinez, Zarela, 27–28, 38–39, 255
Mashed Potatoes with Kale and Olive Oil, 69
Mayer, Jean, 9
McCarthy, Jay, 193
McGee, Harold, 99
McIntosh, W. A., 8
McManus, Kathy, 103–5, 110–11, 255
Mead, 231
Mead, Margaret, 205